D0908208

RETURN TO
SBVMWD
ENG. LIBRARY

LIBRARY

MICROPROCESSORS
AND MICROCOMPUTERS

MICROPROCESSORS AND MICROCOMPUTERS

BRANKO SOUČEK
Professor

State University of New York, Stony Brook, New York
Institute Ruder Bošković, Zagreb

A WILEY-INTERSCIENCE PUBLICATION

JOHN WILEY and SONS
New York • London • Sydney • Toronto

Copyright © 1976 by John Wiley & Sons, Inc.

All rights reserved. Published simultaneously in Canada.

No part of this book may be reproduced by any means,
nor transmitted, nor translated into a machine language
without the written permission of the publisher.

Library of Congress Cataloging in Publication Data:

Souček, Branko.

    Microprocessors and microcomputers.

    "A Wiley-Interscience publication."
    Includes bibliographical references and index.
    1. Microprocessors.   2. Miniature computers.

I. Title.
QA76.5.S657   001.6'4'04   75-33123
ISBN 0-471-81391-5

Printed in the United States of America

10 9 8 7 6 5 4 3 2

To My Mother

PREFACE

The mass production of inexpensive and powerful microprocessors constitutes a major event in both electrical engineering and computer sciences. In the former area, microprocessors are used to replace digital systems and electromechanical logic design. In the latter area, microcomputers are challenging minicomputers and conventional computers.

This book describes the general programming and interfacing techniques common to all microprocessors and then concentrates on detailed descriptions of representative microprocessor families. It is hoped that this volume will be useful to engineers, scientists, and managers in many areas.

The book is written as a textbook for students, as well as a reference work for practicing engineers and scientists. The treatment is kept as straightforward as possible, with emphasis on functions and systems. A minimal background in related areas at the undergraduate level is assumed, although many fundamentals are reviewed.

The book is divided into three parts. Part 1 deals with microprocessor programming and interfacing techniques. It explains digital codes, logical systems, microcomputer organization, simple hexadecimal programming, assembly language programming, and the use of MACRO's and high-level languages. It then concentrates on interfacing techniques and explains input/output transfer modes, direct memory access, interrupt, and interfacing components and chips. This material will provide the basic working knowledge necessary for the design and usage of microprocessor oriented systems.

Part 2 presents detailed descriptions of representative microprocessor families. This part starts with the description of simple 4-bit microprocessors which provide excellent replacement for digital systems and electromechanical logic. A variety of 8-bit microprocessors is described next. The new and powerful 16-bit microprocessors that challenge conventional computers are also described in this part. For each microprocessor family a detailed description of available chips, I/O buses, instruction sets, and addressing modes is given. A large number of programming and interfacing examples is included.

Part 3 presents new microprocessors and special-purpose microsystems. The replacement of powerful minicomputers with the microchip set is

vii

described. Newly developed microprocessors, memory, and I/O chips suitable for a broad range of applications are presented. High-speed microsystems for control applications are also discussed. Bipolar LSI circuits that simplify the construction of microprogrammed central processors and device controllers are presented.

The treatment is rounded out with a large number of illustrations, examples, and references. Many chapters are provided with problems. The examples and problems are designed as practical exercises for students or beginners in the use of microprocessor techniques. In general the book starts at the level of the beginner and then systematically and gradually shifts into the areas of advanced interfacing, programming, and application techniques.

Branko Souček

Stony Brook, New York
Fall 1975

ACKNOWLEDGMENTS

I acknowledge the stimulation gained over a long period from many teachers and colleagues. My thanks are due to Professors L. Braun, G. A. Korn, and J. D. Schoeffler for stimulating discussions. I acknowledge the support received from the following computer lecturers and specialists: S. Brannan, Dr. D. C. Collins, W. B. Cunningham, D. G. Dimmler, E. R. Garen, M. R. Lemas, M. J. Rosenblum, H. Slivjanovski, M. J. Smith, and D. Willard.

In writing a book such as this, it was necessary to borrow some data from the manuals of computer manufacturers. I should like to thank the following companies for giving me the permission to take material from their publications:

Digital Equipment Corporation
Fairchild Camera and Instruments Co.
Integrated Computer Systems
Intel Corporation
Intersil Inc.
Motorola Semiconductor Products, Inc.
National Semiconductor Corporation
Pro-Log Corporation
Rockwell International Corporation
Scientific Micro Systems
Software Research Corporation

CONTENTS

1

NUMBER SYSTEMS AND DIGITAL CODES

Chapter 1 introduces the number systems and digital codes. It concentrates on the binary codes most widely used in computer technology. Arithmetic operations with binary numbers are explained. Different codes for information coding are shown and compared. Octal and hexadecimal number systems, which are widely used during program preparation for microprocessors and microcomputers, are described. Gray code, excellently suited for use in position transducers, is explained. The ASCII character set is defined.

1.1. DECIMAL AND BINARY NUMBER SYSTEMS

Definitions

The fundamental requirement of a computer is the ability to represent and store numbers and to perform operations on the numbers thus represented. The numbers can be represented in different number systems. From early childhood most individuals are trained to represent quantities in the decimal number system. This system counts in units of tens and was probably developed because man has ten fingers. The base of this number system is 10, since ten basic digits are used (ten fingers). The basic digits are 0, 1, 2, 3, 4, 5, 6, 7, 8, and 9. By giving to these digits different positions, or weights, we can express numbers larger than 10. Number 10 is base of the decimal system. One can build a number system with a different base, b.

In general, a number $(N)_b$ in a fixed, positive, integral base b number system is represented in positional notation as

$$(N)_b = (P_n P_{n-1} \cdots P_1 P_0 \cdot P_{-1} P_{-2} \cdots)$$

The number b is the base of the system. This is a positive integer and is fixed throughout the system. The positional digits P_i are integers such that

$$0 \le P_i \le b - 1 \qquad i = \cdots -2, -1, 0, 1, 2 \cdots n$$

3

The value of each position in a number is known as its position coefficient or weight. For example:

$$346 = \begin{array}{rcr} 3 \times 100 & = & 300 \\ 4 \times 10 & = & 40 \\ 6 \times 1 & = & 6 \\ \hline & & 346 \end{array}$$

A simple decimal weighting table is

$$\cdots 10^3 \ 10^2 \ 10^1 \ 10^0 \cdot 10^{-1} \ 10^{-2}$$

In general, in a base b system the successive digit positions, left to right, have the weights

$$\cdots b^3 \ b^2 \ b^1 \ b^0 \cdot b^{-1} \ b^{-2} \cdots$$

The symbol "·" is called the radix point. The portion of the number to the right of the radix point is called the fractional part of the number, and the portion to the left is called the integral part. In the decimal system, the radix point is called the decimal point.

Computing machines can be built on the basis of any number systems. However, all modern digital computers are based on the binary (base 2) system. Why has this new number system been brought into use? The reason is that it is easier to distinguish between two entities than between ten entities. Most physical quantities have only two states: a light bulb is on or off; switches are on or off; material is magnetized or demagnetized; current is positive or negative; holes in paper tape or cards are punched or not punched; and so on. It is easier and more reliable to design circuits which must differentiate between only two conditions (binary 0 and binary 1) than between ten conditions (decimal 0 through 9).

The base of the binary system is 2. The radix point can be called the binary point. The possible digits are 0 and 1. The successive digit positions, left to right, have the weights:

$$\cdots 2^3 \ 2^2 \ 2^1 \ 2^0 \cdot 2^{-1} \ 2^{-2} \ 2^{-3} \cdots$$

This weighting table is used to convert binary numbers to the more familiar decimal system. For example, let us find the decimal equivalent of the binary number 10101 (Table 1.1).

Table 1.1

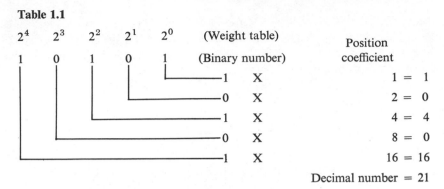

| 2^4 | 2^3 | 2^2 | 2^1 | 2^0 | (Weight table) | Position coefficient |

Decimal number = 21

The process of counting can be used to point out differences and similarities between decimal and binary systems. In the decimal system, counting consists of increasing the digit in a particular position in the order 0, 1, 2, ... 8, 9. When we reach 0 (10) in this position, we carry 1 to the immediate-left position. Since the binary number system utilizes only two digits, particular positions of the number can go only through two changes, and then we carry 1 to the immediate-left position. Thus the numbers used in the binary number system to count up to a decimal value 10 are as shown in Table 1.2.

Table 1.2

Decimal	Binary
0	0
1	1
2	10
3	11
4	100
5	101
6	110
7	111
8	1000
9	1001
10	1010

There are some special names widely used in computer technology, such as "bit," "byte," and "word."

Bit. A *binary digit* is usually referred to as a *bit*. Thus a number such as 1010 is referred to as a 4-bit binary number, and 101 as a 3-bit number, and so on. The bit at the left end of the number is called the most significant bit (it has the largest weight). The bit at the right end of the number is called the least significant bit (it has the smallest weight). Figure 1.1 presents a binary number composed of 16 bits.

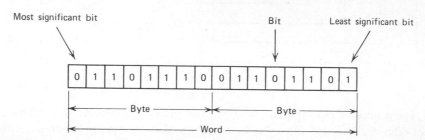

Figure 1.1. Bit, byte, word.

Byte. The evolution of the computer and data equipment has brought about an 8-bit unit for information exchange between devices. Such an 8-bit unit is referred to as a "byte." Many new types of digital computers and controllers thus express the numbers of 8, 16, 24, or 32 bits (1, 2, 3, or 4 bytes). Figure 1.1 presents a binary number composed of 2 bytes.

Word. The computer is composed of a large number of cells or registers for storing binary information. Most of the registers in a given machine are of the same length, n. Each register can be used to store n bits of binary information. Information stored in one register is also called a *word.* Figure 1.1 presents a word of a 16-bit computer.

Decimal-to-Binary Conversion

Decimal numbers can have, in general, an integer part and a fraction part. Each part should be converted separately into a binary equivalent. The complete representation is obtained by combining the two along with the binary point. There are two commonly used methods for converting decimal numbers to binary equivalents, the subtraction method and division-multiplication method.

Subtraction Method. (We follow here the procedure of Ref. 4.) Subtract the highest possible power of two from the decimal number and place a 1 in the appropriate weighting position of the partially completed binary number. Continue this procedure until the decimal number is reduced to 0.

If, after the first subtraction, the next-lower power of 2 cannot be subtracted, place a 0 in the appropriate weighting position. An example for an integer is

$$
\begin{array}{cccccccc}
 & & 2^5 & 2^4 & 2^3 & 2^2 & 2^1 & 2^0 \\
53 & & & & & & & \\
-32 \to 2^5 & 1 & 1 & 0 & 1 & 0 & 1 \\
\hline
21 & & & & & & & \\
-16 \to 2^4 & & & & & & & \\
\hline
5 & & & & & & & \\
-4 \to 2^2 & & & & & & & \\
\hline
1 & & & & & & & \\
-1 \to 2^0 & & & & & & & \\
\hline
0 & & & & & & &
\end{array}
$$

Hence $(53)_{10} = (110101)_2$.

An example for a fraction is

$$
\begin{array}{cccccc}
 & 2^{-1} & 2^{-2} & 2^{-3} & 2^{-4} & 2^{-5} \\
0.5625 & & & & & \\
-0.5 \to 2^{-1} & 1 & 0 & 0 & 1 & 0 \\
\hline
0.0625 & & & & & \\
-0.0625 \to 2^{-4} & & & & & \\
\hline
0.0 & & & & &
\end{array}
$$

Division Method. If a decimal integer should be converted into a binary equivalent, apply a number of divisions by 2. Divide the decimal number by 2. If there is a remainder, put a 1 in the lowest binary digit; if there is no remainder, put a 0 in the lowest binary digit. Divide the result from the first operation by 2 and repeat the process. Continue until the result has been reduced to 0 (Ref. 4). For example:

$$
\begin{array}{rl|l}
2 & 53 & \text{Remainder} \\
2 & 26 & \to \quad 1 \\
2 & 13 & \to \quad 0 \qquad (53)_{10} = (110101)_2 \\
2 & 6 & \to \quad 1 \\
2 & 3 & \to \quad 0 \\
2 & 1 & \to \quad 1 \\
 & 0 & \to \quad 1
\end{array}
$$

Multiplication Method. If a decimal fraction should be converted into a binary equivalent, apply a number of multiplications by 2. If the product is less than 1, the most significant binary digit is zero; if the product is greater than 1, the most significant binary digit is 1. The second digit is obtained according to the same rule, operating this time on the fractional part of the product obtained in the first step. This process is continued until the desired degree of accuracy is reached. For example:

$$
\begin{array}{lll}
 & & \text{Carry} \\
0.5625 \times 2 = 1.1250 & \rightarrow & 1 \\
0.1250 \times 2 = 0.2500 & \rightarrow & 0 \\
0.250 \ \times 2 = 0.5 & \rightarrow & 0 \\
0.5 \ \ \ \times 2 = 1.0 & \rightarrow & 1 \\
0.0 \ \ \ \times 2 = 0.0 & \rightarrow & 0 \\
\end{array}
$$

Hence $(0.5625)_{10} = (.10010)_2$.

1.2.   ARITHMETIC OPERATIONS WITH BINARY NUMBERS

Addition

Binary addition follows the same pattern as decimal addition except that a carry to the next position is not generated after the sum reaches 10, but is generated when the sum reaches 2 $(1 + 1)$. For example:

$$
\begin{array}{rcl}
101 & = & 5_{10} \\
+010 & = & 2_{10} \\
\hline
111 & = & 7_{10} \\
\end{array}
$$

$$
\begin{array}{rcl}
11 & \leftarrow & \text{carries} \\
111 & = & 7_{10} \\
+101 & = & 5_{10} \\
\hline
1100 & = & 12_{10} \\
\end{array}
$$

Let us follow the second example (add 111 to 101). First, $1 + 1 = 0$ plus a carry of 1. In the second column, 1 plus the carry $1 = 0$ plus another carry. The third column is $1 + 1 = 0$ with a carry plus the previous carry, or $1 + 1 + 1 = 11$. Our answer is 1100 (decimal 12), which is the correct solution for $7 + 5$.

The addition of binary numbers in digital machines is performed by a special unit called a *functional adder*.

Subtraction

Binary numbers may be directly subtracted in a manner similar to decimal subtraction. It is entirely possible to design a machine that contains a functional subtractor as well as a functional adder. This procedure is not followed by the computer designers. It has been noted that if one wishes to perform a subtraction operation, one merely changes the sign of the subtrahend and proceeds with an addition operation. It is only important to find the proper way to express the negative numbers.

To see how negative numbers can be represented in the computer, consider a mechanical register, such as a car mileage indicator. If the register rotates forward, it performs addition. If the register rotates backward, it performs subtraction. An example for a 5-digit register rotating backward is[4]

$$
\begin{array}{c}
00004 \\
00003 \\
00002 \\
00001 \\
00000 \\
99999 \\
99998 \\
99997
\end{array}
$$

It should be clear that the number 99997 corresponds to -3. To prove that, we can perform addition

$$
\begin{array}{r}
00004 \\
+\ 99997 \\
\hline
1\ 00001
\end{array}
$$

If we neglect the carry to the left, we have effectively performed the operation of subtracting.

$$4 - 3 = 1$$

The number 99997 in this example is called the ten's complement of 3. Thus in a decimal number system negative numbers can be presented in the form of the ten's complement and the negative sign could be omitted.

In digital machines, in the same manner, the two's complement of binary numbers is used to represent negative numbers and to carry out binary subtraction.

The two's complement of a number is defined as that number which when added to the original number will result in a sum of unity. For example, the binary number 010 110 110 110 has a two's complement equal to 101 001 001 010 as shown in the following addition

$$
\begin{array}{r}
010\ 110\ 110\ 110 \\
101\ 001\ 001\ 010 \\
\hline
1\ 000\ 000\ 000\ 000
\end{array}
$$

In order to obtain two's complement of a number, two steps should be followed.

1. Obtain the one's complement which is formed by getting each bit to the opposite value

$$010\ 110\ 110\ 110 \quad \text{Number}$$
$$101\ 001\ 001\ 001 \quad \text{One's complement of the number}$$

2. Two's complement is equal to the one's complement plus 1

$$
\begin{array}{ll}
101\ 001\ 001\ 001 & \text{One's complement of the number} \\
+ \qquad\qquad\quad 1 & \text{Add 1} \\
\hline
101\ 001\ 001\ 010 & \text{Two's complement of the number}
\end{array}
$$

An example of subtraction:

$$
\begin{array}{ll}
7 - 3 = 4 & \\
0011 & 3_{10} \\
1100 & \text{One's complement of 3} \\
1101 & \text{Two's complement of 3} \\
+ & \\
\underline{0111} & 7_{10} \\
1\ 0100 & 4_{10}
\end{array}
\qquad
\begin{array}{ll}
12 - 5 = 7 & \\
0101 & 5_{10} \\
1010 & \\
1011 & \\
+ & \\
\underline{1100} & 12_{10} \\
1\ 0111 & 7_{10}
\end{array}
$$

Multiplication

In binary multiplication, the partial product is moved one position to the left as each successive multiplier is used. If the multiplier is 0, the partial product is 0; if the multiplier is 1, the partial product is equal to the multiplicand. Examples:

$$
\begin{array}{ll}
5 \times 3 = 15 & \\
101 & 5_{10} \\
\underline{11} & 3_{10} \\
101 & \\
\underline{101} & \\
1111 & 15_{10}
\end{array}
\qquad
\begin{array}{ll}
5 \times 5 = 25 & \\
101 & 5_{10} \\
\underline{101} & 5_{10} \\
101 & \\
000 & \\
\underline{101} & \\
11001 & 25_{10}
\end{array}
\qquad
\begin{array}{ll}
5 \times 10 = 50 & \\
101 & 5_{10} \\
\underline{1010} & 10_{10} \\
000 & \\
101 & \\
000 & \\
\underline{101} & \\
110010 & 50_{10}
\end{array}
$$

Division

Following the rules of binary subtraction and multiplication, one can perform binary division in the same way as decimal division. Examples:

$$18 : 2 = 9 \qquad\qquad 10 : 5 = 2 \qquad\qquad 14 : 4 = 3.5$$

$$
\begin{array}{r}
1001 \quad 9_{10} \\
2_{10}\ \ 10\overline{)10010} \quad 18_{10} \\
\underline{10} \\
00 \\
00 \\
\overline{01} \\
00 \\
\overline{10} \\
10 \\
\overline{0}
\end{array}
\qquad
\begin{array}{r}
10 \quad 2_{10} \\
5_{10}\ \ 101\overline{)1010} \quad 10_{10} \\
\underline{101} \\
000 \\
000 \\
\overline{0}
\end{array}
\qquad
\begin{array}{r}
11.1 \quad 3.5_{10} \\
4_{10}\ \ 100\overline{)1110.0} \quad 14_{10} \\
\underline{100} \\
110 \\
100 \\
100 \\
100 \\
\overline{0}
\end{array}
$$

1.3. OCTAL, BINARY-CODED DECIMAL, AND GRAY CODES

Octal Number System

To express a number in the binary system, it is necessary to use substantially more digits than in the decimal system. For example, $(35)_{10} = (100011)_2$. It is very easy for humans to make errors in reading and writing large binary numbers. For easy notation of binary numbers, the octal number system can be used. The base of the octal system is 8, and the digits are 0 through 7. Thus the numbers used in the octal system to count up to a decimal value 10 are as shown in Table 1.3.

Table 1.3

Decimal	Binary	Octal
0	0	0
1	1	1
2	10	2
3	11	3
4	100	4
5	101	5
6	110	6
7	111	7
8	1000	10
9	1001	11
10	1010	12

Since the base of the octal system is $8 = 2^3$, to convert binary numbers into octal numbers one has to separate binary bits into 3-bit groups. These 3-bit groups can be represented by one octal digit using the table of equivalents in Table 1.3. For example:

110101111001	Binary number
110 101 111 001	3-bit groups
6 5 7 1	Octal equivalent for each group

Hence $(110 \ 101 \ 111 \ 001)_2 = (6571)_8$.

Conversion of a decimal number into an octal equivalent, and arithmetic operations with octal numbers, follow the same philosophy as for binary numbers.

It is important to notice that computers do not operate on the basis of the octal number systems. Computers operate in binary number systems. Octal notation is used sometimes as a help for humans to avoid reading and writing large binary numbers.

Binary-Coded Decimal Numbers (BCD)

It is obvious that the handiest system for humans is the decimal number system. Hence many computer input-output devices will operate in such a way that on the computer side they will transmit/receive the binary number, and on the human side they will receive/transmit the decimal number. This code conversion requires either extra electronics or computational time. Required code conversion can be minimized by using a hybrid representation called *binary-coded decimal* (BCD) representation.

BCD codes are base-10 oriented and may be directly related to decimal numbers. At the same time, they use only binary digits 0 and 1.

BCD representation is formed by replacing each decimal digit in a decimal number by a 4-bit binary representation of that digit. For example, 6_{10} will be represented as 0110. Hence integers 0 to 9 will be represented as shown in Table 1.4.

Table 1.4

Decimal	Binary	BCD
0	0	0000
1	01	0001
2	10	0010
3	11	0011
4	100	0100
5	101	0101
6	110	0110
7	111	0111
8	1000	1000
9	1001	1001

The BCD representation of decimal numbers is formed by direct replacement of digits with their BCD counterpart. For example:

$$0110 \quad 0011 \quad 0100 \quad 0111$$
$$6 \qquad 3 \qquad 4 \qquad 7$$

Example. Convert BCD number 0101 0111 (decimal 57) into binary equivalent.

$$\text{Weights} \quad (8\ 4\ 2\ 1) \times 10 \qquad (8\ 4\ 2\ 1) \times 1$$
$$0\ 1\ 0\ 1 \qquad\qquad 0\ 1\ 1\ 1$$

We express as $8 + 2$ the weighting factor 10 to simplify multiplication. Hence the BCD number 0101 0111 is equivalent to

$$[(0101) \times (8 + 2)] + (0111) \times 1$$

Binary addition and multiplication will be

$$
\begin{array}{rl}
0111 & \times\ 1 \\
0101 & \times\ 2 \\
+\ 0101 & \times\ 8 \\
\hline
0111001 &
\end{array}
$$

This is the binary equivalent of decimal 57 as it should be. Hence circuits for binary addition can be used to convert BCD codes into binary codes.

Two BCD digits are often used together to encode letters and symbols as well as numbers. For example, consider the two-digit decimal numbers 00, 01, 02 . . . 09 to represent the numbers 0, 1, 2 . . . 9. The remaining two-digit numbers, 10 to 99, can be used to represent A, B, . . . Y, Z, and other symbols (such as $+$, $-$, ?). By the use of first decimal-encoding the letters and symbols and then BCD-encoding the decimal code, any number, letter, or symbol can be simply expressed in a binary representation to a digital system.

Excess-3 BCD Numbers. The excess-3 BCD representation is sometimes employed in computers and particularly in electronic tabulating machines to simplify formation of the nine's complement. Every digit is found by adding 3 to the digit and converting to its 4-bit binary representation. A table of excess-3 digits and their nine's complement appears in Table 1.5. Note that the nine's complement is found by just changing all the 1's to 0's and vice-versa.

Hexadecimal Numbers. This is an extension of the natural BCD representation, using extra symbols for six combinations of 4 bits, which is illegal in BCD. Thus we must become accustomed to a counting scheme of 16

Table 1.5

Decimal	Excess-3	Excess-3 Nine's Complement
0	0011	1100
1	0100	1011
2	0101	1010
3	0110	1001
4	0111	1000
5	1000	0111
6	1001	0110
7	1010	0101
8	1011	0101
9	1100	0011

symbols and invent 6 new number symbols. The usual hexadecimal counting scheme is

$$0, 1, 2, 3, 4, 5, 6, 7, 8, 9, A, B, C, D, E, F$$

where $A-F$ represents 1010 through 1111 (decimal values 10–15) of the 4-bit group. Hexadecimal numbers are shown in Table 1.6.

Gray Code

While binary codes are excellently suited for use in performing calculations, they might present a serious problem in applications where transitions between two adjacent binary-coded positions are sampled. An example is computer control of the angular position of shafts or the linear position of a rod. Two adjacent positions of the encoder, coded in binary code, may differ in many 1's and 0's. For example, positions 7 and 8 will have codes 0111 and 1000. There is often momentary ambiguity at the exact transition point between encoder segments as to which position is correct. As a result, the system may produce outputs like 1010, 0101, 1100, and so on. These outputs differ widely from both the old position 0111 and the new position 1000. The digital control system will interpret such transient information as a positionary error and will generate the driving force to correct the position.

The transient error can be reduced in the following way. The code for two adjacent positions should differ only in 1 bit. Since all other bits are unchanged during the transient, the reading at the transient instant can represent only the old position or a new position. Hence the ambiguity is reduced to within either the old or new position and not anywhere in the entire position of the encoder, as encountered with binary codes.

The Gray code is one of a series of codes known as reflected binary codes and is excellently suited for use in position transducers. The Gray code resembles the binary code to the extent that it always has the same bit length and the same most significant bit. The major difference from the binary code is that two adjacent numbers in the Gray code differ in only 1 bit. A series of numbers in both codes is shown for a comparison in Table 1.6.

Table 1.6

Decimal	Binary	Gray	Hexadecimal
0	0000	0	0
1	0001	01	1
2	0010	11	2
3	0011	10	3
4	0100	110	4
5	0101	111	5
6	0110	101	6
7	0111	100	7
8	1000	1100	8
9	1001	1101	9
10	1010	1111	A
11	1011	1110	B
12	1100	1010	C
13	1101	1011	D
14	1110	1001	E
15	1111	1000	F

1.4. DATA FORMAT

The computer is designed to operate upon binary information, which it conveniently represents with electronic components and stores in the memory. Binary information can represent fixed-point numbers, floating-point numbers, binary-coded alphabetic characters, and computer instructions.

Fixed-Point Numbers

Most of the computers operate with two's complement arithmetic. In this case the computer word can be used to store positive as well as negative numbers in the following way. The most significant bit of the word is a sign bit. The 0 is used for positive numbers; 1 is used for negative numbers. The rest of the word presents the magnitude of the number: for positive values it presents the number; for negative values it presents the two's complement of the number. Hence, if the computer word has n bits, $n - 1$ bits are used to present the value of the number which can be any integer between 0 and 2^{n-1}.

An example for 12-bit computer:

Positive numbers:	000 000 000 000	0_{10}
	000 000 000 001	1_{10}
	000 000 000 010	2_{10}
	011 111 111 111	$2^{11} - 1 = 2047_{10}$
Negative numbers:	111 111 111 111	-1_{10}
	111 111 111 110	-2_{10}
	100 000 000 001	$-(2^{11} - 1) = -2047_{10}$
	100 000 000 000	$-2^{11} = -2048_{10}$

Thus the 12-bit word computer can represent directly the numbers between -2048_{10} and $+2047_{10}$. To represent larger values, two computer words can be used, or the number can be presented in floating-point form.

Floating-Point Numbers

In floating-point notation, the number is divided into two parts, namely a mantissa (number part) and an exponent (to some base). In the decimal number system, for example, the number 15 can be written in the following ways:

Mantissa		Exponent
0.15	$\times$	10^2
1.5	$\times$	10^1
15.0	$\times$	10^0
150.0	$\times$	10^{-1}
1500.0	$\times$	10^{-2}

The computer floating-point presentation makes use of a representation similar to the above example. However, since the computer works with binary information, both the mantissa and the exponent are presented as binary numbers. Since both the mantissa and the exponent can be either positive or negative, 2 bits are reserved for signs. Figure 1.2 shows the fixed-point and floating-point presentations of numbers for 36-bit word length. For a small computer, more than one word can be used to present floating-point numbers.

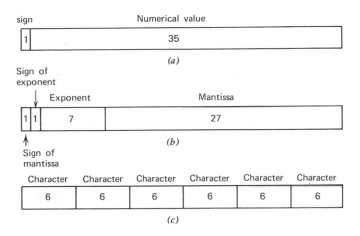

Figure 1.2. Format. (*a*) Fixed point; (*b*) floating point; (*c*) alphanumeric characters.

Alphanumeric Characters

There are occasions when it is necessary to have the computer represent the characters of the alphabet and punctuation marks. Binary codes are used to represent such characters. There are 26 letters and 10 numerals, so that if 6 bits are used for each character, allowing 64 characters, many special symbols can be accommodated. The most frequently used code is the ASCII code (an abbreviation for USA Standard Code for Information Interchange). The ASCII code can use 6, 7, or 8 bits. Table 1.7 presents 6- and 8-bit ASCII codes. Bits are grouped into the 3-bit groups, with each group presenting an octal digit. Table 1.8 presents a 7-bit ASCII code and also a BCD code. Figure 1.2*c* shows the six, 6-bit characters packed into one 36-bit computer word.

Table 1.7. ASCII[a] Character Set

Character	8-Bit Octal	6-Bit Octal	Character	8-Bit Octal	6-Bit Octal
A	301	01	!	241	41
B	302	02	"	242	42
C	303	03	#	243	43
D	304	04	$	244	44
E	305	05	%	245	45
F	306	06	&	246	46
G	307	07	'	247	47
H	310	10	(	250	50
I	311	11	)	251	51
J	312	12	*	252	52
K	313	13	+	253	53
L	314	14	'	254	54
M	315	15	-	255	55
N	316	16	.	256	56
O	317	17	/	257	57
P	320	20	:	272	72
Q	321	21	;	273	73
R	322	22	<	274	74
S	323	23	=	275	75
T	324	24	>	276	76
U	325	25	?	277	77
V	326	26	@	300	
W	327	27	[	333	33
X	330	30	\	334	34
Y	331	31	]	335	35
Z	332	32	↑	336	36
0	260	60	←	337	37
1	261	61	Leader/Trailer	200	
2	262	62	LINE FEED	212	
3	263	63	Carriage RETURN	215	
4	264	64	SPACE	240	40
5	265	65	RUBOUT	377	
6	266	66	Blank	000	
7	267	67	BELL	207	
8	270	70	TAB	211	
9	271	71	FORM	214	

From "Introduction to Programming," Digital Equipment Corporation, Maynard, Mass., 1969.

[a] An abbreviation for USA Standard Code for Information Interchange.

Table 1.8. Binary Coded Decimal Format

Kennedy 1406/1506 ASCII-BCD Conversion

Symbol[a]	BCD (octal code)	ASCII Equivalent (octal code)	Symbol	BCD (octal code)	ASCII Equivalent (octal code)
(Space)	2Ø	Ø4Ø	A	61	1Ø1
!	52	Ø41	B	62	1Ø2
#	13	Ø43	C	63	1Ø3
$	53	Ø44	D	64	1Ø4
%	34	Ø45	E	65	1Ø5
&	6Ø	Ø46	F	66	1Ø6
’	14	Ø47	G	67	1Ø7
(	34	Ø50	H	7Ø	11Ø
)	74	Ø51	I	71	111
*	54	Ø52	J	41	112
+	6Ø	Ø53	K	42	113
’	33	Ø54	L	43	114
-	4Ø	Ø55	M	44	115
.	73	Ø56	N	45	116
/	21	Ø57	O	46	117
			P	47	12Ø
Ø	12	Ø6Ø	Q	50	121
1	Ø1	Ø61	R	51	122
2	Ø2	Ø62	S	22	123
3	Ø3	Ø63	T	23	124
4	Ø4	Ø64	U	24	125
5	Ø5	Ø65	V	25	126
6	Ø6	Ø66	W	26	127
7	Ø7	Ø67	X	27	13Ø
8	1Ø	Ø7Ø	Y	30	131
9	11	Ø71	Z	31	132
:	15	Ø72	[	75	133
;	56	Ø73	\	36	134
<	76	Ø74	]	55	135
=	13	Ø75			
>	16	Ø76			
?	72	Ø77			
@	14	1ØØ			

From "A Pocket Guide to the Hewlett-Packard Computers," Hewlett-Packard Company, Palo Alto, Cal., 1970.

[a] Other symbols which may be represented in ASCII are converted to spaces in BCD (20)

PROBLEMS

1. Perform the following binary additions:

   (a) 10110
       + 101

   (b)   100
       + 10

   (c) 1011101
         + 1

   (d)   1111
          101
       + 1000

   (e) 1011011
       1110011
       + 1100

   (f)   11011011
          11011011
       + 11011011

   (g)   1111111
          1111111
       + 1111111

   (h)   1000001
          1000001
       + 1000001

2. Find one's complement and the two's complement of the following:
   (a) 011 100 110 010
   (b) 010 111 011 111
   (c) 000 000 000 001
   (d) 111 111 111 111
   (e) 111 111 111 110
   (f) 000 000 000 111
   (g) 100 000 000 000
   (h) 100 000 000 001
   (i) 000 000 000 000
   (j) 000 100 100 100

3. Convert the following decimal numbers into binary form:

   5, 3, 1000, 2047, 409, 33, 65, 1, 7, 1500

4. Find the binary equivalent for decimal numbers of problem 3 if those numbers are negative. Use 12-bit word size.

5. Perform the following subtractions by two's complement method:
   (a) 10111   (b) 1011101   (c) 11011011011   (d) 11111111
       − 11   − 101   − 100000   − 100001

6. Multiply the numbers from problem 5.
7. Divide the numbers from problem 5.

REFERENCES

1. Ware, W. H., *Digital Computer Technology and Design*, Vol. I, Wiley, New York, 1963.
2. Chu, Y., *Digital Computer Design Fundamentals*, McGraw-Hill, New York, 1962.
3. Flores, I., *The Logic of Computer Arithmetic*, Prentice-Hall, Englewood Cliffs, N.J., 1962.
4. *Introduction to Programming*, Digital Equipment Corporation, Maynard, Mass., 1969.

2

LOGICAL OPERATIONS, DIGITAL CIRCUITS, AND MICROCHIPS

Chapter 2 deals with logical operations and digital circuits. It starts with a definition of binary variables and then explains basic logical operations. Fundamental concepts of digital-system design are introduced through consecutive levels: basic logical circuits, basic functional circuits, examples of the design of digital systems, and computer-aided digital-system design. The chapter ends with the description of the basic organization of digital computers, storage devices, and input-output devices. Microprocessors chips, and read only and random access memories are described.

2.1. BASIC LOGICAL CIRCUITS

Numerical data and instructions for operations are represented in the computer in the binary number system. A binary signal can be either 1 or 0, and it may be considered as a special kind of variable, Fig. 2.1a. Binary variables can be represented by a letter. Let us suppose that a binary variable is denoted by A. To distinguish between possible states 1 and 0, we can use notation A and $\overline{A}$, respectively. $\overline{A}$ is called the complement of the variable A.

To solve different problems, computers use logical operations between binary variables. Logical operations between binary variables are treated by a special branch of mathematics which is called Boolean algebra.

Figure 2.1b presents a general logical system with binary variables A, B, ..., N as inputs. Boolean algebra can be used to find out the output of the system.

Input-output relationships of a logical system can also be expressed through the truth table. The truth table consists of two parts. The first part of the truth table is related to the inputs and presents a complete listing of all possible combinations of inputs A, B, ..., N.

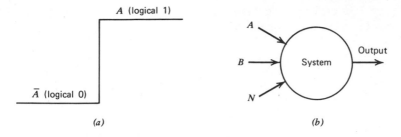

(a)   (b)

Figure 2.1. Binary variable.

The second part of the truth table is the output state as a function of combinations of inputs.

All logical systems can be reduced to a few basic logical circuits which will now be defined.

INVERTOR

The invertor is one input circuit which produces the output, the state of which is equal to the complement of the input. Thus, if the input is a 0, the output is a 1; if the input is 1, the output is 0. Figure 2.2 shows the truth table of the invertor and a standard symbol which is used to indicate the invertor in block diagrams.

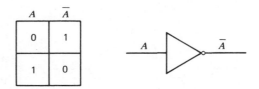

Figure 2.2. Invertor.

AND

The AND circuit has two or more inputs. Figure 2.3a presents a simple circuit with two switches which illustrate the AND operation. If switch A is closed, the variable A has a value of 1. If the switch A is open, the variable A has a value of 0. The current can flow through the circuits only if both switches are closed (the output is 1, only if both variables A and B are 1). The AND operation is often indicated as $A \cdot B$. Thus the AND operation of three variables, A, B, and C, is indicated as $A \cdot B \cdot C$.

Figure 2.3*b* presents a standard symbol for the AND circuit. Figure 2.3*c* presents the truth table for the AND circuit.

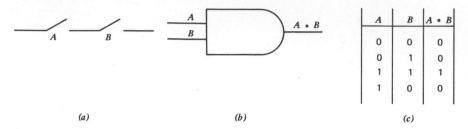

A	B	$A \cdot B$
0	0	0
0	1	0
1	1	1
1	0	0

(a)   (b)   (c)

Figure 2.3. AND circuit.

OR

The OR circuit has two or more inputs. Figure 2.4*a* presents a simple circuit with two switches which illustrates the OR operation. The current will flow if either of the switches A or B is closed. This operation is indicated by a plus sign between the variables. The truth table and block diagram are shown in Fig. 2.4 for two variables.

The three basic circuits, INVERTOR, AND, and OR, are sufficient to design a digital computer. These circuits can be combined to produce elaborate functions. Some of those functions, which are very frequently used, will be listed next.

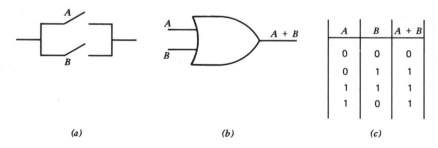

A	B	$A + B$
0	0	0
0	1	1
1	1	1
1	0	1

(a)   (b)   (c)

Figure 2.4. OR circuit.

NOR

The NOR circuit is a combination of the OR and INVERTOR. Figure 2.5*a* shows the truth table of the NOR circuit and two block diagrams for the

NOR operation. The output is expressed as $\overline{A + B}$. This is simply the result of first performing the OR function $A + B$, and then the INVERT function. Because of the inversion, the output of the truth table for NOR circuit is exactly opposite of the output of the OR circuit. The truth table is composed of the truth tables for OR and INVERTOR as indicated in Fig. 2.5a.

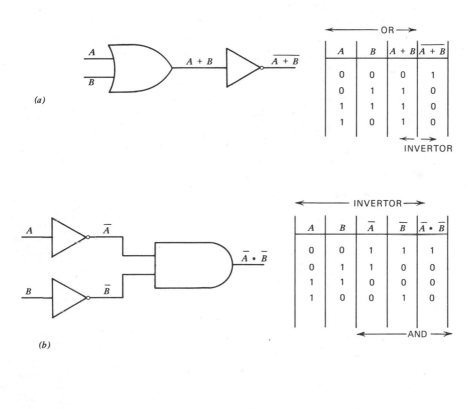

(a)

←	OR	→	
A	B	$A + B$	$\overline{A + B}$
0	0	0	1
0	1	1	0
1	1	1	0
1	0	1	0

← INVERTOR →

(b)

←	INVERTOR	→		
A	B	$\overline{A}$	$\overline{B}$	$\overline{A} \cdot \overline{B}$
0	0	1	1	1
0	1	1	0	0
1	1	0	0	0
1	0	0	1	0

← AND →

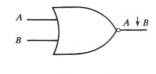

(c)

Figure 2.5. NOR circuit.

One can also perform NOR operation by different combinations of circuits (Fig. 2.5b). This circuit is composed of invertors and an AND gate, but one can see that its truth table gives the same output as the one in Fig. 2.5*a*. In the second circuit, the output is expressed as $\overline{A} \cdot \overline{B}$. This is the result of first performing the INVERT functions $\overline{A}$, $\overline{B}$, and then the AND function. We see that

$$\overline{A + B} = \overline{A} \cdot \overline{B} \tag{2.1}$$

Equation 2.1 can be written in a more general form which is known as de Morgan's theorem and presents a fundamental theorem of Boolean algebra. This theorem states that the complement of a function is obtained by complementing each of the variables and interchanging the operations of OR and AND. The general form of de Morgan's theorem is

$$\overline{f(A_1, A_2, \ldots, +, \cdot)} = f(\overline{A}_1, \overline{A}_2, \overline{A}_3, \ldots, \cdot, +) \tag{2.2}$$

The bottom of Fig. 2.5 presents a symbol for NOR operation.

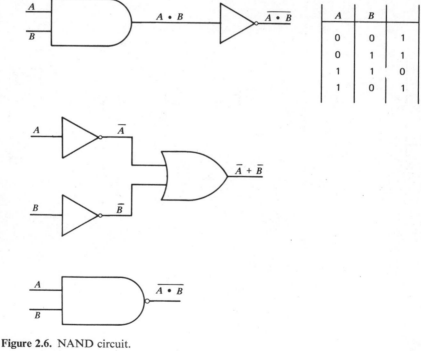

Figure 2.6. NAND circuit.

NAND

The NAND circuit is a combination of the AND and INVERTOR. Figure 2.6 shows the truth table and two block diagrams for NAND operations. In the first diagram, NAND operation has been expressed as $\overline{A \cdot B}$. In the second diagram, NAND operation has been expressed as $\overline{A} + \overline{B}$. This is another example where de Morgan's theorem, Eq. 2.2, can be used

$$\overline{A \cdot B} = \overline{A} + \overline{B} \qquad (2.3)$$

The bottom of Fig. 2.6 shows a symbol for NAND operation.

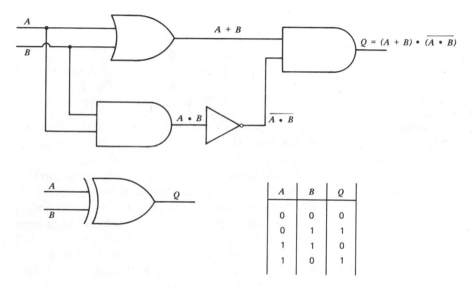

Figure 2.7. Exclusive OR circuit (EOR).

EOR

The EOR circuit presents the exclusive OR operation. The exclusive OR is similar to OR, with the exception that one set of conditions for A and B is excluded; if both A and B are in the state 1, the output will not go into the state 1 but will take the state 0.

Figure 2.7 presents a truth table, block diagram, and symbol of the EOR circuit.

The output of EOR circuit, according to the block diagram, is given by

$$Q = (A + B) \cdot (\overline{A \cdot B}) \qquad (2.4)$$

The operations INVERTOR, OR, AND, NOR, NAND, and EOR can be applied to binary numbers.

A binary number in the computer is composed of a number of bits. Each bit can be treated as one binary variable. Hence logical operations can be performed between two binary numbers, treating each pair of bits as two binary variables. For example:

$$
\begin{array}{lcccccccccccccl}
 & A_{12} & & & & & & & & & & A_2 & A_1 & \\
A = & 1 & 0 & 1 & 0 & 0 & 0 & 1 & 1 & 0 & 0 & 1 & 0 & \text{First number} \\
B = & 0 & 1 & 1 & 1 & 0 & 1 & 0 & 1 & 1 & 0 & 1 & 1 & \text{Second number} \\
 & B_{12} & & & & & & & & & & B_2 & B_1 &
\end{array}
$$

results in

$$
\begin{array}{lccccccccccccl}
A \cdot B = & 0 & 0 & 1 & 0 & 0 & 0 & 0 & 1 & 0 & 0 & 1 & 0 & \text{AND} \\
A + B = & 1 & 1 & 1 & 1 & 0 & 1 & 1 & 1 & 1 & 0 & 1 & 1 & \text{OR} \\
\overline{A \cdot B} = & 1 & 1 & 0 & 1 & 1 & 1 & 1 & 0 & 1 & 1 & 0 & 1 & \text{NAND} \\
\overline{A + B} = & 0 & 0 & 0 & 0 & 1 & 0 & 0 & 0 & 0 & 1 & 0 & 0 & \text{NOR} \\
(A + B) \cdot (\overline{A \cdot B}) = & 1 & 1 & 0 & 1 & 0 & 1 & 1 & 0 & 1 & 0 & 0 & 1 & \text{EOR}
\end{array}
$$

Timing. The truth tables of logical circuits show a steady state of input-output relationships. However, when electrical pulses are applied as inputs, it takes some time for the output to reach the steady-state level because of the internal delays in the circuits. The delay of one circuit is usually small, in the order of a few nano-seconds (10^{-9} sec). In the computer, binary signals of the pulse pass through many circuits, and delays might become substantial. In this situation, it is crucial to allot a specific amount of time for each step of an operation. If the operation is completed before this time has elapsed, the machine waits. In this way the speed of operation is somewhat slowed down, but high reliability is achieved because the synchronism between many parallel-going operations is guaranteed.

Logical 1

Logical 0

Figure 2.8. Clock.

This basic synchronism for a computer is derived from a clock. This is normally a free-running oscillator designed to produce pulses with stable constant frequency (Fig. 2.8). Two levels of pulses correspond to two logical states of binary variables, 0 and 1. Almost all operations in the machine are gated with the clock pulses.

However, input-output transfers between computer and peripheral devices are usually asynchronous.

2.2. FLIP-FLOP

The main active elements in the computer are the flip-flops, which are binary storage devices, each capable of storing a single bit of information. The flip-flop is also called a binary trigger, latch, bistable multivibrator, or, simply, bistable.

Figure 2.9 explains a basic principle of a device having two stable states.

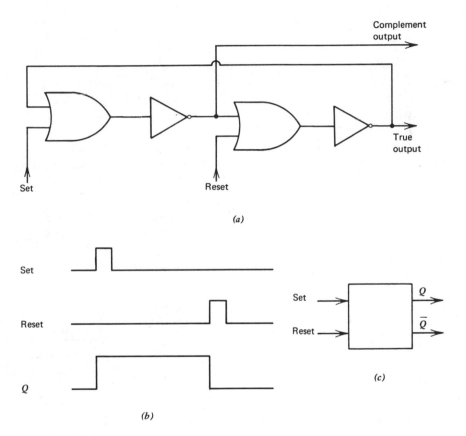

Figure 2.9. Flip-flop.

The circuit has two inputs, the SET and RESET. Normally, both the SET and RESET inputs are at 0. If the SET input is brought to 1, the circuit output goes to 1. Even when the input is removed, the circuit stays in the state 1, due to the internal feedback.

Figure 2.9*a* shows the flip-flop composed of OR circuits and invertors, and it explains the feedback action which keeps the circuit in the stable state. If the RESET input is brought to 1, the circuit goes to the opposite stable state and the true output goes to 0. The same feedback from the output will keep the circuit in the state 0 when the RESET input is removed.

Figure 2.9*b* shows the input-output relationship for the flip-flop. Figure 2.9*c* shows a symbolic presentation of the flip-flop.

A flip-flop can be easily designed from INVERTORS and OR gates, as shown in Fig. 2.9. However, since the flip-flops are very frequently used, they are produced as standard integrated units. Flip-flops are produced in few versions, which differ in triggering arrangements.

RS Flip-Flop. This flip-flop is especially designed to operate under clock control. Its schematic presentation is shown in Fig. 2.10*a*. Inputs *S* (set) and *R* (reset) are used to determine the state of the flip-flop, but the clock pulses must be applied to sample those inputs. The timing is shown in Fig. 2.10*b*. The clock looks at *R* and *S* lines. If *R* is active, the clock will switch the flip-flop into the state 0 (reset). If *S* is active, the clock will switch the flip-flop into the 1 (set) state. Inputs *R* and *S* are not allowed to be active at the same time because the state of the flip-flop would not be clearly defined.

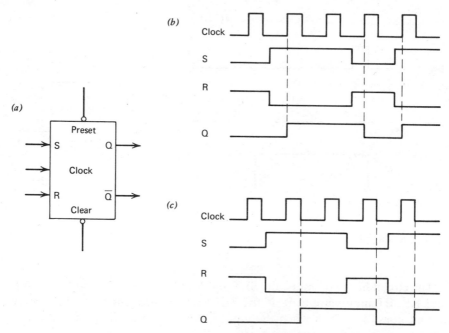

Figure 2.10. RS flip-flop. (*a*) Symbol; (*b*) timing; (*c*) timing for master-slave RS.

RS flip-flop has two auxiliary inputs, PRESET and CLEAR, which are not under clock control. These inputs are normally at a logical 1 level. If the CLEAR input is grounded, the flip-flop is forced in the 0 state. If the PRESET input is grounded, the flip-flop is forced in the 1 state.

RS Master-Slave Flip-Flop. Two *RS* flip-flops are integrated in the same chip. The leading edge of the clock samples the input *R*, *S* lines, and the information is stored into the first flip-flop. The trailing edge of the clock transfers the information on the second flip-flop whose outputs are used as the outputs of the unit. Timing is shown in Fig. 2.10*c*.

Complement Flip-Flop. This kind of flip-flop has only one input. A pulse applied on the input line causes the circuit to switch states (complement action). If the state is 1, it becomes 0; if 0, it becomes 1. Hence the output changes with every two transitions of the input. Timing and schematic presentation are shown in Fig. 2.11*a* and *b*, respectively.

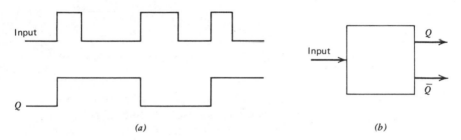

(a)   (b)

Figure 2.11. Complement flip-flop.

JK Flip-Flop. This is basically a complement flip-flop designed to operate under clock control. Its schematic presentation is shown in Fig. 2.12*a*. The clock looks at *J* and *K* lines. If only *K* is active, the clock will switch the flip-flop into the state 0 (reset). If only *J* is active, the clock will switch flip-flop into the state 1 (set). If both *J* and *K* are active, the clock will complement the state of the flip-flop. The timing is shown in Fig. 2.12*b*. *JK* flip-flop is also provided with preset and clear inputs.

JK Master-Slave Flip-Flop. Two *JK* flip-flops are connected together. The output is delayed by the duration of the CLOCK pulse. Timing is shown in Fig. 2.12*c*.

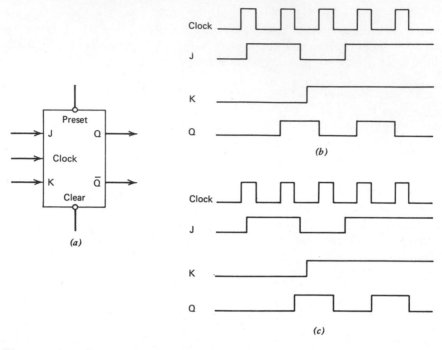

Figure 2.12. JK flip-flop. (a) Symbol; (b) timing; (c) timing for master-slave JK.

D-Flip-Flop. This is basically a set-reset flip-flop with only one data line (D). The leading edge of the clock samples the data line. If D input is high, the clock will switch the flip-flop into the 1 state. If D input is low, the clock will switch the flip-flop into the 0 state.

Schematic presentation and timing are shown in Fig. 2.13a and b, respectively. The D-flip-flop is also provided with preset and clear inputs.

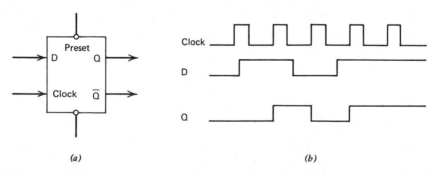

Figure 2.13. D flip-flop.

Latch Circuit. This circuit operates as a digital sample and hold circuit. It has two inputs, data (*D*) and CLOCK (*C*). Information presented at the data (*D*) input is transferred to the *Q* output when the clock is high (1). When the clock goes low, the information that was present at the data input at the time that transition occurred is retained at the *Q* output. Hence the trailing edge of the CLOCK samples the data line, and the circuit holds (stores) the binary information. Schematic presentation and timing are shown in Fig. 2.14*a* and *b* respectively.

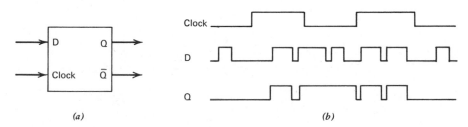

(a)   *(b)*

Figure 2.14. Latch circuit.

Note the following design features of the flip-flops. If nothing is connected to the flip-flop inputs *R*, *S*, *J*, *K*, *D*, CLOCK, PRESET, or CLEAR, the inputs will be at a high level. The grounding of the PRESET input will force the flip-flop in the state 1. The grounding of the CLEAR input will force the flip-flop in the state 0. *R* and *S* inputs must always be in opposite states. *J* and *K* inputs, if both are at high levels, will enable the CLOCK to complement the flip-flop.

The basic flip-flops will trigger on the leading (positive-going) edge of the CLOCK input. The master-slave flip-flops, due to internal transfer between first and second stage, produce the output, as if triggered on the trailing (negative-going) edge of the CLOCK.

Those inputs which switch the flip-flop when low (CLEAR, PRESET, and CLOCK for master-slave flip-flop), are marked on block diagram as _____.

2.3. BASIC FUNCTIONAL CIRCUITS

Computer processes can be synthesized with only a few simple binary devices: flip-flops, AND gates, OR gates, and invertors. Through combinations of those basic units we can design the registers for storing, shifting, or counting, units for arithmetic operations, selectors, decoders, memories, and so on.

Register. A flip-flop can be used to store one bit of information. Binary numbers can be, in general, composed of n bits, and it is necessary to provide the storage for n bits. This can be achieved by putting together n RS flip-flops. Such a combination is called n-bit register (Fig. 2.15a).

The R, S lines are used for parallel input of n-bit information. Since R and S lines must always be on complementary levels, invertors are used to provide this condition. Registers can be built using separate flip-flops, but they are also available as standard integrated units. Figure 2.15b shows a schematic presentation of a 4-bit integrated register with parallel inputs and outputs.

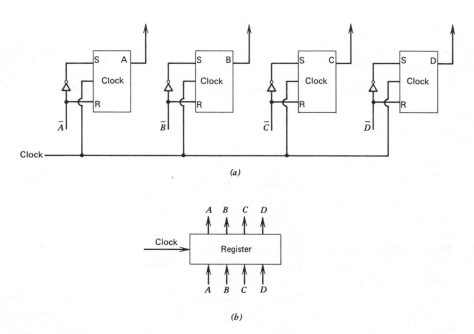

(a)

(b)

Figure 2.15. Register.

Shift Register. Shifting presents one of the basic operations in the digital computer. A shift register is a circuit which is able to shift its contents within itself and without altering the order of the bits. Provision can be made to shift right or left and to shift one position, two positions, or any number of positions. Figure 2.16a shows a logical diagram of a 4-bit shift register with the ability to shift right one position. Figure 2.16b gives a symbolic presentation. The shift register is composed of RS master-slave flip-flops. A binary number is entered into the shift register through the PRESET inputs. Each

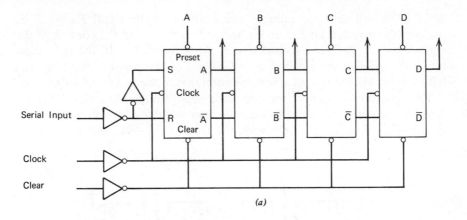

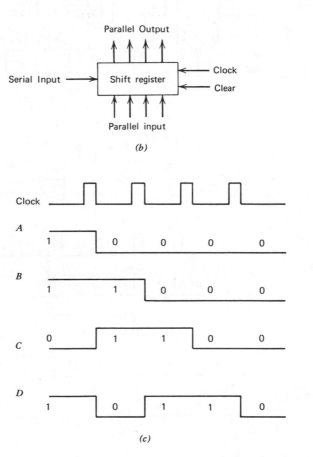

Figure 2.16. Shift register.

clock pulse will shift the number one position to the right. Figure 2.16c presents the number 1101 stored in the shift register and the content of the register after 1, 2, 3, and 4 clock cycles. After the first shift, the right-most bit of the original information is shifted out of the register and lost. The left-most bit will become zero, because nothing is connected to the serial input.

The operation of shifting for one place goes through the following steps. The leading edge of the clock will sample lines A and $\overline{A}$ and write information in the B flip-flop. In the same way, the transfers $B \rightarrow C$ and $C \rightarrow D$ will

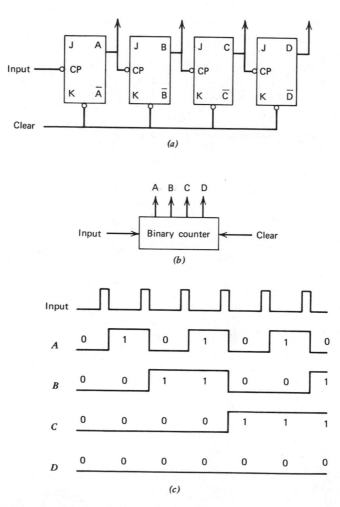

Figure 2.17. Binary counter.

occur. The trailing edge of the clock will set the information onto the output lines of RS master-slave flip-flops, preparing it for the next shift.

Shift registers can be built using separate flip-flops, but they are also available as standard integrated units.

Binary Counter. A counter is a flip-flop register storing a binary number. Whenever a pulse occurs on the counter input, the counter must increment the stored number by 1. A 4-bit counter is presented in Fig. 2.17a. It is composed of four RS master-slave flip-flops. A clear line can be used to reset the counter. If k pulses enter the counter at the input, the states of the four stages will present binary number k. The negative-going (trailing) edge of the first pulse will set the flip-flop A into state 1. The output of the counter, after the first pulse, will read 0001.

The negative-going edge of the second pulse will put flip-flop A into state 0. The negative transition at the output A will set flip-flop B into state 1. The output of the counter after the second pulse will read 0010. Figure 2.17b shows the schematic presentation and Fig. 2.17c the timing for a few input pulses.

Binary counters can be built using separate flip-flops, but they are also available as standard integrated units. Figure 2.18b shows the truth table for the binary counter.

Decade Counter. Another standard integrated unit is a decade counter. It has count input, clear input, and 4-bit output (Fig. 2.18a). This counter will present results in binary-coded decimal form (BCD). The BCD count sequence is achieved through proper feedback between binary triggers and is presented in Fig. 2.18b. Note the difference between the binary sequence and the BCD sequence. The two sequences are the same for counts 0, 1 . . . 9. After 9 counts, binary sequence proceeds while the BCD sequence is reset. Hence the output of the BCD counter is a decimal digit expressed by four binary digits.

Full Adder. Adding is much more complicated than the processes discussed up to now because of the carry problem. The addition process for bit position $n + 1$ involves adding the digits from A_{n+1} and B_{n+1} and the carry C_n from the right; the result is a digit for the sum and possibly a digit to be carried to the left (carry C_{n+1}). Full adders are now available as integrated units. Figure 2.19 shows a schematic presentation of 1-bit and 4-bit full adders. A 1-bit adder has inputs for a $(n + 1)$th bit of a number A and for $(n + 1)$th bit of a number B and the carry input C_n. It provides the outputs for the sum $\sum$ and $\overline{\sum}$, and carry C_{n+1} to the possible next bit to the left.

A 4-bit adder has inputs $A_1A_2A_3A_4$, $B_1B_2B_3B_4$, and carry-in C_n. It provides the outputs $\sum_1\sum_2\sum_3\sum_4$ and carry-out C_{n+4}.

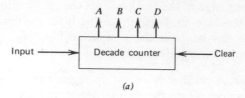

(a)

Count	Binary Counter Output				BCD Counter Output			
	D	C	B	A	D	C	B	A
0	0	0	0	0	0	0	0	0
1	0	0	0	1	0	0	0	1
2	0	0	1	0	0	0	1	0
3	0	0	1	1	0	0	1	1
4	0	1	0	0	0	1	0	0
5	0	1	0	1	0	1	0	1
6	0	1	1	0	0	1	1	0
7	0	1	1	1	0	1	1	1
8	1	0	0	0	1	0	0	0
9	1	0	0	1	1	0	0	1
10	1	0	1	0	0	0	0	0
11	1	0	1	1	0	0	0	1
12	1	1	0	0	0	0	1	0

(b)

Figure 2.18. Decade counter. (a) Schematic presentation; (b) count sequence.

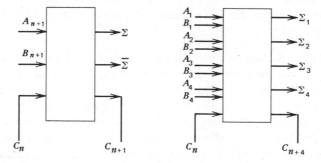

Figure 2.19. Full adder.

38

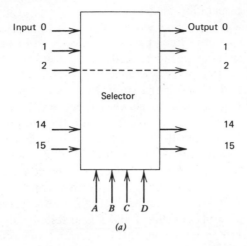

(a)

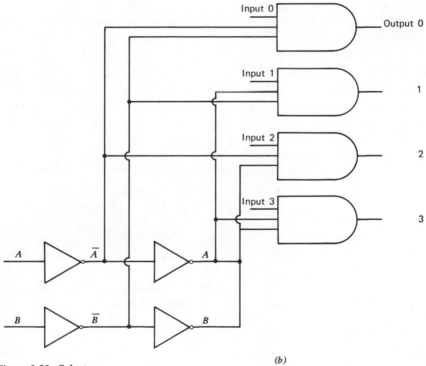

(b)

Figure 2.20. Selector.

Selector. During the operation of the computer, it is necessary from time to time to select a part of a machine and to connect it to another part. This operation is done by a selector. Each part to be selected must have a "house number," or destination address. Figure 2.20*a* presents a 4-bit selector which can select between $2^4 = 16$ different destination addresses. This selector has four control inputs, *A*, *B*, *C*, *D*. If the control inputs are, say, in the state 0010, the selector will open the gate between input #0010 (2) and output #0010. The other 15 gates will stay closed because they have different addresses from the selected one, 0010. This selector can be used to select one of 16 different sources and to connect it to one of 16 different "customers"; or it can select one of 16 sources and connect it to the common customer; or it can be used to connect one common source to one of 16 different customers. Figure 2.20*b* shows a block diagram of a 2-bit selector. Addresses 01 should be selected when *A* is in state 1 and *B* is in state 0, ($\overline{B} = 1$). Hence wires $\overline{B}$ and *A* are used to open the gate #01. In the same way, one can follow the connections to other gates.

Selectors can be built using separate gates, but they are also available as standard integrated units. The integrated selector has additional *strobe input* connected to the AND gates. The strobe is normally low, keeping the outputs at a low level. When the strobe goes high, the selected output becomes high. Also, outputs of the AND gates are ORed into one common output.

Decoder. The digital information can be coded in different ways. One way is, for example, the binary system. The 16 numbers, say 0, 1 . . . 15, can be expressed by four binary digits, *A*, *B*, *C*, *D*. If those digits are, say, in the state 0011, they present the binary code of the number 3. The 4-bit decoder is a device with 4 inputs, *A*, *B*, *C*, *D*, and 16 outputs. If the inputs are in the state 0011, only the output #3 will be high and all other outputs should be low. Figure 2.21*a* presents a 4-bit decoder. Figure 2.21*b* presents a logical diagram of a 2-bit decoder.

If the input digits *AB* are, say, in the state 11, the last AND gate should produce the output. This will happen if all inputs to the gate are in state 1.

In the same way, one can follow the connections to other gates. Knowing the truth table between inputs and outputs, one can build the decoder using separate gates. Some standard decoders are also available as ready-made integrated units (4-line to 10-line or binary to BCD decoder; 4-line to 16-line decoder; BCD to 7-segment decoder for display, and so on).

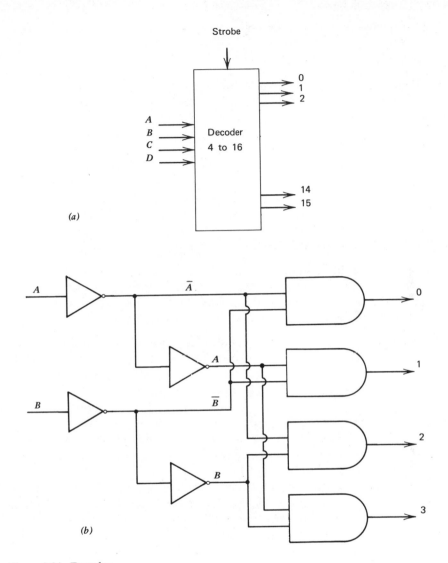

Strobe

A
B
C
D

Decoder
4 to 16

0
1
2

14
15

(a)

A $\overline{A}$ 0

A   1

B $\overline{B}$

B   2

3

(b)

Figure 2.21. Decoder.

41

2.4. DIGITAL SYSTEM DESIGN

Theorems

A digital system can be defined in two ways: through the truth table or by logical equation. Both ways are used to design the system using standard basic circuits.

In a few cases, we have seen that the same digital operation can be performed through different combinations of circuits. Figure 2.5 presents two different combinations producing the same NOR function. Figure 2.6 presents two different combinations producing the same NAND function. If the system has more than two inputs and performs more elaborate functions, it can be composed, usually, through many different combinations of basic circuits.

A digital system designer has to solve two problems:

1. To define input-output relationships and to find the combination of basic circuits which will perform the desired operation of the system.

2. To check that the chosen combination is composed of a minimum number of basic circuits—this step is called minimization.

Minimization can be a very complicated procedure especially for an elaborate system design. There are a number of sophisticated minimization techniques. Minimization is especially important if the system should be reproduced many times, in which case it is of interest to have the minimal number of circuits in the system. A minimal number of circuits will reduce the cost and may increase the speed and reliability of the system.

Laboratory digital systems are usually simple and are not reproduced in large quantities. In this situation minimization, if necessary, can be done by following a few basic theorems of Boolean algebra.

Table 2.1 presents a list of important theorems which one can prove through the combinations of the truth tables of basic circuits. A, B, and C are binary variables. The left-hand half of the table presents theorems for OR operations ($+$). The right-hand half of the table presents corresponding theorems for AND operations ($\cdot$).

Let us explain the first theorem for OR operation

$$A + 0 = A$$

This theorem says if an OR circuit has two inputs, the first of which is constantly connected to 0, the output will always follow the second input. This theorem is obvious from the definition of OR function; in Fig. 2.4a, if the switch B is open all of the time ($B = 0$), the output is equal to A.

Table 2.1

1	$A + 0 = A$	$A \cdot 1 = A$
2	$A + B = B + A$	$AB = BA$
3	$A + BC = (A + B)(A + C)$	$A(B + C) = AB + AC$
4	$A + \overline{A} = 1$	$A \cdot \overline{A} = 0$
5	$A + A = A$	$A \cdot A = A$
6	$A + 1 = 1$	$A \cdot 0 = 0$
7	$\overline{1} = 0$	
8	$A + AB = A$	$A(A + B) = A$
9	$\overline{\overline{A}} = A$	
10	$A + (B + C) = (A + B) + C$	$A(BC) = (AB)C = ABC$
11	$A + \overline{A}B = A + B$	$A(\overline{A} + B) = A \cdot B$
12	$\overline{A + B} = \overline{A} \cdot \overline{B}$	$\overline{A \cdot B} = \overline{A} + \overline{B}$
13	$AB + \overline{A}C + BC = AB + \overline{A}C$	$(A + B)(\overline{A} + C)(B + C)$ $= (A + B)(\overline{A} + C)$

Let us explain the first theorem for AND operation

$$A \cdot 1 = A$$

This theorem says if an AND circuit has two inputs, the first of which is constantly connected to 1, the output will always follow the second input. This theorem is obvious from the definition of the AND function; in Fig. 2.3a, if the switch B is closed all of the time ($B = 1$), the output is equal to A.

In a similar way, one can explain the other theorems. Those theorems and de Morgan's theorem, Eq. 2.2, present the basis for the digital system design.

Example 1: Design of a 1-bit functional adder. The block diagram of the adder is shown in Fig. 2.19. The adder has inputs for 1-bit for variable A, for variable B, and for the carry C_n. It produces outputs for the sum and a carry output C_{n+1}. Following the basic principle of addition of binary numbers, we can form the truth table for the adder, Fig. 2.22a. The addition can be explained for two different cases. (a) "Half adder": carry $C_n = 0$

A	B	C_{in}	S_1	C_{out}	S
0	0	0	0	0	0
0	1	0	1	0	1
1	0	0	1	0	1
1	1	0	0	1	0
0	0	1	0	0	1
0	1	1	1	1	0
1	0	1	1	1	0
1	1	1	0	1	1

(a)

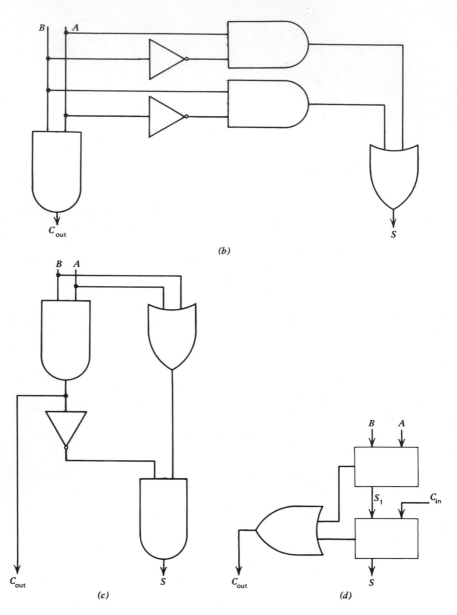

(b)

(c)   (d)

Figure 2.22. One-bit functional adder. (a) Truth table; (b), (c), (d), circuits.

(the low-order bit position of the number). (b) "Full adder": C_n can be either 0 or 1 (all other bit positions of the number).

Let us first examine the case a, which is represented by the first four lines of the table in Fig. 2.22a. A functional device that will perform the operation of adding a single bit position to another single bit position is called a *half adder*. Such a device will have two input lines, *A* and *B*, and two output lines, one called the sum line and the other called the carry line. According to the rules for adding binary numbers, and from Table 2.1, the sum line will be a 1 if either *A* or *B* is 1, but not if both *A* and *B* are 1.

$$S = A\overline{B} + \overline{A}B \tag{2.5}$$

This is a Boolean equation and is read in the following manner: *S* is equal to *A* and not *B* or not *A* and *B*. This equation states that *S* will be a 1 when *A* is a 1 and *B* is a 0, or when *A* is a 0 and *B* is a 1. The carry line will be a 1 only if both inputs are 1's.

$$C_{\text{out}} = A \cdot B \tag{2.6}$$

This equation reads: *C* is equal to *A* and *B*. The circuit implementation of those two equations is shown in Fig. 2.22*b*.

Now, let us try to minimize the number of basic circuits in the half adder. The half adder is composed of two parts corresponding to the Eqs. 2.5 and 2.6. We can try to modify Eq. 2.5 so that it will contain, in itself, Eq. 2.6. In this way, the half adder would be composed of only one part.

$S = A\overline{B} + \overline{A}B$	Start
$S = A\overline{A} + A\overline{B} + \overline{A}B + B\overline{B}$	Theorem 4, left, Table 2.1
$S = A(\overline{A} + \overline{B}) + (B(\overline{A} + \overline{B}))$	Theorem 3, right
$S = (A + B) \cdot (\overline{A} + \overline{B})$	Theorem 3, right
$S = (A + B) \cdot (\overline{A \cdot B})$	de Morgan's theorem

$$S = (A + B) \cdot (\overline{A \cdot B}) \tag{2.7}$$

Now we can implement the Eq. 2.7 for *S* and the Eq. 2.6 for C_n. The implementation of those two equations is shown in Fig. 2.22*c*.

Digital systems presented in Fig. 2.22*b* and *c* will perform exactly the same function—the half adder. However, the first system is composed of six basic units while the second system is composed of only four basic units.

As a second example of the transformation of Boolean expressions, let us start with Eq. 2.7 and try to obtain its equivalent, Eq. 2.5:

$S = (A + B) \cdot (\overline{A \cdot B})$	Start
$S = (A + B) \cdot (\overline{A} + \overline{B})$	de Morgan theorem
$S = A(\overline{A} + \overline{B}) + B(\overline{A} + \overline{B})$	Theorem 3, right
$S = A\overline{A} + A\overline{B} + \overline{A}B + B\overline{B}$	Theorem 3, right
$S = A\overline{B} + \overline{A}B$	Theorem 4, left

There are no fixed rules as to which theorems to use or in what order. The exercises are the best school. One usually wants to transform a Boolean equation in one of two forms:

$$f_1(A, B, C, D \ldots) = (A \cdot B \cdots) + (B \cdot C \cdots) + (\ ) + (\ ) \quad (2.8)$$

$$f_2(A, B, C, D \ldots) = (A + B \cdots) \cdot (B + D + \cdots) \cdot (\ ) \cdot (\ ) \quad (2.9)$$

The function f_1 presents the system composed of many parts ( ), which are ORed together (+). The function f_2 represents the system composed of many parts ( ) which are ANDed together (·).

In the first example shown, we transformed the function f_1 into its equivalent f_2 (Eq. 2.5 into Eq. 2.7). We started with theorem 4, and then used theorem 3. This theorem has a special name, the distribution law. It may be generally useful to try those steps in transforming the f_1 form into the f_2 form.

In the second example shown, we transformed the f_2 form into the f_1 form, starting with de Morgan's theorem and then used the distribution law. It may be generally useful to try those steps in transforming the f_2 form into the f_1 form.

As a further example, we now design the full adder which has two inputs, A and B, and a carry input, C_{in}. The full adder is explained by the whole table in Fig. 2.22a.

The sum bit of a full adder may be obtained by listing the input conditions from the table in Fig. 2.22a that will produce a 1 output.

$$A \cdot \overline{B} \cdot \overline{C}_{in} \qquad \overline{A} \cdot B \cdot \overline{C}_{in} \qquad \overline{A} \cdot \overline{B} \cdot C_{in} \qquad A \cdot B \cdot C$$

Since either of those terms will produce the desired output S, they should be ORed together giving

$$S = A \cdot \overline{B} \cdot \overline{C}_{in} + \overline{A} \cdot B \cdot \overline{C}_{in} + \overline{A} \cdot \overline{B} \cdot C_{in} + A \cdot B \cdot C \quad (2.10)$$

In the same way, the carry C_{out} can be obtained

$$C_{out} = A \cdot B \cdot \overline{C}_{in} + A \cdot \overline{B} \cdot C_{in} + \overline{A} \cdot B \cdot C_{in} + A \cdot B \cdot C_{in} \quad (2.11)$$

These two equations can be reduced to obtain the form

$$S = (S_1 + C_{in}) \cdot (\overline{S_1 \cdot C_{in}}) \qquad (2.10a)$$
$$C_{out} = C_1 \cdot C_2 \qquad (2.11a)$$
where
$$S_1 = (A + B) \cdot (\overline{A \cdot B}) \qquad (2.12)$$
$$C_1 = A \cdot B \qquad (2.13)$$
$$C_2 = S_1 \cdot C_{in} \qquad (2.14)$$

One can see that Eqs. 2.10a and 2.12 describe the operation of half-adder summation and are identical in form. Also, Eqs. 2.13 and 2.14 describe the half-adder carry generation and are identical in form. Hence two half adders and an OR circuit described by Eq. 2.11*a* will implement a full adder as shown in Fig. 2.22*d*.

The output S_1 of the first half adder is called the partial sum and is listed in Fig. 2.22*a*.

Through the design of the full adder we showed the basic steps in the design of digital systems. Most laboratory systems are simpler than the adder and can be designed with elementary Boolean theorems or directly from the truth table, using integrated digital modules.

Example 2: Design of a digital comparator. A digital comparator is a circuit which compares two *n*-bit digital numbers, *A* and *B*. If two numbers are identical, the output of the comparator is 1. If two numbers are different, the output of the comparator is 0.

Let us first design the comparator for 1-bit variables *A* and *B*. The output should be 1 if both *A* and *B* are 1, or if both *A* and *B* are 0:

$$Q = A \cdot B + \overline{A} \cdot \overline{B} \tag{2.15}$$

Figure 2.23*a* shows the circuit implementation of Eq. 2.15. This is an f_1-type of circuit as defined by Eq. 2.8. As an exercise, let us convert it into an f_2-type of circuit as defined by Eq. 2.9.

$$Q - AB + \overline{A} \cdot \overline{B} \qquad \text{Start}$$
$$Q = \overline{(\overline{A} + \overline{B})} \cdot (A + B) \qquad \text{de Morgan}$$
$$Q = \overline{(\overline{A \cdot B})} \cdot (A + B) \qquad \text{de Morgan}$$
$$Q = \overline{(\overline{A \cdot B})} \cdot (A + B) \tag{2.16}$$

Equation 2.16 presents the complement of Eq. 2.4 for exclusive OR gate. Figure 2.23*b* shows the circuit implementation of Eq. 2.16 using a standard EOR element.

This is a circuit of a 1-bit digital comparator. In order to compare two *n*-bit numbers, *n* such circuits should be used. The output is 1 only if the outputs $Q_1, Q_2, \ldots Q_n$ of all *n* circuits are 1:

$$Q = Q_1 \cdot Q_2 \cdots Q_n \tag{2.17}$$

Figure 2.23*c* shows the circuit implementation of the *n*-bit comparator according to Eq. 2.17 (f_2-type circuit).

Again, let us see the f_1-type equivalent of this circuit. De Morgan's theorem gives

$$Q = Q_1 \cdot Q_2 \cdots Q_n = \overline{\overline{Q}_1 + \overline{Q}_2 + \overline{Q}_3 + \cdots \overline{Q}_n} \tag{2.18}$$

Figure 2.23*d* shows the circuit implementation of Eq. 2.18. This is the *n*-bit comparator, built from basic logic circuits.

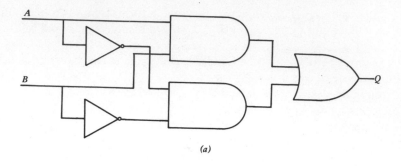

(a)

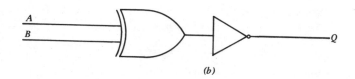

(b)

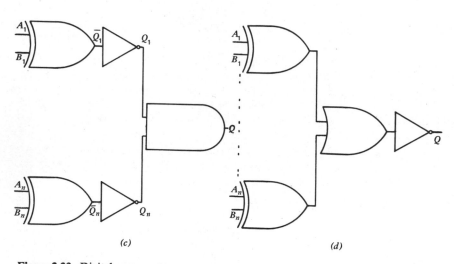

(c)

(d)

Figure 2.23. Digital comparator.

Example 3: Serial-parallel transmission system. There are two common modes of operation of digital systems, the parallel and the serial. Up to now, we discussed only parallel modes. In the parallel mode, each bit that is needed to represent the information occurs on a separate wire simultaneously with other bits on other wires. In the serial mode, the pulses (or absence of pulses) occur serially, one after another, and the information conveyed by this pulse sequence can be transmitted from one place to another over a single communication link (in the simplest case, one data wire and one ground wire).

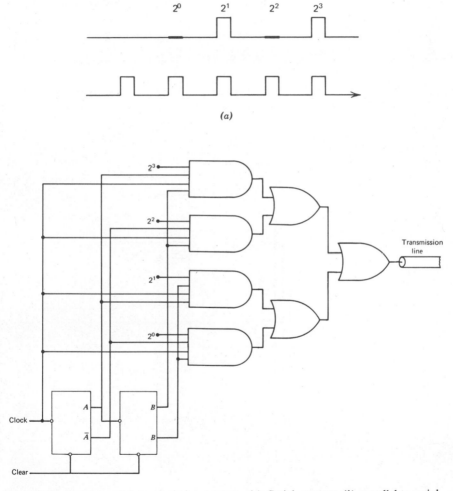

Figure 2.24. Serial-parallel transmission system. (*a*) Serial output; (*b*) parallel-to-serial transformation.

Figure 2.24a shows the serial presentation of a binary number, 1010. Now we show the design of circuitry to transform a parallel bit code into a serial code. The circuit will have $2^2 = 4$ inputs (parallel data) and one output. This circuit can be composed of one 2-bit counter, Fig. 2.17, and one 2-bit selector, Fig. 2.20. The whole circuit is shown in Fig. 2.24b. Parallel information is steadily available at the input. The clock will advance the counter through the states 0, 1, 2, and 3. As a result, the counter will select the gates 0, 1, 2, and 3. As a result, first bit 0 will be sampled and will appear as a pulse (or no pulse) at the output, then bits 1, 2, and 3. Figure 2.24a shows the serial output.

Next, we show the design circuitry to transform a 2-bit serial code into a parallel code. The circuit will have 1 input (serial data) and $2^2 = 4$ outputs. This circuit is similar to the one described above. Figure 2.24c shows a 2-bit serial to parallel transformation system.

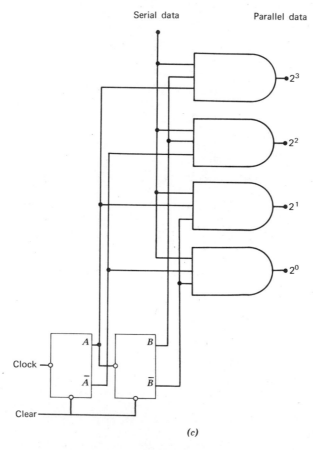

(c)

Figure 2.24. (*Cont'd.*) (*c*) serial-to-parallel transformation.

Computer-Aided Digital System Design

Digital system design follows a defined set of rules. These rules can be programmed into a digital computer. Computer programs are now available for various stages of digital system design.

Minimization. The input to the minimization program is the truth table. The program will find the minimized equation and type the solution (desired output) in the form of Eq. 2.8. At the present state of the art, programs are available for systems with up to 11-input variables (e.g., LOGMIN, Tymshare, Inc.; TRUMIN, Brookhaven National Laboratory).

Simulation. When a digital system is designed on paper, it is of interest to follow its operation before building the system. Simulation programs enable one to define each block of the system, status of each block, connections between blocks, and delays through the blocks. The program will print the status of each block as a function of time. Figure 2.25 shows the simulation of the decade counter. Figure 2.25*a* shows the counter, as envisaged by the designer (4 flip-flops; after 10 counts, the feedback resets the counter; CLK = clock generator; RST = flip-flop; $R = 1$ reset; $S = 1$ set; $T = 1$, complement; SS = single shot; –o– = inversion). Figure 2.25*b* shows the input to the program; F and T mean false and true, respectively. Each line defines one of eight blocks. The program will understand this message in the following way:

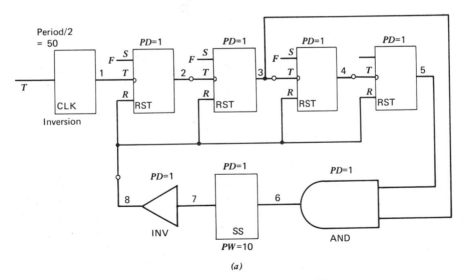

Figure 2.25. Computer simulation of the decade counter. (*a*) The counter.

Block 1: Clock generator; clock cycle = 50 time units; T = true at t = 0.

Block 2: RST, flip-flop; internal delay = 1 time unit; T input will trigger on output from block 1; S input is false; R input will trigger on inverted output from block 8.

Block 6: AND gate; delay 1 unit; inputs connected to blocks 3 and 5.

Block 7: Single shot; delay 1 unit; produced pulse 10 units; triggered from block 6.

Block 8: Invertor; delay 1 unit; input from block 7.

```
BLK DES:  1,CLK,50,T
BLK DES:  2,RST,1,1,F,-8
BLK DES:  3,RST,1,-2,F,-8
BLK DES:  4,RST,1,-8,F,-8
BLK DES:  5,RST,1,-4,F,-8
BLK DES:  6,AND,1,3,5
BLK DES:  7,SS,1,10,6
BLK DES:  8,INV,1,7
BLK DES:  END
```

(b)

TIME	BLK	TYP	STATE
1	8	INV	T
50	1	CLK	T
51	2	RST	T
100	1	CLK	F
150	1	CLK	T
151	2	RST	F
152	3	RST	T
200	1	CLK	F
250	1	CLK	T
251	2	RST	T
300	1	CLK	F
350	1	CLK	T
351	2	RST	F
352	3	RST	F
353	4	RST	T
400	1	CLK	F
450	1	CLK	T
451	2	RST	T
500	1	CLK	F
500	STOP AT TIME LIMIT		

(c)

Figure 2.25. (*Cont'd.*) (*b*) Input to the simulation program; (*c*) output of the program.

Figure 2.25c shows the output of the program for the first 10 clock cycles. One can follow the state of each block as a function of time. This is an example of the program LOGSIM, Tymshare, Inc.

Truth Table Generation. Input to the program will define the system. The program will then generate the truth table.

The simulation programs are conversational and easy to use even for a nonexperienced user. Those programs present substantial help in the digital system design.

2.5. INTEGRATED LOGICAL CIRCUITS

Basic logical circuits and flip-flops are built from transistors, diodes, and resistors in discrete or integrated versions. They are grouped into the following categories:

> *TTL*—transistor-transistor logic.
> *RTL*—resistor transistor logic.
> *DTL*—diode transistor logic.

In conventional discrete circuitry, *TTL* logic has not found wide acceptance simply because transistors are more expensive than either diodes or resistors. In integrated circuits, on the other hand, transistors are easier and cheaper to fabricate than resistors. As a result, *TTL* is the most common type of integrated logic.

On the basis of de Morgan's theorem, Eq. 2.2, it is clear that the OR function can be performed with a NAND gate; also an AND function can be performed with a NOR gate. AND and OR logic is sometimes called positive logic. NAND and NOR logic is called negative logic. NAND and NOR gates consume less power, and as a result most *TTL* gates are NAND and NOR gates.

In order to distinguish negative logic from positive, a small circle in the diagrams is used (Fig. 2.26). This circle signifies the inversion. If the circle is on the output side, it inverts the output level. As an example, compare the truth table for AND, Fig. 2.26a–c, with the truth table for NAND, Fig. 2.26a–f.

If the circle is on the input side, it inverts the inputs before they perform basic gate functions. As an example the OR gate, Fig. 2.26b–e, with inputs A, B will produce the same output as the gate in Fig. 2.26b–f with inputs $\overline{A}$, $\overline{B}$. We can rephrase the same statement. The OR gate, Fig. 2.26b–e, will produce the output H(high) if one or more inputs are high. The gate in Fig. 2.26b–f will produce the output H if one or more inputs are low.

Figure 2.26 illustrates the applications, functions, and truth tables of two variables and their equivalents.

The basic circuits are sometimes produced in a so-called *open-collector* version. That means no resistor is connected internally between the circuit output and power supply. The user can connect the outputs of two or more circuits in parallel and supply a loading resistor. The functions with an increased number of input variables can be performed in this way.

Transistors in logical circuits are not ideal switches. As a result, each logical unit presents a load for the unit on the output of which is connected. This load is called the fan-in factor. Also, each unit can drive only limited numbers of units. This driving capability is expressed as a fan-out factor. These factors are normalized to a unit current. Manufacturers provide design loading

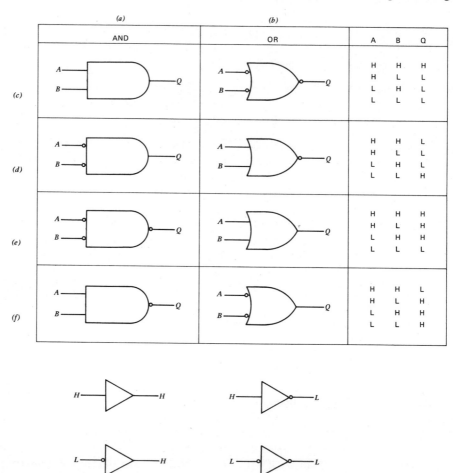

Figure 2.26. Positive and negative logic. (Adapted from Digital Equipment Corp.)

charts for logical circuits. For a typical NAND gate, fan-in can be 1, fan-out can be 10. This number means that such a NAND gate can drive the inputs of up to 10 similar gates simultaneously.

Different integrated circuits are available for different speeds. Since various sections of data processing systems have different speed requirements, it is usually possible to improve performance, reduce power consumption, and hold down overall costs by combining more than one series of circuits in a single system. When combining circuits of different series, however, one should check that they are compatible and are loaded properly.

2.6. DIGITAL COMPUTER

Basic Organization

A most elaborate digital system is a stored-program digital computer. A hypothetical computer that demonstrates the logic and technique of programming was first introduced by Turing. Modern computers, designed for a wide variety of applications, differ from each other in many ways. However, in solving a given problem all modern computers perform the same basic functions: *input* of information; *storage* of information; *arithmetic* and logical operations; *output* of information, and finally *control* of operations. The block diagram of a digital computer is shown in Fig. 2.27*a*.

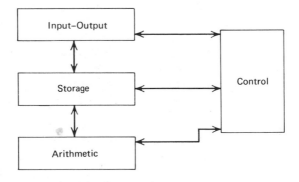

Figure 2.27. (*a*) Block diagram of digital computer.

Input Unit. Input devices are used to supply the data needed for calculation as well as the program to tell the computer how to operate on data. Input unit requirements vary greatly from machine to machine. Standard input units are manual keyboard, punched paper-tape reader, and card reader.

Input may be also in a magnetic tape, disk, or drum or through a display tube. Direct channels are used to accept data when a computer is used for measurement or control of processes.

Output Unit. The results of computer operations are supplied to the user through the output units. Standard output units are teletypewriter, paper-tape punch, card punch, line printer, and plotter. Output may be also via a magnetic tape, disk, or drum. If immediate output of results is necessary, a display tube is used. When the computer is used for measurement or control of processes, data channels provide outputs which may be used to initiate, control, or stop physical action (e.g., to adjust a pressure valve setting).

Storage Unit. This unit contains data necessary for calculation, inter-mediate data, and final data before output. It also holds the instructions which tell the computer what to do with data. The digital computer is a relentless follower of instructions. It does exactly what it is instructed to do.

Arithmetic Unit. This unit performs the actual work of computation and calculation. The arithmetic unit can receive the numbers and performs on them arithmetic or logical operations such as addition, subtraction, multi-plication, division, AND, OR. The arithmetic unit will have some registers for storing sequences of digits, the exact number and type of these registers depending on the particular machine. The main register is called an accumu-lator. At the beginning of the operation, the accumulator stores one of the operands. At the end of the operation, the accumulator usually stores the result.

Control Unit. All the action in the computer should be synchronized and should follow the instructions of the program. The computer has a relatively small number of operations that it can perform. The control unit is an ad-ministrative or switching section. It receives the instruction from the memory and decides how and when to perform operations. It knows for each unit when the generation is completed and tells the unit what to do next.

Storage Devices

The storage unit, or memory, of the computer contains a large number of *memory cells* or *memory locations*. Each location can be used to store n-bits of binary information. Information stored in one memory location is also called a *word*. The number of bits used, n, presents the word size and generally refers to the accuracy with which a single number can be represented. It is always possible to achieve any desired accuracy by using more than one word to represent the number. However, it is usually better to chose the machine with the word size which matches the need of a particular application. The word size varies from machine to machine. Small computers have a word size of 4 to 16 bits. Larger machines have longer words.

The memory can be composed of a few thousand locations or words. Small computers are usually designed in memory blocks of 4096 words (4 kilowords). Hence the memory can have 4096 or 8192 or 12288, and so on, words. Modern, larger computers can have memories with tens of thousands of words. The memory can be thought of as a village composed of many houses. One house corresponds to one memory location. Each house holds one word or one item of information. Each house has its unique address by which it is identified.

Figure 2.27b presents a block diagram of the memory composed of many cells or locations. Each location is permanently labeled with a unique number called its *address*. Access to a particular location is obtained by specifying the address of the location. Hence to obtain an item of information from the memory it is necessary to know the address at which this information is stored. Only one location can be addressed at a time.

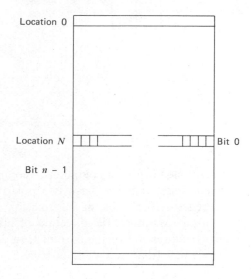

Figure 2.27. (*Cont'd.*) (*b*) Memory.

The most straightforward way of building a memory would be to use semiconductor flip-flop registers. One *n*-bit register can be used to present one word of the memory. Such semiconductor memories are built only in small sizes where a limited number of words or locations is necessary. Larger computer memories use magnetic materials to store binary information.

The computer handles all information in binary form, that is, as a number representable by only two digits, zero and one. The ferromagnetic material has the ability to store the binary information.

Figure 2.28a presents a hysteresis loop of a ferromagnetic material. If the material is initially an NS magnet, a magnetizing force, F_d, is required to change the polarity to an SN magnet. When the magnetizing force is removed, magnetization follows the hysteresis loop from the point d to the point e and stays permanently magnetized SN. Few types of magnetic memories are in current use, such as core memories, drum, disk, and magnetic tape.

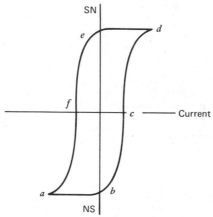

Figure 2.28. (a) Hysteresis loop of a ferromagnetic material.

Core Memory. The main memory of a computer is composed of a large number of small magnetic cores that can have two polarities, NS or SN. Each core element is used to store a bit of information. By threading a current-carrying wire through the core, the direction of magnetization can be reversed by changing the direction of the current (Fig. 2.28b). Since the mass of the core is very small (diameter of approximately 0.03 in.), little

Figure 2.28. (*Cont'd.*) (b) Magnetization of ferrite cores.

magnetizing force is required to switch the state, thus permitting fast switching speeds (hundreds of nanoseconds).

The magnetic state remains indefinitely after the current is removed. Hence the core presents a bistable element and presents a basic unit for storage of 1 bit of information.

One n-bit word is composed of n cores. The reading or writing of information in a word is done parallel to all n cores. The time required to locate and transmit the information is known as the *memory access time*. The memory access time of new core memories is very short—of the order of less than 1 μsec. The computer can address any location of the core memory at any time and can go from one address to another in a random fashion. We say that the core memory is a random access memory. Because of the easy and fast access to the information stored, core memory is used to store the program and the data frequently needed during the operation.

Drum Memory. In the magnetic drum storage, the magnetic material is deposited on the surface of a cylindrical drum that revolves at high speeds, Fig. 2.29. The drum surface is divided into rows and tracks. Each track is provided with two heads, read head and write head. As the drum rotates at a constant speed about its axis, the successive rows pass under the two sets of heads. Reading and writing processes must be synchronized with the drum movement. The access time to any particular row depends on the position of this row relative to the heads at the time the computer wants the information. It may take from a fraction of the revolution to the full revolution to access the row. Average access time is half the revolution time, which is usually in the order of 2 to 10 msec. The information on the drum is organized in records. The record is a group of words sequentially recorded on the

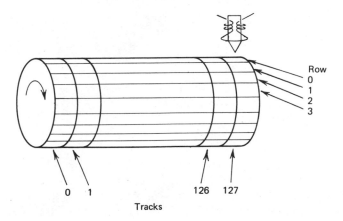

Figure 2.29. Drum memory.

drum surface. The transfer of the record of words between the computer and the drum can be achieved with relatively high speed. Millisecond access time may be necessary to find the beginning of the record, but after that the transfer proceeds in the microsecond range.

The drum memory can be used to store the program prior to its execution and to store large quantities of data. Drums for small computers usually have up to 128 tracks and up to a quarter of a million words of capacity.

Disk Memory. This memory is composed of a number of disks coated with magnetic material (Fig. 2.30). It generally has one set of read-write heads per disk surface. This set is reconnected on an arm which must be moved in and out across the disk in order to scan the entire surface of the disk. The access time is composed of a positional time which may take 100 msec and of the rotational delay which can be 10 msec. The main use of magnetic disks is for auxiliary storage. The data are stored in records, and high transfer rates between disk and core storage are possible.

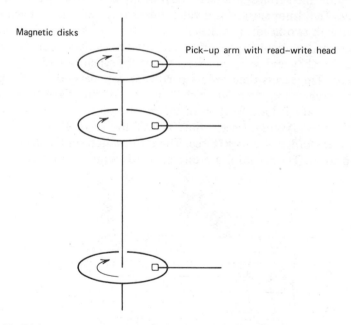

Figure 2.30. Disk memory.

Magnetic Tape. When vast amounts of storage are required, computers generally make use of magnetic tape. The tape has the advantage of being able to store as many data as necessary, because more tape can always be

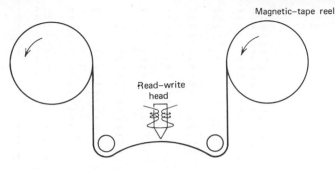

Figure 2.31. Magnetic tape memory.

added. Figure 2.31 gives a schematic representation of magnetic-tape storage. To gain access to a particular item of information, the tape must be started and rewound. It can take several seconds or even minutes to gain access to any particular datum, depending on the speed of the tape. However, the continuous transfer can be at very high rates, up to half a million bits per second. Magnetic tapes are used for auxiliary storage and to input and output large numbers of data.

Input-Output Devices

There are basically two different types of communication with a computer: communication between computer and user, and communication between computer and some other kind of electronic device. Here the communication with the user will be described. Input and output techniques vary widely among computers, but punched cards, punched paper tape, and printed output sheets are the most prevalent media.

Input processes involve two steps. First, the cards or the tape must be punched on special keypunch units which are not connected to the computer. Second, a prepared card or tape is read into the computer through the electromechanical input units.

The output process goes the opposite way. First, the electromechanical output units of the computer will punch paper tape or cards. Second, the cards or tapes will be read by auxiliary units not connected to the computer if a printed record is required.

The most common device for communication with the user on the small computer is the teletype unit. The teletype unit contains a keyboard, printer, paper-tape reader, and paper-tape punch. The teletype unit can use either the keyboard or the paper-tape reader to input information to the computer and cause either the printer or the paper-tape punch to accept output information from the computer.

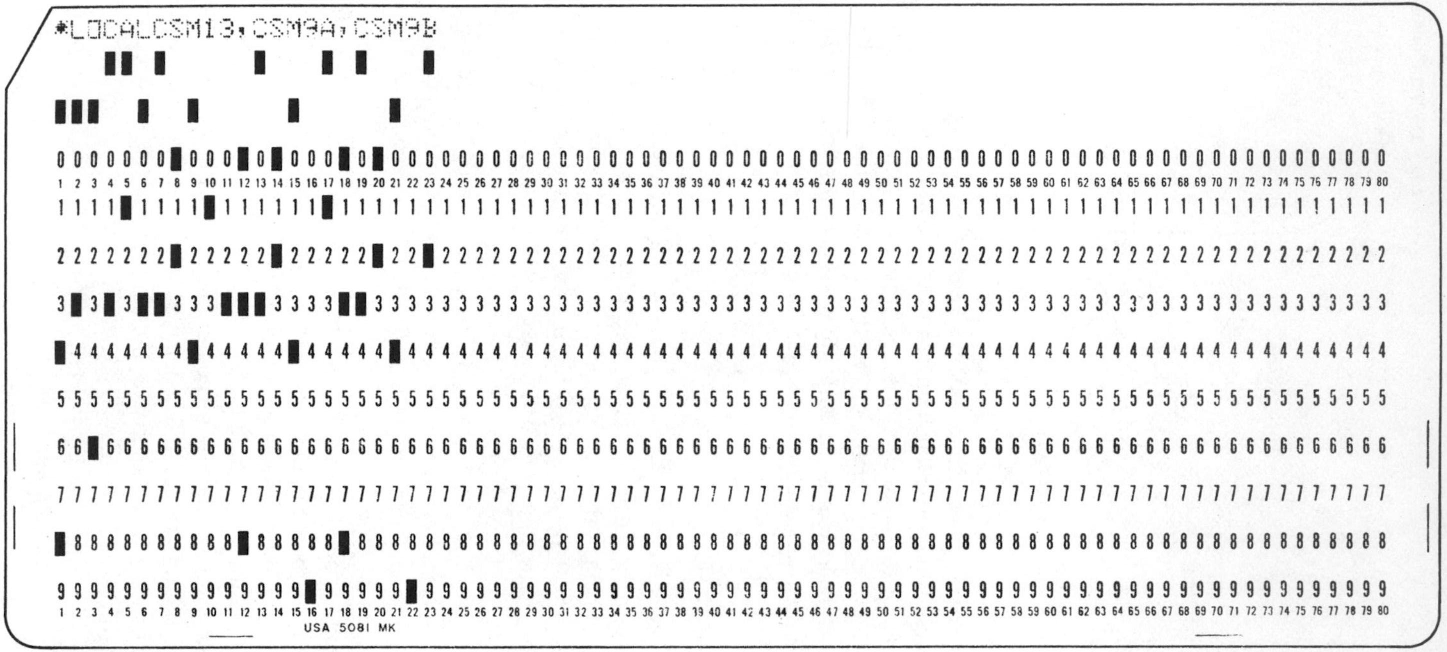

Figure 2.32. Punched cards.

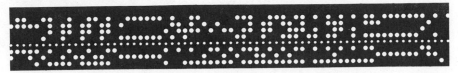

Figure 2.33. Punched tape.

Punched Cards. Card inputs are, in general, the most widely used input media. Punched cards are digital devices. Each descriptive position on the card is a potential hole that is either punched or not punched. On a standard IBM card the positions are arranged in 80 columns and 12 rows. Normally, a column contains the punched code for one numeral, letter, or symbol. On the top of the card, the same character may be printed for the user's convenience. Figure 2.32 shows such an example of a punched card.

Punched Tape. Paper tape, like punched cards, utilizes holes for coding purposes. Paper tape usually has eight channels, as shown in Fig. 2.33, but tape with five, six, or seven channels is sometimes encountered. The binary code on the tape can be arbitrary depending on the mechanical design of the equipment. The most frequently used is ASCII code, which is presented in Table 1.7. Eight holes are grouped into the group of $2 + 3 + 3$ with each group representing an octal digit. Note that the code for the octal digits, 0 through 7, is the sum of the digit plus 260_8.

Line Printer. If a large number of data are to be printed, the line printer is the most desirable unit because it yields the printed result at a reasonably high speed. This machine typically prints a complete line of 60 or more characters at one time and operates at a maximum rate of 1000 lines per minute.

There are a number of other less frequently used input-output media, and new devices are under development.

2.7 MICROPROCESSOR AND MEMORY CHIPS

Chip Technologies

Microprocessors are new semiconductor components. Each semiconductor chip constitutes one basic building block of the computing system. By connecting together a few large-scale integration (LSI) chips, one can build all kinds of microcomputing systems. Although small in size and inexpensive, such microcomputing systems are quite powerful.

The applications of microprocessors can be divided into two categories.

Microprocessors Replacing Digital Logic Design. Instead of designing digital logic circuits, the designer can take a simple, mass-produced microprocessor and program it to perform the required task.

Microcomputers Replacing Minicomputers. In many applications minicomputers are too powerful for a given task. Simple microcomputers will do the job.

Microprocessors have already found applications in many areas:

- Microcomputers
- I/O channels for large computers
- Computer terminals
- Distributed computers
- Telecommunications
- Inventory control
- Point-of-sale terminals
- Machine control
- Smart instruments
- Automotive and avionic controllers
- Biomedical systems
- Optical character recognition (OCR)
- Consumer products
- Calculators
- Automated testing equipment
- Robots

Figure 2.34 shows a basic microcomputer system connected to typical external modules. The basic elements of the system are as follows: central processing unit, read only program memory, random access data memory, I/O structure, and clock. Each of those elements is now available as a semiconductor chip.

Today three basic technologies are used for microprocessor chip fabrication: bipolar, MOS, and I²L.

Bipolar or TTL technology produces gates composed of bipolar transistors. Bipolar chips are very fast, with a gate propagation delay of a few nanoseconds. However, packing density and power consumption are not very good. Bipolar microprocessors have instruction cycle times of 0.1–1 μsec.

Metal oxide semiconductor (MOS) technology produces gates composed of field-effect transistors. The packing density is excellent, but the gate propagation delay is substantial (it can be a fraction of a microsecond). The MOS microprocessors have instruction cycle times of 2–20μsec.

Integrated injection logic (I²L) technology combines the packing density of MOS with the high speed of bipolar processing. Hence I²L technology is a strong challenger of both MOS and bipolar, and thus appears set to play a key role in microprocessor chip technology.

Semiconductor Random Access Memories (RAM's)

Bipolar and MOS technologies are now utilized in memory fabrication.

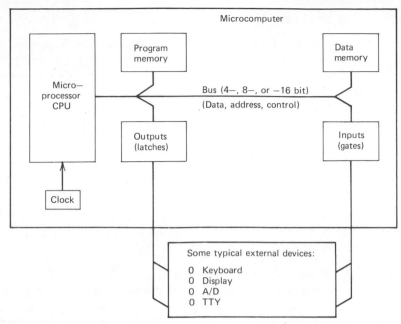

Figure 2.34. Basic microcomputer system connected to typical external modules.

The computer can address any location of the semiconductor memory at any time and can go from one address to another in a random fashion. We say that the semiconductor memory, as well as the core memory, is a random access memory (RAM). The computer can perform with the RAM both read and write operations. For each bit of storage, one flip-flop is used. Each flip-flop is composed of two cross-coupled gates, as shown in Fig. 2.9. Such memories are called *static* memories: once the bit pattern is stored in the memory, it is safe as long as the power is on. When the power is switched off, however, the memory content is lost. Hence semiconductor memories represent a volatile type of storage. The solution to the RAM volatility problem is a battery-backup power.

Some MOS memories use capacitor storage elements. Here the data are stored as a charge on the capacitance inherent in MOS transistors. The charge must be refreshed at the minimum frequency required to recharge these cells to maintain the data. Such memories are called *dynamic* memories. The main advantage of dynamic memories is very low power dissipation, in the microwatt per bit range.

The RAM's are used in microprocessors for data storage. They are available as chips, with 256, 1024, or 4096 bits.

Semiconductor Read Only Memories (ROM's)

In microprocessors the program is usually stored separately from the data. In many applications the same program is used day after day and hence must be stored in the nonvolatile memory. Typically the microprocessor reads the instructions of the program and executes them. The microprocessor does not write any new information into the program memory; the program is left unchanged. For this kind of job a read only memory (*ROM*) is used.

The *ROM* has many advantages over the *RAM*:

- Extremely large memories per chip (2048 × 8 @ $28).
- Low cost.
- Low power.
- Nonvolatile storage.
- Fast access time (35 to 1200 nsec).

Figure 2.35 shows a simplified diagram of the *ROM*. Storage of a 1 is equivalent to connection of the diode, and storage of a 0 is equivalent to no connection of a diode. To read the word line X, it is enough to apply the voltage corresponding to 1 to the line X; the output lines will show the stored bit pattern.

The programming of *ROM*'s is permanent and irreversible. Usually the current is used to melt open thin metal conductors in order to remove gate connections (Fig. 2.35*a*). The user develops the bit pattern of the program and sends it to the manufacturer to burn the required *ROM* mask. Since the mask charge is over $1000, *ROM*'s are ordinarily used only in large-quantity production.

Some *ROM*'s use electric field or electromagnetic radiation to inject charge into an oxide trap above the gate region of a connecting MOS transistor (Fig. 2.35*b*). Such memories, which can be reprogrammed using special equipment, are known as programmable read only memories (*PROM*'s). The main characteristics of the *PROM* are:

- Rapid turn-around time during the system development phase.
- Expensive programming equipment.

The *PROM*'s are used in low-quantity production.

Programmed Logical Arrays (PLA's)

In *ROM*'s and *RAM*'s, the internal built-in address selectors are used to select one out of many memory locations. For example, 12-bit address inputs would define all the addresses from 0 to $2^{12} = 4096$. In other words, if the *ROM* has 12-bit address input, it should have 4096 words.

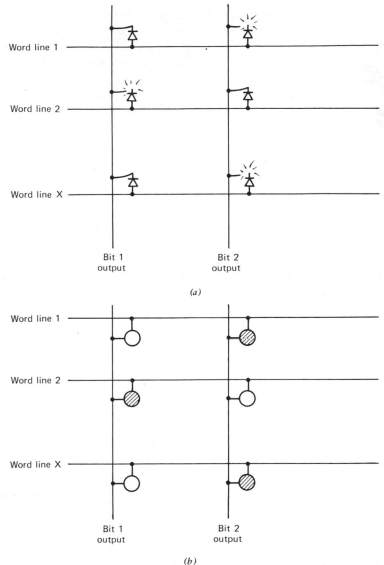

Figure 2.35. Principle of the read only memory operation. (a) Mask programmable *ROM*;
(b) Field Programmable *ROM* (*PROM*)

In some applications not all input addresses are available. Consider the
case of using the *ROM* for punched cards to ASCII code conversion.
The cards are using 12 rows, and the ASCII is an 8-bit code. Hence the
ROM with the 12-bit address bus, and with 8-bit word length, would do
the job ($2^{12} = 4096 \times 8 = 32,768$-bit *ROM* is needed). However, we know

that the 12 bits on the cards are not used to define 4096 different codes. They actually define only 96 meaningful codes. Most bit combinations are never used. Only one of the first seven rows on the card is ever punched.

Instead of *ROM* for such applications a programmed logical array (*PLA*) could be used. With the *PLA* the designer specifies not only an output bit pattern for each word, but also the word address. Hence the designer does not need the memory words for those addresses that never occur as the inputs. In the example of punched-card-to-ASCII code conversion, 96-word *PLA* with 12 inputs and 8 output will do the job. Each of the 96 input addresses the designer defines will correspond to a valid punch card code.

Three State Logic

Some of the microprocessors are using the three state logic on their buses. The source that controls a given line could force the line into one of the three states:

- logical one (true)
- logical zero (false)
- off or high impedance state

In the off, or high impedance state, the line is available for other devices to put the information on it without affecting the original source that drives the line.

PROBLEMS

1. Two flip-flops provide the outputs A, $\overline{A}$ and B, $\overline{B}$. Design the circuit $Q = A + B$. Use only NAND and NOR gates.
2. Two flip-flops provide the outputs A, $\overline{A}$ and B, $\overline{B}$. Design the circuit $Q = A \cdot B$. Use only NAND and NOR gates.
3. Four flip-flops provide the outputs A, $\overline{A}$, B, $\overline{B}$, C, $\overline{C}$, D, $\overline{D}$. Design the circuit $Q = A + B + C + D$. Use only NAND and NOR gates with two inputs per gate.
4. Four flip-flops provide the outputs A, $\overline{A}$, B, $\overline{B}$, C, $\overline{C}$, D, $\overline{D}$. Design the

circuit $Q = A \cdot B \cdot C \cdot D$. Use only NAND and NOR gates with two inputs per gate.

5. Prove the 13 theorems of Table 2.1. After proving the first theorem, use it to prove the second, and so on. Use de Morgan's theorem.

6. Find the sum of products (Eq. 2.8) of the following functions:
   (a) $(AC + B) \cdot (CD + \overline{D})$
   (b) $(\overline{AC} + D) \cdot (\overline{B + CE})$

7. Design two registers of 6 bits each in such a way that the clock pulse will exchange their contents.

8. Four-bit binary reversible counter will count in the following way: 0, 15, 14, 13 . . . 2, 1, 0. Write the truth table for 4 bits, A, B, C, D, and design the counter using the master-slave flip-flops.

REFERENCES

1. Millman, J., and H. Taub. *Pulse, Digital and Switching Waveforms*, McGraw-Hill, New York, 1965.

2. McCluskey, E. J. *Introduction to the Theory of Switching Circuits*, McGraw-Hill, New York, 1965.

3. Hill, F. J., and G. R. Peterson. *Introduction to Switching Theory and Logical Design*, Wiley, New York, 1968.

4. *Small Computer Handbook*, Digital Equipment Corporation, Maynard, Mass., 1970.

3

BASIC MICROCOMPUTER INSTRUCTIONS

Chapter 3 introduces microcomputer instructions. It is shown that instructions commonly used in small scientific computers can be grouped into the following classes: word transmission, arithmetic and logical operations, control, register reference, and input-output. Definitions and examples of the use of the basic instructions are given. Different modes of computer addressing are explained.

3.1. INTRODUCTION

Every machine built by man is designed for a specific job: power generation, temperature measurement, voltage transformation and so on. A general-purpose digital computer is not designed for one fixed job. It can be used for a large variety of jobs, but it has to go through the procedure of "training," that is, it has to learn how to perform a given task. Man trains the computer through programming.

The program for the computer is composed of a number of instructions. Each instruction commands the computer to select one of its built-in operations. The number of elementary instruction-operations depends on the computer. Very small digital computers can have as few as eight elementary instructions. Large machines have a few hundred different instructions. Each basic instruction can perform one operation, such as ADD, MULTIPLY, and STORE.

To be able to program on a digital computer, one does not have to understand in detail the internal electrical structure of the machine. However, it is necessary to know its basic logical organization and to distinguish the parts of the machine which are accessible to the programmer. The logical organization of a computer and those parts which are directly involved in

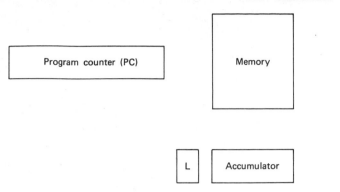

Figure 3.1. Basic parts of the computer.

programming are shown in a very simplified form in Fig. 3.1. These are memory, program counter, accumulator, and link.

Memory

The main memory is composed of a large number of words or locations. Each memory location has an address. If the memory has 4096 words, the addresses will be 0, 1, 2, . . . 4095. One word or location can be used to store one binary number (datum) or one instruction of the program, coded in binary form. The user is to decide which part of the memory will be used for data and which part will be used for the program. Instructions of an elementary program are stored in the memory in consecutive locations. The computer will read one instruction from the memory and perform an operation. It will then read the next instruction, from the next location, and perform another operation, and so on. Here we shall deal with a memory composed of 4096 words, each of them having 12 bits.

Program Counter

This register is used to keep track of the location of the program in the memory. At the end of each cycle the program counter indicates the address of the memory location containing the next instruction of the program. Ordinarily, instructions are stored in numerically consecutive locations. When one instruction is finished, the program counter is advanced by 1, and it automatically points to the address of the next instruction. In some cases the contents of the program counter can be changed by the program itself. In this way a transfer of command to another portion of the stored program takes place. Here we shall deal with a 12-bit program counter that can address up to 4096 memory words.

Accumulator

The accumulator (A) is the prime component of the arithmetic unit of the computer. It is composed of a number of flip-flops, and it can keep one word of binary information. It is surrounded by electronic circuits to perform arithmetic and logical operations under the direction of the control unit. The computer can perform an arithmetic or logical operation involving only two operands at a time. The first operand usually comes from the location of the memory specified by the instruction, while the second operand comes from the accumulator. The result of the operation usually remains in the accumulator.

The computer can test the result in the accumulator, and based on this test it can make different decisions.

Here we shall deal with a 12-bit accumulator. Whenever an operation, such as binary addition, causes a carry out of the most significant bit, the carry is lost from the accumulator. This carry is recorded in a 1-bit link register.

Link

The link (L) is a 1-bit register, which acts as an extension of the accumulator and is complemented by any carry out of the accumulator. It is sometimes called an extend or carry register. It is used not only to represent an extension of the accumulator but also to connect in loop the most significant and the least significant end of the accumulator. This loop can be used to shift the information right or left under the program control. The state of the link can be tested for decisions.

Example

A job to be programmed for the computer should be divided into elementary steps described by the instruction set of the computer. A small computer when performing an arithmetic operation usually deals with only two operands. The first operand is stored in the accumulator. The second operand is stored in the computer memory. The instruction must specify the address of the memory location where the operand is.

The instructions are

• CLEAR. This instruction will set the contents of the accumulator to be zero.

• ADD 100. This instruction will add the contents of the location with address 100 to the contents of the accumulator and will leave the result in the accumulator.

Example. Program to calculate $77 + 22 + 15 = 114$. The program is shown in Table 3.1.

Table 3.1

Location	Contents	Comment
200	CLEAR	Accumulator contains 0000
201	ADD 300	Accumulator contains 77
202	ADD 301	Accumulator contains 99
203	ADD 302	Accumulator contains 114
204	HALT	
⋮		
300	77	
301	22	
⋮	15	
400		

The program and the data should be written in the memory of the computer. We have arbitrarily decided that the program should be stored starting with location address 200, data should be stored starting with location address 300, and the result should be stored in location 400. The instructions and the data should be coded in binary form, but in this example, for the sake of simplicity, we shall use symbolic notation for instructions.

To execute the program, the program counter should be set to point to the first instruction stored in location 200. The instruction CLEAR will clear the accumulator to zero. At the end of this instruction the program counter is advanced by 1, and the next instruction will come from location 201. This instruction, ADD 300, will add the contents of location 300 to the contents of the accumulator. At the end of this instruction the accumulator contains the number 77. Again the program counter is advanced by 1, and the next instruction comes from location 202. This instruction, ADD 301, adds the contents of location 301 to the existing contents of the accumulator and leaves the result in the accumulator. At the end of this instruction the accumulator contains $77 + 22 = 99$. The next instruction is ADD 302. It adds the contents of location 302 to the existing contents of the accumulator. The accumulator contains $99 + 15 = 114$.

The last instruction, HALT, stops the program counter and that is the end of the program.

3.2. PROGRAM CODING

All operations in a digital computer are performed in the binary number system. All items of information stored in the computer memory should also be presented in binary form. Instructions of which the program is composed should also be presented to the computer in binary form. However, during the procedure of writing the program, instructions can be written in some other form. In general, the program can be coded in four ways: binary form, octal form, hexadecimal form and symbolic or mnemonic form.

Binary Coding

The binary form of an instruction is the only form the computer is able to understand. Each computer has a set of instructions in binary code which are understandable to it. For each instruction the computer has prewired circuits that obey the operation dictated by the instruction. The binary form of the instruction is identical with the binary form of data. The computer cannot distinguish the instruction from the data. The programmer tells the machine whether to interpret the binary configuration as an instruction or as a datum.

Table 3.2 shows part of the computer memory. The left-hand column contains the addresses of locations in binary form. The right-hand column represents the contents of locations in binary form. Each location or word has 12 bits. In this particular machine the most significant 3 bits of the instruction tell the computer what to do. For example, code 001 signifies the operation addition. Nine least significant bits of the instruction present the address of the location keeping the operand.

Table 3.2

Location	Contents
000000000100	001000000111
000000000101	000000000000
000000000110	000000000000
000000000111	101010101010

If the program counter points to location 000 000 000 100 instruction 001 000 000 111 will be executed. This instruction will cause the contents of the memory location 000 000 111 to be added to the contents of the accumulator. That means that number 101010101010 will be added to the accumulator.

Octal Coding

It is clear from the above example that it would be very tedious and confusing to write computer programs in binary form. A longer program, for example, would be composed of several hundreds or thousands of 0's and 1's. Here the octal number system can be of substantial help. Octal numbers will represent binary numbers used by the computer. Table 3.3 shows the program from Table 3.2 coded in octal system. The programmer can follow octal coding more easily than binary coding. It is important to remember that some other form. In general, the program can be coded in four ways: binary form, octal form, hexadecimal form, and symbolic or mnemonic form.

Table 3.3

Location	Contents
0004	1007
0005	0000
0006	0000
0007	5252

Table 3.4 gives another small program coded in octal form. We shall show in this program that the computer cannot distinguish between a number and an instruction[2].

Table 3.4

Location	Contents
0031	1032
0032	1040
⋮	
0040	0100

Assume that the initial value of the accumulator is zero and that the program counter points to location 0031. The first instruction 1032 will add the contents of location 0032 to the accumulator. The contents of that location 1040 are treated as a number and are added to the accumulator.

The program counter will be advanced by 1 and will take the second instruction from location 0032. The contents of that location 1040 are now treated as an instruction; the computer instruction, 1040, will cause the contents of location 0040 to be added to the existing contents of the accumulator. After the execution of the two instructions number 1140_8 is in the accumulator. Thus the above program treats the binary information 1040 first as a binary number and then as an instruction.

Mnemonic Coding

Octal coding presents an obvious improvement in comparison with binary coding. However, octal coding would also be inconvenient for larger programs. The programmer would have to learn by heart octal codes for all instructions available for a given computer. The computer might have a few hundred different instructions, and it would be difficult to remember a few hundred different octal codes.

To simplify the process of writing, debugging, and reading the program, mnemonic or symbolic coding has been invented. Its basic principle follows.

Each computer instruction is presented by a simple 3- or 4-letter mnemonic symbol. Mnemonic symbols are considerably easier to relate to a computer operation, since they can be chosen in such a way as to suggest the definition of the instruction. In fact, we have already used some kind of symbolic instructions in the small program shown in Table 3.1. Each computer has a fixed set of symbolic instructions.

Table 3.5 shows a computer instruction presented in three forms: binary, octal, and symbolic. This is the same instruction as that used in Tables 3.2 and 3.3. It belongs to the instruction set of the PDP-8 minicomputer. Binary code 001 in this computer is used for the operation of two's complement addition. Hence the symbolic name TAD has been given to this instruction. It is much easier to remember that two's complement addition can be coded TAD than to remember binary code 001.

Table 3.5

Operation	Address			
001	000	000	111	Binary
1	0	0	7	Octal
TAD			7	Symbolic

Symbolic coding, while very convenient for the programmer, cannot be understood by the computer. The only language the computer can understand is binary coding. Hence it is necessary to translate the symbolic program to its binary equivalent. This can be done by hand using tables with the instruction set for a given computer; each mnemonic instruction can be replaced by its binary equivalent.

In practice, this translation is performed by a special computer program called an *assembler*. By using a binary code to represent alphanumeric characters, the programmer is able to store alphabetic mnemonic instructions in the computer memory. The assembler will compare each mnemonic instruction with a table of instructions and will replace it with a binary equivalent. This process of translation is called the *program assembling*.

Hexadecimal Coding and Hand Assembling

Hexadecimal coding follows the same philosophy as octal coding, except that hexadecimal numbers are used as short-hand representations of binary numbers (Table 1.6): 4 binary bits are presented as one hexadecimal character. Clearly, 8 binary bits are presented as two hexadecimal characters, and so on. Here are a few examples.

Binary Bits	Hexadecimal Characters
0000	0
0011 1110	3E
0000 1111 1111	0FF
1111 0000 0101	F05

The following is an example of the program to perform this operation: Add the number AB89 to the number 4523, using microprocessor 4004.

Multiple-Precision Addition

ADR	INSTR	LABEL	MNEMONIC	OPERAND	COMMENTS
0	F1	(ADD)	CLC		ADD AB89 TO 4523
1	A9		LD	9	ADD REG 9 TO REG 3
2	83		ADD	3	
3	B3		XCH	3	
4	A8		LD	8	ADD REG 8 TO REG2 WITH CARRY
5	82		ADD	2	
6	B2		XCH	2	
7	AB		LD	B	ADD REG B TO REG5 WITH CARRY
8	85		ADD	5	
9	B5		XCH	5	
A	AA		LD	A	ADD REG A TO REG4 WITH CARRY
B	84		ADD	4	
C	B4		XCH	4	
D	C0		BBL	0	RETURN

Courtesy Pro-Log Corporation

The program is stored at the addresses 0 to D. The column "instr" presents the hexadecimal coding for instructions. The column "mnemonic" presents the mnemonic coding for the same instructions; for example, the mnemonic instruction CLC (CLEAR CARRY) has the hexadecimal code F1. For short programs like this one, the translation from mnemonic (symbolic) coding into hexadecimal coding can be done by hand, using the instruction tables for a given computer. For larger programs the assembler will perform the translation.

Let us take one more look at the instructions of this example:

CLC (CLEAR CARRY)   = F1
ADD 3 (ADD content of register 3 to the accumulator) = 83
LD 8 (LOAD content of register 8 to the accumulator) = A8

It is clear that symbolic coding is closer to the programmer than hexa-decimal coding because the symbolic name of the instruction is related to the operation performed. For this reason symbolic coding is used even in the case of hand assembling. The programmer first writes the program in a symbolic form and only then consults the instruction tables to convert the symbolic codes into hexadecimal codes. The resulting hexadecimal object program can be directly entered into the microcomputer memory. It will set the binary bit pattern necessary for the program execution.

Flow Charts

The first step in writing the program is to make a logical block diagram or flow chart. A flow chart can be used to plan the structure of the program, to specify all contingencies, and to decide for different paths the program will take following each possible outcome. A flow chart enables one to break the problem into self-contained logical units and to make changes and modifications prior to writing the program. When logical units are clearly defined on the flow chart, instruction-by-instruction programming can be easily done.

A flow chart is basically a collection of boxes and lines. Boxes are of

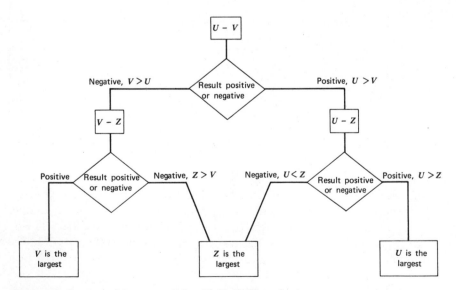

Figure 3.2. Largest of three quantities, U, V, Z. Flow chart.

various shapes, representing the action to be performed in the program. A rectangle with one input and one output indicates a block of processing; a diamond indicates a choice point. A more detailed description of flow-chart symbols is given in Appendix A.

Lines are used to connect boxes and to indicate the sequence of operations. A straight-line program is the simplest case in which there is a straight-line progression through the processing steps with no change in course.

A flow chart is useful not only in writing the program but also in checking the written program for errors. It is also much easier to explain the program to someone by using a flow chart rather than a long list of instructions.

Let us suppose that we want to write the program in order to find the largest of the three numbers U, V, and Z. The first step would be to make a flow chart, as shown in Fig. 3.2. The second step would be to write the instruction-by-instruction program for each box from the flow chart.

Notation

In programming for the computer, it will be necessary to specify the memory location, accumulator, link, and program counter. Whenever possible, we shall use the following general notations, following Flores:[1]

A Accumulator

L Link

PC Program counter

M The operand location, the number appearing in the operand position of the instruction; effective address

I The address from which the instruction was obtained

The following symbols will be used to explain the meaning of instructions

( )   The symbol in parentheses represents the contents of the location specified by the symbol. (121) refers to the contents of memory location 121; (A) refers to the contents of the accumulator.

[ ]   The bracketed symbol represents the location where the symbol within the bracket is stored. [7] refers to the location where number 7 is stored. It is clear that ( ) and [ ] have reverse meanings. Thus, if (121) = 7, then [7] = 121.

$\rightarrow$ A single arrow represents the copy operation and is used to describe the moving of data between the source and the destination. Thus, (121) $\rightarrow$ A means that the contents of location 121 are duplicated in the A register. The data-moving operation leaves the contents of the source unchanged. The original contents of the destination are lost and are replaced by the contents of the source.

$\Rightarrow$ The double arrow is used to represent the sequence of instructions in the program. Normally, after the computer has taken the instruction from location I, it will take the next instruction from location $I + 1$, which would be indicated as $\Rightarrow I + 1$. However, if the program has branches, it might jump from location I to location M, which would be indicated as $\Rightarrow M$.

src   Source address

dst   Destination address

$\wedge$ Boolean AND function

$\vee$ Boolean OR function

$\veebar$ Boolean "exclusive OR" function

$\sim$ Two's complement

$\uparrow$ One item is popped from the stack. The whole stack of items has been moved by one position up.

$\downarrow$ One item is pushed onto the stack. The whole stack of items has been moved by one position down.

3.3.   CLASSIFICATION OF INSTRUCTIONS

The computer is built to recognize and perform an explicitly stated number of specific instructions. In writing the program the programmer is restricted to these specific instructions. The number and type of instructions will vary, depending on the size and purpose of the computer.

Instructions can be divided into groups to answer the following question. Which part of the computer is the instruction addressing or referring to?

There are three types of instructions:

• Memory reference.
• Register reference.
• Input-output reference.

Memory-reference instruction is distinguished by the fact that it commands the computer to proceed to a particular memory location. This instruction tells the computer the address of the memory location. For example, the instruction ADD 300, from Table 3.1, is the memory-reference instruction. It tells the computer to go to address 300 and to use the data stored at this address as the first operand. The second operand is in the accumulator. The two operands should be added.

Register-reference instructions, sometimes called operate microinstructions, perform a variety of operations without any need for reference to a memory location. For example, the instruction CLEAR, from Table 3.1, is this type of instruction. It tells the computer to erase the register-called accumulator to zero. It deals with only one operand, the number stored in the accumulator.

Input-output instructions perform the transfer of data between the computer and the peripheral equipment, such as peripheral memories (disk, tape, drum), printing and punching devices, display units, and data multiplexers. Designing of the input-output transfer is the most difficult part of the job and requires understanding of both programming techniques and logical organization of the machine.

Another way to divide instructions into groups is through the question: What is the basic function the instruction is performing? There are five types of instructions:

- Move data, arithmetic and logical instructions.
- Control instructions.
- Subroutine linking instructions.
- Operate instructions.
- Input-output instructions.

Move-data or word-transmission instructions are concerned with the motion of information back and forth between the core memory and the working register (accumulator). The instruction should specify the direction of motion, the source of data, and/or the destination of data.

Arithmetic and logical instructions are concerned with operations between two operands. The instruction should specify the operation, the source, and the destination. The source keeps the first operand. The destination keeps the second operand. After the operation, the source contents are unchanged, but the destination will keep the result of the operation.

Control instructions are mainly concerned with decision making. A control instruction can test the result of calculation at some point in the program. At this point the program will go into a few branches. On the basis of this test, the control instruction will choose the proper branch of the program to be executed.

Subroutine linking instructions are concerned with linkages of the main program with subprograms and with the return back to the main program.

Operate instructions deal with only one operand. In a small computer, this operand is usually the contents of the accumulator. Hence operate instructions can be used to clear, complement, shift, and so on, the number stored on the accumulator.

Input-output instructions deal with data transfer in and out of the machine.

3.4. BASIC COMPUTER INSTRUCTION SET

Digital computers differ very much in capability, size, and price. Some machines can perform a very limited number of basic operations, while some have repertoires with hundreds of different fancy operations. Theoretically, any computer can be used to solve a given problem. A small computer will solve the problem by going through a large number of very simple operations, and it may take a long time to produce the solution. A larger machine having a variety of operations can solve the same problem in substantially fewer number of steps. Practice has shown which basic operations the computer should have to reach a reasonable compromise between the machine price and its usefulness. In this section we shall define such a minimum-sized hypothetical computer and its basic operations. Similar machines exist and are very useful for simple jobs. It is natural that one should learn computer techniques, starting with such a basic stripped-down machine.

The machine we shall consider is a high-speed general-purpose computer operating with 12-bit binary numbers. It is a single-address parallel machine using two's complement arithmetic. In this section we shall define the basic computer instruction set. We shall define all instructions, except input-output instructions, which will be described later.

In defining our basic computer we shall start from a real, widely used minicomputer, the well known PDP-8, and microprocessor IM6100. Our basic computer resembles the PDP-8 or IM6100, stripped down to its most elementary functions. We shall use this basic computer to explain the machine instructions, programming fundamentals, and interfacing fundamentals. Detailed description of the PDP-8 and IM6100 is given in Chapter 16.

Move Data: Arithmetic and Logical Instructions

Small computers have at least one instruction for moving data, one instruction for arithmetic operations, and at least one instruction for logical operations. The most frequently used instructions are STORE, ADD, and AND.

STORE M

This is a move-data instruction. It takes the contents of the accumulator and stores them into the specified memory location M. The contents of the accumulator remain unchanged. The accumulator is the source and the memory location is the destination. In brief

$$(A) \rightarrow M$$

The example in Table 3.6 shows the contents of the accumulator, link, and location 57, before and after executing instruction STORE 57: Note:

1. The state of the accumulator and link is not altered.
2. The original contents of the addressed location are replaced by the contents of the accumulator.

Table 3.6

	Link	Accumulator	Location 57
Before	0	4567	1234
After	0	4567	4567

ADD M

This is an arithmetic instruction. It performs binary addition between the contents of the source (specified memory location *M*) and the accumulator. It leaves the result on the accumulator. If a carry out of the most significant bit of the accumulator should occur, the state of the link bit is complemented. In brief

$$(A) + (M) \rightarrow A$$

The example in Table 3.7 shows the contents of the accumulator, link, and location 47, before and after executing instruction ADD 47. Note:

The data word in the referenced location is not affected.

Table 3.7

	Link	Accumulator	Location 47
Before	0	1234	1122
After	0	2356	1122

AND M

This is a logical instruction. It causes a bit-by-bit Boolean AND operation between the contents of the accumulator and the contents of the source location *M* in the memory. The result is left in the accumulator.

In brief

$$(M) \wedge (A) \rightarrow A$$

The example in Table 3.8 shows the contents of the link, the accumulator, and location 52, before and after executing instruction AND 52. To point out the bit-by-bit operation, numbers are presented in binary form. Note:

1. The contents of the referenced location are not affected.
2. The state of the link bit is not affected.

Table 3.8

	Link	Accumulator	Location 52
Before	0	101010101010	111111000000
After	0	101010000000	111111000000

Control Instructions

A large number of scientific problems are much more complicated than mere straightforward calculation. Scientific programs as a rule will be composed of many branches and decision points. The program will continue to follow one branch or another, depending on the result obtained prior to the decision point. Decisions and branching are performed by control instructions, which truly serve as the crux of a modern computer. The basic control instructions are HALT, JUMP, SKIP IF, and Increment and Skip if Zero (ISZ).

HALT

The simplest control instruction is the instruction HALT. This instruction will tell the computer to stop the advancing of the program counter. It is often used when the programmer would like the computer to stop for a moment, in order to check the results obtained thus far in the program. The programmer can then decide whether to continue calculations or to make some alterations in the program or data. The programmer can press the START key on the computer console if he wants the program to continue.

JUMP M

The JUMP instruction deals with the program counter. It loads the address part of the instruction M into the program counter. As a result, the next instruction of the program will come from the location M. In brief

$$\Rightarrow M$$

The example in Table 3.9 illustrates the jump operation. The execution of the instruction in location 100 (JUMP 145) causes the program to jump over the instructions in locations 101 to 144. After executing the instruction in location 100, the program counter will point to the instruction in location 145, and the program will continue from this point. Note:

The jump instruction does not affect the contents of the accumulator, link, or any memory location.

Table 3.9

Location	Contents
100	JUMP 145
⋮	⋮
145	ADD 150
⋮	⋮

SKIP (if Condition) Instructions

The SKIP instruction examines some condition in the computer. If the condition is fulfilled, the instruction following the SKIP is skipped. If the condition is not fulfilled, the instruction following the SKIP is performed. The computer usually has a variety of SKIP instructions, such as

SKIPP

Skip if the contents of the accumulator are positive. That means if the skip instruction is in location J, get the next instruction from $I + 2$, if $(A) = +$; otherwise get it in the usual way from $I + 1$. In brief

$$(A) = + \Rightarrow I + 2$$
$$(A) \neq + \Rightarrow I + 1$$

SKIPZ

Skip if zero instruction. In brief

$$(A) = 0 \Rightarrow I + 2$$
$$(A) \neq 0 \Rightarrow I + 1$$

SKIPN

Skip if negative instruction. In brief

$$(A) = - \Rightarrow I + 2$$
$$(A) \neq - \Rightarrow I + 1$$

SKIPL

Skip if link set instruction. In brief

$$(L) = 1 \Rightarrow I + 2$$
$$(L) = 0 \Rightarrow I + 1$$

SKIP

Unconditional skip. The next instruction is always skipped. In brief

$$\Rightarrow I + 2$$

The example in Table 3.10 illustrates the skip operation: if the datum at location 150 is 0, add 10 to it. Otherwise continue the program at location 106. Note:

The SKIP instruction does not affect the contents of the accumulator, link, or any memory location.

Table 3.10

Location	Contents
100	CLEAR
101	ADD 150
102	SKIPZ
103	JUMP 106
104	ADD 151
105	STORE 150
106	
⋮	⋮
150	1234
151	0010

ISZ M

Increment and skip if zero instruction performs two operations: it adds 1 to the contents of the memory location M, and then examines the result of addition. If the result is zero, the next instruction is skipped. If the result is not zero, the next instruction will be executed. In brief

$$(M) + 1 \to M$$
$$(M) = 0 \Rightarrow I + 2$$
$$(M) \neq 0 \Rightarrow I + 1$$

The example in Table 3.11 illustrates the ISZ operation[2]. It performs the multiplication 10×2 by adding 10 to itself 2 times. Location 150 keeps the first number 10. Location 151 keeps the number -2, and it will be used as a counter. The program has the shape of a loop; each pass performs one addition. In the first pass the execution of ISZ 151 increments the contents of location 151 from 7776 (decimal -2) to 7777 (decimal -1), and then the program executes the next instruction, JUMP 100. In the second pass, the execution of ISZ 151 increments the contents of location 151 from 7777 to 0000. As a result, the instruction JUMP 100 is skipped and the program is transferred to the instruction HALT. Note:

1. ISZ instruction does not affect the contents of the accumulator or the link.
2. The ISZ instruction increments the contents of specified memory location and then checks for a zero result.
3. If ISZ instruction is used for looping k-times, then $-k$ should be stored in the counting location.

Table 3.11

	Location	Contents
1st pass	→100	ADD 150
	101	ISZ 151 ⸺
	102	JUMP 100	2nd pass
	103	HALT ◄
	⋮	
	150	0010
	151	7776

Subroutine Linkage Instruction

In a large program, the same sequence of instructions is often needed at several different places. For example, the sequence to calculate the square root is likely to be needed in many parts of the program for calculating areas. Instead of writing the sequence every time it is needed, the JMS instruction (jump to subroutine) is used.

The sequence can be written as a subroutine and located outside the main program. Whenever the main program needs a subroutine, the JMS instruction will be used. This instruction provides the linkage between the main program and the subroutine. For example, suppose that the main program needs the subroutine when it reaches location 100 and suppose that the subroutine is in locations 150 to 170, Table 3.12.

Table 3.12

Location	Contents	Comment
100	JMS 150	This instruction stores 101 in location 150 and transfers program control to location 151.
⋮	⋮	
150	. . .	After JMS 150 is executed, this location contains 101.
151	CLEAR	
152	⋮	
170	JUMP I 150	This instruction finds the return address (101) stored in location 150, and transfers the program back to the main program.

The program counter keeps track of the address of the next instruction to be executed. Just before JMS 150 is executed, the program counter keeps address 100. During the execution of the instruction JMS 150 the program counter is advanced to point to the next address 101. The JMS 150 instruction takes the value of the program counter and stores it in the first location of the subroutine. Hence location 150 will now have the contents equal 101. Upon the execution of the subroutine, the first location (150) will be used as a pointer for a return to the main program.

Next, instruction JMS 150 will place address 151 into the program counter. Hence the program control is transferred to the second location of the subroutine.

The last instruction of the subroutine will provide for the return to the main program. It finds the return address 101 stored in location 150 and transfers the control to location 101. This instruction uses indirect addressing, which will be discussed later.

The three steps just described are shown in Fig. 3.3.

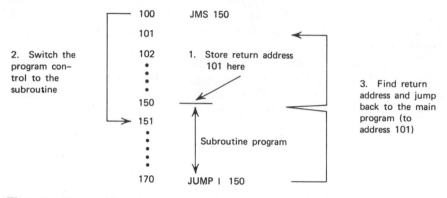

Figure 3.3. Subroutine linkage.

Operate Instructions

This group of instructions deals with only one operand. The source of the operand is the same as the destination of the result. The general form of the operate instruction is

$$\text{OPR dst}$$

In a small computer the destination is usually the accumulator, and it does not have to be specified in the instruction. For some instructions, the destination can be the link register, and in this case an L will be attached to the OPR:

Destination $\equiv$ accumulator	Destination $\equiv L$
OPR	OPRL

The basic operate instructions are CLEAR, INCR, COMPL, ROTL, and ROTR.

CLEAR

The CLEAR instruction sets the accumulator to all zeros. In brief

$$0 \rightarrow A$$

CLEARL

The CLEARL instruction sets the link to zero. In brief

$$0 \rightarrow L$$

INCR

The INCR instruction adds a 1 to the contents of the accumulator. In brief

$$(A) + 1 \rightarrow A$$

COMPL

The COMPL instruction sets the accumulator to the one's complement of its original value, that is, all 1's become 0's and all 0's become 1's. In brief

$$(\overline{A}) \rightarrow A$$

COMPLL

The COMPLL instruction complements the link register. In brief

$$(\overline{L}) \rightarrow L$$

ROTL

The ROTL instruction treats the accumulator and the link as a closed loop and shifts all bits in the loop by one position to the left. This operation is illustrated in Fig. 3.4.

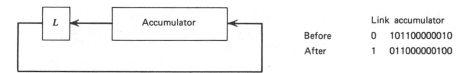

	Link	accumulator
Before	0	101100000010
After	1	011000000100

Figure 3.4. Rotation to the left.

ROTR

The ROTR instruction treats the accumulator and the link as a closed loop and shifts all bits in the loop by one position to the right. This operation is illustrated in Fig. 3.5.

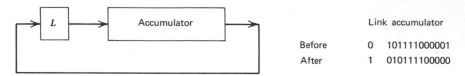

	Link	accumulator
Before	0	101111000001
After	1	010111100000

Figure 3.5. Rotation to the right.

All basic computer instructions are listed in Table 3.13.

3.5. BASIC COMPUTER ADDRESSING

All instructions addressing the memory have a common name—memory reference instructions. The general form of memory reference instructions used up to now is

OPR M

In fact, each memory reference instruction in a small computer should contain three items, *OPR*, *D*/tag:

> operation code *OPR*
> operand address or displacement *D*
> addressing tags

The operation code (*OPR*) tells the computer what to do. The displacement *D* gives some information as to where the operand is. The addressing tags tell the computer how to calculate the real or effective address from the displacement supplied in the instruction.

The effective address is the address with which the instruction performs an operation. For most instructions, the effective address is the address keeping the operand. For the jump instruction, the effective address is the one to which the program control is switched.

In many cases the effective address is equal to the displacement *D*. In fact, in the examples given up to now we showed only simple cases in which the effective address is identical with *D*.

Table 3.13

Type	Mnemonic	Description	In brief
Move data	STORE M	Store (A) into M; A unchanged	$(A) \rightarrow M$
Arithmetic	ADD M	Add (M) to A; result in A	$(M) + (A) \rightarrow A$
Logical	AND M	"And" (M) to A; result in A	$(M) \wedge (A) \rightarrow A$
	HALT	Halt program	
	JUMP M	Jump, unconditionally to M	$\Rightarrow M$
	SKIPP	Skip on positive accumulator	$(A) = + \Rightarrow I + 2; (A) \neq + \Rightarrow I + 1$
	SKIPZ	Skip on zero accumulator	$(A) = 0 \Rightarrow I + 2; (A) \neq 0 \Rightarrow I + 1$
Control	SKIPN	Skip on negative accumulator	$(A) = - \Rightarrow I + 2; (A) \neq - \Rightarrow I + 1$
	SKIPL	Skip if link is set to one	$(L) = 1 \Rightarrow I + 2; (L) = 0 \Rightarrow I + 1$
	SKIP	Skip, unconditionally	$\Rightarrow I + 2$
	ISZ M	Increment (M); skip if result zero	$(M) + 1 \rightarrow M$ $(M) = 0 \Rightarrow I + 2; (M) \neq 0 \Rightarrow I + 1$
Subroutine linkage	JMS M	Jump to subroutine, save PC	$(PC) \rightarrow M; \Rightarrow M + 1$
	CLEAR	Clear A	$0 \rightarrow A$
	CLEARL	Clear link	$0 \rightarrow L$
	COMPL	Complement A	$(\overline{A}) \rightarrow A$
	COMPLL	Complement L	$(\overline{L}) \rightarrow L$
Register	INCR	Increment A by 1	$(A) + 1 \rightarrow A$
Reference	ROTL	Rotate A with L left 1 bit	
	ROTR	Rotate A with L right 1 bit	
Input	CLEAR02	Clear flag in the device (02)	$0 \rightarrow F02$
	SKIP02	Skip if flag set in the device (02)	$(F02) = 1 \Rightarrow I + 2; (F02) = 0 \Rightarrow I + 1$
Output	READ02	Read the data from the device (02) into A	$(02) \rightarrow A$
	WRITE02	Write the data from A into the device (02)	$(A) \rightarrow 02$
	GO02	Activates an output of the selector (02)	

There are different kinds of addressing, determined by addressing tags. Figure 3.6 shows an example of a 12-bit computer instruction; 3 bits are used for operation code, 2 bits are tag bits, and 7 bits are used as displacement D.

The right hand tag bit is called the page-addressing bit.
The left hand tag bit is called the indirect-addressing bit.

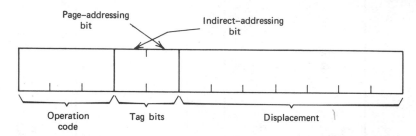

Figure 3.6. Instruction format for the memory reference instructions.

Hence the two tag bits can determine four ways of addressing.

Tag bits are 00, direct addressing; 01, page-relative addressing; 10, indirect addressing; and 11, page-relative and indirect addressing.

In each case the effective address will be calculated from the displacement D, but using another rule. Hence in general

$$M, \text{ effective address } = F(D),$$

where F is determined by the address tag bits.

Direct Addressing

If both tag bits are zero, the displacement D is directly used to address the memory. An example is shown in Table 3.14.

$$M, \text{ effective address } = D$$

Direct addressing is the simplest way of addressing, but it has an obvious disadvantage—in the example of Fig. 3.6 the displacement has only 7 bits. By using 7 bits one can directly address only $2^7 = 128_{10} = 200_8$ memory locations. To address the larger part of the memory, a longer command word with more bits would be needed. In small computers, which should be simple and cheap, other methods of addressing are used to overcome this difficulty.

Table 3.14

Location	Contents	Accumulator
10	ADD 20	1234
⋮		
20	1234	1234

Page-Relative Addressing

To make the best use of the available bits of the operand address, a small computer utilizes a division of a memory into blocks, or pages. In a given example of a computer with 7 bits for displacement, each page will have $128_{10} = 200_8$ locations. The displacement can now be used to address any location on a given page relative to the beginning of the page. The address of the beginning of the page is the base address to which the displacement should be added. The pages are

Memory locations	
Page 0	0–177
Page 1	200–377
Page 2	400–577

The effective address is given by

M, effective address = starting address of the current page + D

The example in Table 3.15 shows the meaning of page addressing.

If the instruction ADD 20 is in location 201, the computer will interpret it as add from the twentieth location relative to 200. If the same instruction ADD 20 is in location 406, the computer will interpret it as add from the twentieth location starting from location 400. In both cases the page bit in the instruction is set to indicate page addressing.

If the page bit is zero, the computer will use the displacement for direct-addressing locations 0-177, that is, it will address the zero page. Hence the page bit instructs the computer to address either the current page on which the instruction itself is stored or the zero page (0-177).

To address another part of the memory, indirect addressing should be used.

Table 3.15

	Location	Contents	Accumulator
	200	CLEAR	0000
	201	ADD 20	1234
	⋮		
Page 1	220	1234	
	⋮		
	377		
	400		
	⋮		
	405	CLEAR	0000
	406	ADD 20	7654
Page 2	⋮		
	420	7654	
	⋮		
	577		

Indirect Addressing

In indirect addressing the displacement indicates the operand's address instead of the operand. An indirect address (pointer address) identifies the location that contains the desired address (effective address).

For indirect addressing the indirect-addressing bit in the instruction word should be set. In writing mnemonic programs, a special character is used to indicate indirect addressing. Here we shall use the character I. During the assembly of the program, the presence of I will result in an indirect bit of the instruction being set to 1.

Examples in Tables 3.16 and 3.17 show the difference between direct and indirect addressing.

Table 3.16

Location	Contents	Accumulator
30	500	0000
⋮		
100	ADD 30	0500
⋮		
500	7771	

Table 3.17

Location	Contents	Accumulator
30	500	0000
⋮		
100	ADD I 30	7771
⋮		
500	7771	

The first example shows direct addressing. In the instruction ADD 30, 30 is the effective address. Hence the data from address 30 will be added to the accumulator.

The second example shows indirect addressing. In the instruction ADD I 30, 30 is the pointer address. It points to location 30, keeping the effective address 500. As a result the data from the effective address 500 will be added to the accumulator.

Hence the effective address is the contents of the displacement

$$M, \text{effective address} - (D)$$

There are many applications of indirect addressing in data acquisition, sorting, and retrieval problems. In small computers indirect addressing also provides the means for returning to the main program from a subroutine, as shown in the example in Table 3.12.

The instruction JMS 150 will store the return address 101 into location 150. The first instruction of the subroutine is in location 151. The last instruction of the subroutine is JUMP I 150. The pointer address 150 keeps the return address 101. Hence this instruction will cause the jump to location 101, that is, back to the main program.

Page-Relative and Indirect Addressing

If both tag bits are set, we have a combination of page-relative and indirect addressing. In this case the effective address is calculated in two steps.

Page addressing: address 1 = starting address of the current page + D
Indirect addressing: M, effective address = (address 1)

A few examples are shown in Table 3.18.

Table 3.18

Location	Contents	Accumulator
200	CLEAR	0000
201		
⋮		
210	ADD I 20	1234
⋮		
220	300	
⋮		
300	1234	
⋮		
400	CLEAR	0000
⋮		
405	ADD I 20	7654
⋮		
420	500	
⋮		
500	7654	

The instruction ADD I 20, stored in page 200:

$$\text{Address } 1 = 200 + 20 = 220$$
$$\text{Effective address} = (220) = 300$$

Hence the data from location 300 are added to the accumulator.
The instruction ADD I 20, stored in page 400:

$$\text{Address } 1 = 400 + 20 = 420$$
$$\text{Effective address} = (420) = 500$$

Hence the data from location 500 are added to the accumulator.

PROBLEMS

1. What are the contents of the accumulator and locations 55, 56, and 57 after execution of the following program?

Location	Contents
50	CLEAR
51	ADD 55
52	ADD 56
53	STORE 57
54	HALT
55	1234
56	1100
57	0000

2. What are the contents of the accumulator and locations 55, 56, and 57 after execution of the program from problem 1 if the instruction ADD 56 is changed to AND 56?

3. Write the program to complement the contents of location 200. The program should start at location 300.

4. Write the program to move the data from location 150 into location 151. The program should start at location 110.

5. What are the contents of the accumulator and locations 55, 56, and 57 after execution of the following program?

Location	Contents
50	CLEAR
51	ADD I 55
52	ADD I 56
53	STORE 57
54	HALT
55	60
56	61
57	0000
60	10
61	25
62	0000

6. What are the contents of the accumulator after execution of the following program?

Location	Contents
200	
⋮	
220	0012
⋮	
320	7000
⋮	CLEAR
377	ADD 20
400	ADD 20
⋮	HALT
420	1200
⋮	

7. Write the program to add three numbers stored in locations 300, 310, and 1000. The program should start at location 200.

8. Write the program to extract the most significant bit of the data stored in location 300. Store this bit in location 301. Use the instructions for rotation and skip.

9. Solve problem 8 using AND instruction.

10. Make a logical OR operation on data in locations 200 and 201 and store the result into location 202. Use de Morgan's theorem.

REFERENCES

1. I. Flores, *Computer Programming*, Prentice-Hall, Englewood Cliffs, N.J., 1966.
2. *Introduction to Programming*, Digital Equipment Corporation, Maynard, Mass., 1969.
3. H. D. Leeds, G. M. Weinberg, *Computer Programming Fundamentals*, McGraw-Hill, New York, 1966.

4

PROGRAMMING MICROPROCESSORS

Chapter 4 deals with programming. The basic procedures of programming are presented in logical order. The programming of control operations, loops, subroutines, arithmetic and logical operations, and input-output operations is explained. The chapter concentrates on the symbolic programming of those operations, and then explains briefly the corresponding FORTRAN statements. In this way, the reader learns symbolic coding and the meaning of operations as well as the philosophy of programming in algebraic language. For each operation, a few examples of short programs are given. As microprocessors are replacing digital logic design, programming becomes the major tool for system designers. Programming techniques common to all microprocessors and minicomputers are described.

4.1. LANGUAGE

From the classification of instructions of the computer, we can conclude that the computer is capable of performing operations such as moving the data inside the machine; performing arithmetic and logical operations; making decisions based on the results; and transferring the data in and out of the machine. The computer can perform each of those tasks, but the programmer should decide which task is needed, and the programmer decides that through writing the program.

The program is a list of instructions for the computer to follow to arrive at a solution for a given problem. Each instruction in the program will activate the proper circuitry in the machine and perform a small, simple operation. A small computer has a moderate number of simple instructions. A problem to be programmed should be divided into very small elementary steps which can be expressed with the computer instruction set. The elementary nature of the machine requires the programmer to specify the calculation procedure in minute detail. Every instruction step should be specified with complete accuracy. The machine will respond to instructions like an obedient clerk and will do exactly what it is instructed to.

Since the repertoire of built-in operations in the computer is quite small, even a relatively simple calculation will be composed of a number of instruction steps. It is quite normal that the program should be composed of hundreds, even thousands, of instructions. The programmer's job proceeds through the following phases: very accurate definition of the problem to be programmed; determination of the most feasible solution method; flowcharting the problem; writing the program instruction by instruction; and program check-out.

When the program is finished, it should be read in the computer and stored in the computer memory. The computer will read an instruction from the memory and will perform an operation. It will then read the next instruction, perform another operation and so on until it reaches the end of the program.

Source and Object Program

It is important to recall that the computer works in the binary number system and understands the information coded only in the binary system. Hence the instruction stored in the computer memory is also a binary piece of information composed of zeros and ones. It would be very unpractical if the programmer had to write a program composed of hundreds of instructions using zero and one coding. Hence other ways have been invented to write the program. In general, in programming a computer two programming languages are employed:

• The language used by the programmer, or the source language.
• The language used by the computer, or the object language. The object language is also called the machine language.

The source language is composed of a clearly defined set of symbolic instructions. Each instruction has a mnemonic code, reminding the programmer of the operation to be performed. For example, in a given computer the symbolic instruction ADD can be used to signify the operation addition. No other codes will be allowed for the same operation. Hence the codes such as ADDIT or SUM will be meaningless for this particular source language. For each computer instruction, the source language will have one and only one symbolic code.

The object language is the zero and one language used inside the computer. This is the only language the machine can understand.

The programmer writes the program in the mnemonic source language.

The machine understands only the binary, object language. Hence some kind of translation is necessary to translate each symbolic command into its binary equivalent. The translation is performed in the same way as the translation from one human language into another; it is based on the use of the dictionary.

The dictionary lists side by side all the source-language instructions and the corresponding object-language binary codes. The translation is simple because of the following reasons: for a given instruction there is only one code in the source language and one code in the object language; one line of the program keeps one instruction, which is independent of the previous line and the following line.

A line of the instruction dictionary may look like this

$$ADD = 001$$

meaning that the addition in the computer is coded in the source language as ADD and it should be translated into the object language as 001.

The most obvious procedure for writing the program would be

1. The programmer writes the program using the source-language mnemonic instructions.

2. The secretary having no knowledge of programming or mathematical analysis takes the source-object dictionary and translates each source line into the corresponding object line.

3. The obtained object program is loaded into the computer, which then performs the calculation.

We see that the translation procedure is strictly automatic and clearly defined. Hence the computer can be instructed to do the job of the secretary. It is necessary to develop a program that can carry out the translation. Such a program is called the *assembly* program. Today every computer has such a program available.

In order to be able to carry out the translation, the assembly program has a translation dictionary. The assembly program, when loaded into the computer, will read in the source program and translate each mnemonic instruction into its binary equivalent in the object program.

Symbolic Addresses

In all examples shown so far we have been using binary or octal addresses for memory locations. For longer programs such a procedure would be very unpractical. The programmer would have to keep in mind octal addresses of locations and remember for what purpose each location has been used. To simplify the process of writing, debugging, and reading the program, mnemonic coding for addresses has been introduced. The programmer may assign symbolic names to locations, and the assembler will assign address values for him. The programmer can choose symbolic names at free will, keeping in mind the restrictions of the assembler. The first restriction is the number of letters used in the name. If the assembler has a limit of, say, 5 letters, it will ignore additional letters in the name. The second restriction is that the first character of the name should be a letter (A $\cdots$ Z). Other characters can be either letters or digits (0, 1, . . . 9).

The names of locations are chosen to suggest the operand stored in the location. For example, the following symbolic names can be used: VOLTAGE, RESULT, X5, SIGN, WEIGHT and so on.

Symbolic names for addresses become part of the source program. During the translation procedure the assembly program will replace each symbolic address by one binary address. For this purpose, the assembler will *ad hoc* build a dictionary for address translation. The first line of the dictionary will be the first symbolic address used in the program and the binary address of the first memory location available in the machine. Let us suppose that the first symbolic name is VOLTAGE and the first available location has the address 234. Then the first line of the address dictionary will be

$$VOLTAGE = 234$$

In a similar way the assembler will find a binary address for each symbolic address.

Note that the assembly program will have two dictionaries.

- The fixed instruction dictionary which is part of the assembler
- The address dictionary built by the assembler during the procedure of translating the program

Figure 4.1 shows an example of the source-language instruction as written by the programmer and its object-language binary equivalent as stored in the computer.

The following examples show the meaning of symbolic addressing. Let us write the program to perform the calculation $22 + 35 - 13 = 44$. We arbitrarily decide to use the address 100 as the starting point of the program; the addresses 150, 151, 152 for data; and the address 153 for the result.

The elementary instruction set defined earlier has the instruction ADD, which can be used to perform the operation $+35$. However, the subtraction operation cannot be performed directly, because the basic instruction set does not have the instruction for subtraction. At this point we have to recall the two's complement arithmetic. Having the proper presentation for the negative number, subtraction can be performed using the addition:

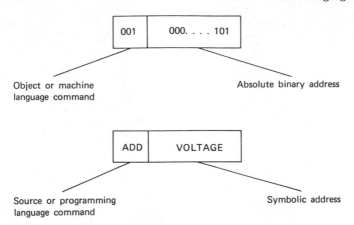

Figure 4.1. Object-language and source-language instructions.

$x - y = x + (-y)$. The proper presentation of the negative number is its two's complement.

The program is shown in Table 4.1.

Table 4.1

Location	Contents
100	CLEAR
	ADD 152
	COMPL
	INCR
	ADD 150
	ADD 151
	STORE 153
	HALT
150	22
151	35
152	13
153	0

Let us now write the same program using symbolic addressing. We choose the names X, Y, and Z for locations to keep the data, and the name RES for the location keeping the result. The beginning of the program will be named START. Table 4.2 shows the program.

Table 4.2

Location	Contents
START	CLEAR
	ADD Z
	COMPL
	INCR
	ADD X
	ADD Y
	STORE RES
	HALT
X	22
Y	35
Z	13
RES	0

The addressing used in Table 4.1 is called absolute addressing. The addressing used in Table 4.2 is called symbolic addressing.

The Assembler Mechanics

The mechanics of assembling and executing the program is shown in Fig. 4.2a and b, respectively. The following steps are involved.

1. Load the assembly program in the computer. A fixed instruction dictionary makes part of the assembler. The assembly program will also reserve empty space at the beginning for the address dictionary.

2. Give the assembler the address of the first memory location to be used by the program. The assembler will build the address list relative to this address.

3. Put the source program in the reading device and start the computer. The assembler will read the source program, translate it, and output the object program. During the translation the assembler will also check to see if there are some formal errors in the program and will mark the lines with errors. Errors might be due to the use of illegal command code, the use of the same symbolic name for two different addresses, failing to assign the symbolic name to an address and so on.

4. If assembling the program has resulted in no errors, the assembler is no longer needed. Load the produced object program in the computer. Load the data (if any). The computer will execute the program and will produce results.

assembling

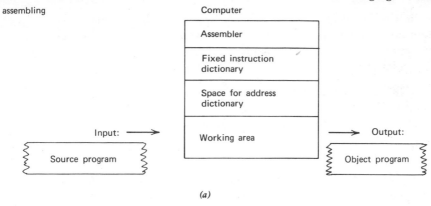

(a)

computing

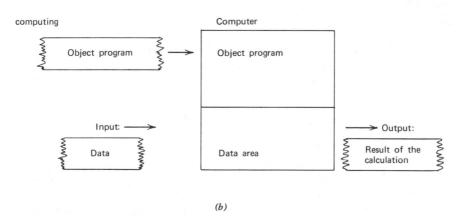

(b)

Figure 4.2. Mechanics of assembling and computing.

Higher Languages and FORTRAN Compiler

The assembler will translate the symbolic source program in the binary object program. If we used the assembler to translate the program shown in Table 4.2, which is composed of 12 lines, the result would be the object program composed of 12 binary-coded words. It is important to notice that the assembler will translate a symbolic source command into a binary object command. Hence the symbolic language, while being more comfortable for the programmer than the binary language, still expresses the problem through a very small elementary instruction set.

In some applications more advanced programming languages can be used, that is, languages that are problem-oriented and allow the programmer to use more meaningful commands than elementary computer instructions. Three languages are of particular importance.

COBOL for common business-oriented language.
ALGOL for algebraic language.
FORTRAN for formula translation language.

Because of its wide use, especially in scientific and technical programming, we have chosen FORTRAN to be presented along with the symbolic language.

A program written in the FORTRAN language should also be translated into the equivalent machine-language program. The program for translation of the FORTRAN language into the machine code is called the *compiler*. The compiler may produce many lines of machine coding for each line written in the FORTRAN. For example the problem shown in Table 4.2 would be expressed in the FORTRAN language by a single statement

$$RES = X + Y - Z$$

The programmer would only write this statement. The compiler would translate it into many lines of machine coding. From this example it is quite clear that it is much easier to write the program in FORTRAN than to code the same problem in the symbolic language. Unfortunately, this is not always possible and also has some drawbacks. Without going into details we should mention the following.

A FORTRAN compiler, being more clever than a symbolic assembler, translates the programming statement into a very general machine program, which will check for all kinds of limits, number of ranges, and overflows; it will use the function generating subroutines, and so on.

Hence the program will occupy the larger part of the memory, and being composed of more instructions, it will take longer time to produce the result than the symbolic program tailored for a particular application. Another problem is the input-output transfer. The FORTRAN is very elegant for input-output programming with standard peripheral equipment, such as magnetic tape, teletype, and line printer. However, the FORTRAN, being fixed for a hardware configuration, cannot be used to program the transfer with customer-designed special devices, such as measuring or control equipment. Major limitations to the use of FORTRAN in measuring and control applications are as follows: lower speed, low efficiency of memory utilization, and input-output limited to standard peripheral devices.

On the other hand, for calculation and simulation purposes where the above factors are not of major importance, the FORTRAN is very convenient. It enables one to express the problem using a few higher-level statements rather than breaking the problem into a very large number of elementary computer instructions.

The FORTRAN is especially useful in calculating arithmetic expressions. The primitive arithmetic functions of addition, subtraction, multiplication, division, and exponentiation are written like algebra, with a special sign between the variables concerned. The signs used are

$$+, \; -, \; *, \; /, \; **$$

For example, the FORTRAN statement for calculation of the equation

$$Y = (A + B) * (C - D)/(E - F)$$

is exactly the same as the equation itself.

One can learn the FORTRAN programming without learning the principles of computer organization and operation.

There are as many symbolic languages as there are varieties of computers. Each computer has its own symbolic language, composed of instructions available on this computer. On the other hand, FORTRAN statements are general, and with slight restrictions, practically the same statement can be used in programming any computer.

In the next few sections we shall show the basic programming techniques, concentrating on the principles rather than on the particular computer or programming language. We shall program the examples, whenever possible, in the symbolic language using the basic computer instruction set, and then for comparison we shall solve the problem using the FORTRAN statements.

4.2. CONTROL OPERATIONS

One of the most important features by which to distinguish a digital computer from a desk calculator is the ability to program the computer to make decisions. It is quite possible to have a useful program in which there are no arithmetic operations or a program without input-output transfer, and so on. On the other hand, practically every program has to make at least a few decisions.

Without decision-making the program would be composed of a number of commands, which would be executed sequentially in the order they are stored in the memory. The decision-making feature enables one to write the program composed of a number of branches, each branch to be executed if a given condition is fulfilled. The program then looks like a tree with many branches and loops, rather than like a straight-line sequence of commands.

Let us suppose that the computer controls an experiment, in which the temperature is the critical variable. The computer can read the temperature

T from the digital voltmeter. The program can be written to compare the temperature T with the prescribed value T_0. Three possible outcomes may result: $T < T_0$; $T = T_0$; $T > T_0$. The computer program can have three different branches, and it can decide which branch of the program to execute. There should also be a general control program which is the thread binding together separate parts and instructions.

In writing the control program, one has to solve three problems: labeling, testing, and directing.

Labeling

Decisions always have more than one outcome. In general, for each outcome it might be necessary to write a separate program branch. Each program branch must have its name or label by which it is called upon. In symbolic coding the label or the name is in fact the symbolic address of the beginning of the program branch. Examples of labels are MAX, MIN, EQUAL, X7.

Testing

The program can make decisions and branching using a special set of instructions. Those are control instructions. Control instructions do not affect data and do not transmit them. They simply test some condition or result in the computer and guide the computer through the program in fixed or in variable sequences. In small computers, control instructions usually test the contents of the accumulator or the link register. Such instructions are SKIPN, SKIPZ, SKIPL.

Directing

When testing is finished, the program should be directed to one of a few possible branches, depending on the result of the test. Speaking in terms of machine-language programming, that means that the program counter should be set to point to the starting address of the program branch needed. Instructions such as JUMP are used to direct the program.

It is important to remember that in some machines and in some languages there are occasions when testing and directing merge into one step and are performed with one instruction or with one programming statement.

Simple Decisions

Example. Test the memory location T. If $(T) = 0$, store (X) into *RES*. If $(T) \neq 0$, store (Y) into *RES*. Figure 4.3 shows the flow diagram and Table 4.3 shows the program.

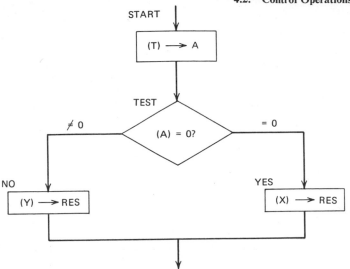

Figure 4.3. $A = 0$, or $A \neq 0$, flow chart.

Table 4.3

Location	Contents
START	CLEAR
	ADD T
TEST	SKIPZ
	JUMP NO
YES	CLEAR
	ADD X
	STORE RES
	JUMP OUT
NO	CLEAR
	ADD Y
	STORE RES
OUT	HALT
T	1177
X	1
Y	0
RES	0

Notice the following points concerning the example:

1. The program is divided into four blocks labeled START, TEST, YES, and NO. START and TEST can be omitted from the program without affecting it in any way. We use those labels only for simpler identification of the blocks from flow-charts. The labels YES and NO are necessary and are used to identify two possible branches of the program.

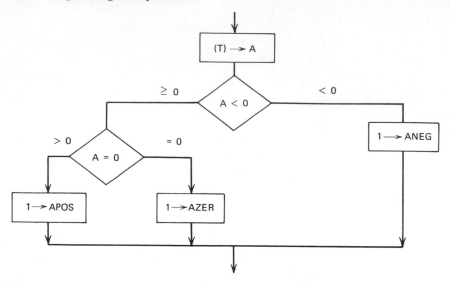

Figure 4.4. $A = 0$, or $A > 0$, or $A < 0$, flow chart.

2. The instruction SKIPZ is used for testing and decision.
3. Direction is achieved using the instruction JUMP.

Example. Find if (T) is positive, negative, or zero. If $(T) > 0$, add 1 to APOS. If $(T) = 0$, add 1 to AZER. If $(T) < 0$, add 1 to ANEG. Figure 4.4 shows the flow diagram and Table 4.4 shows the program.

Table 4.4

Location	Contents	
	CLEAR	
	ADD	T
	SKIPN	
	JUMP	TEST2
	ISZ	ANEG
	JUMP	OUT
TEST2	SKIPZ	
	JUMP	POSIT
	ISZ	AZER
	JUMP	OUT
POSIT	ISZ	APOS
OUT	HALT	
T	1234	
ANEG	—	
APOS	—	
AZER	—	

Note the following points regarding the example.

1. Only the labels absolutely necessary for coding are used.

2. Two control instructions are used, SKIPZ and SKIPN, dividing the program into three branches.

Example. Three numbers are stored at *X*, *Y* and *Z*, respectively. Sort them in ascending order and store in locations OUT1, OUT2 and OUT3. Figure 4.5 shows the flow diagram and Table 4.5 shows the program.

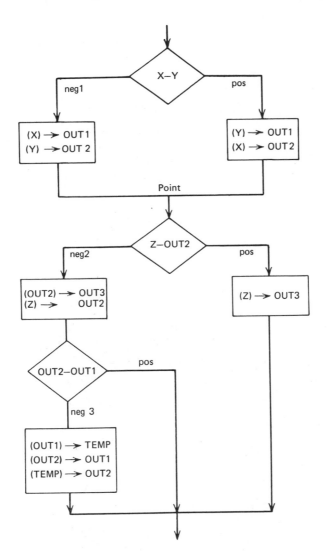

Figure 4.5. *X*, *Y*, *Z* in order, flow chart.

Table 4.5

START	CLEAR	
	ADD	Y
	COMPL	
	INCR	
	ADD	X
	SKIPP	
	JUMP	NEG1
	CLEAR	
	ADD	Y
	STORE	OUT1
	CLEAR	
	ADD	X
	STORE	OUT2
POINT	CLEAR	
	ADD	OUT2
	COMPL	
	INCR	
	ADD	Z
	SKIPP	
	JUMP	NEG2
	CLEAR	
	ADD	Z
	STORE	OUT3
	HALT	
NEG1	CLEAR	
	ADD	X
	STORE	OUT1
	CLEAR	
	ADD	Y
	STORE	OUT2
	JUMP	POINT

This example shows the importance of flow charts. Although the program is relatively simple, it would be difficult to code it without breaking it into small blocks. The flow chart shows the operations to be performed in each block as well as the relationships between the blocks.

4.3. CONTROL OPERATIONS IN FORTRAN

The major formal difference between the symbolic coding and the FORTRAN coding is the following.

Table 4.5 (*Continued*)

NEG2	CLEAR	
	ADD	OUT2
	STORE	OUT3
	CLEAR	
	ADD	Z
	STORE	OUT2
	CLEAR	
	ADD	OUT1
	COMPL	
	INCR	
	ADD	OUT2
	SKIPP	
	JUMP	NEG3
	HALT	
NEG3	CLEAR	
	ADD	OUT1
	STORE	TEMP
	CLEAR	
	ADD	OUT2
	STORE	OUT1
	CLEAR	
	ADD	TEMP
	STORE	OUT2
	HALT	
X	5	
Y	7	
Z	3	
OUT1	0	
OUT2	0	
OUT3	0	

• In symbolic coding the program is composed of individual instructions. In the absence of any special provision, the control always passes from one instruction to its successor.

• In the FORTRAN, the program is composed of statements. Each statement is one line of the program. In the absence of any special provision, the control always passes from one statement to its successor.

• In symbolic coding we use octal notation for data and for addressing. In FORTRAN we use decimal notation.

In writing the FORTRAN control operations, one again encounters problems of labeling, testing, and directing.

Labeling

In FORTRAN any statement may be identified by a number written to the left of the statement. For example

$$71 \quad Z = X + Y$$

The number 71 presents the label of this statement. In this program no other statement is allowed to be labeled with the same number. The statement number in FORTRAN does not mean the memory address; its sole purpose is to be used to identify the statement when we wish to transfer the control to that statement.

Testing

In the FORTRAN language there is one basic conditional control statement that can be used for testing and at the same time for directing the program control. This is the IF statement. This statement will test the specified quantity if this quantity is less than zero, equal to zero or greater than zero, and it will provide a three-way branching. For example, the statement

$$IF(Y) \quad 11, \ 12, \ 71$$

will test the variable Y and will transfer the program control to one of the three statements 11, 12, or 71

If $Y < 0$; statement 11 will be executed next.
If $Y = 0$; statement 12 will be executed next.
If $Y > 0$; statement 71 will be executed next.

Directing

In the FORTRAN language there is one basic unconditional directing statement, GO TO. If at some point in the program we wish to have the control transferred to statement 71, we should write the statement

$$GO \ TO \ 71$$

Now we shall repeat the examples shown in Figs. 4.3, 4.4, and 4.5 using the FORTRAN language.

Example. Code the problem of Fig. 4.3 in the FORTRAN language. The solution is shown in Table 4.6.

Table 4.6

5	IF(T) 10, 20, 10
10	RES = Y
64	GO TO 75
20	RES = X
75	STOP

Notice the following points concerning the example.

1. The statement numbers 5, 10, 64, 20, and 75 correspond to the blocks START, TEST, YES, NO, and OUT, respectively. The labels 5 and 64 can be omitted from the program, because those two statements are entered in the usual way upon the execution of the previous statement. The labels 10, 20, and 75 are necessary, because they are used in control statements IF(T) 10, 20, 10, and GO TO 75.

2. The statement *RES = Y* states that the old value of the variable *RES* is to be replaced by the present value of the variable *Y*.

3. The STOP statement terminates the program.

Example. Code the problem of Fig. 4.4 in the FORTRAN. The solution is shown in Table 4.7.

Table 4.7

	IF(T) 1, 2, 3
1	ANEG = ANEG + 1
	GO TO 4
2	AZER = AZER + 1
	GO TO 4
3	APOS = APOS + 1
4	STOP

Notice the following points relevant to the example.

1. Only one IF statement is enough to split the program into three branches.

2. The statement ANEG = ANEG + 1 states that the value of the variable ANEG should be incremented by one.

Example. Code the problem of Fig. 4.5 in the FORTRAN language. The solution is shown in Table 4.8.

Table 4.8

	IF (X − Y) 10, 10, 11
10	OUT1 = X
	OUT2 = Y
	GO TO 12
11	OUT2 = X
	OUT1 = Y
12	IF (Z − OUT2) 20, 20, 21
20	OUT3 = OUT2
	OUT2 = Z
	IF(OUT2 − OUT1) 30, 30, 31
30	TEMP = OUT1
	OUT1 = OUT2
	OUT2 = TEMP
	GO TO 31
21	OUT3 = Z
31	STOP

Notice the following point with regard to the example.

The first IF statement performs its test on the numerical difference between the quantities in X and Y, as specified by the expression $X − Y$.

Computed IF and GO TO Statements

In general one can include any arithmetic expression in the IF statement. The IF statement will perform the test on the result of the expression. For example, the statement

$$IF(X + Y − 2 * Z)\ 1,\ 2,\ 36$$

will test the result of the expression $(X + Y − 2 * Z)$. According to the result, which can be negative, zero, or positive, the IF statement will switch the control to the statement 1, 2, or 36, respectively.

Somewhat different is the generalized form of the GO TO statement:

$$GO\ TO\ (7,\ 2,\ 36,\ 14),\ M$$

This statement will cause a transfer of the control to the statement 7 if $M = 1$, to 2 if $M = 2$, to 36 if $M = 3$, or to 14 if $M = 4$. The variable M should be determined in another statement prior to the GO TO statement.

4.4. LOOPS

The program loop is a set of commands which is repeatedly executed. Looping is one of the most powerful techniques in programming the computer. Often the computer has to perform the same task but on different sets of data. In such situations the program can be repeated in the loop, rather than writing the same set of commands for each set of data.

Example. Add 100 numbers stored in locations DATA up to DATA + 143. Here we mean 100_{10}. Recall that addresses are in octal, and that 100_{10} = 144_8.

This problem can be solved by simply repeating the command for addition 100 times, as shown in Table 4.9. It is quite clear that such programming is not efficient. We repeat the same operation ADD 100 times writing 100 identical instructions. If we wished to add a list of say 10000 data, the program would be composed of 10000 instructions, and it would occupy the substantial part of the memory.

Table 4.9

	CLEAR	
	ADD	DATA
	ADD	DATA + 1
	ADD	DATA + 2
	$\vdots$	
	ADD	DATA + 143
	STORE	RES
	HALT	
RES	0	
DATA		
$\vdots$		
DATA + 143		

The same problem can be solved in a more elegant way writing the program in the form of a loop, as shown in Table 4.10 and Fig. 4.6.

Table 4.10

	CLEAR	
	ADD CONST	
	STORE COUNT	
	CLEAR	Initialize
	ADD ADATA	
	STORE POINT	
	CLEAR	
	ADD I POINT	Processing
	ISZ POINT	List advance
	ISZ COUNT	}
	JUMP .−3	} Testing and directing
	STORE RES	
	HALT	
ADATA	DATA	
POINT	0	
CONST	7634	Minus 100, in octal form
COUNT		
DATA		
	⋮	

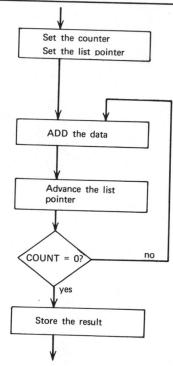

Figure 4.6. Loop to add a list of data.

118

Notice the following points concerning the example.

The program is subdivided into four blocks, each performing a special task. Those tasks are initialization, processing, list advance, and testing and directing.

Initialization

Initialization is part of the program before the loop. It prepares the parameters of the loop. In the example, the program sets the counter which will be used to count the number of loops; the location COUNT is set to -100. The program also sets the pointer to the first datum from the list, to be used in the loop. In other words, we initialize the pointer to point at the beginning of the data list; the contents of the location ADATA are transferred into the location POINT, which is the pointer location of the loop. These contents are the first address of the list DATA.

Processing

Processing is the main part of the loop program performing the basic operation. In the example, the instruction ADD I POINT performs the basic operation; in the ith loop it takes the contents of the ith location of the DATA list and adds these contents to the accumulator. Processing constitutes the actual job we want the computer to do and includes operations within the loop and whatever we want to be done repetitively. The other three tasks are to ensure that processing is performed the right number of times and on the right data.

List Advance

The loop usually performs the operation with the list of data. The operation is performed with the first item of the list. In the next passage the operation should be performed with the second item of the list and so on. In the example, the list is addressed indirectly, through the pointer location POINT. In each passage the instruction ISZ POINT adds 1 to the contents of the location POINT. Hence in the first passage the contents are DATA, in the second DATA $+$ 1 and so on. The instruction is used only to increment the pointer. It will never skip, since the pointer will never reach zero. In this example the step of the list advance is equal to one. In general, the list can be advanced in a step different from one.

Testing and Directing

The loop should be repeated a fixed number of times, and then the program should be directed out of the loop. In the example the program simply counts the number of loops. The location COUNT is set to -100. The instruction ISZ COUNT adds 1 to it during each passage of the loop. After the hundredth passage, COUNT goes to zero, and the program skips the JUMP instruction. Hence the program will execute the JUMP instruction during each iteration and return back for the next loop. However, at the hundredth passage the program will execute the STORE RES instruction.

In this example the exit out of the loop has been achieved by testing to see if the processing has been repeated a given number of times. There are also other conditions which can be tested for possible exit.

Flowcharting the Loop. Indexing

Loops usually operate on lists of data. They perform the same operation on the first item from the data list, then on the second, on the ith and so on. Hence in the ith passage the program takes the ith item from the data list D_i and performs an operation $F(D_i)$.

In flowcharting the loop it is very important to indicate the position of the data. Figure 4.7 shows the flow chart of the example of adding a list of data using i to designate the position of data. In the first pass $i = 1$, and the operation is performed with the data item $DATA_1$; in the second pass $i = 2$, and so on. The subscript i tells which set of data should be used. The

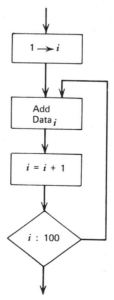

Figure 4.7. Flowcharting the loop.

third block on the diagram represents the fact that each time around the loop we proceed to the next data item on the list. The last block represents the testing for the end of the list.

Operations with data lists and subscripts are called indexing. The loop performs a number of passages. In the ith passage the operation is performed on the ith item from the list and then the subscript or index i is changed by one step. The step is usually equal to 1, but it can be 2 (taking every second term), -1 (backward processing of the list), and so on.

In the example of Table 4.10 we changed the index by ISZ POINT instruction. We also checked for the end of the program by the ISZ COUNT instruction.

In many computers there is a special built-in provision for indexing, usually by the use of the so-called index register. Besides direct and indirect addressing, such machines also have the indexed mode of addressing. In this mode the effective address is the sum of the displacement part of the instruction and the number stored at the index register.

Every time an indexed instruction is executed, the contents of the index register are automatically incremented (or decremented). In this way the programming of loops and list operations is greatly simplified. The computer can have more than one index register, facilitating the writing of programs using more than one subscript. Such an operation can have the general form

$$X_i = F(Y_j)$$

The use of index registers and the examples of programs with indexed addressing will be shown later.

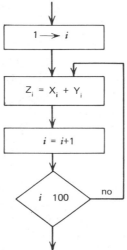

Figure 4.8. Loop termination through counting.

Table 4.11

	CLEAR	
	ADD CONST	
	STORE COUNT	
	CLEAR	
	ADD AX	
	STORE PX	
	CLEAR	Initialize
	ADD AY	
	STORE PY	
	CLEAR	
	ADD AZ	
	STORE PZ	
	CLEAR	
	ADD I PX	
	ADD I PY	Processing
	STORE I PZ	
	ISZ PX	
	ISZ PY	List advance
	ISZ PZ	
	ISZ COUNT	Testing
	JUMP .-10	
	HALT	
AX	X	
AY	Y	
AZ	Z	
PX	—	
PY	—	
PZ	—	
COUNT	—	
CONST	7634	Minus 100 octal
X	3	List X
X + 1	5	
X + 2	7	
⋮		
Y	6	List Y
Y + 1	0	
Y + 2	4	
⋮		
Z	0	List Z
Z+1	0	
Z + 2	0	
⋮		

Loop Termination Through Counting

The most frequently used way of stopping the loop is to count the number of passes. This way was also used in the example of Fig. 4.6. This way can always be used when the same operation is unconditionally performed over and over on all items of the list whose length is known.

Example. Perform the operation $Z_i = X_i + Y_i$; Fig. 4.8 shows the flow chart and Table 4.11 shows the program for the list of 100 items. The flow chart indicates only the basic operations without going into details. So, for example, the initialization is indicated by $1 \rightarrow i$. That means prepare the condition to reach the 1th item from lists X and Y. In fact, in the program the initialization is performed with the first 12 instructions. Note that the counting is used to exit from the loop.

Loop Termination through Condition Testing

In some applications the loop can be terminated before processing all items on the list. This is often the case in loops searching for a particular value of the item on the list. In this case the program is required to loop until the specific condition is found.

Example. Search a list of 100 items to find the first occurrence of the

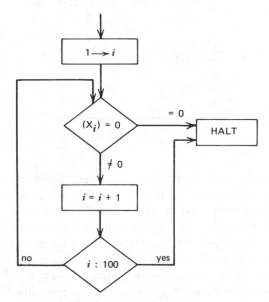

Figure 4.9. Loop termination through special condition.

number 0. The program is shown in Table 4.12 and the flow chart is shown in Fig. 4.9. Note:

There are two exits out of the loop, normal and conditional. The normal exit is used if all items of the list are processed and none of them is zero. There is a special exit when the program finds one item to be zero. The condition the program was looking for is fulfilled, and there is no need to process the list any further.

Table 4.12

	CLEAR	
	ADD	CONST
	STORE	COUNT
	CLEAR	
	ADD	AX
	STORE	POINT
	CLEAR	
	ADD I	POINT
	SKIPZ	
	SKIP	
	HALT	
	ISZ	POINT
	ISZ	COUNT
	JUMP.	−7
	HALT	
CONST	7634	
COUNT	—	
AX	X	
POINT	—	
X	—	

Address Modification

In all examples shown up to now we have been using indirect addressing through the pointer location in order to reach the items on the list. The list advancing has been performed by incrementing the pointer.

Another technique for advancing through the list is address modification; the address part of the processing instruction is altered every time the program performs the loop. The simplest way is to increment the contents of the location keeping the processing instruction. Now we shall repeat the example of Table 4.10 using this technique. The program should add 100 numbers stored in locations from DATA to DATA + 143.

The program is shown in Table 4.13.

Table 4.13

	CLEAR	
	ADD	CONST
	STORE	COUNT
	CLEAR	
PROC	ADD	DATA
	ISZ	PROC
	ISZ	COUNT
	JUMP	PROC
	HALT	
CONST	7634	
COUNT	—	
DATA		

It should be noted that the actual processing instruction stored in location PROC is incremented to perform the program modification:

Instruction ISZ PROC adds one to location PROC

in each pass through the loop. Hence the contents of PROC in the 1, 2, ith pass are ADD DATA, ADD DATA + 1, ADD DATA + i.

In this example the address modification is performed using the ISZ instruction. Computers having an index register can perform address modification in a more elegant way by using indexed addressing, as it will be shown later.

4.5. LOOPS IN FORTRAN

Lists in FORTRAN. DIMENSION Statement

As a problem-oriented language, FORTRAN is very elegant in dealing with lists. List processing and looping can be performed with statements we have thus far learned. We still have to learn the statement for space allocation: DIMENSION statement.

A DIMENSION statement is an instruction to the compiler, not to the machine. It is used to reserve space for the list. Thus to reserve space for the list X of 100 items, we write the statement

DIMENSION X(100)

To reserve space for the list X of 100 items, and for the list Y of 56 items, we write the statement

DIMENSION X(100), Y(56)

The statement can also be used for a variable with more than one subscript. Thus to reserve space for a two-dimensional array X_{ij} of 10 by 36 items, we write

$$\text{DIMENSION X(10, 36)}$$

Here we give a few examples of programming lists and loops in the FORTRAN language.

Example. Code in FORTRAN the problem from Fig. 4.7. The program is shown in Table 4.14.

Table 4.14

```
1    DIMENSION DATA(100)
2    I = 1
3    RES = 0
4    RES = RES + DATA(I)
5    I = I + 1
6    IF(I–100) 4, 4, 7
7    STOP
```

Note the following.

1. Statement 1 tells the compiler to reserve space for 100 items of the array called DATA.
2. Statement 2 sets the index of the list to one.
3. Statement 3 sets the initial value of the result, RES = 0.
4. The program performs the loop; in each iteration it adds one item from the list to the existing contents of the RES.
5. The loop index is increased by 1 in each iteration.
6. When the index reaches $I = 100$, the IF statement will switch the control out of the loop, and the program will stop.
7. Not all the statements should have statement numbers. One can omit statement numbers 1, 2, 3, 5, and 6.

Example. Code in FORTRAN the problem from Fig. 4.8. The program is shown in Table 4.15.

Table 4.15

```
     DIMENSION X(100), Y(100), Z(100)
     I = 1
3    Z(I) = X(I) + Y(I)
     I = I + 1
     IF(I–100) 3, 3, 4
4    STOP
```

Example. Code in FORTRAN the problem of Fig. 4.9. The program is shown in Table 4.16.

Table 4.16

	DIMENSION X(100)
	I = 1
5	IF(X(I)) 10, 20, 10
10	I = I + 1
	IF(I − 100) 5, 5, 20
20	IO = I
	STOP

Counting in FORTRAN. DO Statement

We have seen a few examples of FORTRAN programs of count-controlled loops. All those problems have been coded using the statements we have thus far learned. As count-control loops are very frequently encountered, the FORTRAN language has a special statement for their programming, the DO statement. A DO statement may look like

$$DO \ 4 \ I = 1, \ 20$$

This statement takes care of a few basic operations needed in programming the loop.

1. It initializes the index I. In the above example, the first value of the index will be 1.

2. The DO statement is outside the loop. Statements composing the loop are all statements following the DO statement until the statement specified in the DO statement is reached. In the example, statement 4 is the last statement of the loop.

3. Because of the DO statement, the loop in this example will be executed 20 times. Each time the value of the index I will be increased by one and the Ith item from the list will be processed. After the number of passes specified in the DO statement is finished, the program exits out of the loop.

Example. Code the problem shown in Fig. 4.7 using the DO statement. The program is shown in Table 4.17. Statement 5 will be executing 100 times, each time increasing the index i by one.

First pass	RES = RES + DATA (1)
Second pass	RES = RES + DATA (2)
ith pass	RES = RES + DATA (i)
100th pass	RES = RES + DATA (100)

Table 4.17

	DIMENSION DATA(100)
	RES = 0
	DO 5 I = 1, 100
5	RES = RES + DATA(I)
	STOP

Example. Code the problem shown in Fig. 4.8 using the DO statement. The program is shown in Table 4.18.

Table 4.18

	DIMENSION X(100), Y(100), Z(100)
	DO 3 I = 1, 100
3	Z(I) = X(I) + Y(I)
	STOP

Example. Code the problem shown in Fig. 4.9 using the DO statement. The program is shown in Table 4.19.

Table 4.19

	DIMENSION X(100)
	DO 10 I = 1, 100
	IF(X(I)) 10, 20, 10
10	CONTINUE
20	IO = I
	STOP

This example represents a somewhat different case, since the program has two branches, as shown in Fig. 4.9. If there are several branches within the loop, they must all converge in one statement, the statement mentioned in the DO command. For this purpose, FORTRAN has a dummy statement, CONTINUE. This statement presents no operation and is used only as a merging point. In the example, the last statement in the loop is the statement

10 CONTINUE

This statement indicates that the loop has reached its last statement and should start a new pass.

4.6. SUBROUTINES

The ever-increasing use of computers has been accompanied by a number of different programs. Writing programs may take rather long. Hence it is of interest to have a means for taking advantage of already-written programs and to "steal" from them as much as possible.

Programs solve various problems with a substantially unlimited number of variations of operations and parameters. Hence there is little chance that one can copy somebody's whole program except in the case of exactly the same application. Fortunately, modern programs are written in modular form. It is possible that some modules can be copied from one application to another.

Modularity is achieved by using subroutines in writing programs. A subroutine is the part of the program which by itself solves some basic operation. It can be composed of only a few instructions, but it can also be quite a long program.

The main purpose of writing a subroutine is to use it at different points in the same program, or to copy it from one program to another. It is of utmost importance that a subroutine should provide aid to the programmer who is not capable of developing the required routine himself.

Suppose we want to calculate the sine function of the parameter at a few places in a program. The sine function is a very basic function, but it is not easy to program it by using elementary machine instructions; we shall most probably have to calculate the sine function in a power series.

Since the sine is a function often required, we may be lucky to find somewhere an already-written program for calculating this function. Nowadays there are organized program libraries and organizations collecting programs from many sources and making them available to the users.

The program for the sine function will be written as an independent unit or subroutine. It will clearly define how to enter the parameter in the routine and how to get the result from the routine. In such a case the user can copy the subroutine and use it in his program, without even having to know how the subroutine is written.

If we buy a small computer for laboratory applications, we shall develop a number of programs in the course of time. It is very useful to split programs into subroutines from the very beginning. In this way we can build our own library of subroutines useful for particular applications. When it is necessary to write a new program, we can copy, whenever possible, the subroutines already existing in the library.

Since a subroutine can be used at a later time, or even by another person, it is very important to provide a clear description and definition of the subroutine and, if necessary, to make a flow chart of it.

Open Subroutine

Program subroutines can be very useful even as part of a single program. Suppose that we need a function in different parts of the program. We can write the subroutine programming this function. Whenever we need the function in the program, we can simply insert the same set of instructions, rather than think again and again how to solve the problem.

It is possible that at each insertion the subroutine should be slightly modified to meet the requirements at this point in the program. Hence the sub-

Table 4.20

CLEAR	
CLEARL	
ADD	X1
ADD	X2
ROTR	

Table 4.21

⋮		
CLEAR		
CLEARL		
ADD	X1	Subroutine
ADD	X2	
ROTR		
STORE	XA	
⋮		
CLEAR		
CLEARL		
ADD	Y1	Subroutine
ADD	Y2	
ROTR		
STORE	YA	
⋮		
CLEAR		
CLEARL		
ADD	Z1	Subroutine
ADD	Z2	
ROTR		
STORE	ZA	
⋮		

routine is open to changes, and this kind of subroutine is called an *open subroutine*.

Example. Find the average of $X1$ and $X2$ and store it in XA; after that perform the same operation with $Y1$, $Y2$ and YA, and then with $Z1$, $Z2$ and ZA.

In this program the same function, the average, is needed at three points. We shall first develop the subroutine for one application. This subroutine is shown in Table 4.20. It performs the operation $(X1 + X2)/2$. Recall that the division by 2 is equivalent to moving the binary point by one place. This is achieved by an instruction which rotates the contents of the accumulator $(X1 + X2)$ by one place to the right.

Having the subroutine, we can write the main program. We simply copy the subroutine whenever needed. The program is shown in Table 4.21. We do not have to think about the subroutine every time. We can use the same set of instructions and just adapt them to different addresses.

MACRO Instructions

The procedure shown in Tables 4.20 and 4.21 can be automatized. There is a means for instructing the assembler to insert the subroutine in the program whenever needed.

Every program is composed of machine instructions, each performing a small operation. A modern assembler enables us to define our own new instructions to replace the whole subroutine. So, in the example of Table 4.21, we would like to have a new instruction, say AVERG, which would replace five machine instructions of the subroutine, shown in Table 4.20. Such a big instruction is then called a MACRO instruction. There are two special commands for the assembler, which can be used to define MACRO instructions. Table 4.22 shows those instructions in the example of defining the operation AVERG. The commands MACRO and ENDMACRO tell the assembler that the subroutine between them is defined as a new instruction, called AVERG. Now we can use this new instruction in the main program.

Table 4.22

AVERG	MACRO	FIRST, SEC
	CLEAR	
	CLEARL	
	ADD	FIRST
	ADD	SEC
	ROTR	
	ENDMACRO	

Table 4.23 shows the same program as Table 4.21, written with the MACRO instruction.

Table 4.23

$\vdots$

AVERG X1, X2
STORE XA
$\vdots$

AVERG Y1, Y2
STORE YA
$\vdots$

AVERG Z1, Z2
STORE ZA
$\vdots$

During the procedure of assembling, the assembler will realize that the AVERG is a MACRO instruction. The assembler will look at the way we have defined this instruction. It will replace the MACRO instruction AVERG by the subroutine, as defined and shown in Table 4.22. It will also insert the parameters, as called in the program of Table 4.23. Note:

Tables 4.22 and 4.23 show the program as it would be written by the programmer. The assembler will change the program in the form shown in Table 4.21 and will translate each instruction into binary code.

Example. An open subroutine to multiply by 3. The subroutine is shown in Table 4.24. The multiplication $3 = 2 + 1$ is performed in two steps. The multiplication by 2 is performed by rotating the accumulator by one place. The multiplication by 1 is performed by addition.

Table 4.24

TIMES3	MACRO	
	STORE	TEMP
	CLEARL	
	ROTL	
	ADD	TEMP
	ENDMACRO	

Table 4.25 shows the main program, in which the multiplication by 3 is used at three points with variables X, Y, and Z respectively. As in the previous example, the assembler will understand that the instruction TIMES3 is a MACRO instruction. It will look for its definition and will insert the routine shown in Table 4.24 in the program every time it finds the MACRO instruction TIMES3. Note:

Table 4.25

```
CLEAR
ADD    X
TIMES3
STORE  X3
   ⋮
CLEAR
ADD    Y
TIMES3
STORE  Y3
   ⋮
CLEAR
ADD    Z
TIMES3
STORE  Z3
   ⋮
```

The pseudo-instructions MACRO and ENDMACRO used here will have different names from computer to computer. However, they will serve the purpose described here to define the body of the MACRO subroutine.

Closed Subroutine

The MACRO operation can greatly simplify the procedure of writing the program. This technique can save the programmer's time, but it does not use the memory space of the machine in a better way. We write the MACRO commands, but the assembler inserts actual instructions of the subroutine in the program. Hence if we perform the task, say, three times as in the example of Table 4.21 or 4.23, basically the same set of instructions will be inserted three times in the program.

There is another way of writing subroutines; a subroutine is written outside the main program. It is written in a general way so that it can be used whenever needed. Since the subroutine is a closed unit, it is called a *closed subroutine*.

Figure 4.10 shows the principal difference between the use of open subroutines and closed subroutines. The box represents a subroutine.

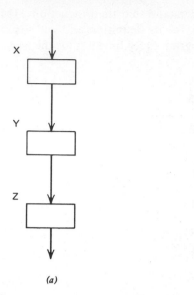

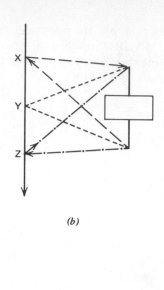

(b)

(a)

Figure 4.10. Subroutines. (a) Open, (b) closed.

An open subroutine is actually inserted in the main program at every point when needed.

A closed subroutine is stored outside the main program and is written only once. The main program, when needed, jumps to the subroutine, uses it, and then returns control to continue the main program.

The jump to the subroutine is performed by a special JMS instruction, defined earlier. The JMS instruction automatically stores the location of the next instruction after the JMS in the location to which the program is instructed to jump, thereby enabling the return.

The return can be achieved using an indirect JUMP to the first location of the subroutine.

Example. A closed subroutine to multiply the contents of the accumulator by 3. The main program and the subroutine are shown in Table 4.26.

Note the following important points.

1. The first location of the subroutine is used by calling instruction JMS. The JMS instruction will store the return address in it. Suppose that the JMS instruction is stored in location 50. Then address 51 will be written by the JMS instruction in location TIMES3.

2. Instructions forming the body of the subroutine are the same as in the case of the open subroutine.

Table 4.26

	CLEAR	
⋮	ADD	X
50	JMS	TIMES3
51	STORE	X3
⋮	⋮	
	CLEAR	
	ADD	Y
64	JMS	TIMES3
65	STORE	Y3
⋮	⋮	
	CLEAR	
	ADD	Z
71	JMS	TIMES3
72	STORE	Z3
⋮	⋮	
TIMES3	—	
	STORE	TEMP
	CLEARL	
	ROTL	Subroutine
	ADD	TEMP
	JUMP	I TIMES3
	⋮	

3. The last instruction of the subroutine, JUMP I TIMES3 will return control to the main program, to location 51 in this example.

4. The same subroutine is called again from location 64, and after having been executed it will return control to location 65. The subroutine is called once more from location 71, and it will return control to location 72.

5. Although the subroutine is used many times, it is stored in the computer only once. This presents a significant saving of memory space over the use of open subroutines.

Getting Data for the Subroutine

In the last example of the subroutine for multiplication by 3, only one item, the number to be multiplied, was moved at a time from the main program to the subroutine. The number was loaded into the accumulator, and then the JMS instruction would call the subroutine.

In general, if there is only one item to be moved between the main program and the subroutine, one can use the accumulator. In machines with more than one accumulator, more items can be moved in this way.

There is another way of moving data, which will be explained by the following example.

Example. A closed subroutine to multiply by 3. Do not use the accumulator for data moving. The program is shown in Table 4.27. Note the following important points:

1. In the main program, the data are stored in the location immediately after the JMS instruction.

2. In the subroutine, the instruction ADD I TIMES3 is used to load the data into the accumulator. The data are stored at the return address in the main program.

3. The ISZ TIMES3 is used to increment the contents of TIMES3 by one, thereby making the return jump (JUMP I TIMES3) proceed to the next instruction after the location which kept the number to be multiplied by 3.

Table 4.27

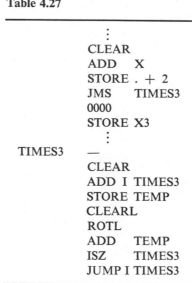

	⋮
	CLEAR
	ADD X
	STORE . + 2
	JMS TIMES3
	0000
	STORE X3
	⋮
TIMES3	—
	CLEAR
	ADD I TIMES3
	STORE TEMP
	CLEARL
	ROTL
	ADD TEMP
	ISZ TIMES3
	JUMP I TIMES3

Such a method of getting data into the subroutine is particularly useful when two or more items are needed in the subroutine.

Example. The subroutine to copy a block of data starting with location 100 into a block starting with address 150. A block of 16 data should be copied. The program is shown in Table 4.28.

Table 4.28

```
                   ⋮
        JMS     COPY
        100
        150
        7760                   Minus 16 octal
                   ⋮
COPY    —
        CLEAR                  Move the parameters 100, 150, and −16
        ADD   I COPY              from the main program into the sub-
        STORE   POINT1           routine locations POINT1, POINT2,
        CLEAR                     and COUNT
        ISZ     COPY
        ADD   I COPY
        STORE   POINT2
        CLEAR
        ISZ     COPY
        ADD   I COPY
        STORE   COUNT
        CLEAR
        ADD   I POINT1         Loop to copy the data
        STORE I POINT2
        ISZ     POINT1
        ISZ     POINT2
        ISZ     COUNT
        JUMP . − 6
        ISZ     COPY          Return to the main program
        JUMP  I COPY
POINT1  —
POINT2  —
COUNT   —
```

The first part of the subroutine uses the technique described above to move the three parameters 100, 150, and −16 from the main program into the subroutine. The second part of the subroutine performs the operation. The third part takes care of the return to the main program.

4.7. SUBROUTINES IN FORTRAN

Since the FORTRAN language is very general and almost machine-independent, there are large libraries of FORTRAN subroutines. This language provides a few ways of defining and using subroutines. The most widely used way is through SUBROUTINE, RETURN, and CALL statements.

The first two statements are equivalent to the MACRO and ENDMACRO pseudocommands; they are used to define the body of the subroutine.

Example. The FORTRAN subroutine to copy the block of data from the array SOURCE to the array DEST. The block has N words. The subroutine is shown in Table 4.29.

Table 4.29

SUBROUTINE COPY (SOURCE, DEST, N)
DO 15 I = 1, N
15   DEST(I) = SOURCE(I)
RETURN
END

The CALL statement is used to link the main program with the subroutine. It is equivalent to the JMS instruction in the symbolic language.

Example. Copy the array $X1$ into the array $X2$ (300 words), the array $Y1$ into $Y2$ (100 words), and the array $Z1$ into $Z2$ (1000 words). A segment of the program is shown in Table 4.30.

Table 4.30

$\vdots$
CALL COPY (X1, X2, 300)
CALL COPY (Y1, Y2, 100)
CALL COPY (Z1, Z2, 1000)

4.8. ARITHMETIC AND LOGICAL OPERATIONS

Even a computer with a very elementary instruction set can be programmed to perform a variety of arithmetic operations. Arithmetic operations deal with numbers. We should recall that numbers in the machine can be presented either as normal binary numbers (integers or fractions) or as floating-point numbers.

Basic computer instructions deal with normal binary numbers. In performing arithmetic operations, the machine does not recognize a binary point. It is entirely up to the programmer to decide the position of the binary point.

Arithmetic operations will be correct provided that numbers are within the limits of the machine. We should recall that the machine with n bits can represent numbers in the range

$$(-2^{n-1}) - 0 - (+2^{n-1}-1)$$

Hence a 12-bit machine can represent the largest negative number and the largest positive number, -2048_{10} and $+2047_{10}$, respectively (4000_8 and 3777_8). If the operation produces a result outside this range, the result will be incorrect.

Let us see what will happen if we calculate the expression

$$Z = U + V$$

Table 4.31 shows four examples for different values of U and V for a 12-bit word computer. In the first example two positive numbers are added producing a good result.

Table 4.31

U	V	L	Z	Sign of the result
2422	1122	0	3544	+
3001	1010	0	4011	−
4000	4010	1	0010	+
7100	7700	1	7000	−

In the second example two positive numbers are added producing a result which exceeds the range of the machine. The result will be treated as a negative number.

In the third example, two negative numbers are added producing too big a result, which looks like a positive number.

In the last example, two negative numbers are added producing too big a result, which looks like a negative number. In both cases with negative numbers, the overflow has set the link bit (L) to one.

Because of situations like those in the last three examples in Table 4.31, the programmer must consider the size of the numbers used in calculations. By checking the sign bit of the operands and the result, and examining the link bit, the programmer can detect the overflow. One can write the subroutine to correct the result, or at least to indicate the error.

Arithmetic and logical operations, which can be readily programmed even on a very small computer, are addition, subtraction, multiplication, division, AND, OR, EOR.

Addition can be performed with the instruction for addition.

Subtraction can be performed by using addition and two's complement representation for negative numbers.

Multiplication and division can be performed by special instructions, if available, but they can also be performed by subroutines. Multiplication can be programmed using the operations of addition and rotation. Division can be programmed using the operations of subtraction and rotation.

For logical operations the computer has at least one instruction, for example, AND.

On the basis of de Morgan's theorem, having one logical instruction as well as a complementing instruction, one can program other logical operations.

Next we show a few examples of programming arithmetic operations.

Illustrative examples follow the principles of the PDP-8 programs. For original PDP-8 programs see Ref. 2.

Absolute Value and the Sign

Example. Write the program to extract the sign bit and the absolute value of the operand stored in the memory location *U*. The sign bit should be stored

Table 4.32

	CLEAR	
	CLEARL	
	ADD	U
	ROTL	
	SKIPL	
	JUMP	POS
	ROTR	
	COMPL	
	INCR	
	SKIP	
POS	ROTR	
	STORE	ABS
	CLEAR	
	ADD	U
	ROTL	
	CLEAR	
	ROTR	
	STORE	SIGN
	HALT	
U	1234	
ABS	—	
SIGN	—	

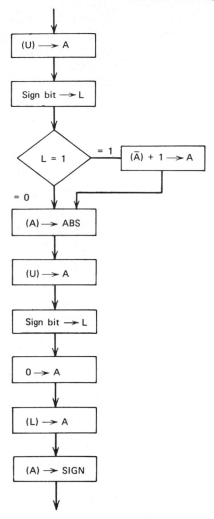

Figure 4.11. Absolute value and sign.

in location SIGN and the absolute value in location ABS. Table 4.32 shows
the program. Figure 4.11 shows the flow chart of the program. The first half
of the program extracts the absolute value; the second half extracts the
sign bit.

Powers of Two

Example. Given the integers N and M. Write the program to calculate the
value $Z = M \times 2^N$. In the decimal number system multiplication by 10^N
means moving the decimal point by N places to the right. Similarly in the

binary system, multiplication by 2^N means moving the binary point N places to the right. This is the same as moving the number N places to the left (relative to the binary point). Multiplication is performed by loading the accumulator by the number M and rotating left N times. The operation will be correct if the result can be expressed with 12 bits. For larger numbers, significant bits rotated out of the accumulator would be lost. The program is shown in Table 4.33. The flow diagram is shown in Fig. 4.12.

Table 4.33

Location	Contents	Comment
MULTIP	CLEAR	Clear Accumulator
	ADD N	Take N
	COMPL	One's complement
	INCR	Two's complement
	STORE COUNT	Setting the loop counter
	CLEAR	Clear Accumulator
	ADD M	Take M
LOOP	CLEARL	Clear carry
	ROTL	Rotate left (multiply by 2)
	ISZ COUNT	Sufficient number of times?
	JUMP LOOP	No, do again
	STORE Z	Yes
	HALT	
N	7	
M	212	
Z	0000	
COUNT	0000	

Multiplication

Example. Write the program to multiply U by V by adding V to itself U times. The program is shown in Table 4.34.

We have shown two methods of multiplication: multiplication through rotation, which is suitable for multiplying by powers of two; multiplication through addition, which is suitable for all numbers but is rather lengthy.

The best multiplication procedure is the one based on the principle of multiplication by binary numbers: the partial product is moved one position to the left as each successive multiplier bit is used. If the multiplier bit is 0, the partial product is 0; if the multiplier bit is 1, the partial product is equal to the multiplicand.

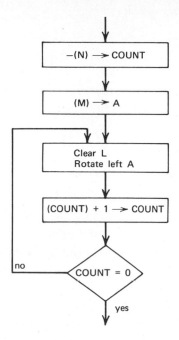

Figure 4.12. Multiplication by power of two.

Table 4.34

Location	Contents	Comment
START	CLEAR	Clear accumulator
	CLEARL	Clear carry
	ADD U	Take the multiplicand
	COMPL	One's complement
	INCR	Two's complement
	STORE COUNT	Set the loop counter
	CLEAR	Clear accumulator
LOOP	ADD V	Add the multiplier
	ISZ COUNT	Sufficient number of times?
	JUMP LOOP	No, do again
	STORE Z	Yes
	HALT	
U	0012	
V	0017	
Z	0000	
COUNT	0000	

Example: $\qquad$ $5 \times 5 = 25$

$$
\begin{array}{ll}
101 & 5_{10} \\
\underline{101} & 5_{10} \\
101 & \\
000 & \\
\underline{101} & \\
11001 & 25_{10}
\end{array}
$$

Note: If we multiply the number XXX by the number XXX, the product will have the length XXXXXX or XXXXX. In other words, by multiplying two numbers of n-bits, we can generate a product of $2n$ bits.

The multiplication subroutine is shown in Table 4.35 and its flow chart in Fig. 4.13. Note the following important points:

1. The multiplier and the multiplicand are stored in memory locations $M1$ and $M2$, respectively.

Table 4.35

Location	Contents		Comment
MULTPL	CLEAR		Clear accumulator
	ADD	MIN12	Take $(-12)_{10}$
	STORE	COUNT	Set loop counter (12 bits)
	CLEARL		Clear link
LOOP	CLEAR		Clear accumulator
	ADD	M1	Add multiplier
	ROTR		Rotate right
	STORE	M1	Store multiplier and part of the product
	CLEAR		Clear accumulator
	ADD	M5	Take product
	SKIPL		Is it least sign bit of multiplier $= 1$
	SKIP		No
	ADD	M2	Yes, add multiplicand
	CLEARL		Clear link
	ROTR		Rotate right the product
	STORE	M5	Save the product
	ISZ	COUNT	Enough times?
	JUMP	LOOP	No, do again
	HALT		
M1	0011		
M2	0020		
M5	0000		
COUNT	0000		
MIN12	7764		$(-12)_{10}$

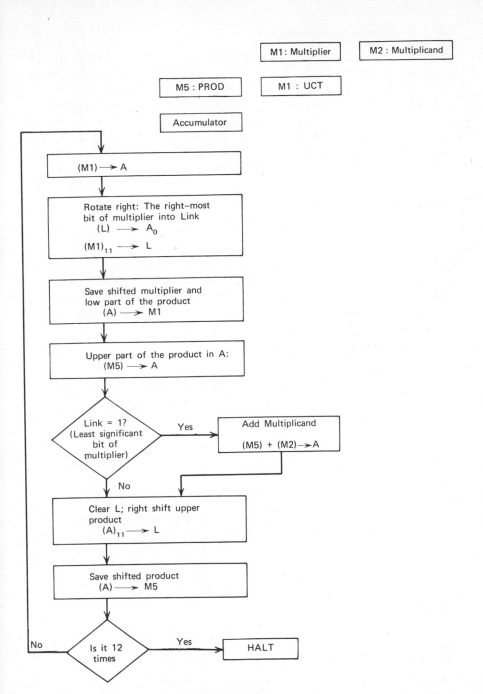

M1 : Multiplier   M2 : Multiplicand

M5 : PROD   M1 : UCT

Accumulator

$(M1) \longrightarrow A$

Rotate right: The right-most
bit of multiplier into Link
$(L) \longrightarrow A_0$
$(M1)_{11} \longrightarrow L$

Save shifted multiplier and
low part of the product
$(A) \longrightarrow M1$

Upper part of the product in A:
$(M5) \longrightarrow A$

Link = 1?
(Least significant
bit of
multiplier)

Yes

Add Multiplicand
$(M5) + (M2) \longrightarrow A$

No

Clear L; right shift upper
product
$(A)_{11} \longrightarrow L$

Save shifted product
$(A) \longrightarrow M5$

No   Is it 12
times

Yes

HALT

Figure 4.13. Multiplication by shifting and adding.

145

2. First the multiplication with the least-significant bit is performed. The multiplier is loaded into the accumulator and rotated right, so that the bit by which to multiply comes into the link.

3. The multiplication is performed through twelve loops, for 12 bits.

4. The product is a double-length word to be stored at locations $M5$ and $M1$ at the end of the operation. As the program is looping, the multiplier is shifted out of the $M1$ and the lower half of the product is shifted into $M1$.

5. The program will perform multiplication for two positive numbers.

Double-Precision Arithmetic

Two memory words are used to express double-precision numbers. If still better precision is needed, three or more words can be used.

Example. Program to add two double-precision numbers. The program is shown in Table 4.36. Note that if the addition of UL and VL produces the carry, it will appear in the link. The link is rotated into the least-significant bit of the accumulator. The values of UH and VH are then added to the carry. The double-precision result is stored in ZL and ZH.

Table 4.36

Location	Contents		Comment
DUBADD	CLEARL		Clear link
	CLEAR		Clear accumulator
	ADD	UL	Add U low
	ADD	VL	Add V low
	STORE	ZL	Store the sum
	CLEAR		Clear accumulator
	ROTL		Get link into accumulator
	ADD	UH	Add U high
	ADD	VH	Add V high
	STORE	ZH	Store the sum
	HALT		
UL			
UH			
VL			
VH			
ZL			
ZH			

Example. Program to subtract two double-precision numbers. The program is shown in Table 4.37. Recall that the two's complement of the number is equal to the one's complement plus one. Hence in order to form the two's complement of a double precision number composed of two halves *BL* and *BH*, we proceed as follows: form the one's complement of *BL*; add one to it; form the one's complement of *BH*, but do not add one to it.

Table 4.37

DUBSUB	CLEAR	
	CLEARL	
	ADD	BL
	COMPL	
	INCR	
	ADD	AL
	STORE	CL
	CLEAR	
	ROTL	
	STORE	CARRY
	CLEAR	
	ADD	BH
	COMPL	
	ADD	AH
	ADD	CARRY
	STORE	CH
	HALT	
AH		
AL		
BH		
BL		
CH		
CL		
CARRY		

Logical Information Processing

Most of the instructions and operations shown up to now deal with a computer word as a unit. There are occasions when only part of the computer word is needed. One of the examples is packing the codes for alphanumeric characters into the computer memory.

Alphanumeric characters can be presented in different codes; BCD code and ASCII code are most frequently used. In ASCII code there are modifications, depending on whether 6, 7, or 8 bits are used for the coding of one character. Those codes are shown in Tables 1.7 and 1.8. Since the computer word has more bits than the code for one character, more than one character can be packed in the word. In this way a message coded in alphanumeric codes can be stored in the computer memory.

When the message is needed, the computer program must take one character at a time and deliver it to the input-output equipment. Packing and unpacking information is only an example of operations which do not deal with the whole computer word as a unit.

Example. A 6-bit ASCII code for characters *A–Z* is used to code the word OK. Two characters are stored in one computer word of 12 bits, with the symbolic address SIX. Write the program to unpack the characters, to change the code to 8-bit ASCII, and to store the characters in two locations, FIRST and SEC. The program is shown in Table 4.38.

Table 4.38

	CLEARL	
	CLEAR	
	ADD	SIX
	ROTR	
	ROTR	
	ROTR	
	ROTR	
	ROTR	
	ROTR	
	AND	MASK
	ADD	POS300
	STORE	FIRST
	CLEAR	
	ADD	SIX
	AND	MASK
	ADD	POS300
	STORE	SEC
	HALT	
SIX	1713	
MASK	0077	
POS300	0300	
FIRST	—	
SEC	—	

The example illustrates the following important points:

1. Characters O and K are coded in 6-bit ASCII code as 17 and 13, respectively, and packed together in location SIX. Hence the contents of SIX are 1713.

2. Using the instruction ROTR 6 times, the contents of the accumulator become 1317.

3. The code for the first character O is obtained by logical AND operation between the contents of the accumulator and the contents of the location MASK. The MASK has 6 leading bits equal to zero and the last 6 bits equal to one (octal 0077). Hence the bit-by-bit logical AND operation will leave on the accumulator only the bits covered by one's in the mask. The result of the AND operation is 0017 on the accumulator.

4. The difference between 6- and 8-bit ASCII codes for the characters A–Z is octal 300; see Table 1.7. Hence 300 is added to the unpacked code for O, and code 317 is stored in location FIRST.

5. To unpack the second character, the contents of location SIX are again loaded in the accumulator, but are not rotated. The same mask will now extract the last 6 bits, 13. Adding the 300, we get the 8-bit code 313, which will be stored in location SEC.

6. The input-output program can now transmit the unpacked codes, one by one, to the input-output device (to be printed, for example).

4.9. FORTRAN ARITHMETIC

FORTRAN is especially designed for programming problems that can be expressed by simple mathematical formulas. The basic operations of addition, subtraction, multiplication, division, and exponentiation are written like algebra, with a special sign between the variables concerned. The signs used are

$$+, -, *, /, **$$

Hence the arithmetic expression in FORTRAN may look like

$$Y = (X1 + X2) * (X3 - X4)/(X5 ** 3)$$

The computer, like a high school student, will first perform the calculation within the parentheses and then the operations between the parentheses. An additional fact should be remembered for the FORTRAN compiler: some operations will take precedence over the others. The priority will be

> Exponentiation.
> Multiplication and division.
> Addition and subtraction.

Hence the equation

$$Y = 3.0 * X1 + X2$$

will be treated by the compiler as

$$Y = (3.0 * X1) + X2$$

Although we did not indicate the parentheses, multiplication takes precedence over addition.

The equation

$$Y = X1 + X2/X3$$

will be treated by the compiler as if it were written

$$Y = X1 + (X2/X3)$$

The compiler will first perform division and then it will add $X1$ to the quotient.

The computer recognized two different kinds of numbers, integers and floating-point numbers. While basic machine instructions deal with integers, FORTRAN can be used to perform calculations with either integers or with floating-point numbers. Some means must be provided to distinguish between those two presentations.

In writing numerical values, the rule is simple: a floating-point number must have the decimal point, and an integer must not. Thus 35. is treated by the compiler as a floating-point number, and 35 as an integer.

Also in naming the variables, the programmer must know if the variable is an integer or a floating-point number. The rule is as follows: a named quantity that is to be treated as an integer must have a name starting with one of the letters I, J, K, L, M, and N.

The examples are MAX, MIN, NX, I and so on.

A name starting with any other letter is treated as a floating-point number.

The examples are AVERG, DELTA, VOLT, AT, X, Y, U3 and so on.

If we recall the examples of FORTRAN programs shown up to now, we shall notice the following:

Most of the variables used in calculations are floating-point numbers. The use of floating-point presentation relieves the programmer of essentially all concern about the size of the numbers under manipulation, or of the decimal point, since the range of floating-point numbers is very large.

Indices used in loops and arrays are integers. Often some calculation must be performed with indices, as in the example

$$N = I - 3 * (I/3) + 1$$
$$GO\ TO\ (7,\ 109,\ 2),\ N$$

If such two statements are written in the middle of the DO loop, with index I, the values of N in the first, second, and third loop will be 1, 2, and 3, and the GO TO statement will switch the control to statements 7, 109, and 2, respectively.

If the programmer feels restricted with the choice of names for integers and floating-point numbers, FORTRAN enables him to use statements INTEGER and REAL and to define any name he wishes for his variable.

For example, the compiler will understand the statement

INTEGER SUM

as to treat the variable SUM as an integer, although its name does not start with one of those characters reserved for integers.

In the same way, the compiler will understand the statement

REAL MAX

as to treat the variable MAX as a floating-point number, although its name starts with M.

Without going into details, we may list a few more useful FORTRAN statements:

DOUBLE PRECISION expresses the number over a double number of bits for high precision

FUNCTION defines the routine name, which can be called upon in the program

LOGICAL statements enable one to perform logical operations with variables. The variable may take only one of the two values, TRUE or FALSE

4.10. INPUT-OUTPUT PROGRAMMING

Input-output refers to the transfer of data between the computer and peripheral devices. In early computers, input-output programming was quite an elaborate task, requiring a knowledge of programming techniques as well as computer structure. There has been a tendency towards simplifying the input-output transfer. In some modern machines, one can program the input-output transfer basically in the same way as data moving between core locations and accumulators. Most of the small machines have input-output instructions to perform the transfer of data.

A detailed description of input-output transfers will be given separately. Here we shall deal only with the basic transfer for which the following facts should be remembered.

1. The output transfer moves data from the computer accumulator into the data register of the peripheral device. After the data reach the data register the I/O instruction also starts the electromechanical system of the

device (for example, if the device is a printer, the electromechanical system for printing the character is started).

2. The input transfer moves the data from the peripheral device data register into the computer accumulator. The I/O instruction also starts the electromechanical system of the device (for example, if the device is a paper-tape reader, the electromechanical system for reading the punched tape is started).

In general, the I/O instruction of a small computer has three parts, as shown in Fig. 4.14: the operation code, device selection code, and the command code.

The operation code deals primarily with the computer and is used to distinguish the I/O instruction from other instructions.

The device selection code and the command code deal primarily with the peripheral device.

| Operation Code | Device selection | Command |

Figure 4.14. Input-output transfer; instruction format.

Device Selection

As a rule, many peripheral devices can be connected to the same computer. There must be a means for selecting with the I/O instruction the device with which the computer has to communicate. This is achieved using the device selection code as part of the I/O instruction. The device selection code is transmitted simultaneously to all peripheral devices connected to the computer. Each device has a built-in device selector. The selector monitors the device codes. When the selector receives the code belonging to the device, it will couple the selected device to the computer. All other devices will have some other codes and will stay uncoupled.

Figure 4.14 shows an I/O instruction with 6 bits used for a device selection code. Hence in this example up to 64 different devices can be coupled to the machine. The devices can have selection codes (or "house numbers") such as 02, 03 . . . 62, 63.

Command

With an I/O instruction the computer can perform many kinds of communications with the peripheral device. It can send data, receive them, but it can also instruct the peripheral device to perform some special task or test the status of the device. For this purpose the I/O instruction uses a few bits as command bits. Command bits are sent to all peripheral devices, but only the selected device will react to the command.

Figure 4.14 shows an I/O instruction with 3 bits used for a command code. It is up to the designer of the peripheral device to decide how to use command bits.

In general, each peripheral device should be capable of recognizing at least three basic commands and performing three basic tasks: data transfer, testing the device flag, and clearing the device flag.

Data Transfer

The data transfer command will cause data to be moved between the accumulator and the data buffer register of the selected device. We shall use two symbolic names, READ and WRITE, for input and output data transfer, respectively. Thus the instruction

READ04

will perform data transfer from the device 04 into the accumulator. On the other hand, the instruction

WRITE03

will perform data transfer from the accumulator into the device 03.

Device Flag

Digital computers are extremely fast machines, with the basic cycle time of an order of 1 μsec. Most peripheral devices using electromechanical parts are much slower, sometimes with a speed in the millisecond range. Some provision is necessary to synchronize operations between the computer and the peripheral device.

The input device must signal the computer that it has completely assembled the information and is now ready to transfer it to the computer.

The output device must signal the computer that it has completely finished the previous operation and is now ready to accept a new piece of information from the computer.

Without such signals the computer would perform data input or output with a speed that the device could not follow, which would result in erroneous operation.

In order to ensure correct operation, each peripheral device has a device flag. This is a 1-bit register (the flip-flop) that is set to 1 when the device is ready. For an output device the flag is set when the device can be used. For an input device the flag is set when the device has assembled the data.

If the device keeps its flag cleared (set to 0), the device is busy; the output device is still processing the previous command; the input device is still assembling the data.

The I/O instruction can be used for testing the device flag. Such an I/O command operates in a way similar to the SKIP instructions: if the flag F is set (device ready), the next instruction in the program is skipped; if the flag F is cleared (device busy), the next instruction in the program is executed. In short

$$(F) = 1 \Rightarrow I + 2$$
$$(F) = 0 \Rightarrow I + 1$$

We shall use the symbolic name SKIP, device, for the I/O command which tests the flag. This instruction, like any other I/O instruction, will be accepted only by the selected peripheral device. Thus the instruction

SKIP04

will test the flag of the peripheral device 04. If flag 04 is set, the next instruction in the program will be skipped.

We need another instruction to clear the flag and in this way to initialize the peripheral device. The instruction

CLEAR03

will clear (set to 0), the flag in the device with the selection code 03.

We have defined four symbolic I/O instructions, READ, WRITE, SKIP, and CLEAR. We have in fact been using the same I/O instruction. Different operations are achieved with different combinations of command bits only, Fig. 4.14. The designer must know which bit is used for a given operation. When the I/O instruction is transmitted to the peripheral device, this bit will activate the action.

Examples of I/O Programming

Example. The program to read one character from the teletype keyboard. The keyboard selection code is 03. The program is shown in Table 4.39. The example illustrates the following important points.

1. The first two instructions clear the accumulator and the flag in the device 03, respectively.

2. The instructions SKIP03; JUMP.–1 perform the loop. The computer will test the flag 03 again and again, until the key on the teletype unit is pressed, or paper tape is loaded into the reader. The teletype will assemble

the ASCII code for the character in the keyboard buffer register and will set the flag. As a result the program will skip out of the loop.

3. The instruction READ03 will transfer data from the teletype buffer register into the accumulator. The next instruction will store data in the core memory.

Table 4.39

INPUT	CLEAR
	CLEAR03
	SKIP03
	JUMP.− 1
	READ03
	STORE X
	HALT
X	0

Example. The program to print out an ASCII character (the letter *L*) on the teletype printer. The printer selection code is 04. The program is shown in Table 4.40. The example illustrates the following important points.

1. The first two instructions are used to transfer zero to the printer buffer register. When this operation is completed, the flag will be set by the printer.

2. Instruction ADD X takes the ASCII code for the character (*L*) to be printed in the accumulator.

3. Instructions SKIP04, JUMP.−1 perform the loop until the flag 04 signifies that the printer is ready for new transfer.

4. Instruction WRITE04 transfers the code in the teletype buffer. The character is then printed on the paper.

Table 4.40

OUTPUT	CLEAR
	WRITE04
	ADD X
	SKIP04
	JUMP.− 1
	WRITE04
	HALT
X	314

4.11. FORTRAN INPUT-OUTPUT

FORTRAN is concerned primarily with mathematical problems in which input and output are of a rather simple nature. The programmer need not understand the structure of the computer input-output channels. The data transfer is achieved with the statements, such as

READ (device, format) variable,
WRITE (device, format) variable.

For example, the statement

READ(4,5)X

will read one datum from the device number 4 and will store it as the variable X. During the read-in operation the data will be formatted as dictated by the format statement number 5. The formatting will be explained later.

Another example:

WRITE(2,7) A,B,C

This statement will write the data from three words *A*, *B*, *C* on the peripheral device 2, using the format 7.

Format

The FORMAT statement enables the user to specify the form and arrangement of data on a selected external device. The most frequently used formats are the following: *E*, *F*, *I*, and *H*.

E w.d Format

This format is used to present the data in floating-point form using the exponent. The *w* is the total number of places to be used. The *d* is the number of places right of the decimal point.

Example. Write the data $X = 12.34$ using different *E* formats

WRITE (4,5)X
5   FORMAT (E 9.3)

The result is $\wedge$ .123E + 02. The E + 02 means the 10 to power 2. Note that nine places are typed, of which three are to the right of the decimal point.

The caret symbol, $\wedge$, is used to indicate the presence of a space.

WRITE (4,6)X
6   FORMAT (E 7.3)X

The result is .12E + 02.

F w.d Format

This format is used to present data in floating-point form without an exponent. The *w* is the total number of places to be used. The *d* is the number of places right of the decimal point.

Example. Write the data $Y = 12.34$ using different F formats

$$WRITE\ (4,5)Y$$
$$5\quad FORMAT\ (F\ 10.3)$$

The result is $\wedge \wedge \wedge \wedge 12.340$

$$WRITE\ (4,5)Y$$
$$5\quad FORMAT\ (E\ 4.5)$$

The result is 12.3.

I w Format

This format is used to present data as a *w*-digit integer.
  Example. Write the data MIN $= 1234$ in the I format

$$WRITE\ (4,7)\ MIN$$
$$7\quad FORMAT\ (I\ 6)$$

The result is $\wedge \wedge 1234$.

n H h_1h_2—h_n Format

This format can be used with the WRITE statement to transmit *n* alphanumeric data following the *H*.
  Example.

$$WRITE\ (6,\ 11)$$
$$11\quad FORMAT\ (14\ H\ GOOD\ MORNING)$$

As a result the sentence GOOD MORNING is written on the output unit number 6.

For a more detailed description of input-output statements and for device numbers to be used, one should consult the FORTRAN manual of the computer installation to be used.

PROBLEMS

1. The list contains five items stored in locations $X1$ to $X5$. Sort those items in ascending order and store them in locations $Y1$ to $Y5$.

2. Write the program to put 0 into memory locations 2000 up to 2777.

3. Write the program to pick up every second term from list X and store it in list Y. The lists have storage spaces of 100 and 50 places, respectively.

4. Write the subroutine to complement a block of data. In the calling program, the JMS instruction should be followed by two parameters: the starting address of the block and the number of words in the block.

5. Write a MACRO subroutine to extract the Nth bit from the word in the accumulator. N can be any number between 0 and 11.

6. Write a program to add two triple precision numbers $X + Y = Z$. Each number has three parts, high, medium, and low: XH, XM, XL; YH, YM, YL; ZH, ZM, ZL.

7. Write the program to put 0 into memory location 1000, -1 into 1001, -2 into 1002 and so on up to location 1777.

8. Write the MACRO subroutine which will resemble the FORTRAN IF statement. It will check the number in the accumulator. If the number is negative, the program will jump to location NEG; if it is zero, the program will jump to location ZER; if it is positive, the program will jump to location POZ.

9. Write a program to find how many of the numbers stored in a table from address 2000 to address 2777 are negative, positive, or zero. Use the MACRO subroutine from problem 8.

10. Write the FORTRAN program for problems 1, 3, 4, and 9.

REFERENCES

1. I. Flores, *Computer Programming*, Prentice Hall, Englewood Cliffs, N.J., 1966.
2. *Introduction to Programming*, Digital Equipment Corporation, Maynard, Mass., 1969.
3. H. D. Leeds, G. M. Weinberg, *Computer Programming Fundamentals*, McGraw-Hill, New York, 1966.

5

INTERFACING
MICROPROCESSORS

Chapter 5 discusses interfacing and describes direct connection of the small computer to the external devices. Basic computer organization, implementation of instructions, and circulation of instructions and data between memory and main registers are explained. Basic modes of data transfer in and out of the computer are described: unconditional, conditional, and interrupt programmed transfer and direct memory access. For each mode, examples of programming and interfacing are given for typical laboratory operations. It is shown that through simple selection and timing many devices can simultaneously communicate with the microcomputer. Some methods for comparison of the small computer input-output systems are given.

5.1. BASIC COMPUTER ORGANIZATION

This section is intended to introduce the basic blocks of the computer and to illustrate their functional interrelationships. The basic structure of the computer is composed of the memory, data buses, and registers.

The memory is the focal point of the computer; it provides the storage for the program, the data, and the intermediate results. The instructions of the program and the data are stored in the memory as binary-coded numbers. The computer fetches the instruction from the memory and performs the operation dictated by the instruction. The instruction might also tell the computer the address of the data. The computer then takes the data from the specified memory location.

Data buses provide the way for moving the binary information between different parts of the computer. Data buses can be one-directional or two-directional, and they are composed of many wires, one wire for each bit.

Registers are used to store the binary information during the execution of the instruction. The register is composed of a number of flip-flops, one flip-flop per bit. The computer can have many registers. The basic registers

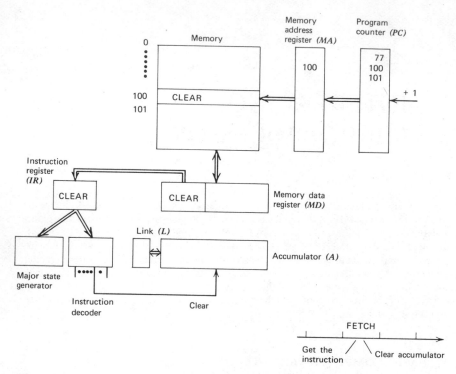

Figure 5.1. Functional registers and units of the small digital computer. Implementation of the single-cycle instruction.

are accumulator, link, memory data register, program counter, memory address register, and the instruction register.

Figure 5.1 shows the basic structure of the computer: memory, registers and data ways between different parts of the machine.

The Accumulator (*A*)

The *A* register is the prime component of the computer. At the beginning of the operation the accumulator may keep one of the operands. The second operand, if needed, will come from the memory. At the end of the operation, the accumulator keeps the result. Here we shall consider a machine having a 12-bit word length. Hence the accumulator will also be composed of 12 bits.

The Link (L)

The L register has only one bit and is used to connect in loop the most significant and the least significant end of the accumulator and to receive the carry from the accumulator.

The Memory Data (MD) Register

The MD register is used for reading the data out of the memory, or for writing the data into the memory. It has the same number of bits as the memory word (12). The MD provides the way to get the information in or out of the memory. Once a word of information is in the MD register, it is accessible to arithmetic operations and to transfers to the other registers. Also, if the data from any register should be stored in the memory, they must first be transferred to the MD register.

The Program Counter (PC)

The PC register contains the address of the core memory location from which the next instruction will be taken. It has 12 bits and can address up to 4096 memory locations. In a normal operation, the PC goes through a step-by-step counting sequence and causes the computer to read successive memory locations. The contents of the addressed location are then transferred to the MD register, and they instruct the computer as to what to do. In some cases, the count on the program counter can be changed under the program control. This is the case during the execution of the jump instructions. In this way a transfer of command to another part of the stored program is encountered.

The Memory Address (MA) Register

The MA register is the only means of addressing specific memory locations. It has 12 bits for addressing 4096 words of the core memory. If the computer looks for the instruction, then the contents of the PC will be transferred to the MA to address the location where the instruction is stored. If the computer looks for data, then the address may come from the MD register. To get the data, the address must be transferred to the MA register.

It is obvious that the MA and the PC perform somewhat similar operations. The reason for the two registers is the following: the PC is used to keep track of the location of the current instruction and to point to the next instruction. If the instruction is a memory-reference type, the computer must address the memory to get the operand without disturbing the contents of the PC. For this purpose, the MA is used. Consider the following example:

100   ADD   150
101   :

The *PC* keeps the address 100, from which the instruction will come. During the execution of this instruction, the *MA* is used to address location 150. After that the *PC* points to address 101 for the next instruction.

Instruction Register (*IR*)

The *IR* is used to keep the operation code of the instruction currently being performed by the machine. If the operation code has 3 bits, the *IR* will also have 3 bits. The instruction comes from the memory into the *MD* register. The 3 bits presenting the operation code are then transferred to the *IR*. The *IR* decodes the operation code and initiates the steps necessary for the execution of the instruction.

Major State Generator

All operations in the computer are performed step by step. One step represents the basic computer cycle, and in modern machines it lasts about 1 μsec. There are instructions which are performed in a single cycle. Other instructions are performed in two or three cycles. Not all the cycles will be used for the same purpose. The programmed instruction controls the computer state generator with three possible states: fetch, defer, and execute. Each state is used for other purposes. The basic actions during each of these states follow.

Fetch. The fetch state is used to read the instruction from the memory and to decode it. It goes through the following steps:

•   The contents of the memory locations specified by the *PC* are read in the *MD* register.

•   The contents of the *PC* are incremented by one.

•   The operation code of the instruction is transferred into the *IR* to cause enactment.

•   If a one-cycle instruction is fetched, the operations specified are performed during the last part of the fetch cycle.

Defer. If the memory-reference instruction uses indirect addressing, the defer state is entered after the fetch state. It is used to read the address of the operand from the memory. It goes through the following steps:

•   The address part of the instruction is transferred from the *MD* into the *MA*.

• The contents of the addressed memory location are read in the MD register. The contents present the address of the operand.

Execute. The execute state is used in all memory-reference instructions except jump.

• For instructions which need an operand from the memory, the execute state is used to read the operand into the MD and to perform the operation specified by the operation code of the instruction, leaving the result on the accumulator. These instructions are ADD, AND, ISZ.

• For the STORE instruction, this state is used to deposit the contents of the accumulator in the specified memory location.

• For the jump-to-subroutine instruction, during this state the contents of the PC are transferred into the core memory address designated by the instruction. Also, the address designated by the instruction is transferred into the PC in order to change the program control.

Each control state lasts for one computer cycle. It is further divided into smaller time slices which can be used to perform sequential logical operations. Each instruction determines the major states the computer must enter for the execution of that instruction. A few examples of the execution of typical instructions illustrate the operation of the computer.

5.2.   IMPLEMENTATION OF INSTRUCTIONS

Single-Cycle Instructions

A single-cycle instruction is fetched from the memory and executed during the same basic computer cycle. All one-operand or register-reference instructions shown up to now are single-cycle instructions. During the execution of this instruction the computer is in the fetch state.

Figure 5.1 shows an example of the execution of the CLEAR instruction. The program is stored in the core memory. The instruction CLEAR is stored in the location with address 100. The instruction is stored in binary form, but for simplicity we use its symbolic form. Let us suppose that the instructions are stored in sequence in the memory and that the program counter points from one instruction to the next. Eventually the PC will contain address 100. During a single computer cycle the following operations occur:

• Address 100 is transferred from the PC to the MA.

• The PC is incremented by one, and it points to the next instruction 101.

• The MA addresses the memory location. The contents of the location are read into the MD.

•   The *MD* contents are now the instruction to be executed (CLEAR). This instruction has only an operation code but has no address part. The operation code is transferred into the *IR*.

•   The *IR* and decoder decode the instruction and start the part of the machine required for the execution of that particular instruction. In this simple case, it might start the clear pulse, in order to clear the accumulator. In this way the instruction is executed.

Jump Instructions

Each computer can have a number of conditional and unconditional jump instructions. The jump instruction can be executed in only one machine cycle but in a way different from the register-reference instruction. Figure 5.2 shows an example of the execution of the JUMP instruction. The instruction JUMP 150 is stored in the memory location with address 100. During a single computer cycle, the following operations occur:

•   Address 100 is transferred from the *PC* to the *MA*.

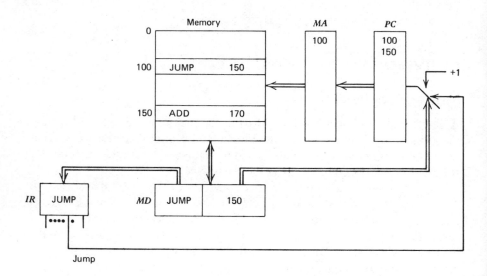

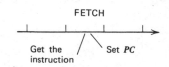

Figure 5.2. Implementation of the jump instruction.

• The MA addresses the memory location. The contents of the location are read into the MD.

• The MD contents are now the instruction to be executed, JUMP 150. This instruction has the operation code JUMP and the address part 150.

• The operation code is transferred into the IR, where the instruction is decoded, and prepares the necessary circuits; in a simplified picture it starts the jump pulse which will switch for a moment the switch S from the normal $+1$ position, to the low position.

• The address part of the instruction, 150, is transferred through the established data way into the PC. In this way the instruction is executed. The next instruction comes from the address stored in the PC, that is, from the memory address 150.

Memory-Reference Instructions

The memory-reference instruction takes one operand from the memory. It is clear that the computer will have to deal with the memory two times, the first time to fetch the instruction and the second time to get the operand. Two computer cycles will be needed. During the first cycle the machine is in the FETCH state. During the second cycle the machine is in the EXECUTE state. Figure 5.3 shows an example of the execution of the ADD instruction. The instruction ADD 105 is stored in the memory location with address 100. During the two computer cycles, the following operations occur:

FETCH cycle:

• Address 100 is transferred from the PC to the MA.

• The PC is incremented by one.

• The MA addresses the memory location. The contents of the location are read into the MD.

• The MD contents are now the instruction to be executed, ADD 105. This instruction has the operation code ADD and the address part 105.

• The operation code is transferred into the IR, where the instruction is decoded, and it prepares the necessary circuits for addition.

• The address part of the instruction, 105, is transferred from the MD into the MA.

EXECUTE cycle:

• The MA addresses the memory location. The contents of the location are read into the MD.

• The MD contents are now the operand, 0071.

• The prepared circuits perform the operation ADD. Hence the number 0071 will be added to the existing contents of the accumulator (0004), and the result will be stored in the accumulator. In this way the instruction is executed.

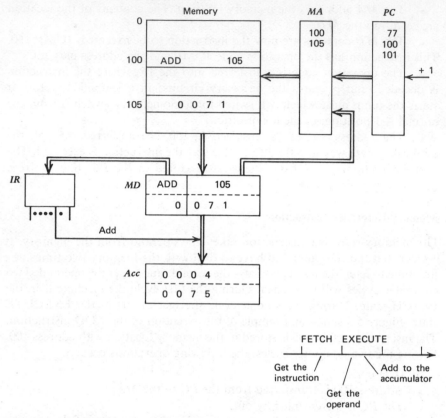

Figure 5.3. Implementation of the memory-reference instruction.

Page-Relative Addressing

We should recall that the memory-reference instruction has the form

OPR, tag bits, displacement.

The first tag bit is used for the page-relative mode of addressing. The second tag bit is used for the indirect-mode of addressing.

For the operation of the page-relative addressing, the *MA* and the *PC* are split into two parts each (Fig. 5.4):

*MA: MA*1 (5 bits) and *MA*2 (7 bits).
*PC: PC*1 (5 bits) and *PC*2 (7 bits).

Now let us consider two cases determined by the page-relative bit.

Page-Relative Bit Equals Zero. In this case the effective address is equal to the displacement. The instruction addresses page zero. Figure 5.4a shows the execution of the instruction ADD 20.

To form the effective address, the displacement 20 is transferred into MA2, and zero is transferred into MA1. In this way the twentieth location of the page zero is addressed.

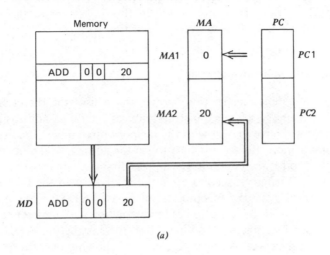

(a)

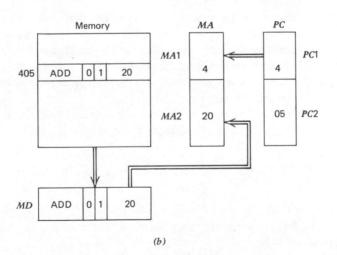

(b)

Figure 5.4. Implementation of the instruction with page-relative addressing. (a) Instruction addresses the zero page; (b) instruction addresses the current page.

Page Relative Bit Equals One. In this case the effective address is equal to the displacement plus the starting address of the page on which the instruction itself is stored. The address of the instruction is on the *PC*. The *PC*1 is used to count pages; the *PC*2 is used to count the locations within the pages. Hence if the instruction is stored in location 405, this address is written on the *PC*, as shown in Fig. 5.4*b*.

To form the effective address, the displacement 20 is transferred into *MA*2 and the *PC*1 is transferred into *MA*1. In this way the twentieth location relative to the address 400 is addressed (location 420).

Instructions with Indirect Addressing

The memory-reference instruction shown above uses the direct-addressing mode. If the memory-reference instruction uses a indirect-addressing mode, the computer will have to deal with the memory three times: the first time to fetch the instruction; the second time to get the address of the operand; and the third time to get the operand. During the first cycle the machine is in the FETCH state. During the second cycle the machine is in the DEFER state. During the third cycle the machine is in the EXECUTE state. Figure 5.5 shows the example of the execution of an instruction with indirect addressing. In the memory location with address 100, the instruction ADD I 105 is stored. During the three computer cycles, the following operations occur:

FETCH cycle:
- Address 100 is transferred from the *PC* to the *MA*.
- The *PC* is incremented by one.
- The *MA* addresses the memory location. The contents of the location are read into the *MD*.
- The *MD* contents are now the instruction to be executed ADD I 105. This instruction has the operation code ADD and the address part I 105.
- The operation code is transferred into the *IR*, where the instruction is decoded, and prepares the necessary circuits.
- The address part of the instruction 105 is transferred from the *MD* into the *MA*. The indirect bit *I* instructs the machine to enter the DIFER state.

Note: The *MA* address is formed as in Fig. 5.4, dictated by the page-relative bit.

DEFER cycle:
- The *MA* addresses the memory location. The contents of the location are read into the *MD*.
- The *MD* contents are now the address 200.

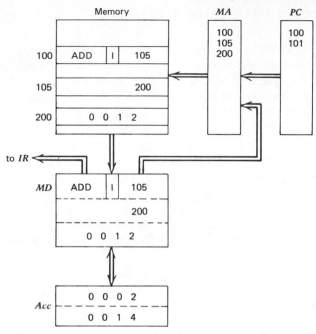

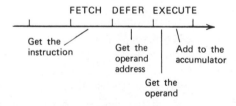

Figure 5.5. Implementation of the instruction with indirect addressing.

- The *MD* contents are transferred to the *MA*.

EXECUTE cycle:

- The *MA* addresses the memory location. The contents of the location are read into the *MD*.
- The *MD* contents are now the operand 0012.
- The prepared circuits perform the operation ADD. Hence the number 0012 will be added to the existing contents of the accumulator (0002). In this way the instruction is executed and the result is stored in the accumulator (0014).

5.3.   PROGRAMMED INPUT/OUTPUT TRANSFER

One of the major applications of small computers is in the domain of process control, data collection, and measurement. For those applications it is of importance that the computer be capable of communicating with the devices of the measuring and control chains. The exchange of information between the peripheral device and the computer is controlled either by the computer program or by specially designed elements of the peripheral device. Input-output transfers controlled by the computer program are called *programmed data transfers*. The transfer controlled by the peripheral device is performed without program intervention through special data channels which steal time slices from the central processor whenever necessary. Hence such a transfer is called the *cycle stealing* transfer. In some machines this transfer is called by other names, such as data break, data channel, and direct memory access (*DMA*). In this section we shall discuss only programmed data transfers.

A programmed data transfer is performed by the I/O transfer instruction. A small computer has at least one IOT instruction. This instruction can be used for the following tasks:

- To send the *command* to the peripheral device, instructing the device what to do. For example, a magnetic tape unit can be instructed to backspace the tape by one record.
- To receive and test the information describing the *status* of the peripheral device. An example is a test to determine if a magnetic tape transport is rewinding or if it is ready for recording.
- To *output* the data from the computer to the peripheral device. An example is the output of X and Y data to be used as coordinates of the point to be displayed on the cathode ray tube.
- To *input* the data from the peripheral device to the computer. An example is the input of the digitized data from the measured process.

The above tasks can be performed in one of the three ways called unconditional transfer, conditional transfer, and program interrupt.

Unconditional Transfer

This transfer is rarely used, only for processes whose timing is fixed and known. The peripheral device must be ready for communication. The program for unconditional transfer is simple and straightforward, as shown schematically in Fig. 5.6a. The IOT instruction is inserted in the program between other instructions at the place where the transfer is needed.

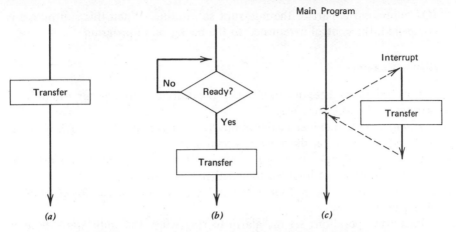

Figure 5.6. Programmed input-output transfer. (a) Unconditional; (b) conditional; (c) program interrupt.

Conditional Transfer

This transfer is used very often. It is performed under program control, but only if the peripheral device is ready for communication. The computer program is shown schematically in Fig. 5.6b; two IOT instructions are usually used to perform the transfer. The first instruction is used to bring into the computer the information describing the status of the peripheral device. The program then tests the status and makes the decision. If the device is not ready, the program can perform the loop and check the status repeatedly. When the device becomes ready, the program executes the second IOT instruction, which performs the desired action. The main advantage of the conditional transfer is that it enables the synchronization between the computer operation and the peripheral-device operation. The main disadvantage is the waste of computer time if one has to wait for the device to become ready.

Program Interrupt

Program-interrupt transfer makes more efficient use of the computer time possible. The transfer will be performed under the program control, but the computer does not have to check repeatedly if the device is ready for transfer. The computer program can perform a calculation which is independent of the transfer. Let us call this program the background job. When the peripheral device is ready, it will interrupt the computer and cause it to leave its background program for a moment and to perform a special interrupt subroutine for transfer. This operation is shown schematically in Fig. 5.6c. The

IOT command is part of the interrupt subroutine. When this subroutine is completed, the control is returned to the background program.

Simple Example

Let us compare the unconditional, conditional, and program-interrupt transfer in the following way.

Example. One member of the family is "programmed" to watch over the milk and to take it off the stove when cooked.

Unconditional operation: go in the kitchen at, say, 8:25 and take the milk off the stove, without caring whether it is cooked.

Conditional operation: look at the milk once every minute. When cooked, take it off the stove.

Interrupt operation: set the alarm to ring when the milk starts boiling. Perform the background job of writing homework. When the alarm rings, interrupt the background job for a moment and take the milk from the stove. Resume the background job from the point where interrupted.

Party Line I/O

Normally, peripheral devices are slower than the computer. Hence a computer can communicate, if necessary, with a number of peripheral devices.

The I/O lines of a computer form a bus to which all the peripheral devices are connected.

Figure 5.7 shows the computer bus with a number of peripheral devices. This mode of operation is called the party line operation. The input/output lines from the computer are bused to all devices on the party line, so the

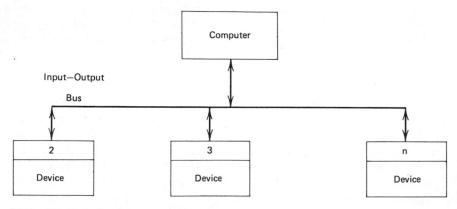

Figure 5.7. Party line input-output transfer.

devices appear as a single device to the computer. Each peripheral device must have its own controller. The controller must have a device selection address, so that the computer can call a specific device for transfer.

The controller must take care of the following:

- To decode the device selection code received from the computer and to respond only if the code is identical with its address.
- To decode the command code received from the computer and to initiate operations.
- To send the computer the information describing the status of the peripheral device.
- To perform the gating for data transfer between the computer and the device.

IOT Instruction

The computer communicates with the controller through the IOT instruction. An example of the IOT instruction is shown in Fig. 5.8. The instruction has three parts: operation code, device selection address, and command code.

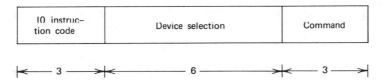

Figure 5.8. Instruction format for input-output transfer.

Operation Code. In the example, 3 bits are used for operation code and one out of eight possible combinations of those bits is the code of the IOT instruction. These bits are loaded in the computer instruction register. The specific action for the I/O instruction is initiated.

Device Selection Address. In the example, 6 bits are used for device selection address. Hence this computer can identify up to 64 different devices. The decoding is performed in the peripheral device.

Command Code. In the example, 3 bits are used for the command code. Hence this computer can send up to eight different commands to the peripheral device. The decoding is performed in the peripheral device.

Figure 5.9 shows the information flow which affects a programmed data transfer with the peripheral device. The IOT instruction, like any other instruction of the program, is read from the core memory into the *MD*

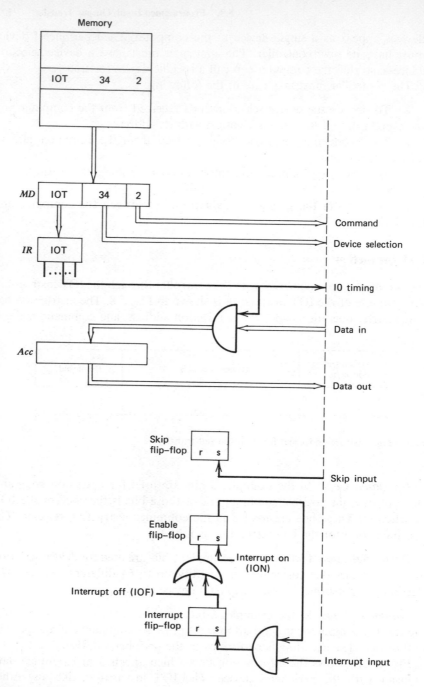

Figure 5.9. Parts of the small computer involved in the programmed input-output transfer.

buffer register. The operation code (first 3 bits) are transferred in the *IR*. The instruction decoder activates the IOT timing generator. As a result, the computer enters the I/O state.

I/O State and Timing Signals

The I/O state is characteristic of the I/O instruction in the same way as the FETCH, DEFER and EXECUTE are characteristic of all other instructions.

During the I/O state, the computer generates a number of timing signals which are used to perform the operations needed for communication with the peripheral device, for strobing the data lines and gating the command lines.

Device Selection Lines

The device selection bits of the I/O instruction sit in the memory data register *MD*. Using those bits, the I/O instruction selects the peripheral device. These bits are transmitted over the party line bus to all peripheral devices. The device selection code presents the key to the peripheral device. Each peripheral device has its specific lock, called the device selector. The device selection code will match with only one device selector; hence only one device will be coupled for communication with the computer. In the example, 6 bits are used for device selection; hence six device selection lines go out of the computer (DS0–DS5 lines).

Command Lines

The command code of the I/O instruction sits in the memory data register. Using those bits, the I/O instruction tells the selected peripheral device what to do.

The command lines are connected to all peripheral devices. However, the device address code will couple only one device to the bus. Hence the command will be received only by the peripheral device selected by the device selection part of the I/O instruction. In the example 3 bits are used for command code; hence three command lines go out of the computer (C0–C2 lines).

Data Lines

The data transfer is performed between the peripheral device and the accumulator. Twelve input and twelve output lines present the data way. Data lines are connected to all peripheral devices. Each peripheral device has the gating logic for data lines. Only the device selected by the device selection part of the I/O instruction will open the gates for data lines.

The output lines are provided with driving amplifiers. These lines present the contents of the accumulator throughout the operation. The selected peripheral device should strobe these lines into its data buffer register.

The input lines bring the data from the peripheral device. These lines are gated inside the computer, so that they do not disturb the contents of the accumulator. Only during the execution of an I/O transfer instruction will the computer strobe the input lines into the accumulator.

Skip Line

The computer has one skip input. The computer senses the flag of the peripheral device through this input. The flag is a 1-bit register (flip-flop) in the peripheral device. If the device is ready for communication, it will set its flag. If the device is not ready, it will keep its flag reset.

If the flag shows that the device is ready, the computer may issue an I/O instruction and it can perform the transfer. On the other hand, if the flag shows that the device is not ready, the computer will have to delay the I/O transfer for some later time. The flags of all peripheral devices are connected to the same one skip line. Each device has a gating logic between the flag and the skip line, controlled by the device selector.

The computer examines the flag by issuing an I/O command with the address of the device. The selected device connects its flag to the skip line.

The states of the flag will be copied through the skip line into the skip flip-flop in the computer. The computer is so wired that each I/O instruction checks the skip flip-flop.

If the skip flip-flop is in the state zero, after the I/O instruction is performed, the program counter will point to the next instruction in the program.

If the skip flip-flop is in the state one, after the I/O instruction is performed, the program counter will be incremented by two and the next instruction will be skipped. In brief

$$(\text{Skip}) = 0 \quad \Rightarrow I + 1$$
$$(\text{Skip}) = 1 \quad \Rightarrow I + 2$$

In this way the program can be split in two branches: the first branch, if the device is busy, and the second one, if the device is ready for transfer.

Interrupt Line

The computer has one interrupt line. The computer receives requests from peripheral devices through this line. Upon receiving a request, the computer stops the background program and performs the interrupt routine for the peripheral device. The interrupt line is connected directly without gating, to the flags of the peripheral devices. As a result, if any of the peripheral devices requests the interrupt service, the computer will receive the request.

A simplified interrupt logic is composed of the input gate, enable flip-flop, and interrupt flip-flop, Fig. 5.9.

The input gate is controlled by the enable flip-flop, and is closed if the flip-flop is not set.

The enable flip-flop is under program control. The computer has the instruction interrupt on (ION) which will set the enable flip-flop. Another instruction, interrupt off (IOF) will reset the enable flip-flop. Hence by the program control it is possible to disconnect (disable) or to connect (enable) the interrupt line from the computer. (The two interrupt instructions, IOF and ION, belong to the class of I/O instructions with a special code.)

If the programmer wants to use the interrupt feature, the ION instruction must be issued. The input gate will be open and will wait for a signal on the interrupt line.

The signal on the interrupt line will set the interrupt flip-flop. Each computer instruction examines the interrupt flip-flop. When the interrupt flip-flop is set, the following takes place:

- The computer will complete the current instruction of the program.
- The contents of the program counter will be automatically deposited in a specific memory location, for example in address 0.
- The specific address, for example, 1, will be set in the program counter.

The two characteristic interrupt addresses are fixed for a given computer. In our example we use addresses 0 and 1.

The features described above can be used to transfer the program control from the background program to the specific interrupt routine whenever the device sets the request. Upon the execution of the interrupt routine, the background job is resumed.

5.4. INTERFACE COMPONENTS FOR PROGRAMMED INPUT-OUTPUT TRANSFER

Device Selector

Each peripheral device connected to the party line bus must have a device selector. Device selection address lines are connected to all device selectors, Fig. 5.10. Each device selector is assigned a select code and is enabled only when the assigned code is present on the bus. The selector with the proper code will open the gates to allow the command pulses to enter the selected device.

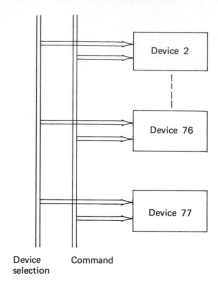

Device   Command
selection

Figure 5.10. Command lines and device-selection address lines.

Figure 5.11 shows an example of the device selector. Six pairs of device selection address lines (DS0–DS5) from the bus are connected to an AND gate. Let us suppose that this selector should accept the address 34_8 (binary 011100). Hence the gate should produce the output logical 1 if the device address bits (DS0–DS5) satisfy the equation:

$$OUT = \overline{DS0} \cdot DS1 \cdot DS2 \cdot DS3 \cdot \overline{DS4} \cdot \overline{DS5}$$

Each bit (DS) is present on the bus. Hence if we want to design the device selector for the code described by the equation, we should connect the items present in the equation to the AND gate. This case is shown in Fig. 5.11a.

If one wants to change the address assigned to the device, it is enough to slightly modify the connections in the device selector. Figure 5.11b shows the selector for the code 17_8 (binary 001111).

The output of the device selector is used to gate the command lines and to activate different actions in the device.

(a)   (b)

Figure 5.11. Simple device selector. (a) Selector for address 34_8; (b) selector for address 17_8.

Command Decoder

The command lines are connected to all peripheral devices. In the device, the command lines are gated by the device selector output. Hence only the selected device receives the command from the computer.

The device must have some kind of a command decoder. Decoding depends on the functions the device must perform. The device which should perform, say, only three functions, may have a simple 3-to-3 decoder, which is in fact only the gate controlled by the device selector. Such a simple gating for the command lines is shown in Fig. 5.12a. When the computer issues the I/O command with bit C0 set, the command 0 line in the selected device will become active and the device will perform the specific job zero. In the same way the computer can issue the command for job one or for job two, using bits C1 and C2, respectively.

Often the device must perform more than three functions. In this case the 3–8 decoder provides the possibility to activate up to 8 different jobs. A simple 3–8 command decoder is shown schematically in Fig. 5.12b. The integrated decoders are available on the market. For the internal structure of the decoder see Fig. 2.21.

It is entirely up to the designer of the peripheral device controller how to use the commands as well as which code to use for a given task. In our examples we shall restrict ourselves to the use of up to five commands, to which we give the symbolic names CLEAR, SKIP, READ, WRITE and GO. These can be, for example, the commands with codes 0 to 4, respectively. The designer can define some other functions from the codes 5 to 7, if needed.

The CLEAR command will be used to reset the flag flip-flop in the selected device. Hence the command CLEAR32 will clear the flag of the device 32.

The SKIP command will be used to connect the flag of the selected device to the skip line. Hence the command SKIP12 will connect the flag of the device 12.

The READ command will be used to gate the data buffer register of the selected device into the accumulator. Hence the command READ10 will transfer the data of the device 10 into the accumulator.

The WRITE command will be used to gate the accumulator into the data register of the selected device. Hence the command WRITE10 will transfer the data from the accumulator into the device 10.

The GO command will be used to activate a line in the interface. The designer can use such an instruction for various purposes. Hence the command GO70 will activate one line in the selector 70.

In all our examples we shall use only those commands. Not all the commands will be needed in each peripheral device. For example, a device such as a paper-tape reader does not need the WRITE command because it does not have a facility to receive the data from the computer.

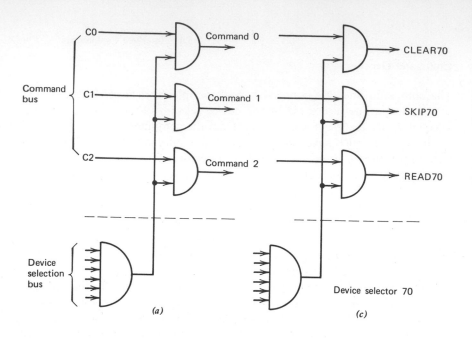

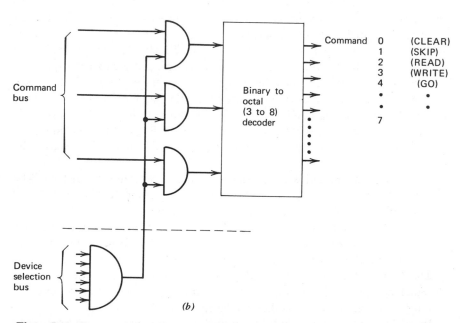

Figure 5.12. Command decoder. (*a*) One-to-one decoding; (*b*) three-to-eight decoding; (*c*) device selector for address 70 and command decoder with 3 outputs: CLEAR70, SKIP70, and READ70.

Figure 5.12c shows an example of the device selector and command decoder for a device with the selection code 70. The designer has decided to define the commands in the following way:

> I/O instruction, with selection address 70, and command code 1,
>   (binary 001) ≡ CLEAR70
> I/O instruction, with selection address 70, and command code 2,
>   (binary 010) ≡ SKIP70
> I/O instruction, with selection address 70, and command code 4,
>   (binary 100) ≡ READ70.

In our example we leave it up to the designer to choose the code he wants for a given command. In some minicomputers specific codes are always used for specific commands, as it will be shown later. However, this fact does not change the principles of operations.

Flag Flip-Flop

As it was pointed out, the flag is a 1-bit register in the peripheral device. If the device has performed all actions necessary before the transfer and is ready for communication with the computer, the device will set its flag, Fig. 5.13.

The flag can be connected either to the interrupt line or to the skip line.

Through the interrupt input the device requests the computer to perform a special service with this particular device. If the interrupt input is enabled, the computer has to accept the interrupt request at the moment when it is set by the device.

Through the skip input the computer can examine the flag at the time when the computer wants. To do that, the computer must issue an I/O instruction, SKIP. This command will copy the state of the flag flip-flop of the selected device into the skip flip-flop of the computer. For example, the I/O instruction SKIP70 will cause the following (Fig. 5.13):

- The device code 70 will be recognized only by the device selector 70;
- The command line, to which the name SKIP has been given, will be gated by the selector and it will be active only in the device 70. The line SKIP70 will open the gate on the skip line in the device 70;
- If the flag flip-flop 70 is in the state 1, it will set the skip flip-flop in the computer through the skip line.

After the computer has received the flag information and has started the action, it should clear the flag. The CLEAR I/O instruction is used for this purpose. For example, if the instruction CLEAR70 is issued, the CLEAR70 output of the command decoder will reset the flag flip-flop 70. Note the following important features:

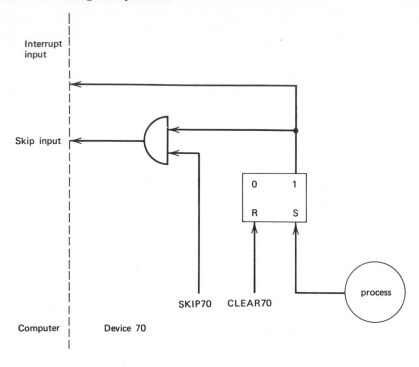

Figure 5.13. Flag flip-flop in the peripheral device.

1. The flag is set by the action in the peripheral device.

2. The flag is tested by the computer through issuing the SKIP I/O instruction, with a proper device selection code. This instruction connects the flag to the skip input of the computer.

3. The flag can be used for interrupt request. For this purpose the flag is directly connected to the interrupt input of the computer.

4. The flag is cleared by the computer through issuing the CLEAR I/O instruction, with a proper device selection code.

Device Data Register

The data transfer is performed between the accumulator and the device data register (DR). The data from this register can be used for different purposes in the input and output transfer.

As an example of the input transfer, let us consider a digital voltmeter connected to the computer, Fig. 5.14a. The voltmeter measures the analog quantity, the voltage, and converts it into a digitized quantity, the number.

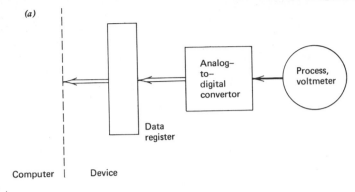

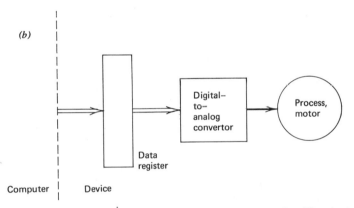

Figure 5.14. Data registers in the peripheral device. (*a*) Input transfer; (*b*) output transfer.

Such digitized data are stored into the device data register. At this point the device can set the flag, signifying to the computer that it has the data ready for the input to the machine.

As an example of the output transfer, let us consider a motor for angle positioning, controlled by the computer, Fig. 5.14*b*. The computer supplies the angle as a digitized quantity into its accumulator. The digitized datum is transferred into the device data register. A digital-to-analog-leader network connected to the data register will convert the datum into an analog voltage for driving the motor.

The I/O transfer is performed between this device register (*DR*) and the accumulator. For each bit one data line is provided on the bus for output transfer, and one data line for input transfer.

It is important to notice that the transfer through only one line will merge (OR) the incoming data from the source with the data already existing at the destination. Figure 5.15*a* shows the one-line transfer of data between one flip-flop of the source *S* and one flip-flop of the destination *D*. The transfer command pulse will open the gate between the logical 1 output of *S* and the set input of *D*. If *S* is in the state 1, it will force the *D* to the state 1. However, if *S* is in the state 0, it will not affect the existing state of the *D*. Hence the result of the transfer is the inclusive OR of the previous contents in *D* and the contents transferred from *S*. This kind of transfer is called the MERGE or OR transfer.

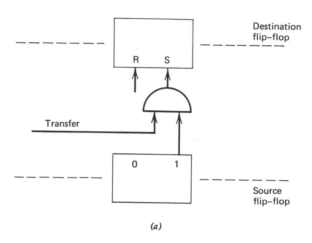

(*a*)

Figure 5.15. Register-to-register data transfer. (*a*) Merge (OR) transfer.

Another kind of transfer is COPY or LOAD or JAM. In this transfer the data from the source are copied at the destination and the original contents of the destination are lost. The copy transfer can be achieved in two ways.

In Fig. 5.15*b* the copy transfer is achieved by connecting the source and the destination flip-flop with two wires. If the *S* is in the logical 1 state, this state will be transferred to *D* through the set input. If *S* in the logical 0 state, this state will be transferred to *D* through the reset input. This kind of transfer has a drawback: it asks for two lines per bit per direction. That is why this kind of connection is avoided whenever possible.

In Fig. 5.15*c* the copy transfer is achieved using only one data line but performing the transfer in two steps: first, the reset pulse is sent to reset the destination flip-flop. Then the transfer pulse is used to copy the data from the source into the destination.

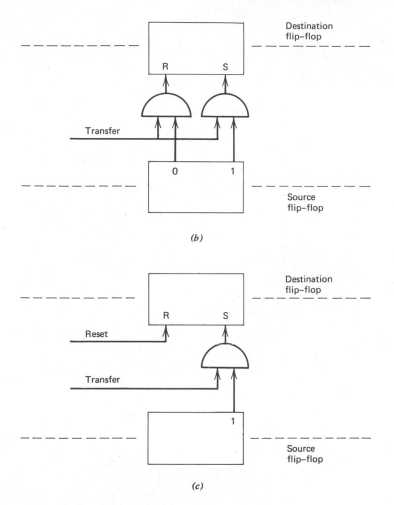

Figure 5.15. (*Cont'd.*) (*b*) Copy or load or jam transfer through two data wires; (*c*) copy transfer using only one data wire.

The resetting can be performed by sending a pulse from the interface electronics into the reset line of the destination register. In the case of input transfer, where the destination is the accumulator, the computer instruction CLEAR can be used to clear the accumulator prior to the I/O instruction.

Input Data Gates

The accumulator has an input line for each bit flip-flop. The peripheral device register *DR* has an output line for each bit flip-flop. Those output lines are

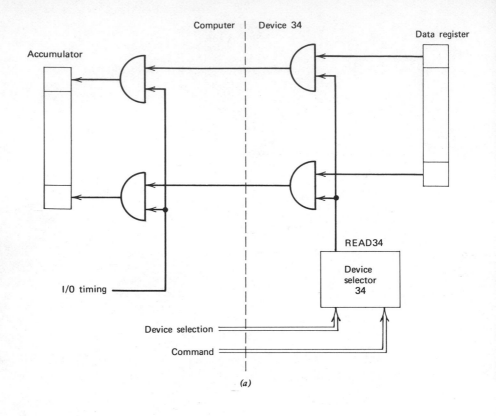

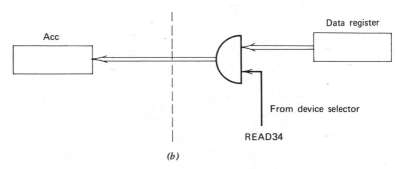

Figure 5.16. Input data gates. (*a*) Details; (*b*) simplified presentation.

186

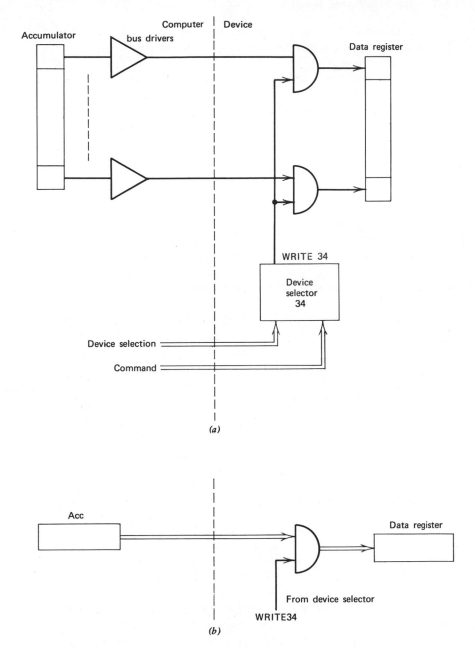

Figure 5.17. Output data gates. (*a*) Details; (*b*) simplified presentation.

gated by the signal from the peripheral device selector, as shown in Fig. 5.16a.

When it is the time for transfer, the computer program sends the device address and command codes on the bus through the I/O instruction. Only the selected device opens the data gates and in this way the data are transferred from the selected device data register into the accumulator.

Figure 5.16b shows a simplified way of presenting the same operation. Instead of drawing one line and one gate for each data wire, a double arrow notation is used to represent all data lines. A single arrow is used to present the control input to the gate.

If the computer and the device are physically separated, the data gates should have drivers to drive the data input bus.

Output Data Gates

The accumulator has an output line for each bit flip-flop.

The peripheral device register has an input line for each bit flip-flop. Those lines are gated by the signal from the peripheral device selector, as shown in Fig. 5.17a.

The accumulator is loaded with the word. Then an I/O instruction is issued to perform the transfer. The I/O instruction sends the device address and the command code onto the bus. Only the selected device opens the data gates and in this way the data are transferred from the accumulator to the selected device data register.

Figure 5.17b shows a simplified way of presenting the same operation.

5.5. UNCONDITIONAL, CONDITIONAL, AND INTERRUPT PROGRAMMED TRANSFERS

Unconditional Transfer

Here we show a simple example of the data transfer between the computer and the peripheral devices. The computer collects the data from three measuring points. Each measuring point has its data register. The data from the three points should be transferred to the computer and stored into three consecutive locations in the memory.

The designer should design an interface between the measuring points and the computer and should write the program for transfer.

Each measuring point is treated as an independent peripheral device. A selection address must be assigned to each device. Let us suppose that the designer has decided to use selection addresses 40, 41, and 42. A block diagram of an interface is shown in Fig. 5.18.

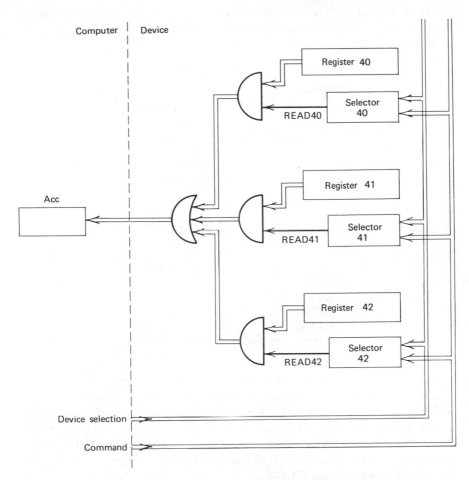

Figure 5.18. Interface components for unconditional programmed transfer.

The computer program should send three I/O instructions with selection addresses 40, 41, and 42, respectively. The only task the I/O instruction should perform is to transfer the data. Any command code can perform this task. We have decided to use the code octal 1. That means the command bits in the I/O instruction should be 001. For this command we define the name READ. Hence the three I/O instructions will be of the form:

$$I/O401 \equiv READ40$$
$$I/O411 \equiv READ41$$
$$I/O421 \equiv READ42$$

Let us suppose that we want to store the data from the three measuring points in locations DEV40, 41, and 42. The program can then have a form as shown in Table 5.1

Table 5.1

Location	Content
	CLEAR
	READ40
	STORE DEV40
	CLEAR
	READ41
	STORE DEV41
	CLEAR
	READ42
	STORE DEV42
	$\vdots$
DEV40	—
DEV41	—
DEV42	—

The program is composed of three identical parts for three devices. The first instruction will clear the accumulator. The I/O instruction READ40 will send address 40 and the command 1 onto the bus. Only selector 40 will be enabled by this code and the command 1 pulse will open the gates of the device 40 register. The data from this register will be transferred into the accumulator. The instruction STORE DEV40 is used to deposit the data in the core memory location DEV40.

In a similar manner, the following three instructions will move the data from the device 41 into the memory location DEV41. The last three instructions will move the data from the device 42 into the memory location DEV42. With this the transfer is finished and the program can continue using the data for calculation.

Conditional Transfer

It may happen that the peripheral device is busy performing the last computer command when a new command comes. For example, if the last command to the magnetic tape unit was to rewind the tape, it will take some time before the operation of rewinding is finished. If in the meantime the program issues an instruction for reading the data from the tape, an incorrect operation will result. It is important that the computer should somehow test the status of the peripheral device and decide whether the transfer can be performed or not.

The peripheral device has the flag flip-flop. If the device is ready for transfer, it sets the flag flip-flop. If the device is busy performing the last operation, or preparing the data, it keeps the flag flip-flop reset.

The output of the flag flip-flop is gated by the peripheral device selector,

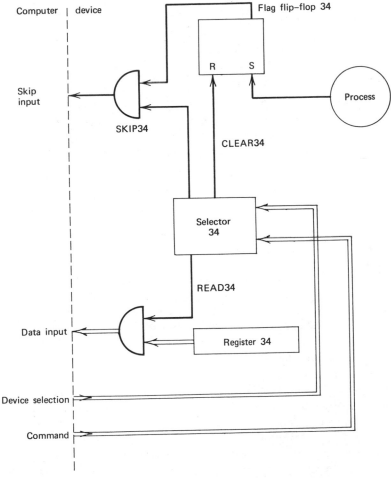

Figure 5.19. Interface components for conditional programmed transfer.

as shown in Fig. 5.19, on the party line bus skip wire. All devices are connected to the same skip wire. This wire enters into the computer and activates the I/O skip logic.

To test the flag, the computer issues an I/O instruction with the address to select the device. Only the flag of the selected device will be gated to the computer. If the flag is set, the computer may issue the second I/O instruction to perform the transfer.

Figure 5.19 shows an example of the interface for conditional transfer. Three I/O instructions with three different command codes are used. If the device has selection code 34, we can define the following three commands:

$$I/O341 \equiv CLEAR34$$
$$I/O342 \equiv SKIP34$$
$$I/O344 \equiv READ34$$

The program is shown in Table 5.2.

Table 5.2

Location	Content
	SKIP34
	JUMP . -1
	CLEAR
	READ34
	STORE RES
	CLEAR34
	$\vdots$
RES	—

The first instruction, SKIP34, connects the flag flip-flop of the device 34 to the I/O skip line. Let us suppose that the device is not ready for transfer. Hence the I/O skip line is in the logical zero state and the program counter points to the second instruction. The second instruction, JUMP . -1, instructs the computer to go back and read the flag again. The program will perform the loop until the peripheral device becomes ready and sets the flag flip-flop. The I/O skip wire will be in the logical one state. After executing the instruction SKIP34, the computer will skip the next instruction. The rest of the program will clear the accumulator and then transfer the data from the selected device into the accumulator using the instruction READ34. At the end, the I/O instruction CLEAR34 will reset the flag in the device 34.

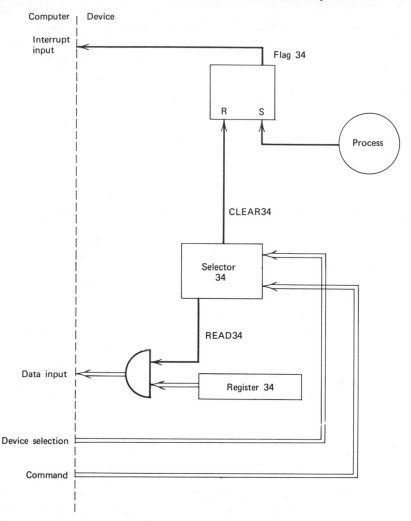

Figure 5.20. Interface components for program-interrupt transfer.

In this example the computer asks the selected device to perform three different operations, hence three command codes are used:

Code 2, in the instruction SKIP34, is used to gate the flag of the selected device to the computer.

Code 4, in the instruction READ34, is used to gate the data of the same device to the computer.

Code 1, in the instruction CLEAR34, is used to reset the flag 34.

Those instructions with the same address selection code but with a different command code will energize three different output wires in the device selector; see Fig. 5.12. These wires are connected to the skip gate, data gate and flag reset, as shown in Fig. 5.19.

Program Interrupt Transfer

If there is a large difference in speed between the computer and the peripheral device, or a large amount of computing is required, the testing, if the device is ready, would be a waste of time. The waiting loops such as in the example of Table 5.2 should be avoided. The program interrupt can be used to notify the computer when the device is ready, or requests service. The main characteristic of the program interrupt is that the communication between the computer and the device is made upon request from the device.

The device flag flip-flop is used to signal the computer that the device requests service or transfer.

The flag flip-flop is connected on the party bus INTERRUPT wire, as shown in Fig. 5.20. This wire enters the computer and activates the interrupt logic.

The interrupt logic switches the program control from the background program to a specific interrupt routine that services the device. This operation is shown in the example of Table 5.3 and Fig. 5.20. The computer performs the long calculation using the background program stored in the address 200 up. The computer is connected to the device with the selection address 34. This device contains a nuclear detector producing random pulses. When a pulse occurs, its digitized amplitude is stored in the device data register, and also the flag flip-flop is set. In this way the device sends the request to the computer to read in the data.

The request can interrupt the computer at any time. Let us suppose that the request has occurred during the execution of the instruction in address 234.

After the execution of this instruction, the program counter will point to address 235. The interrupt logic stores the contents of the *PC* in location 0 and it sets address 1 in the *PC*. It also resets the interrupt flip-flop in the computer.

In address 1 the instruction JUMP INTR is stored and commands the computer to go to the interrupt routine starting at the address INTR. The interrupt routine is shown in Table 5.3. Note the following important facts regarding the interrupt routine:

1. The I/O instruction CLEAR34 resets the flag because the request is accepted and the requested operation is in progress.

2. The contents of the accumulator belong to the background job. The instruction STORE SAVEA saves the contents of the accumulator.

Table 5.3

Location	Content	Comment
0		It will keep the PC, (235)
1	JUMP INTR	Enter interrupt routine
	⋮	
INTR	CLEAR34	
	STORE SAVEA	
	CLEAR	
	READ34	Interrupt routine
	STORE RES	
	CLEAR	
	ADD SAVEA	
	ION	
	JUMP I 0	
	⋮	
SAVEA	0	
RES	0	
200	CLEAR	
	⋮	
234	—	Background program interrupted at 234
235	—	

3. The next three instructions, CLEAR, READ34, STORE RES transfer the data from the peripheral device into the memory location RES.

4. Before the return to the background job the previous contents of the accumulator are restored using the instructions CLEAR, ADD SAVEA.

5. Examining Fig. 5.9 one can see that the interrupt flip-flop, when set, will reset the enable flip-flop. In this way, when an interrupt request is accepted, the interrupt line is disabled for additional requests. Hence before completing the interrupt routine, the instruction ION should be executed. This instruction will enable the interrupt system for future use.

6. The last instruction is JUMP I 0. It will jump to the address stored at address 0. In this example, this address is 235. Hence the background program will continue from the point where it was interrupted. Next time the interrupt request can occur at some other place of the main program and will result in similar operations.

7. Two specific memory locations are used in connection with the interrupt. The first memory location keeps the return address for the background program. The second memory location keeps the first instruction of the interrupt routine. This is usually the linking instruction—JUMP INTR in this example. The routine can then be stored in some other part of the memory.

Multiple Interrupt Structure

In many applications, more than one device is connected to the computer. Requests for service from all devices are ORed to the single INTERRUPT line. The computer cannot know which device requests service. The computer interrupt routine must execute a number of I/O SKIP instructions and in this way examine which device has the flag flip-flop in the set state. When the program identifies the device, it branches into the service routine of this particular device.

Let us repeat the example from Fig. 5.18 and Table 5.1: devices 40, 41, and 42 ask for input transfer. This time instead of the programmed unconditional transfer, we shall use the interrupt transfer. When the device has the data prepared, the device will set the flag flip-flop and will request service through the interrupt line.

Figure 5.21 shows the interface for transfer. Figure 5.22 shows the flowchart of the interrupt routine. Table 5.4 shows the program of the interrupt routine. Note the following characteristic features of the multiple interrupt structure:

1. All interrupt requests are simply ORed to the interrupt bus. In this way the computer receives the interrupt request regardless of its origin.

2. The flag information is always gated with the device selector. In this way the computer can use the address selection scheme and examine one device flag after another in order to find out which of them is set and requests service.

3. Three I/O instructions are sent to each peripheral device. The command SKIPn is used to read the flag of the device n in the computer. The command CLEARn is used to clear the flag when a particular device is serviced. The command READn is used to read the data in the computer.

5.6.   DIRECT MEMORY ACCESS

Principle

Direct memory access (DMA) provides the possibility for I/O transfer without program intervention. The transfer is performed through special channels which steal time slices from the central processor whenever necessary. During each stolen time slice one transfer is performed. This kind of transfer is also known by other names, such as data channel, data break, and cycle stealing transfer.

The computer logic performing the DMA is basically independent of the logic involved in the programmed transfer. The main point is that the DMA

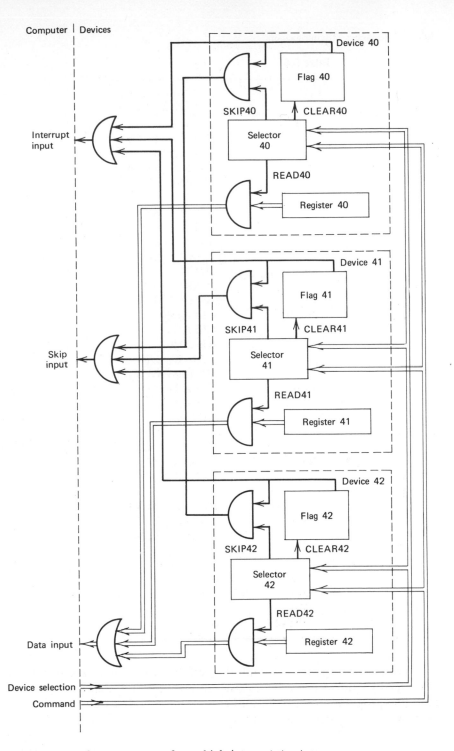

Figure 5.21. Interface components for multiple-interrupt structure.

Table 5.4

Location	Content
0	—
1	JUMP INTR
	:
INTR	STORE TEMP
	SKIP40
	SKIP
	JUMP SR40
	SKIP41
	SKIP
	JUMP SR41
	SKIP42
	JUMP OUT
	JUMP SR42
SR40	CLEAR40
	CLEAR
	READ40
	STORE DEV40
	JUMP OUT
SR41	CLEAR41
	CLEAR
	READ41
	STORE DEV41
	JUMP OUT
SR42	CLEAR42
	CLEAR
	READ42
	STORE DEV42
OUT	CLEAR
	ADD TEMP
	ION
	JUMP I 0
TEMP	0
DEV40	0
DEV41	0
DEV42	0

does not perform the transfer with the accumulator. Rather the transfer is performed via the memory data register directly with the computer memory. Since the program execution is not involved in the *DMA* transfer, the computer working registers are not disturbed.

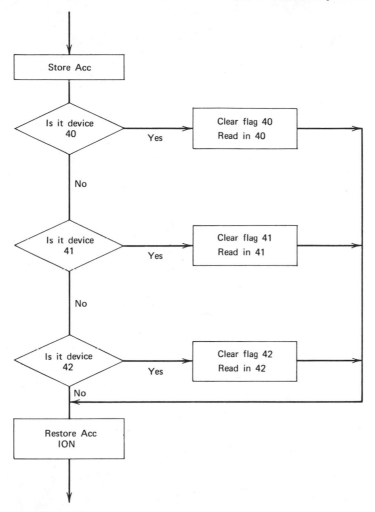

Figure 5.22. Flow chart of the interrupt routine searching for the source of interrupt.

Each basic step of *DMA* is under the control of the peripheral device which sets the request for transfer. For inputting the data in the computer, the device sets the request when the data are prepared; for outputting the data from the computer, the device sets the request when it needs the data and is ready to receive them.

Having the *DMA* facility, the computer can perform in parallel two jobs which might be entirely independent:

- Programmed job.
- *DMA* transfer.

The computer examines the *DMA* requests during the execution of every instruction of the programmed job. If the *DMA* request is received, the next time slice is given to the *DMA* transfer. The programmed job is delayed for this time slice.

Figure 5.23 shows the principle of cycle stealing. The upper line presents the time slices during which the computer performs the programmed job. The arrows indicate the *DMA* requests, received from the peripheral device. The lower line presents the time slices stolen from the programmed job and given for execution of the *DMA* transfer.

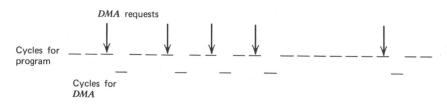

Figure 5.23. Principle of cycle stealing for direct memory access.

The *DMA* transfer is particularly useful for devices with high speed and a large amount of data in block form. An example is the high-speed magnetic tape system or high-speed drum memories.

The Computer and the *DMA* Bus

The computer has a special bus for *DMA* transfer. This bus is primarily intended for high-speed transfer of blocks of data. The transfer of blocks of data usually deals with a block of memory locations. During each transfer one datum is moved between one memory location and the peripheral device. Next time the transfer is performed with the next location in row and so on until the end of the block is reached.

For each transfer the peripheral device communicates with the computer through the lines which provide the following information, (Fig. 5.24):

- The request from the device for *DMA* transfer
- The accept response from the computer
- The address of the memory location to be involved in the transfer
- The data
- The direction of the transfer

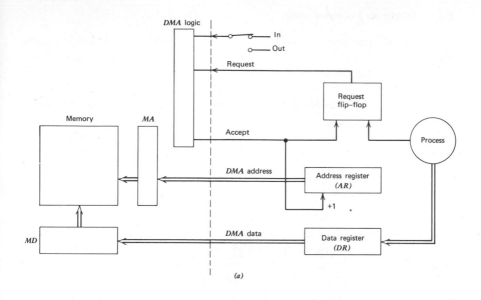

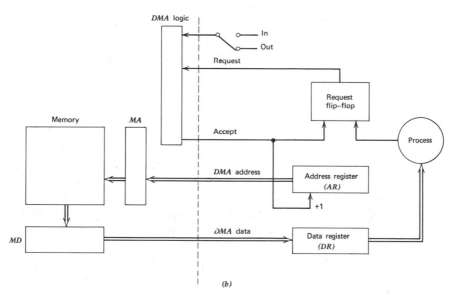

Figure 5.24. Direct memory access. (*a*) Input transfer; (*b*) output transfer.

The request line enters the DMA logic of the computer and is tested during the execution of each instruction. If the line is activated by the device, the next cycle will be given to the DMA.

The accept line brings the computer's response to the peripheral device. It is activated during the DMA cycle and can be used to clear the source of the request in the device.

The DMA address lines specify the memory location involved in the transfer. The address is supplied by the peripheral device. The DMA address lines are strobed into the memory address register of the computer during the DMA cycle.

The data transfer to the computer is achieved through the DMA input lines, Fig. 5.24a. The data are supplied by the peripheral device. The DMA input lines are strobed into the memory data register during the DMA cycle. Afterwards the data are written in the same cycle in the memory location, as specified by the memory address register.

The data output transfer, Fig. 5.24b, is achieved through the DMA output lines. The data are supplied by the computer: the contents of the memory location specified by the memory address register are read into the memory data register and buffered into the DMA output lines. The peripheral device should strobe those lines into its data register during the same DMA cycle.

The direction of the transfer line is used to specify if the device requests an input or an output transfer.

The Peripheral Device in DMA transfer

The basic components of the peripheral device controller for DMA transfer are: request flip-flop, address register (AR) and data register (DR).

The request flip-flop is controlled by the process in the peripheral device. When the device wants to send the request for DMA transfer it sets the request flip-flop. The computer receives the request and enters the DMA cycle. It activates the accept line, which can be used to reset the request flip-flop.

The address register (AR) is used to supply the address of the memory location involved in the transfer. DMA usually deals with a block of data. At the beginning of the operation, the AR should keep the starting address of the block. The contents of the AR are incremented by one during each cycle of the transfer. Hence the next transfer deals with the next memory location in the row. The accept signal can be used to increment the AR.

The data register (DR) has different functions in the input and in the output transfer. In the input transfer, the DR keeps the data supplied by the peripheral device. In the DMA cycle, these data are strobed in the computer through the DMA input lines. In the output transfer, the DR receives

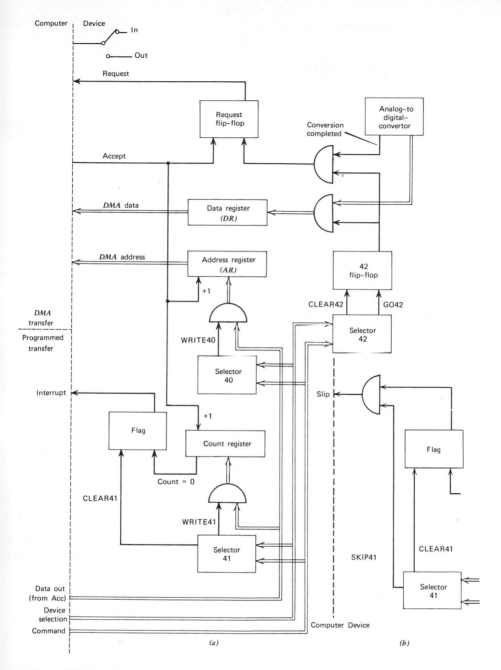

Figure 5.25. Interface components for direct memory access. (*a*) Interrupt is used for the termination of the transfer of the block of data; (*b*) skip test is used for the transfer termination.

203

the data from the computer via the *DMA* output lines. The accept signal can be used to strobe *DMA* output lines into the *DR*.

Example of *DMA* transfer

Figure 5.25 shows an example of the *DMA* input transfer. The detector measures the pulses coming at random from the measured process. Each pulse is converted by the analog to digital convertor into digital form. We want to receive 100 pulses and store their digitized values in 100 successive memory locations, starting with location 2000 and using the *DMA* transfer.

One can recognize the basic components needed for *DMA* transfer: request flip-flop, address register (*AR*), and the data register (*DR*). There are also some other parts which are used for auxiliary tasks.

Thus far we have concentrated only on the basic *DMA* operation—cycle stealing. The whole job of transferring a block of data is in fact composed of more tasks in the following order:

- Initialize the *DMA* logic
- Start
- Repeated cycle stealing
- Termination

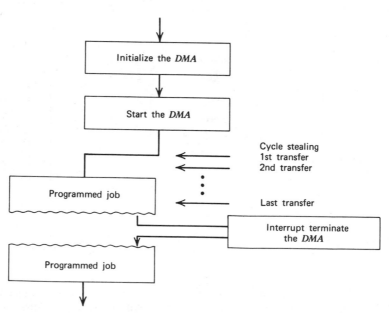

Figure 5.26. Tasks in the DMA transfer: initialize; start; cycle stealing; termination.

Figure 5.26 shows schematically those steps: the computer program is used to initialize and to start the *DMA*. After that the computer can perform the program which is entirely independent of the transfer. During the execution of this program, the *DMA* will steal the cycles whenever requested and perform the transfer. When the transfer is finished, the interrupt can be used to switch the control to the routine for termination of the *DMA*. The basic program can then be continued.

Initialize the *DMA* Logic

Before the *DMA* logic can operate it must be told which direction to transfer the data (in or out), where in the memory to put or take the data, and how many data to transfer. These facts are given by means of a small program which initializes the *DMA* operation. In this program, the programmed I/O transfer is used for the following operations: reset the interface, load the starting address, load the word count.

Table 5.5 shows the program to initialize the *DMA* logic of Fig. 5.25*a*.

Table 5.5

Location	Content	Comment
0	—	
1	JUMP INTR	
	⋮	
	CLEAR41	
	CLEAR42	
	CLEAR	
	ADD ADDRESS	
	WRITE40	Initialize
	CLEAR	
	ADD COUNT	
	WRITE41	
	GO42	
	ION	Start
	JUMP JOB	
JOB	⋮	Cycle stealing during this
	⋮	program, 100 times
ADDRESS	2000	
COUNT	7123	Octal − 100_{10}
	⋮	
INTR	CLEAR42	
	CLEAR41	Termination
	JUMP I 0	

The reset of the interface is achieved by the first two instructions, which clear the flag flip-flop and the flip-flop 42.

The reading of the starting address is achieved with the next three instructions. The starting address is loaded into the accumulator and transferred into the address register of the peripheral device. To distinguish the address register from other parts of the interface, the device selection scheme is used. In this example the selection code of the address register is 40.

The loading of the word count is achieved with the next three instructions. The word count in the form of two's complement of the number of items to be transmitted is loaded in the count register. The selection code of the count register in this example is 41.

Now the interface is ready and the transfer can start.

Start the DMA Logic

When the interface is initialized, the *DMA* transfer can start. This is usually done by allowing the process to send requests. In our example, the I/O instruction GO42 connects the analog to digital converter to the interface by setting the flip-flop 42. From now on, whenever the analog to digital converter finishes the conversion, it will send the digitized data into the data register, and with the signal, conversion completed, it will set the request flip-flop. The instruction GO42 is followed by the instruction ION which turns on the computer interrupt system. The interrupt will be used to notify the termination of the *DMA* transfer.

From now on, no programmed instructions are needed for the *DMA* transfer. Hence the program can perform some other job independently of the transfer.

Cycle Stealing

The detector receives a random pulse. The analog to digital converter converts the pulse into a number. When the conversion is completed, the request flip-flop is set. The next cycle of the computer time is stolen from the programmed job and one transfer is performed into the memory location, as specified by the address register. The accept signal from the computer is used for three operations:

- To clear the request flip-flop.
- To increment the address register by one.
- To increment the counter register by one.

Termination of the *DMA* through the Interrupt

At the beginning the counter register is loaded with the two's complement of the word count. During each transfer cycle the contents of the count register are incremented by one. A simple logic tests the contents. When the contents become zero, the flag flip-flop is set and the interrupt request is sent to the computer. The interrupt switches the program from the basic job into the interrupt routine for transfer termination.

In this simple example, the termination is achieved by disconnecting the analog to digital converter from the interface: the I/O instruction CLEAR42 is used to reset the flip-flop 42. The instruction CLEAR41 resets the flag flip-flop.

At the end of the interrupt routine the program control is switched back to the main program.

Termination of the *DMA* Using the Skip Test

If there is no need for another programmed job to go in parallel with the *DMA* transfer, the skip input can be used to test if the transfer is finished. The flag flip-flop in this case is connected to the skip input of the computer.

Selector 41 must have the third output, SKIP41, to gate the flag to the

Table 5.6

Location	Content	Comment
START	CLEAR41	
	CLEAR42	
	CLEAR	
	ADD ADDRESS	Initialize
	WRITE40	
	CLEAR	
	ADD COUNT	
	WRITE41	
	GO42	Start
	SKIP41	Cycle stealing during
	JUMP . −1	this program
	CLEAR42	Termination
	CLEAR41	
	HALT	
ADDRESS	2000	
COUNT	7634	

skip line. The program for this case is shown in Table 5.6. During the *DMA* transfer the computer is just wasting time in the loop SKIP41, JUMP.−1.

The skip input is shown in Fig. 5.25*b*. The other parts of the interface are the same as in Fig. 5.25*a*.

5.7. CONTROL WORD AND STATUS WORD

Control Word

A simple peripheral device, which can perform only a few operations, can be instructed what to do through the command code of the I/O instruction. The commands, such as READ, WRITE, SKIP, CLEAR, GO can be used to initiate different operations in the peripheral device.

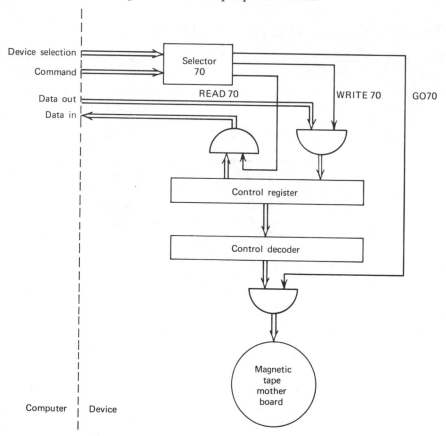

Figure 5.27. Interface components for the control-word transfer.

There are devices that can perform a large variety of operations. For example, the magnetic tape controller with four magnetic tape transports can perform at least 8 different operations with each transport. This presents a total of 32 different operations. In this case the command can be sent to the tape controller not only using the I/O instruction but also using the control word.

The device has a register called the control register, Fig. 5.27. The control register contents are decoded by the control decoder. The outputs of the decoder control different parts of the equipment. Each bit in the control register controls one operation, or one unit. In the example, 2 bits are used to specify the tape transport unit. Hence any of the four transports can be connected to the computer by specifying the unit number.

Another 3 bits are used to specify the operation. Table 5.7 shows an example of operations for the magnetic tape. By combining the unit selection bits and the operation bits one can instruct any unit to perform any operation.

Table 5.7

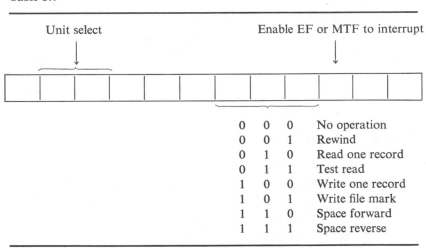

0	0	0	No operation
0	0	1	Rewind
0	1	0	Read one record
0	1	1	Test read
1	0	0	Write one record
1	0	1	Write file mark
1	1	0	Space forward
1	1	1	Space reverse

To instruct the device to perform an operation, the computer loads the control register with the control word with the proper bit configuration. The loading is performed in the standard way as in the programmed data transfer.

A selection code is assigned to the control register. In the example, the code 70 is used.

The control word is loaded in the accumulator and the instruction WRITE70 will transfer it into the control register. In a similar way, if the program should know what the last control word was, the instruction

READ70 can be used. It will transfer the contents of the control word in the accumulator.

When a proper bit configuration is loaded in the control register, the device is ready for operation. To start the operation, an I/O instruction is issued to strobe the outputs of the control decoder in the device. In the example the GO70 instruction is used.

Operating the peripheral device through the use of the control word is shown schematically in Fig. 5.28.

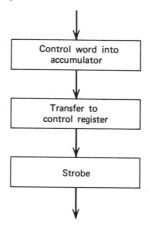

Figure 5.28. Procedure in the use of the control word.

Operating the Magnetic Tape

Example. Instruct the magnetic tape controller to rewind the tape unit 2. The program is shown in Table 5.8.

Table 5.8

	CLEAR	
	WRITE70	
	ADD	CONTR
	WRITE70	
	GO70	
	:	
CONTR	2010	

The first two instructions are used to transfer zero in the control register (resetting). The second two instructions fetch the control word and transfer it to the control register. The bit configuration of the control word is 2010 (octal). According to Fig. 5.27 and Table 5.7, we see that the first octal digit specifies the tape unit (2) and the third octal digit specifies the operation (1 ≡ rewind).

The last instruction strobes the control decoder output into the device, and in this way it starts the operation: rewinding the tape unit 2.

Example. Write the end of the file mark on the tape unit 3. The program is shown in Table 5.9. The only difference from the previous case is the bit configuration in the control word: 3050. We can see that this is the code for the unit 3 and for the operation—write end of file.

Table 5.9

	CLEAR	
	WRITE70	
	ADD	CONTR
	WRITE70	
	GO70	
	⋮	
CONTR	3050	

Example. Read 1 record from the tape unit 1 using the *DMA*. The word count is 100; the starting address of the memory block into which the data should be read is 2000. The address register and the count register are connected as in Fig. 5.25.

The flow chart of the program is shown in Fig. 5.29 and the program is shown in Table 5.10.

Table 5.10

	CLEAR	
	ADD	ADDRESS
	WRITE40	
	CLEAR	
	ADD	COUNT
	WRITE41	
	CLEAR	
	ADD	CONTR
	WRITE70	
	GO70	
	⋮	
ADDRESS	2000	
COUNT	7634	
CONTR	1020	

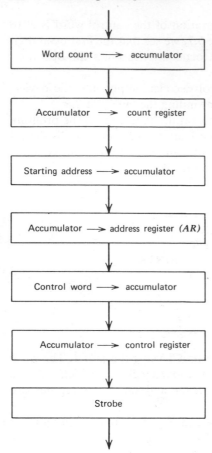

Figure 5.29. Operating the magnetic tape using control word. Flow chart.

The first three instructions load the starting address into the device address register. The next three instructions load the word count into the device count register. The next three instructions load the control word into the device control register. The last instruction strobes the control into the device and the *DMA* transfer will start.

The control word is 4020, meaning the unit number 4 and the operation—read the record.

Status Word

A simple peripheral device which can perform only a few operations can inform the computer about its status using the flag flip-flop. The flag flip-flop is most frequently used to show if the device is busy or ready for transfer.

There are devices which can perform a large variety of operations. In this case the device status cannot be expressed using one bit of information only. Let us consider, for example, the magnetic tape controller. Various situations may arise during the operation of the controller and the computer should be informed about that. These situations may be: parity error, illegal command, end of tape, operation completed and so on.

To inform the computer about the status of the device, the status word is used.

The device has a register called the status register, Fig. 5.30. Whenever a particular situation arises, the device sets a specified bit in the status register. Table 5.11 shows an example of the status word for the magnetic tape controller.

To find out the status of the device, the computer reads the status word. The reading is performed in the standard way as in the programmed data transfer:

A selection code is assigned to the status register. In the example, the code 71 is used. The instruction READ71 will transfer the contents of the status register into the accumulator. The computer program can then be used to examine which bits in the status word are set, and it can make the decision. For example, if the error bit is set, the program can instruct the tape controller to repeat the operation.

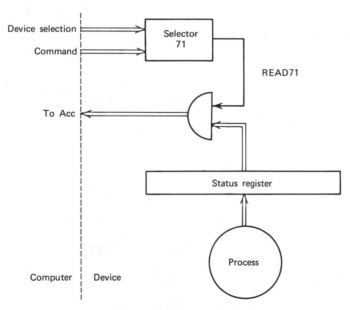

Figure 5.30. Interface components for the status-word transfer.

Table 5.11

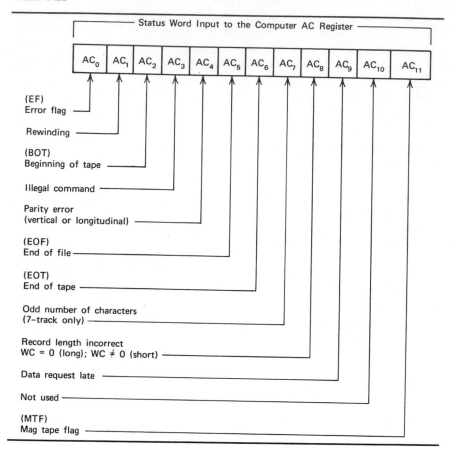

Table 5.12

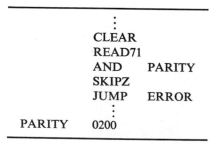

Testing Magnetic Tape Operation

Example. The magnetic tape has finished the transfer of one record using the *DMA*. Test if a parity error has occurred during the operation. The program is shown in Table 5.12.

The first two instructions are used to transfer the status word into the accumulator. The next instruction presents the logical AND operation with the mask containing one in the bit position reserved for the parity error. The mask is 0200. From Table 5.11 we see that this bit corresponds to the parity-error bit. In this way all other bits of the status word are cleared to zero. The last two instructions are used for testing and branching. If the parity-error bit is set, the program will go in the error routine. If the parity-error bit is zero, the program will continue.

Example. Find if the magnetic tape is in the position—beginning of tape. The program is shown in Table 5.13.

Table 5.13

	⋮	
	CLEAR	
	READ71	
	AND	BEGNE
	SKIPZ	
	JUMP	ERROR
	⋮	
BEGNE	1000	

The main difference from the previous case is the mask used to extract the specified bit from the status register. The proper mask is 1000, as one can see from Table 5.11.

Comparison of Different Kinds of Transfer

In the programmed transfer, a great many tasks are performed by the program, while relatively simple tasks are performed by the interface. As a result, the interface is simple. On the other hand, a number of programmed steps is used for each task, thus limiting the speed of the transfer. Typical maximum data transfer rates for programmed operations are below 100 kHz. It is supposed that the whole computer word is transferred but without data formatting and condition checking. Any operation of this kind can considerably decrease the transfer rate. Still, for many typical laboratory processes and control applications, the rates of the programmed data transfer will be adequate.

In the *DMA* transfer, the basic task of the transfer is performed entirely by the hardware. As a result, the interface is substantially more complex than for the programmed transfer. On the other hand, each transfer step is performed in only one computer cycle and the computer can transfer the information more efficiently than through programmed means. The maximum transfer rate of the *DMA* facility can be as high as 500 kHz. Of course, no data formatting and condition checking by the program is possible, since the transfer is performed by hardware only.

Conclusion:

1. Make the estimate of the transfer data rate needed for a given application.

2. See what kind of data formatting and condition checking should be done on each datum during the transfer.

3. Use the programmed transfer whenever possible. It is slower, but it requires a less complicated interface. Also, since the greater number of tasks is performed by the program rather than by the fixed wired interface, it is possible to make adaptations and modifications.

4. Programmed interrupt transfer might provide some advantages over conditional transfer, mainly a more efficient use of the computer time. Also the interrupt is more complicated to program and requires a more elaborate interface design.

5. Direct memory access (*DMA*) is the most efficient way of transferring the data. It enables high-speed transfer but without any data formatting. The *DMA* interface is more complicated than the interface for programmed transfer.

PROBLEMS

1. The following program is stored in the computer:

```
100   CLEAR
101   ADD    I 105
102   COMPL
103   STORE I 106
104   HALT
105   111
106   105
107   000
110   000
111   0001
```

(*a*) What will the contents of the memory address register be after the second instruction is executed? (*b*) What are the contents of the accumulator after the third instruction is executed? (*c*) What are the contents of locations 105 and 106 at the end of the program?

2. The data in peripheral device 40 should be shifted to the left by three places and transferred into peripheral device 41. Design the interface and write the computer program for this task (*a*) using unconditional transfer, (*b*) using conditional transfer, and checking both devices for ready.

3. Peripheral device 37 interrupts the computer at random times. Each time the datum should be stored in the next location of list *X*. When 100 data are received, the device should be disconnected. Design the interface and write the program.

4. Devices 60, 61, and 62 interrupt the computer at random times. The data from the three devices should be stored in lists *X*, *Y*, and *Z*, respectively. Each list is 100 locations long. If any of the lists receives 100 items, further procedure should be stopped.

5. A nuclear detector generates pulses with random amplitudes in the range 0–50. Sort the pulses and count how many times the pulse of a given amplitude has occurred (form the histogram or amplitude probability distribution).

Use program interrupt.

6. Five detectors generate random pulses which should be counted in five memory locations, COUNT0 to COUNT4. Design the interface and write the program, using interrupt transfer.

7. List *T* keeps 200 items which present the temperatures. These items should be transferred one after the other to the peripheral device 50 for experiment control. Design the interface and write the program for conditional transfer. After the one hundredth item has been transferred, the whole process should start from the beginning.

8. Solve problem 7, using the *DMA* transfer. Whenever the device 50 is ready to receive the next datum, it should set the *DMA* request. Use interrupt for *DMA* termination.

9. Write one record on the tap unit 2, using the *DMA*. The word count is 200; the starting address of the memory block is 3000. The address register, count register, and control register are connected as in Figs. 5.25 and 5.27.

10. Use the status word and the control word to perform the following operations on magnetic tape: rewind tape unit 1. Check and wait until tape 1 is at the beginning of tape position. Write one record on tape unit 1. Check for parity. If parity, space reverse the tape and try to write again. Try up to 10 times. If OK, write end of file mark. Otherwise

halt the program. Use the *DMA* transfer, as in problem 9. The status register is connected as in Fig. 5.30.

REFERENCES

1. *Small Computer Handbook*, Digital Equipment Corporation, Maynard, Mass., 1971.
2. E. Burgess, Ed., *On-line Computing Systems*, American Data Processing, Inc., Detroit, 1965.
3. K. H. Beckurts, W. Gläser, G. Krüger, Eds., *Automatic Acquisition and Reduction of Nuclear Data*, Gesellschaft für Kernforschung m.b.H., Karlsruhe, 1964.
4. B. Soucek and A. D. Carlson, *Computers in Neurobiology and Behavior*, John Wiley, New York 1976.

PART II

Detailed Description of Representative Microprocessors

4004/4040 Microprocessors.
8008/8080 and MCOM-8 Microprocessors.
M6800 Microprocessor.
PPS-4 Microprocessor.
PPS-8 Microprocessor.
IMP 4/8/16 and PACE Microprocessors.

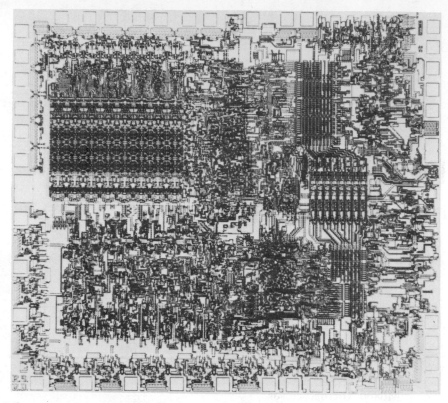

Microprocessor, new tool in instrumentation and process control. The Intel 8080 CPU chip, smaller than 1 cm², performs the functions of thousands of individual logical circuits. (Courtesy of Intel Corporation.)

6

4004/4040
MICROPROCESSORS

Chapter 6 presents 4-bit microprocessors Intel 4004/4040. Basic *CPU*, *ROM*, and *RAM* chips are described. The connection of the basic chips into the microcomputer system is shown. This processor has a 4-bit bus which is used for both address and data. Bus timing is described. The instruction repertoire consists of machine, accumulator, I/O, and *RAM* instructions. A few programming examples are given, including the implementation of a simple logic function.

The material* in this chapter has been adapted in part from a publication of Intel Corporation. The material so published herein is the full responsibility of the author.

6.1. MICROCHIPS

General Description

This new concept in LSI technology makes the power of a general-purpose computer available to almost every logic designer and represents a strong attack on the dependency of systems manufacturers on complicated random logic systems. This component computer from Intel can provide the same arithmetic, control, and computing functions as a minicomputer in as few as two 16-pin dual in-line packages (DIP's) and in less expensive by nearly 2 orders of magnitude.

The set is not designed to compete with the minicomputer, but rather to extend the power of the concept into new ranges of applications. For example, many systems built of SSI and MSI TTL can now be implemented with a totally self-contained system built around this set of devices.

The heart of each system is a single-chip central processor unit (*CPU*) which performs all control and data processing functions. Auxiliary to the

---

* Programs, figures, and tables are courtesy and copyright © 1975 by Intel Corporation. All rights reserved.

CPU are ROM's, which store microprograms and data tables; RAM's, which store data and instructions; and shift registers (SR's), which can expand the I/O capacity of the system. The MCS-4 system communicates with circuits and devices outside the family through "ports" provided on each RAM and ROM.

A system using this set of devices will usually consist of one CPU, from 1 to 16 ROM's, up to 16 RAM's, and an arbitrary number of SR's. A minimum system could be designed with just one CPU and one ROM. With these components, one can build distributed computers, dedicated computers, or personalized computers and can utilize the almost infinite combinations of microprogramming. The designer buys standard devices, and with microprogramming of the ROM fulfills his own unique circuit requirements.

The MCS-4 microcomputer set consists of the following four chips, each packaged in a 16-pin DIP package (Fig. 6.1):

1. A central processor unit chip (CPU): 4004.
2. A read only memory chip (ROM): 4001.
3. A random access memory chip (RAM): 4002.
4. A shift register chip (SR): 4003.

The CPU contains the control unit and the arithmetic unit of a general-purpose microprogrammable computer. The ROM stores microprograms and data tables, the RAM stores data and instructions, and the SR is used in conjunction with I/O devices to effectively increase the number of I/O lines.

The MCS-4 set has been designed for optimum interfaceability; the CPU communicates with the RAM's and ROM's by means of a four-line data bus (D_0, D_1, D_2, D_3). This single data bus is used for all information flow between the chips except for control signals, which are sent to RAM and ROM over five additional lines. One CPU controls up to 16 ROM's (4K x 8 words), 16 RAM's (1280 x 4 words), and 128 I/O lines without requiring any interface circuit. Wi h the addition of a few gates, up to 48 ROM's and RAM's combined and 192 I/O lines can be controlled by one CPU.

The I/O function, although different from the ROM and RAM functions, is physically located in the ROM and RAM chips. Each 4001 and 4002 has four I/O lines for communication with I/O devices (Fig. 6.2).

4001—ROM. The 4001 is a 2048-bit metal-mask-programmable ROM providing custom microprogramming capability for the MCS-4 micro-

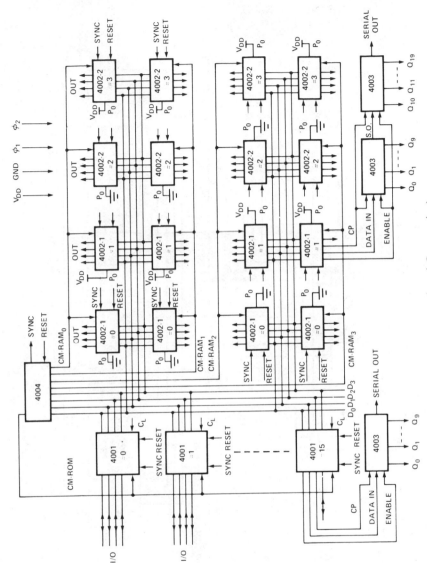

Figure 6.1. MCS-4 system interconnection. (Courtesy of Intel Corporation).

223

224

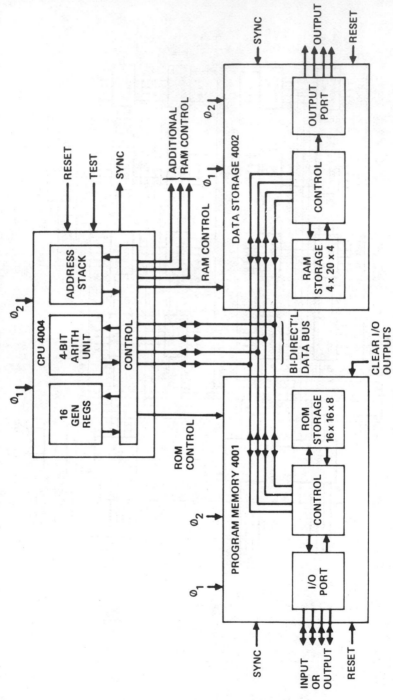

Figure 6.2. Connection of the 4004 *CPU*, *ROM*, and *RAM*. (Courtesy of Intel Corporation).

computer set. Each chip is organized as 256 x 8 bit words which can be used for storing programs or data tables. Each chip also has a 4-bit I/O port, which serves to route information to and from the data bus lines in and out of the system.

4002—RAM. The 4002 performs two functions. As a *RAM*, it stores 320 bits arranged as four registers of 20 4-bit characters each. As a vehicle of communication with peripheral devices, it is provided with four output lines and associated control logic to perform output operations.

4003—SR. The 4003 is a 10-bit serial-in/parallel-out, serial-out shift register. Its function is to increase the number of output lines to interface with I/O devices such as keyboards, displays, printers, teletypewriters, switches, readers, and analog/digital converters.

4004—CPU. The 4004 is a central processor unit designed to work in conjunction with the other members of the MCS-4 microcomputer set to form a completely self-contained system. The *CPU* communicates with the other members of the set through a four-line data bus and with the peripheral devices through the *RAM, ROM,* or *SR* I/O ports. The *CPU* chip contains five command control lines, four of which are used to control the *RAM* chips (each line can control up to 4 *RAM* chips for a total system capacity of 16 *RAM*'s) and one of which controls a bank of up to 16 *ROM*'s.

A typical system composed of the basic four chips is shown in Fig. 6.1. The interconnection between *ROM, RAM,* and *CPU* chips is shown in Fig. 6.2.

Timing

For correct operation of the system two nonoverlapping clock phases—ϕ_1, ϕ_2—must be externally supplied to the 4001, 4002, and 4004. The 4004 will generate a SYNC signal every eight clock periods and will send it to the 4001's and 4002's. The SYNC signal marks the beginning of each instruction cycle. The 4001's and 4002's will then generate internal timing, using SYNC and ϕ_1, ϕ_2.

Basic instruction execution requires 8 or 16 cycles of a 750-kHz clock. In a typical sequence, the *CPU* sends 12 bits of address (in three 4-bit bytes on the data bus) to the *ROM*'s in the first three cycles (A_1, A_2, A_3). This address selects 1 out of 16 chips and 1 out of 256 8-bit words in that chip. The selected *ROM* chip sends back 8 bits of instruction (OPR, OPA) to the *CPU* in the next two cycles (M_1, M_2). This instruction is sent over the four-line data bus in two 4-bit bytes. The instruction is then interpreted and executed in the final three cycles (X_1, X_2, X_3). (See Fig. 6.3.)

When an I/O instruction is received from the *ROM*, data are transferred to or from the *CPU* accumulator on the four *ROM* I/O lines during X_2 time.

A set of four *RAM*'s is controlled by one of four command control lines from the *CPU*. The address of a *RAM* chip, register, and character is stored in two index registers in the *CPU* and is transferred to the *RAM* during X_2, X_3 time when a *RAM* instruction is executed. When the *RAM* output instruction is received by the *CPU*, the content of the *CPU* accumulator is transferred to the four *RAM* output lines.

The *CPU*, *RAM*'s, and *ROM*'s can be controlled by an external RESET line. While RESET is activated, the contents of the registers and flip-flops are cleared. After RESET, the *CPU* will start from address 0 and *CM-RAM₀* is selected.

6.2. CENTRAL PROCESSING UNIT

A block diagram of the 4004 *CPU* is shown in Fig. 6.4. The pin connection is shown in Fig. 6.5.

Four-Bit Adder

The 4-bit adder is of the ripple-through carry type. One term of the addition comes from the TEMP register, which communicates with the internal bus on one side and can transfer data or $\overline{\text{data}}$ to the adder. The other term of the addition comes from the accumulator and carry flip-flop. Both data and $\overline{\text{data}}$ can be transferred. The output of the adder is transferred to the accumulator and carry FF. The accumulator is provided with a shifter to implement rotate-right and rotate-left instructions. The accumulator also communicates with the command control register, special *ROM*'s, the condition flip-flop, and the internal bus. The command control register holds a 3-bit code used for *CM-RAM* line switching. The special *ROM*'s perform a code conversion for DAA (decimal adjust accumulator) and KBP (keyboard process) instructions. The special *ROM*'s also communicate with the internal bus. The condition logic senses ADD = 0 and ACC = 0 conditions, the state of the carry FF, and the state of an external signal (TEST) to implement JCN (JUMP on condition) and ISZ (INCREMENT index register, SKIP if zero) instructions.

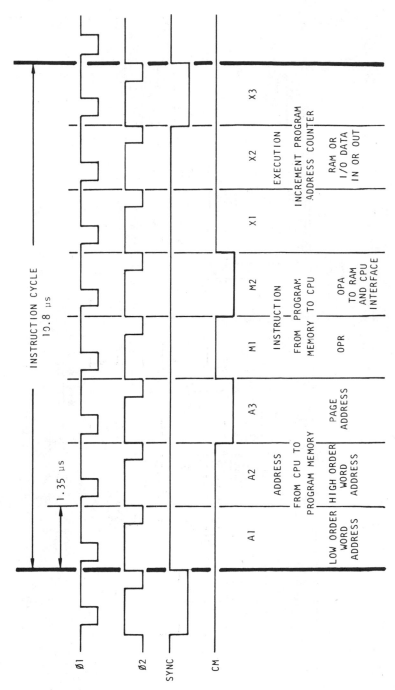

Figure 6.3. MCS-4 basic instruction cycle. (Courtesy of Intel Corporation).

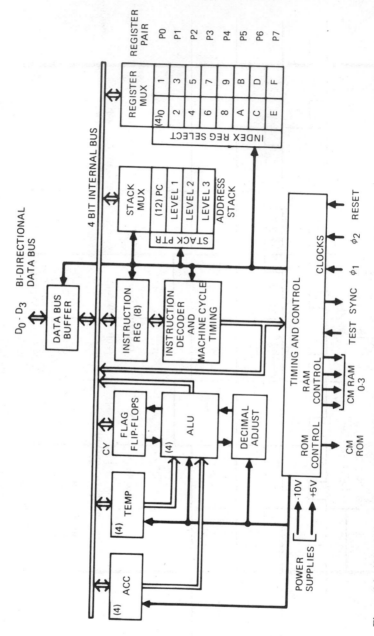

Figure 6.4. 4004 *CPU* block diagram. (Courtesy of Intel Corporation).

228

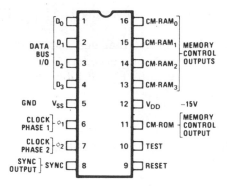

Figure 6.5. 4004 *CPU* pin connection. (Courtesy of Intel Corporation).

Instruction Register Decoder and Control

The instruction register (consisting of the OPR register and OPA register, each 4 bits wide) is loaded with the contents of the internal bus (at M_1 and M_2 time in the instruction cycle) through a multiplexer and holds the instruction fetched from *ROM*. The instructions are decoded in the instruction decoder and appropriately gated with timing signals to provide the control signals for the various functional blocks.

Address Register (Program Counter and Stack) and Address Incrementer

The address register is a dynamic *RAM* cell array of 4 x 12 bits. It contains one level used to store the instruction address (program counter) and three levels that serve as a stack for subroutine calls. The stack address is provided by the effective address counter and by the refresh counter, and it is multiplexed to the decoder.

The address when read is stored in an address buffer and is demultiplexed to the internal bus during A_1, A_2, and A_3 in three 4-bit slices (see Fig. 6.3 for the basic instruction cycle). The address is incremented by a 4-bit carry look-ahead circuit (address incrementer) after each 4-bit slice is sent out on the data bus. The incremented address is transferred back to the address buffer and finally written back into the address register.

Index Register

The index register is a dynamic *RAM* cell array of 16 x 4 bits and has two modes of operation. In one mode the index register provides 16 directly addressable storage locations for intermediate computation and control. In the second mode the index register provides 8 pairs of addressable storage locations for addressing RAM and ROM, as well as for storing data fetched from ROM.

The index register address is provided by the internal bus and by the refresh counter and is multiplexed to the index register decoder.

Individual 4-bit registers R_x carry the names 0 to F, and 8-bit register pairs P_x carry the names 0 to 7.

6.3. RANDOM ACCESS MEMORIES, READ ONLY MEMORIES, AND INPUT/OUTPUT PORTS

Program Memory (ROM)

Program memory stores the instruction to be executed by the CPU and is defined by the CPU instruction set as a page-oriented memory of 256 words per page, as shown in Fig. 6.6. The CPU addresses the page and word, and the program memory sends the 8-bit word at that address to the CPU.

The 12-bit addressing capability of the CPU allows direct access to 16 pages with the four $A3$ bits used as page address. The eight bits at $A1$ and $A2$ are used for the word address within a page. It is important to understand the page organization in terms of the address control instructions (jumping and branching). Certain address instructions use the full 12 bits of address and may be used to change control within a page or from page to page. Other address control instructions use only 8 bits of address and are limited to changing control within a page.

Data Storage (RAM)

The microsystems use the Intel 4002 RAM register devices for program-controlled data storage. Each 4002 is organized as four registers of 20 characters apiece, as shown in Fig. 6.7. Each 20-character register consists of 16 individually addressable characters of main storage plus 4 instruction-selectable status characters.

The instruction capability of the CPU allows addressing up to 32 of the 4002 RAM devices. This is accomplished through an organization of eight banks, each of four RAM chips. RAM banks are selected by the DCL instruction that specifies which of the four CM-RAM lines out of the CPU will be active. In turn, the active CM-RAM line designates which RAM bank will respond to the SRC instruction. The SRC instruction selects the RAM chip, register, and character. A summary of RAM addressing is given in Table 6.1.

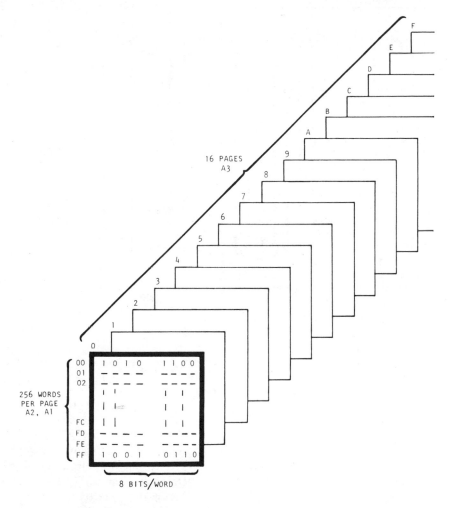

Figure 6.6. *ROM* organization as defined by the *CPU* instructions. (Courtesy of Pro-Log Corporation).

Table 6.1. *RAM* **Addressing**

Level	Instruction
RAM bank	DCL
RAM chip	SRC, even register high-order bits
RAM register	SRC, even register low-order bits
RAM character	SRC, odd register 4 bits

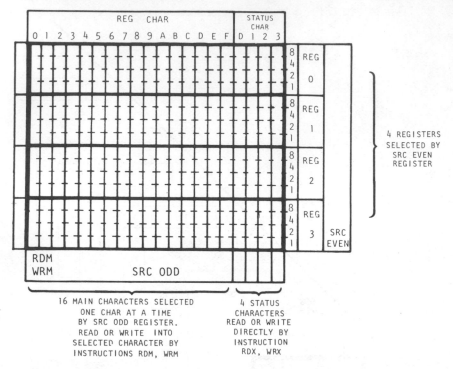

Figure 6.7. *RAM* organization. (Courtesy of Pro-Log Corporation).

Inputs and Outputs

The flow of data into and out of microsystems is accomplished through I/O ports of four lines each. To accomplish an input or output function a port must first be addressed by the *CPU* instruction SRC. The even register of the SRC pair contains the address of the port to be selected. Once a port has been addressed, it remains selected for as many input or output operations as desired until another port is addressed.

There are two types of output ports and one type of input port. Each *RAM* register device has an output port packaged physically within the device. This port shares chip-select addressing with the *RAM* but has its own instruction WMP for the transfer of data from the accumulator to the port. The port latches any data sent to it and retains them as a stable output until a subsequent WMP instruction changes the data. The *RAM* port lines are MOS low-level active outputs capable of driving one low-power TTL load.

6.4. INSTRUCTION SET

The instruction repertoire of the 4004 consists of:

(*a*) 16 machine instructions (5 of which are double length)
(*b*) 14 accumulator group instructions
(*c*) 15 input/output and *RAM* instructions

The three groups of instructions are listed in Tables 6.2, 6.3, and 6.4. Conditional codes for the JUMP instructions are shown in Table 6.5. Most of the instructions are clearly defined in the tables. Here are more detailed descriptions for some instructions.

JUMP ON CONDITION   JCN

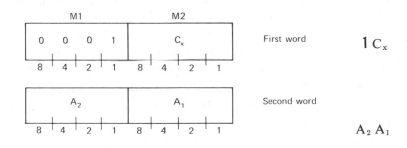

If the designated condition (C_x) is true, program control is transferred to the instruction located at the 8-bit address, A_2, A_1, of the current page; otherwise program control continues in sequence. If the JCN occupies the last two positions of a page or overlaps the page boundary, program control is transferred to the 8-bit address on the next page in sequence.

JCN is one of the two decision-making instructions of the *CPU*, the other being ISZ. JCN allows a decision on the following tests:

Test accumulator for zero or nonzero.
Test carry bit for logic one or zero.
Test external input lead for high or low.

Table 6.5 provides detailed definitions of conditions C_x.

Table 6.2. Sixteen Machine Instructions

Hex Coding		Mnemonic		Description of Operation
		OPR	OPA	
0	0	NOP		No operation.
1	C_x	JCN	C_x	Jump on condition C_x to the program memory
A_2	A_1		LABEL	address A_1, A_2; otherwise continue in sequence.
2	P_x0	FIM	P_x	Fetch immediately from program memory data
D_2	D_1	D_2	D_1	D_1, D_2 to index register pair P_x.
2	P_x1	SRC	P_x	Send register control. Send the contents of index register pair P_x to I/O ports and RAM register as chip-select and RAM character address.
3	P_x0	FIN	P_x	Fetch indirectly. Send contents of register pair 0 out as a program memory address. Data fetched are placed into register pair P_x.
3	P_x1	JIN	P_x	Jump indirectly. Jump to the program memory address designated by contents of register pair P_x.
4	A_3	JUN		Jump unconditionally to program memory ad-
A_2	A_1		LABEL	dress A_1, A_2, A_3.
5	A_3	JMS		Jump to subroutine located at program memory
A_2	A_1		LABEL	address A_1, A_2, A_3. Save previous address (push down in stack).
6	R_x	INC	R_x	Increment contents of register R_x.
7	R_x	ISZ	R_x	Increment and step on zero. Increment contents
A_2	A_1		LABEL	of register R_x: if result is not 0 go to program memory address A_1, A_2; otherwise step to the next instruction in sequence.
8	R_x	ADD	R_x	Add contents of register R_x to accumulator.
9	R_x	SUB	R_x	Subtract contents of register R_x to accumulator with borrow.
A	R_x	LD	R_x	Load contents of register R_x to accumulator.
B	R_x	XCH	R_x	Exchange contents of index register R_x and accumulator.
C	D_x	BBL	D_x	Branch back one level in stack to the program memory address stored by a prior JMS instruction. Load data D_x to accumulator.

Table 6.2.   (*Continued*)

Hex Coding	Mnemonic OPR	OPA	Description of Operation
D D_x	LDM	D_x	Load data D_x to accumulator.
E X	I/O and RAM register instructions		
F X	Accumulator Instructions		

A_1 Low-order address bits
A_2 High-order address bits
A_3 Chip select
P_x1 Register pairs P_0 through P_7, designated by odd characters 1, 3, 5, 7, 9, B, D, F
P_x0 Register pairs P_0 through P_7, designated by even characters 0, 2, 4, 6, 8, A, C, E
R_x Register $0 \rightarrow F$
D_x Data
D_1 Data for odd register
D_2 Data for even register
C_x JUMP conditions

FETCH IMMEDIATE   FIM

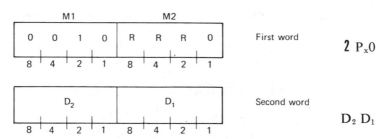

Load the 8 bits of data from the second word, D_2, D_1 to the designated pair of index registers P_x0, where D_2 is data for the even register and D_1 is data for the odd register.

FIM uses the even register numbers to designate a pair. The only valid operand codes for P_x0 are 0, 2, 4, 6, 8, A, C, and E. FIM provides the most efficient way to initialize a pair of index registers.

RRR defines one of the eight register pairs $P0$ through $P7$. The 0 following RRR is part of the command decoding and distinguishes the FIM from the SRC.

Table 6.3.   Accumulator Instructions

HEX CODING	MNEMONIC OPR	OPA	DESCRIPTION OF OPERATION
F 0	CLB		Clear both. (Accumulator and carry.)
F 1	CLC		Clear carry.
F 2	IAC		Increment accumulator.
F 3	CMC		Complement carry.
F 4	CMA		Complement accumulator.
F 5	RAL		Rotate left. (Accumulator and carry.)
F 6	RAR		Rotate right. (Accumulator and carry.)
F 7	TCC		Transmit carry to accumulator and clear carry.
F 8	DAC		Decrement accumulator.
F 9	TCS		Transfer carry subtract and clear carry.
F A	STC		Set carry.
F B	DAA		Decimal adjust accumulator.
F C	KBP		Keyboard process. Converts the contents of the accumulator from a one out of four code to a binary code.
F D	DCL		Designate command line.
F E			
F F			

SEND REGISTER CONTROL   SRC

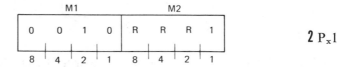

2P_x1

Send the contents of index register pair P_x1 to the I/O ports and *RAM* registers as chip select and/or *RAM* character select. SRC uses the odd register numbers to designate a pair. The only valid operand codes for P_x1 are 1, 3, 5, 7, 9, B, D, and F.

RRR defines one of the eight register pairs $P0$ through $P7$. The 1 following RRR is part of the command decoding and distinguishes the SRC from the FIM.

Table 6.4. I/O and RAM Register Instructions

HEX CODING	MNEMONIC OPR	OPA	DESCRIPTION OF OPERATION
E 0	WRM		Write the contents of the accumulator into the previously selected RAM register character.
E 1	WMP		Write the contents of the accumulator into the previously selected RAM output port. (Output lines.)
E 2	WRR		Write the contents of the accumulator into the previously selected output port. (I/O lines.)
E 3	WPM		Write the contents of the accumulator into the previously selected RAM program memory.
E 4	WR0		Write the contents of the accumulator into the previously selected RAM status character 0.
E 5	WR1		Write the contents of the accumulator into the previously selected RAM status character 1.
E 6	WR2		Write the contents of the accumulator into the previously selected RAM status character 2.
E 7	WR3		Write the contents of the accumulator into the previously selected RAM status character 3.
E 8	SBM		Subtract the previously selected RAM register character from accumulator with borrow.
E 9	RDM		Read the previously selected RAM register character into the accumulator.
E A	RDR		Read the contents of the previously selected input port into the accumulator. (I/O lines.)
E B	ADM		Add the previously selected RAM register character to accumulator with carry.
F C	RD0		Read the previously selected RAM status character 0 into accumulator.
E D	RD1		Read the previously selected RAM status character 1 into accumulator.
E E	RD2		Read the previously selected RAM status character 2 into accumulator.
E F	RD3		Read the previously selected RAM status character 3 into accumulator.

It is necessary to address the I/O port or *RAM* register character using an SRC instruction before an I/O operation or a *RAM* register operation can be performed. The same SRC instruction can be used to address both I/O ports and *RAM* registers; however, the meaning of the address in the designated pair $P_x 1$ is different for each, as shown in Fig. 6.8.

The I/O port is addressed by the contents of the even register designated as P_x. The odd register does not serve any purpose in selecting I/O ports.

Table 6.5. C_x Condition Table for JCN Instruction

JCN HEX	C_x MNEMONIC	C_8	C_4	C_2	C_1	Invert Jump Condition Jump if Accumulator = 0 Jump if Carry Bit = 1 Jump if Test Input = 0 (High)
10		0	0	0	0	NO OPERATION
11	TO	0	0	0	1	Jump if test = 0 (High)
12	C1	0	0	1	0	Jump if CY = 1
13	TO+C1	0	0	1	1	Jump if test = 0 or CY = 1
14	AO	0	1	0	0	Jump if AC = 0
15	TO+AO	0	1	0	1	Jump if test = 0 or AC = 0
16	C1+AO	0	1	1	0	Jump if CY = 1 or AC = 0
17	TO+C1+AO	0	1	1	1	Jump if test = 0 or CY = 1 or AC = 0
18		1	0	0	0	Jump Unconditionally
19	T1	1	0	0	1	Jump if test = 1 (Low)
1A	CO	1	0	1	0	Jump if CY = 0
1B	T1CO	1	0	1	1	Jump if test = 1 and CY = 0
1C	A1	1	1	0	0	Jump if AC $\neq$ 0
1D	T1A1	1	1	0	1	Jump if test = 1 and AC $\neq$ 0
1E	COA1	1	1	1	0	Jump if CY = 0 and AC $\neq$ 0
1F	T1COA1	1	1	1	1	Jump if test = 1 and CY = 0 and AC $\neq$ 0

The *RAM* chip select is addressed by the high-order 2 bits of the even register, the *RAM* register within the selected chip is addressed by the low-order 2 bits of the even register, and the character within the *RAM* register is addressed by the 4 bits of the odd register.

Addressing of the I/O port and *RAM* registers by the even register is tabulated in Fig. 6.8. The table covers any one bank of *RAM* registers. To select other *RAM* banks refer to the DCL instructions.

JUMP to SUBROUTINE   JMS

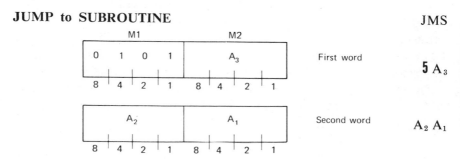

$$5 A_3$$

$$A_2 A_1$$

ELEMENT ADDRESSED	REGISTER PAIR P_X	
	EVEN REGISTER	ODD REGISTER
I/O PORT	PORT SELECT 8 4 2 1	NOT USED 8 4 2 1
RAM REGISTER	CHIP SELECT / REGISTER SELECT 8 4 2 1	CHARACTER 8 4 2 1

CONTENTS OF EVEN REGISTER	I/O PORT SELECTED	RAM # AND RAM REGISTER SELECTED			
		RAM #	REGISTER	RAM DEVICE TYPE	RAM PIN 10 WIRED
0	0	0	0		
1	1	0	1	4002-1	HIGH
2	2	0	2		
3	3	0	3		
4	4	1	0		
5	5	1	1	4002-1	LOW
6	6	1	2		
7	7	1	3		
8	8	2	0		
9	9	2	1	4002-2	HIGH
A	A	2	2		
B	B	2	3		
C	C	3	0		
D	D	3	1	4002-2	LOW
E	E	3	2		
F	F	3	3		

Figure 6.8. Input/output port and *RAM* selection for one bank by even register contents, as Used with SRC instruction.

239

The subroutine address stack is pushed down one level. The program address counter, containing the 12-bit address of the instruction following the second word of the JMS, is transferred to the topmost stack level. Program control is transferred to the instruction located at A_3, A_2, and A_1 from program memory to the program address counter.

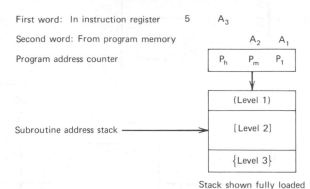

Stack shown fully loaded

BRANCH BACK and LOAD Accumulator   BBL

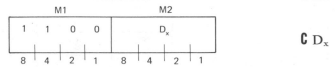

$C\ D_x$

The BBL is used to return from subroutine to main program. The subroutine address stack is pulled up one level. The topmost address is placed in the program address counter, causing program control to be transferred to the sequential instruction following the previous JMS.

6.5. PROGRAMMING EXAMPLES

Addition through Index Registers

Addition of two 4-bit numbers can be performed directly by the ADD or ADM instruction. The ADD instruction adds from one of the index registers to the accumulator, and the ADM adds from the selected *RAM* register into the accumulator (Fig. 6.9).

Numbers longer than 4 bits can be added in multiples of 4 bits. This technique is referred to as *multiple-precision arithmetic*. The carry bit automatically maintains the carry/link between each group of 4 bits to be added. The example shows a routine for adding two 16-bit binary numbers. Note that the first step clears the carry bit. The least significant bits are added

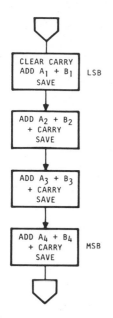

EVEN		PAIR		ODD
E		7		F
C		6		D
A	A_4	5	A_3	B
8	A_2	4	A_1	9
6		3		7
4	B_4	2	B_3	5
2	B_2	1	B_1	3
0		0		1

INDEX REGISTER MAP

Multiple Precision Addition

	ADR	INSTR	LABEL	MNEMONIC	OPERAND	COMMENTS
	0	F1	(ADD)	CLC		ADD AB89 TO 4523
	1	A9		LD	9	ADD REG 9 TO REG 3
	2	83		ADD	3	
	3	B3		XCH	3	
	4	A8		LD	8	ADD REG 8 TO REG2 WITH CARRY
	5	82		ADD	2	
	6	B2		XCH	2	
	7	AB		LD	B	ADD REG B TO REG5 WITH CARRY
	8	85		ADD	5	
	9	B5		XCH	5	
	A	AA		LD	A	ADD REG A TO REG4 WITH CARRY
	B	84		ADD	4	
	C	84		XCH	4	
	D	C0		BBL	0	RETURN

Figure 6.9. Multiple-precision addition: flow chart, register map, and program. (Courtesy of Pro-Log Corporation).

first so that the carry/link will propagate. If an overflow occurs, the carry bit will contain a 1 at the end of the routine.

Generating a Control Pulse

The rectangular pulse should be generated by the program on port 2. The simple program is shown in Fig. 6.10. The FIM instruction is used to load

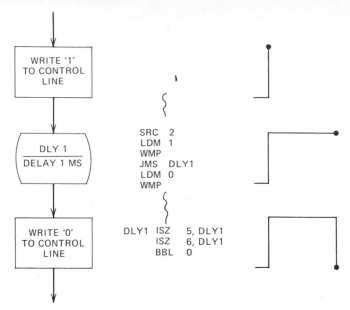

Figure 6.10. Program to generate a pulse. (Courtesy and Copyright © 1975 of Integrated Computer Systems).

the port address into the register, and SRC then selects the port. The LDM instruction brings 1 into the accumulator, and WMP sends it to the selected port. The DLY subroutine uses the INC instruction to create the delay. The INC instruction uses register 5 as a counter. When it overflows, after 16 counts, the counting is cascaded into register 6. This technique can be extended to any number of registers for large counts. Eventually the program returns from the subroutine, and instructions LDM and WMP send the 0 to the selected port.

Sensing Input Lines to Implement a Simple Logic Function

This example shows the implementation of the logic function

$$\text{Output} = (A \cdot B) + (C \cdot D)$$

The flow chart is shown in Fig. 6.11, and the mnemonic code in Table 6.6.

6.6.   4040 CENTRAL PROCESSOR

Additional Features

The 4040 is a single-chip 4-bit parallel MOS central processor. It is intended as an enhanced version of the 4004 and as such retains all of the functional

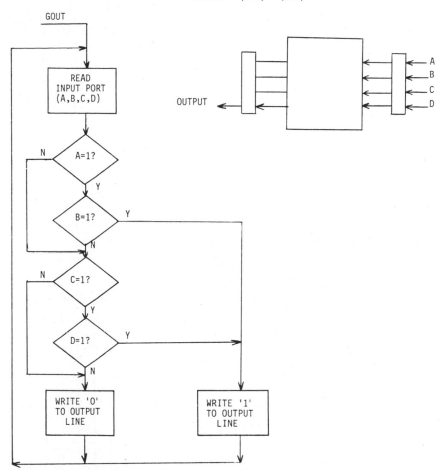

Figure 6.11. Program to emulate simple logic. (Courtesy and Copyright © 1975 of Integrated Computer Systems).

capability of that device. It does, however, provide several significant improvements in hardware and software. These are listed briefly here.

The 4040 software contains all of the 4004 instruction set and includes an additional 14 instructions, providing:

- Halt
- Logical operations
- Interrupt disable, enable functions
- *ROM* bank switching
- Index register bank switching

New 4040 instructions are shown in Table 6.7.

Table 6.6.

ADR	INSTRUCTION BYTE 1	BYTE 2	LABEL	MNEMONIC	OPERAND	COMMENTS
						CY ACC
			GOUT:	FIM	2,0	
				SRC	2	
			LOOP:	RDR		[X] | A B C D
				RAL		[A] | B C D X
				JCN	2,A1	
				RAL		[B] | C D X A
				JUN	CKC	
			A1:	RAL		[B] | C D X A
				JCN	2,OUT	; JUMP IF A,B=1
			CKC:	RAL		[C] | D X A B
				JCN	10,OUT	; JUMP IF C=0
				RAL		[D] | X A B C
			OUT:	TCC		; CY BIT BECOMES OUTPUT
				WMP		
				JUN	LOOP	

Copyright 1975 Integrated Computer Systems. Reprinted with permission.

Table 6.7.

MNEMONIC	OPR $D_3 D_2 D_1 D_0$	OPA $D_3 D_2 D_1 D_0$	DESCRIPTION OF OPERATION
HLT	0 0 0 0	0 0 0 1	Halt — inhibit program counter and data buffers.
BBS	0 0 0 0	0 0 1 0	Branch Back from Interrupt and restore the previous SRC. The Program Counter and send register control are restored to their pre-interrupt value.
LCR	0 0 0 0	0 0 1 1	The contents of the COMMAND REGISTER are transferred to the ACCUMULATOR.
OR4	0 0 0 0	0 1 0 0	The 4 bit contents of register #4 are logically "OR-ed" with the ACCUM.
OR5	0 0 0 0	0 1 0 1	The 4 bit contents of index register #5 are logically "OR-ed" with the ACCUMULATOR.
AN6	0 0 0 0	0 1 1 0	The 4 bit contents of index register #6 are logically "AND-ed" with the ACCUMULATOR
AN7	0 0 0 0	0 1 1 1	The 4 bit contents of index register #7 are logically "AND-ed" with the ACCUMULATOR.
DB0	0 0 0 0	1 0 0 0	DESIGNATE ROM BANK 0. CM-ROM$_0$ becomes enabled.
DB1	0 0 0 0	1 0 0 1	DESIGNATE ROM BANK 1. CM-ROM$_1$ becomes enabled.
SB0	0 0 0 0	1 0 1 0	SELECT INDEX REGISTER BANK 0. The index register; 0 - 7.
SB1	0 0 0 0	1 0 1 1	SELECT INDEX REGISTER BANK 1. The index registers 0* - 7*.
EIN	0 0 0 0	1 1 0 0	ENABLE INTERRUPT.
DIN	0 0 0 0	1 1 0 1	DISABLE INTERRUPT.
RPM	0 0 0 0	1 1 1 0	READ PROGRAM MEMORY.

The 4040 contains the necessary hardware to accept and process single-level interrupts. The interrupt vectors program to location 003, while saving some key processor conditions.

The address stack has been increased from 4 × 12 bits to 8 × 12 bits, allowing up to seven levels of subroutine nesting.

The index register array has been increased from 16 4-bit registers to 24 4-bit registers.

The 4040 is provided with a STOP control which allows the user to halt the processor at an instruction cycle. This feature permits the implementation of a "single-step" operation for program debugging.

The 4040 can address up to 8K × 8-words of *ROM* with no external logic required. This is implemented by having two 4K × 8 memory banks that can be toggled between.

The 4040 is provided with separate power supply pins for the timing circuitry and for the output buffers. These features allow a low-power standby mode by shutting off the main power supply and operating only the timing. Since the output buffers have a separate supply, they can be directly interfaced to other circuit types such as *N*-channel MOS or CMOS. For single-supply systems all three power supply pins can be tied together.

Interrupt Mode

The 4040 is provided with an asynchronous interrupt input and an interrupt acknowledge output. Figure 6.12 presents the basic timing for the interrupt mode. The sequence of events is as follows:

(*a*) During instruction cycle 1 an interrupt occurs and is gated into the interrupt latch during M_2.

(*b*) At A_1 of the next single-cycle instruction the interrupt flip-flop is set. As in the case of the STOP example, if the processor is executing a double-cycle instruction it is allowed to complete it.

(*c*) During instruction cycle 3, the program counter is prevented from incrementing and the data input buffers are inhibited at M_1 and M_2. A JUMP TO SUBROUTINE (JMS) instruction is forced on the internal data bus. The subroutine address is forced to be page 0, location 3. At X_3 the interrupt acknowledge flip-flop is set and its buffered output is available on the interrupt acknowledge pin. The instruction at location 0, 3 begins the interrupt processing routine.

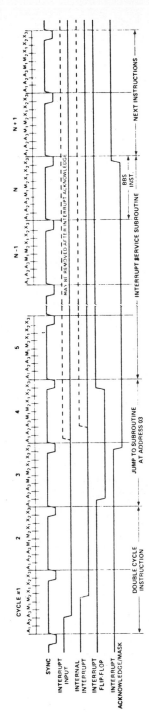

Figure 6-12. 4040 timing. (Courtesy of Intel Corporation).

Table 6.8.

Bank	Page	Word	Instruction	Comment
0	6	82	SRC 4	(IR 8,9) sent to ROM & RAM, Load SRC Reg.
0	6	83	INC 9	Interrupt occurs here.
0	6	84	(JMS 0)	Interrupt acknowledged, 6,84 saved in stack; instruction at 6,84 ignored.
0	6	84	(3)	
0	0	3	SB1	Select IR Bank 1.
0	0	4	XCH 7	(ACC) $\rightarrow$ IR7* — ACC saved.
0	0	5	LCR	(CR) $\rightarrow$ ACC
0	0	6	RAL	(CY) $\rightarrow Acc_0$, $Acc_0 \rightarrow Acc_1$ . . . $Acc_3 \rightarrow$ CY
0	0	7	XCH 6	(ACC) $\rightarrow$ IR6* CY, CR saved.
0	0	8	.	
0	0	9	.	Routine for determining and servicing interrupt is executed here.
.	.	.	.	
0	P	n	XCH 6	(IR6*) $\rightarrow$ ACC
		n+1	RAR	$ACC_0 \rightarrow$ CY — CY restored
		n+2	DCL	$ACC_0 \rightarrow CR_0$, $ACC_1 \rightarrow CR_1$, $ACC_2 \rightarrow CR_2$, CR restored.
		n+3	XCH 7	(IR7*) $\rightarrow$ ACC
		n+4	BBS	Address 6,84 loaded into PC; contents of SRC register sent out;
0	6	84	WRM	program restored.
		.	.	

(*d*) The interrupt acknowledge flip-flop remains set until the interrupt has been processed and the new BRANCH BACK and SRC (BBS) instruction has been executed (instruction cycle *N*). No new interrupt can be entered while interrupt acknowledge is active. Note that the interrupt signal may be removed after interrupt acknowledge occurs.

Saving and Restoring Processor Status

To have an effective interrupt handling capability the processor must be able to save current program and status register values and to restore them when the interrupt processing is complete. In the 4040 the following values must be saved:

- Content of accumulator and carry flip-flop
- Content of command register
- Content of as many index registers as required
- The value of the last SRC address sent out before interrupt
- Content of the program counter
- The current *ROM* bank ($CM\text{-}ROM_0 + CM\text{-}RAM_1$).

Interrupt Processing

An interrupt processing routine is, in general, composed of three parts (Table 6.8):

(*a*) The instructions required to save the current processor status.
(*b*) A portion which determines and services the interrupting device.
(*c*) The instructions required to restore program control to the pre-interrupt conditions.

In the first example, the processor is used with a single *ROM* bank, and index register (*IR*) bank 1 is used to save status [accumulator/carry, command register (*CR*)]. The six remaining registers in *IR* bank 1 are available for interrupt servicing. In addition to being relatively simple, this scheme has the advantage of saving processor status with the fewest number of instructions. Note that, since only one *ROM* bank is available, only the lowest 3 bits of the *CR* need be saved. This allows saving the *CR* and *CY* to be merged in the same register location.

REFERENCES

1. MCS–4 Microcomputer Set, Users Manual, Intel Corp., Santa Clara, Ca., 1974.
2. MCS–40 User's Manual For Logic Designers, Intel Corp., Santa Clara, Ca., 1975.
3. Brewer, M.: *The Designers Guide to Programmed Logic, for PLS 400 Systems*, Pro–Log Corp., Monterey, Cal., 1973.
4. Collins, D. C., E. R. Garen, and M. Lernas,: *Software Development for Microcomputers*, Integrated Computer Systems, Culver City, Ca., 1975.

7

8008/8080 AND MCOM-8 MICROPROCESSORS

Chapter 7 presents 8-bit microprocessors Intel 8008/8080 and Nippon MCOM-8, which are software compatible at the source code level. The basic *CPU* chip is described, as well as a connection into the microcomputer system. The 8080 processor has an 8-bit data bus and a 16-bit address bus. Four modes of memory addressing are described: direct, through the registers, immediate, and through the stack. The instruction repertoire consists of data moving, conditional jump, stack, subroutine, arithmetic, logical, and I/O instructions. A few programming examples are shown, including subroutines and interrupts. Priority interrupts and party-line I/O are described.

The material* in this chapter has been adapted in part from a publication of Intel Corporation. The material so published herein is the full responsibility of the author.

7.1. MICROPROCESSOR 8080

Microprocessor 8080 is presented in block diagram in Fig. 7.1. The pin connection is shown in Fig. 7.2.

General Description

The 8080 is a complete 8-bit parallel central processing unit (*CPU*) for use in general-purpose digital computer systems. It is fabricated on a single LSI chip using Intel's *n*-channel silicon gate MOS process, thus offering much higher performance than conventional microprocessors (2-μsec instruction cycle). A complete microcomputer system is formed when the 8080 *CPU* is interfaced with I/O ports (up to 256 input and 256 output ports) and any type or speed of semiconductor memory.

Although significantly higher in performance than existing microprocessors, the 8080 has been designed to be software compatible at the source

---

* Programs, figures, and tables are courtesy and copyright © 1975 by Intel Corporation. All rights reserved.

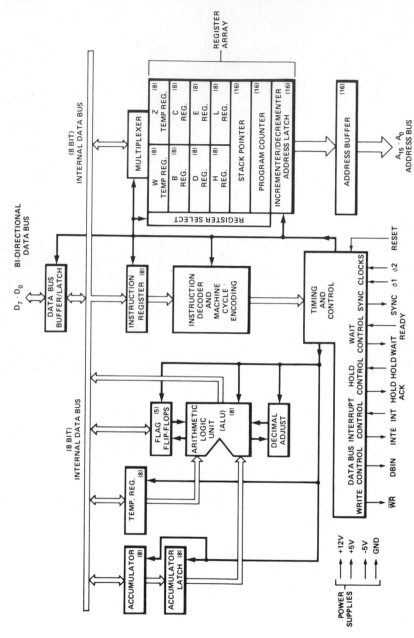

Figure 7.1. 8080 functional block diagram. (Courtesy of Intel Corporation).

252

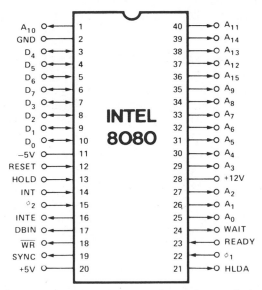

Figure 7.2. 8080 *CPU* pin connection. (Courtesy of Intel Corporation).

code level with Intel's 8008 microprocessor. Like the 8008, the 8080 contains six 8-bit data registers, an 8-bit accumulator, four 8-bit temporary registers, four testable flag bits, and an 8-bit parallel binary arithmetic unit. The 8080 also provides decimal arithmetic capability, and it includes 16-bit arithmetic and immediate operators which greatly simplify memory address calculations and high-speed arithmetic operations.

The 8080 has a stack architecture, wherein any portion of the external memory can be used as a last-in/first-out stack to store/retrieve the contents of the accumulator, the flags, or any of the data registers.

The 8080 also contains a 16-bit stack pointer to control the addressing of this external stack. One of the major advantages of the stack is that multiple-level interrupts can readily be handled, since complete system status can easily be saved when an interrupt occurs and then be restored after the interrupt. Another major advantage is that almost unlimited subroutine nesting is possible.

This processor has been designed to greatly simplify system design. Separate 16-line address and 8-line bidirectional data busses allow direct interface to memories and I/O ports. Control signals, which require no decoding, are provided directly by the processor. All busses, including control, are TTL compatible.

To the programmer, the computer is represented as consisting of the following parts:

1. Seven working registers in which all data operations occur, and which provide one means for addressing memory.

2. Memory, which may hold program instructions or data and which must be addressed location by location in order to access stored information.

3. The program counter, whose contents indicate the next program instruction to be executed.

4. The stack pointer, a register which enables various portions of memory to be used as *stacks*. These in turn facilitate the execution of subroutines and the handling of interrupts as described later.

5. Input/output, which is the interface between a program and the outside world.

Register Map

The 8080 provides the programmer with an 8-bit accumulator and six additional 8-bit "scratch-pad" registers.

These seven working registers are numbered and referenced via the integers 0, 1, 2, 3, 4, 5, and 7; by convention, these registers may also be accessed via the letters *B*, *C*, *D*, *E*, *H*, *L*, and *A* (for the accumulator), respectively.

Some 8080 operations reference the working registers in pairs designated by the letters *B*, *D*, *H*, and *PSW*. These correspondences are shown in Figs. 7.1 and 7.3.

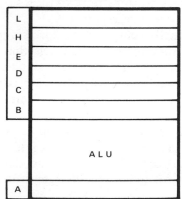

Figure 7.3. 8080 register map. (Courtesy of Intel Corporation).

Pair references are used to deal with 16-bit information, as follows:

Pair Reference	Registers
B	*B–C*
D	*D–E*
H	*H–L*

Typically the register pair keeps an address for *ROM* or *RAM*.

Memory

The 8080 can be used with read only memory, programmable read only memory, and read/write memory. A program can cause data to be read from any type of memory, but can only cause data to be written into read/write memory.

The programmer visualizes memory as a sequence of bytes, each of which may store 8 bits (represented by two hexadecimal digits). Up to 65,536 bytes of memory may be present, and an individual memory byte is addressed by its sequential number from 0 to 65,535D = FFFFH, the largest number which can be represented by 16 bits.

Program Counter

The program counter is a 16-bit register which is accessible to the programmer and whose contents indicate the address of the next instruction to be executed.

Stack Pointer

A *stack* is an area of memory set aside *by the programmer* in which data or addresses are stored and retrieved by stack operations. Stack operations are performed by several of the 8080 instructions, and facilitate the execution of subroutines and the handling of program interrupts. The programmer specifies which addresses the stack operations will operate upon via a special accessible 16-bit register called the *stack pointer*.

Input/Output

To the 8080, the outside world consists of up to 256 input devices and 256 output devices. Each device communicates with the 8080 via data bytes sent to or received from the accumulator, and each device is assigned a number from 0 to 255 which is not under the control of the programmer.

Timing

Instructions in the 8080 contain one to three bytes. Each instruction requires from one to five machine or memory cycles for fetching and execution. Machine cycles are called $M1$, $M2$, ..., $M5$. Each machine cycle requires from three to five states, $T1$, $T2$, ..., $T5$, for its completion. Each state has the duration of one clock period (0.5 μsec). There are three other states (WAIT, HOLD, and HALT) which last from one to an indefinite number of clock periods, as controlled by external signals. Machine cycle $M1$ is always the operation-code fetch cycle and lasts four or five clock periods. Machine cycles $M2$, $M3$, $M4$, and $M5$ normally last three clock periods each. To understand the basic operation of the 8080, refer to the simplified state diagram shown in Fig. 7.4.

During $T1$ the content of the program counter is sent to the address bus, SYNC is true, and the data bus contains the status information pertaining to the cycle that is currently being initiated. $T1$ is always followed by another state, $T2$, during which the condition of the READY, HOLD, and HALT acknowledge signals are tested. If READY is true, $T3$ can be entered; otherwise, the CPU will go into the WAIT state (TW) and stay there for as long as READY is false.

READY thus allows the CPU speed to be synchronized to a memory with any access time or to any input device. Furthermore, by properly controlling the READY line, the user can single-step through his program.

During $T3$, the data coming from memory are available on the data bus and are transferred into the instruction register (during $M1$ only), as shown in the 8080 timing diagram of Fig. 7.4. The instruction decoder and control sections then generate the basic signals to control the internal data transfers, the timing, and the machine cycle requirements of the new instructions.

At the end of $T4$, if the cycle is complete, or else at the end of $T5$, the 8080 goes back to $T1$ and enters machine cycle $M2$, unless the instruction required only one machine cycle for its execution. In such cases, a new $M1$ cycle is entered. The loop is repeated for as many cycles and states as required by the instruction.

It is only during the last state of the last machine cycle that the interrupt request line is tested and a special $M1$ cycle is entered, during which no program-counter increment takes place and interrupt acknowledge status is sent out. During this cycle, one of eight possible restart instructions will be sent to the CPU by the interrupting device.

Instruction state requirements range from a minimum of 4 states for nonmemory referencing instructions, like register and accumulator arithmetic instructions, up to a maximum of 18 states for the most complex instructions (exchange the contents of registers H and L with the contents

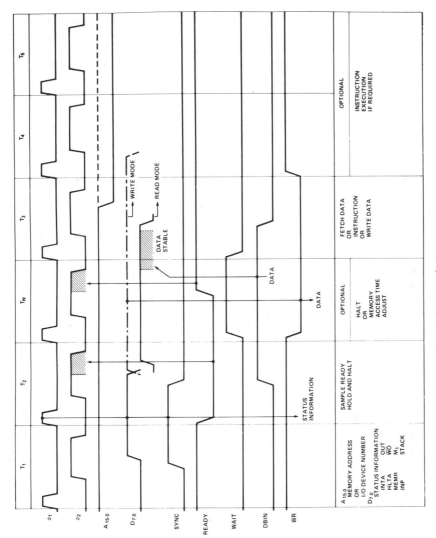

Figure 7.4. Basic timing. (Courtesy of Intel Corporation).

257

of the top two locations of the stack). At the maximum clock frequency of 2 MHz, this means that all instructions will be executed in intervals ranging from 2 to 9 μsec. If a HALT instruction is executed, the processor enters a WAIT state and remains there until an interrupt is received.

Status Information

Instructions for the 8080 require from one to five machine cycles for complete execution. The 8080 sends out 8 bits of status information on the data bus at the beginning of each machine cycle (during SYNC time). The following table defines the status information.

Status Information Definition

Symbol	Data Bus Bit	Definition
INTA[a]	D_0	Acknowledge signal for INTERRUPT request. Signal should be used to gate a restart instruction onto the data bus when DBIN is active.
$\overline{WO}$	D_1	Indicates that the operation in the current machine cycle will be a WRITE memory or OUTPUT function ($\overline{WO}$ = 0). Otherwise, a READ memory or INPUT operation will be executed.
STACK	D_2	Indicates that the address bus holds the push-down stack address from the stack pointer.
HLTA	D_3	Acknowledge signal for HALT instruction.
OUT	D_4	Indicates that the address bus contains the address of an output device and the data bus will contain the output data when $\overline{WR}$ is active.
M_1	D_5	Provides a signal to indicate that the *CPU* is in the fetch cycle for the first byte of an instruction.
INP[a]	D_6	Indicates that the address bus contains the address of an input device and the input data should be placed on the data bus when DBIN is active.
MEMR[a]	D_7	Designates that the data bus will be used for memory read data.

[a] These three status bits can be used to control the flow of data onto the 8080 data bus.

As the status information exists for only a short period on the bus, the designer must provide for its storage. Figure 7.5 shows an example in which the I/O latch is used to store status information. Figure 7.6 shows the typical 8080 system, containing *CPU*, *RAM*, *ROM*, and I/O chips. In this case a special unit, called the *system controller*, serves to store and decode the status information. The status bits are then used to control the flow of the data on the 8080 data bus.

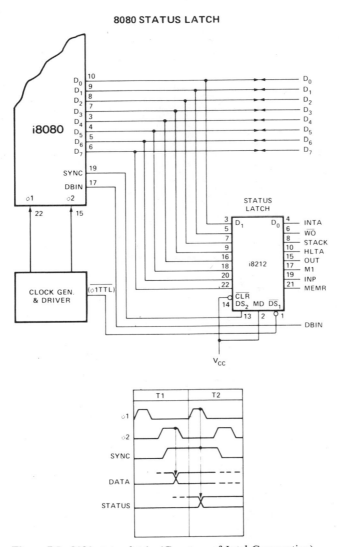

Figure 7.5. 8080 status latch. (Courtesy of Intel Corporation).

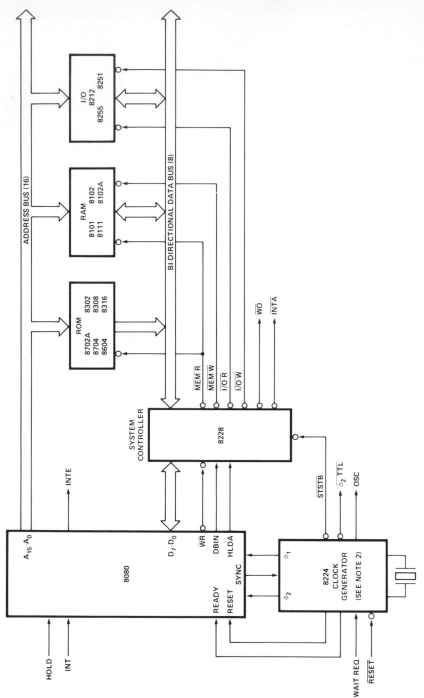

260

Table 7.6. 8080 standard system architecture. (Courtesy of Intel Corporation).

7.2. MEMORY ADDRESSING

Direct Addressing

With direct addressing, an instruction supplies an exact memory address. The instruction:

Load the contents of memory address 1F2A into the accumulator

is an example of an instruction using direct addressing, 1F2A being the direct address.

This would appear in memory as shown in Fig. 7.7.

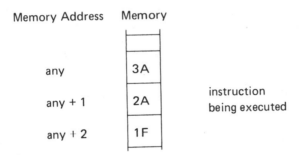

Figure 7.7. Direct addressing. (Courtesy of Intel Corporation).

The instruction occupies three memory bytes, the second and third of which hold the direct address.

Register Pair Addressing

A memory address may be specified by the contents of a register pair. For almost all 8080 instructions, the *H* and *L* registers must be used. The *H* register contains the most significant 8 bits of the referenced address, and the *L* register contains the least significant 8 bits. A one-byte instruction that will load the accumulator with the contents of memory byte 1F2A would appear as shown in Fig. 7.8.

In addition, there are two 8080 instructions which use either the *B* and *C* registers or the *D* and *E* registers to address memory. As above, the first register of the pair holds the most significant 8 bits of the address, while the second register holds the least significant 8 bits. These instructions, STAX and LDAX, are described in the following sections.

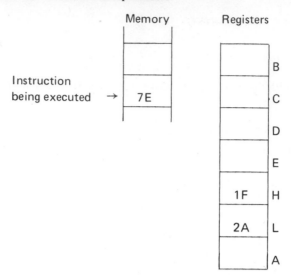

Figure 7.8. Register pair addressing. (Courtesy of Intel Corporation).

Immediate Addressing

An immediate instruction is one that contains data. The following is an example of immediate addressing:

Load the accumulator with the value 2AH.

The above instruction would be coded in memory as shown in Fig. 7.9.

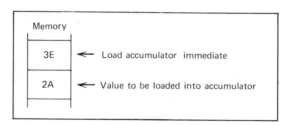

Figure 7.9. Immediate addressing. (Courtesy of Intel Corporation).

Immediate instructions do not reference memory; rather they contain data in the memory byte following the instruction code byte.

Reminder: 2AH = The value 2A, hexadecimal.

Stack Pointer Addressing

Memory locations may be addressed via the 16-bit stack pointer register, as described below.

There are only two stack operations which may be performed; putting data into a stack is called a *push*, while retrieving data from a stack is called a *pop*.

Note: In order for stack push operations to operate, stacks must be located in read/write memory.

Stack Push Operation

Sixteen bits of data are transferred to a memory area (called a *stack*) from a register pair or the 16-bit program counter during any stack push

operation. The addresses of the memory area which is to be accessed during a stack push operation are determined by using the stack pointer as follows:

1. The most significant 8 bits of data are stored at the memory address one less than the contents of the stack pointer.

2. The least significant 8 bits of data are stored at the memory address two less than the contents of the stack pointer.

3. The stack pointer is automatically decremented by two.

For example, suppose that the stack pointer contains the address 13A6H, register *B* contains 6AH, and register *C* contains 30H. Then a stack push of register pair *B* would operate as shown in Fig. 7.10.

Stack Pop Operation

Sixteen bits of data are transferred from a memory area (called a *stack*) to a register pair or the 16-bit program counter during any stack pop op-

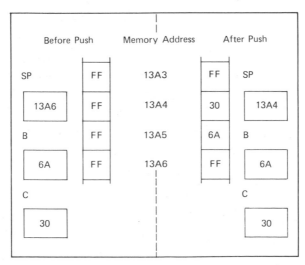

Figure 7.10. Stack pointer addressing: push operation. (Courtesy of Intel Corporation).

eration. The addresses of the memory area which is to be accessed during a stack pop operation are determined by using the stack pointer as follows:

1. The second register of the pair, or the least significant 8 bits of the program counter, are loaded from the memory address held in the stack pointer.

2. The first register of the pair, or the most significant 8 bits of the program counter, are loaded from the memory address one greater than the address held in the stack pointer.

3. The stack pointer is automatically incremented by 2.

For example, suppose that the stack pointer contains the address 1508H, memory location 1508H contains 33H, and memory location 1509H contains 0BH. Then a stack pop into register pair *H* would operate as shown in Fig. 7.11.

The programmer loads the stack pointer with any desired value by using the LXI instruction, LOAD REGISTER PAIR—IMMEDIATE. The programmer must initialize the stack pointer before performing a stack operation, or erroneous results will occur.

Subroutines and Use of the Stack for Addressing

When a subroutine is executed, the sequence of events may be depicted as follows:

Main program
↓
Call instruction
↘ Subroutine
↙
Next instruction
↓

The arrows indicate the execution sequence.

When the CALL instruction is executed, the address of the "next" instruction (i.e., the address held in the program counter) is pushed onto the stack, and the subroutine is executed. The last executed instruction of a subroutine will usually be a "return instruction," which pops an address off the stack into the program counter, and thus causes program execution to continue at the "next" instruction as illustrated in Table 7.1.

Subroutines may be nested up to any depth, limited only by the amount of memory available for the stack. For example, the first subroutine could itself call some other subroutine and so on. An examination of the sequence of stack pushes and pops will show that the return path will always be

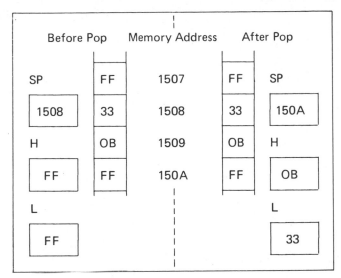

Figure 7.11. Stack pop operation. (Courtesy of Intel Corporation).

identical to the call path, even if the same subroutine is called at more than one level.

7.3. CONDITION BITS

Five condition (or status) bits are provided by the 8080 to reflect the results of data operations. All but one of these bits (the auxiliary carry bit) may be tested by program instructions which affect subsequent program execution. The descriptions of individual instructions in the next section specify which condition bits are affected by the execution of the instruction, and whether the execution of the instruction is dependent in any way on the prior status of the condition bits.

In the following discussion of condition bits, "setting" a bit causes its value to be 1, while "resetting" a bit causes its value to be 0.

Carry Bit

The carry bit is set and reset by certain data operations, and its status can be directly tested by a program. The operations which affect the carry bit are addition, subtraction, rotate, and logical operations. For example,

Table 7.1

Memory Address	Instruction	
0C02		Push address of next
0C03	CALL SUBROUTINE ←	instruction (0C06H)
0C04	02	onto the stack and
0C05	0F	branch to subroutine
0C06	NEXT INSTRUCTION ←	starting at 0F02H
0F00		
0F01		
0F02	FIRST SUBROUTINE	
	INSTRUCTION ←	
0F03		
——		
——	Body of subroutine	
——		
——		Pop return address (0C06H)
0F4E		off the stack and return to
0F4F	RETURN	next instruction

addition of two one-byte numbers can produce a carry-out of the high-order bit:

$$
\begin{array}{rccccccccc}
\text{Bit No.} & 7 & 6 & 5 & 4 & 3 & 2 & 1 & 0 \\
\hline
AE = & 1 & 0 & 1 & 0 & 1 & 1 & 1 & 0 \\
+74 = & 0 & 1 & 1 & 1 & 0 & 1 & 0 & 0 \\
\hline
122 & 0 & 0 & 1 & 0 & 0 & 1 & 0 & 0
\end{array}
$$

→ Carry-out = 1, sets carry bit = 1

An addition operation that results in a carry-out of the high-order bit will set the carry bit; an addition operation that could have resulted in a carry-out but did not will reset the carry bit.

Note: Addition, subtraction, rotate, and logical operations follow different rules for setting and resetting the carry bit. The 8080 instructions which use the addition operation are ADD, ADC, ADI, ACI, and DAD. The instructions which use the subtraction operation are SUB, SBB, SUI, SBI, CMP, and CPI. Rotate operations are RAL, RAR, RLC, and RRC. Logical operations are ANA, ORA, XRA, ANI, ORI, and XRI.

Auxiliary Carry Bit

The auxiliary carry bit indicates carry-out of bit 3. The state of the auxiliary carry bit cannot be directly tested by a program instruction and is present only to enable one instruction (DAA) to perform its function. The following addition will reset the carry bit and set the auxiliary carry bit:

Bit No.	7	6	5	4	3	2	1	0
2E =	0	0	1	0	1	1	1	0
+74 =	0	1	1	1	0	1	0	0
A2	1	0	1	0	0	0	1	0

↳ Carry = 0   ↳ Auxiliary carry = 1

The auxiliary carry bit will be affected by all addition, subtraction, increment, decrement, and compare instructions.

Sign Bit

It is possible to treat a byte of data as having the numerical range -128_{10} to $+127_{10}$. In this case, by convention, the 7 bit will always represent the sign of the number; that is, if the 7 bit is 1, the number is in the range -128_{10} to -1. If bit 7 is 0, the number is in the range 0 to $+127_{10}$.

At the conclusion of certain instructions, the sign bit will be set to the condition of the most significant bit of the answer (bit 7).

Zero Bit

This condition bit is set if the result generated by the execution of certain instructions is zero. The zero bit is reset if the result is not zero.

A result that has a carry but a zero answer byte, as illustrated below, will also set the zero bit:

Bit No.	7	6	5	4	3	2	1	0
	1	0	1	0	0	1	1	1
+	0	1	0	1	1	0	0	1
1]	0	0	0	0	0	0	0	0

Carry-out   ↗   Zero answer
of bit 7

Zero bit set to 1

Parity Bit

Byte "parity" is checked after certain operations. The number of 1 bits in a byte are counted. If the total is odd, "odd" parity is flagged; if the total is even, "even" parity is flagged.

The parity bit is set to 1 for even parity, and is reset to 0 for odd parity.

7.4. 8080 MICROPROCESSOR INSTRUCTION SET

Notation

The following pages present a detailed description of the complete 8080 instruction set (Tables 7.2–7.11).

Symbol	Meaning
$\langle B2 \rangle$	Second byte of the instruction
$\langle B3 \rangle$	Third byte of the instruction
r	One of the scratch-pad register references: A, B, C, D, E, H, L
c	One of the following flag flip-flop references:

Flag Flip-flops
Condition for True
Carry — Overflow, underflow
Zero — result is zero
Sign — MSB of result is one
Parity — parity of result is even

M	Memory location indicated by the contents of registers H and L
( )	Contents of location or register
$\wedge$	Logical product
$\veebar$	Exclusive OR
$\vee$	Inclusive OR
r_m	Bit m of register r
SP	Stack pointer
PC	Program counter
$\leftarrow$	Is transferred to
XXX	A "don't care"
SSS	Source register for data
DDD	Destination register for data

Register No. (SSS or DDD)	Register Name
000	B
001	C
010	D
011	E

Register No. (SSS or DDD)	Register Name
100	*H*
101	*L*
110	Memory
111	*ACC*

Table 7.2. Instructions Using Direct Addressing

Mnemonic	Bytes	Cycles	Description of Operation
STA ⟨B₂⟩ ⟨B₃⟩	3	4	$[\langle B_3 \rangle \langle B_2 \rangle] \rightarrow (A)$ Store the accumulator content into the memory location addressed by byte two and byte three of the instruction.
LDA ⟨B₂⟩ ⟨B₃⟩	3	4	$(A) \rightarrow [\langle B_3 \rangle \langle B_2 \rangle]$ Load the accumulator with the content of the memory location addressed by byte two and byte three of the instruction.

Table 7.3. Instructions Using Register Pair H-L to Address the Memory

Mnemonic	Bytes	Cycles	Description of Operation
ADD M	1	2	$(A) \leftarrow (A) + (M)$ ADD
ADC M	1	2	$(A) \leftarrow (A) + (M) + (carry)$ ADD with carry
SUB M	1	2	$(A) \leftarrow (A) - (M)$ SUBTRACT
SBB M	1	2	$(A) \leftarrow (A) - (M) - (borrow)$ SUBTRACT with borrow
ANA M	1	2	$(A) \leftarrow (A) \wedge (M)$ Logical AND
XRA M	1	2	$(A) \leftarrow (A) \veebar (M)$ Exclusive OR
ORA M	1	2	$(A) \leftarrow (A) \vee (M)$ Inclusive OR
CMP M	1	2	$(A) - (M)$ COMPARE
INR M	1	3	$[M] \leftarrow [M] + 1$ The content of memory designated by registers H and L is incremented by 1. All of the condition flip-flops except carry are affected by the result.
DCR M	1	3	$[M] \leftarrow [M] - 1$ The content of memory designated by registers H and L is decremented by 1. All of the condition flip-flops except carry are affected by the result.

(M) addressed by the contents of registers H and L.
Flags affected are the same as nonmemory reference instructions.

Table 7.4. Immediate Addressing Instructions

Mnemonic	Bytes	Cycles	Description of Operation
ADI $\langle B_2 \rangle$	2	2	$(A) \leftarrow (A) + \langle B_2 \rangle$ ADD
ACI $\langle B_2 \rangle$	2	2	$(A) \leftarrow (A) + \langle B_2 \rangle + (carry)$ ADD with carry
SUI $\langle B_2 \rangle$	2	2	$(A) \leftarrow (A) - \langle B_2 \rangle$ SUBTRACT
SBI $\langle B_2 \rangle$	2	2	$(A) \leftarrow (A) - \langle B_2 \rangle - (borrow)$ SUBTRACT with borrow
ANI $\langle B_2 \rangle$	2	2	$(A) \leftarrow (A) \wedge \langle B_2 \rangle$ Logical AND
XRI $\langle B_2 \rangle$	2	2	$(A) \leftarrow (A) \langle B_2 \rangle$ Exclusive OR
ORI $\langle B_2 \rangle$	2	2	$(A) \leftarrow (A) \langle B_2 \rangle$ Inclusive OR
CPI $\langle B_2 \rangle$	2	2	$(A) - \langle B_2 \rangle$ COMPARE
LXI B $\langle B_2 \rangle$ $\langle B_3 \rangle$	3	3	$(C) \leftarrow \langle B_2 \rangle$; $(B) \leftarrow \langle B_3 \rangle$ Load byte two of the instruction into C. Load byte three of the instruction into B.
LXI D $\langle B_2 \rangle$ $\langle B_3 \rangle$	3	3	$(E) \leftarrow \langle B_2 \rangle$, $(D) \leftarrow \langle B_3 \rangle$ Load byte two of the instruction into E. Load byte 3 of the instruction into D.
LXI H $\langle B_2 \rangle$ $\langle B_3 \rangle$	3	3	$(L) \leftarrow \langle B_2 \rangle$, $(H) \leftarrow \langle B_3 \rangle$ Load byte two of the instruction into L. Load byte three of the instruction into H.

Table 7.5. Register Reference Instructions

Mnemonic	Bytes	Cycles	Description of Operation
INR r	1	1	$(r) \leftarrow (r) + 1$ The content of register r is incremented by 1. All the condition flip-flops except carry are affected by the result.
DCR r	1	1	$(r) \leftarrow (r) - 1$ The content of register r is decremented by 1. All the condition flip-flops except carry are affected by the result.

Table 7.5. (*Continued*)

Mnemonic	Bytes	Cycles	Description of Operation
ADD r	1	1	$(A) \leftarrow (A) + (r)$ Add the content of register r to the content of register A and place the result into register A. (All flags affected.)
ADC r	1	1	$(A) \leftarrow (A) + (r) + (carry)$ Add the content of register r and the contents of the carry flip-flop to the content of the A register and place the result into register A. (All flags affected.)
SUB r	1	1	$(A) \leftarrow (A) - (r)$ Subtract the content of register r from the content of register A and place the result into register A. Two's complement subtraction is used. (All flags affected.)
SBB r	1	1	$(A) \leftarrow (A) - (r) - (borrow)$ Subtract the content of register r and the content of the carry flip-flop from the content of register A and place the result into register A. (All flags affected.)
ANA r	1	1	$(A) \leftarrow (A) \wedge (r)$ Place the logical product of register A and register r into register A. (Resets carry.)
XRA r	1	1	$(A) \leftarrow (A) \veebar (r)$ Place the "exclusive OR" of the content of register A and register r into register A. (Resets carry.)
ORA r	1	1	$(A) \leftarrow (A) \vee (r)$ Place the "inclusive OR" of the content of register A and register r into register A. (Resets carry.)
CMP r	1	1	$(A) - (r)$ Compare the content of register A with the content of register r. The content of register A remains unchanged. The flag flip-flops are set by the result of the subtraction. Equality $(A = r)$ is indicated by the zero flip-flop set to 1. Less than $(A < r)$ is indicated by the carry flip-flop set to 1.
RAL	1	1	$A_{m+1} \leftarrow A_m$, $A_0 \leftarrow (carry)$, $(carry) \leftarrow A_7$ Rotate the content of register A left 1 bit. Rotate the content of the carry flip-flop into A_0. Rotate A_7 into the carry flip-flop.
RAR	1	1	$A_m \leftarrow A_{m+1}$, $A_7 \leftarrow (carry)$, $(carry) \leftarrow A_0$ Rotate the content of register A right 1 bit. Rotate the content of the carry flip-flop into A_7. Rotate A_0 into the carry flip-flop.

(*Continued*)

Table 7.5. (*Continued*)

Mnemonic	Bytes	Cycles	Description of Operation
RLC	1	1	$A_{m+1} \leftarrow A_m$, $A_0 \leftarrow A_7$, (carry) $\leftarrow A_7$ Rotate the content of register A left 1 bit. Rotate A_7 into A_0 and into the carry flip-flop.
RRC	1	1	$A_m \leftarrow A_{m+1}$, $A_7 \leftarrow A_0$, (carry) $\leftarrow A_0$ Rotate the content of register A right 1 bit. Rotate A_0 into A_7 and into the carry flip-flop.
CMA	1	1	(A) $\leftarrow \overline{(A)}$ The content of the accumulator is complemented. The condition flip-flops are not affected.
STC	1	1	(Carry) $\leftarrow 1$ Set the carry flip-flop to 1. The other condition flip-flops are not affected.
CMC	1	1	(Carry) $\leftarrow \overline{(carry)}$ The content of carry is complemented. The other condition flip-flops are not affected.

Table 7.6. **Move Data Instructions**

Mnemonic	Bytes	Cycles	Description of Operation
MOV r_1, r_2	1	1	$(r_1) \leftarrow (r_2)$ Load register r_1 with the content of r_2. The content of r_2 remains unchanged.
MOV r, M	1	2	$(r) \leftarrow (M)$ Load register r with the content of the memory location addressed by the contents of registers H and L.
MOV M, r	1	2	$(M) \leftarrow (r)$ Load the memory location addressed by the contents of registers H and L with the content of register r.
MVI r $\langle B_2 \rangle$	2	2	$(r) \leftarrow \langle B_7 \rangle$ Load byte two of the instruction into register r.
MVI M $\langle B_2 \rangle$	2	3	$(M) \leftarrow \langle B_2 \rangle$ Load byte two of the instruction into the memory location addressed by the contents of registers H and L.

Table 7.7. Conditional Jump Instructions

Mnemonic	Bytes	Cycles	Description of Operation
JMP $\langle B_2 \rangle$ $\langle B_3 \rangle$	3	3	$(PC) \leftarrow \langle B_3 \rangle \langle B_2 \rangle$ Jump unconditionally to the instruction located in memory location addressed by byte two and byte three.
JC $\langle B_2 \rangle$ $\langle B_3 \rangle$	3	3	If (carry) = 1 $(PC) \leftarrow \langle B_3 \rangle \langle B_2 \rangle$ Otherwise $(PC) = (PC) + 3$
JNC $\langle B_2 \rangle$ $\langle B_3 \rangle$	3	3	If (carry) = 0 $(PC) \leftarrow \langle B_3 \rangle \langle B_2 \rangle$ Otherwise $(PC) = (PC) + 3$
JZ $\langle B_2 \rangle$ $\langle B_3 \rangle$	3	3	If (zero) = 1 $(PC) \leftarrow \langle B_3 \rangle \langle B_2 \rangle$ Otherwise $(PC) = (PC) + 3$
JNZ $\langle B_2 \rangle$ $\langle B_3 \rangle$	3	3	If (zero) = 0 $(PC) \leftarrow \langle B_3 \rangle \langle B_2 \rangle$ Otherwise $(PC) = (PC) + 3$
JP $\langle B_2 \rangle$ $\langle B_3 \rangle$	3	3	If (sign) = 0 $(PC) \leftarrow \langle B_3 \rangle \langle B_2 \rangle$ Otherwise $(PC) = (PC) + 3$
JM $\langle B_2 \rangle$ $\langle B_3 \rangle$	3	3	If (sign) = 1 $(PC) \leftarrow \langle B_3 \rangle \langle B_2 \rangle$ Otherwise $(PC) = (PC) + 3$
JPE $\langle B_2 \rangle$ $\langle B_3 \rangle$	3	3	If (parity) = 1 $(PC) \leftarrow \langle B_3 \rangle \langle B_2 \rangle$ Otherwise $(PC) = (PC) + 3$
JPO $\langle B_2 \rangle$ $\langle B_3 \rangle$	3	3	If (parity) = 0 $(PC) \leftarrow \langle B_3 \rangle \langle B_2 \rangle$ Otherwise $(PC) = (PC) + 3$

Table 7.8. Instructions Dealing with Stack

Mnemonic	Bytes	Cycles	Description of Operation
LXI SP $\langle B_2 \rangle$ $\langle B_3 \rangle$	3	3	$(SP_1 \leftarrow \langle B_2 \rangle, (SP)_H \leftarrow \langle B_3 \rangle$ Load byte two of the instruction into the lower-order 8 bit of the stack pointer and byte three into the higher-order 8 bit of the stack pointer.

(Continued)

Table 7.8. (*Continued*)

Mnemonic	Bytes	Cycles	Description of Operation
PUSH PSW	1	3	$[SP - 1] \leftarrow (A), [SP - 2] \leftarrow (F), (SP) = (SP) - 2$ Save the contents of A and F (5-flags) into the push-down stack addressed by the SP register. The content of SP is decremented by 2. The flag word will appear as follows: D_0: CY_2 (carry) D_1: 1 D_2: Parity (even) D_3: 0 D_4: CY_1 D_5: 0 D_6: Zero D_7: MSB (sign)
PUSH B	1	3	$[SP - 1] \leftarrow (B)\ [SP - 2] \leftarrow (C), (SP) = (SP) - 2$
PUSH D	1	3	$[SP - 1] \leftarrow (D)\ [SP - 2] \leftarrow (E), (SP) = (SP) - 2$
PUSH H	1	3	$[SP - 1] \leftarrow (H)\ [SP - 2] \leftarrow (L), (SP) = (SP) - 2$
POP PSW	1	3	$(F) \leftarrow [SP], (A) \leftarrow [SP + 1], (SP) = (SP) + 2$ Restore the last values in the push-down stack addressed by register SP into A and F. The content of SP is incremented by 2.
POP B	1	3	$(C) \leftarrow [SP], (B) \leftarrow [SP + 1], (SP) = (SP) + 2$
POP D	1	3	$(E) \leftarrow [SP], (D) \leftarrow [SP + 1], (SP) = (SP) + 2$
POP H	1	3	$(L) \leftarrow [SP], (H) \leftarrow [SP + 1], (SP) = (SP) + 2$
XTHL	1	5	$(L) \leftrightarrow [SP], (H) \leftrightarrow [SP + 1]$ Exchange the contents of registers H and L and the last values in the push-down stack addressed by register SP. The SP register itself is not changed $(SP) = (SP)$.
SPHL	1	1	$(SP) \leftarrow (H)(L)$ Transfer the contents of registers H and L into register SP.
PCHL	1	1	$(PC) \leftarrow (H)(L)$ JUMP INDIRECT
DAD SP	1	3	$(H)(L) \leftarrow (H)(L) + (SP)$ Add the content of register SP to the content of registers H and L and place the result into H and L. If the overflow is generated, the carry flip-flop is set; otherwise, the carry flip-flop is reset. The other condition flip-flops are not affected. This is useful for addressing data in the stack.
INX SP	1	1	$(SP) \leftarrow (SP) + 1$
DCX SP	1	1	$(SP) \leftarrow (SP) - 1$

Table 7.9. Conditional Subroutine Call and Return Instructions

Mnemonic	Bytes	Cycles	Description of Operation
CALL $\langle B_2 \rangle$ $\langle B_3 \rangle$	3	5	$[SP - 1] [SP - 2] \leftarrow (PC), (SP) = (SP) - 2$ $(PC) \leftarrow \langle B_3 \rangle \langle B_2 \rangle$ Transfer the content of PC to the push-down stack in memory addressed by the register SP. The content of SP is decremented by 2. Jump unconditionally to the instruction located in the memory location addressed by byte two and byte three of the instruction.
CC $\langle B_2 \rangle$ $\langle B_3 \rangle$	3	3/5	If (carry) $= 1$ $[SP - 1] [SP - 2] \leftarrow PC$, $(SP) = (SP) - 2, (PC) \leftarrow \langle B_3 \rangle \langle B_2 \rangle$ Otherwise $(PC) = (PC) + 3$
CNC $\langle B_2 \rangle$ $\langle B_3 \rangle$	3	3/5	If (carry) $= 0$ $[SP - 1] [SP - 2] \leftarrow PC$, $(SP) = (SP) - 2, (PC) \leftarrow \langle B_3 \rangle \langle B_2 \rangle$ Otherwise $(PC) = (PC) + 3$
CZ $\langle B_2 \rangle$ $\langle B_3 \rangle$	3	3/5	If (zero) $= 1$ $[SP - 1] [SP - 2] \leftarrow PC$, $(SP) = (SP) - 2, (PC) \leftarrow \langle B_3 \rangle \langle B_2 \rangle$ Otherwise $(PC) = (PC) + 3$
CNZ $\langle B_2 \rangle$ $\langle B_3 \rangle$	3	3/5	If (zero) $= 0$ $[SP - 1] [SP - 2] \leftarrow PC$, $(SP) = (SP) - 2, (PC) \leftarrow \langle B_3 \rangle \langle B_2 \rangle$ Otherwise $(PC) = (PC) + 3$
CP $\langle B_2 \rangle$ $\langle B_3 \rangle$	3	3/5	If (sign) $= 0$ $[SP - 1] [SP - 2] \leftarrow PC$, $(SP) = (SP) - 2, (PC) \leftarrow \langle B_3 \rangle \langle B_2 \rangle$ Otherwise $(PC) = (PC) + 3$
CM $\langle B_2 \rangle$ $\langle B_3 \rangle$	3	3/5	If (sign) $= 1$ $[SP - 1] [SP - 2] \leftarrow PC$, $(SP) = (SP) - 2, (PC) \leftarrow \langle B_3 \rangle \langle B_2 \rangle$ Otherwise $(PC) = (PC) + 3$
CPE $\langle B_2 \rangle$ $\langle B_3 \rangle$	3	3/5	If (parity) $= 1$ $[SP - 1] [SP - 2] \leftarrow PC$, $(SP) = (SP) - 2, (PC) \leftarrow \langle B_3 \rangle \langle B_2 \rangle$ Otherwise $(PC) = (PC) + 3$
CPO $\langle B_2 \rangle$ $\langle B_3 \rangle$	3	3/5	If (parity) $= 0$ $[SP - 1] [SP - 2] \leftarrow PC$, $(SP) = (SP) - 2, (PC) \leftarrow \langle B_3 \rangle \langle B_2 \rangle$ Otherwise $(PC) = (PC) + 3$
RET	1	3	$(PC) \leftarrow [SP] [SP + 1] (SP) = (SP) + 2$ Return to the instruction in the memory location addressed by the last values shifted into the push-down stack addressed by SP. The content of SP is incremented by 2.

(Continued)

275

Table 7.9. (*Continued*)

Mnemonic	Bytes	Cycles	Description of Operation
RC	1	1/3	If (carry) = 1 (PC) ← [SP], [SP + 1], (SP) = (SP) + 2 Otherwise (PC) = (PC) + 1
RNC	1	1/3	If (carry) = 0 (PC) ← [SP], [SP + 1], (SP) = (SP) + 2 Otherwise (PC) = (PC) + 1
RZ	1	1/3	If (zero) = 1 (PC) ← [SP], [SP + 1], (SP) = (SP) + 2 Otherwise (PC) = (PC) + 1
RNZ	1	1/3	If (zero) = 0 (PC) ← [SP], [SP + 1], (SP) = (SP) + 2 Otherwise (PC) = (PC) + 1
RP	1	1/3	If (sign) = 0 (PC) ← [SP], [SP + 1], (SP) = (SP) + 2 Otherwise (PC) = (PC) + 1
RM	1	1/3	If (sign) = 1 (PC) ← [SP], [SP + 1], (SP) = (SP) + 2 Otherwise (PC) = (PC) + 1
RPE	1	1/3	If (parity) = 1 (PC) ← [SP], [SP + 1], (SP) = (SP) + 2 Otherwise (PC) = (PC) + 1
RPO	1	1/3	If (parity) = 0 (PC) ← [SP], [SP + 1], (SP) = (SP) + 2 Otherwise (PC) = (PC) + 1
RST	1	3	[SP − 1] [SP − 2] ← (PC), (SP) = (SP) − 2 (PC) ← (00000000 00AAA000) Interrupt vector supplied by the external device (see Fig. 7.17)

Table 7.10. Input/Output Instructions

Mnemonic	Bytes	Cycles	Description of Operation
IN $\langle B_2 \rangle$	2	3	$(A) \leftarrow$ (input data) At T_1 time of third cycle, byte two of the instruction, which denotes the I/O device number, is sent to the I/O device through the address lines, and the INP status information, instead of MEMR, is sent out at SYNC time. New data for the accumulator are loaded from the data bus when DBIN control signal is active. The condition flip-flops are not affected.
OUT $\langle B_2 \rangle$	2	3	(Output data) $\leftarrow (A)$ At T_1 time of the third cycle, byte two of the instruction, which denotes the I/O device number, is sent to the I/O device through the address lines, and the OUT status information is sent out at SYNC time. The content of the accumulator is made available on the data bus when the $\overline{WR}$ control signal is 0.
EI	1	1	Interrupt system enable
DI	1	1	Interrupt system disable The Interrupt enable flip-flop (INTE) can be set or reset by using the above instructions. The INT signal will be accepted if the INTE is set. When the INT signal is accepted by the *CPU*, the INTE will be reset immediately. During interrupt enable or disable instruction executions, an interrupt will not be accepted.

Table 7.11. Other Instructions

Mnemonic	Bytes	Cycles	Description of Operation
LDAX D	1	2	(A) ← [(D) (E)] Load the accumulator with the content of the memory location addressed by the content of registers D and E.
INX B	1	1	(B) (C) ← (B) (C) + 1 The content of register pair B-C is incremented by 1. All of the condition flip-flops are not affected.
INX H	1	1	(H) (L) ← (H) (L) + 1 The content of registers H and L is incremented by 1. All of the condition flip-flops are not affected.
INX D	1	1	(D) (E) ← (D) (E) + 1
DAD B	1	3	(H) (L) ← (H) (L) + (B) (C)
DAD H	1	3	(H) (L) ← (H) (L) + (H) (L) (double-precision shift left H and L)
DAD D	1	3	(H) (L) ← (H) (L) + (D) (E)
STAX B	1	2	[(B) (C)] ← (A) Store the accumulator content in the memory location addressed by the content of registers B and C.
STAX D	1	2	[(D) (E)] ← (A) Store the accumulator content into the memory location addressed by the content of registers D and E.
LDAX B	1	2	(A) ← [(B) (C)] Load the accumulator with the content of the memory location addressed by the content of registers B and C.
DCX B	1	1	(B) (C) ← (B) (C) − 1
DCX H	1	1	(H) (L) ← (H) (L) − 1
DCX D	1	1	(D) (E) ← (D) (E) − 1
XCHG	1	1	(H) ↔ (D) (E) ↔ (L) Exchange the contents of registers H and L and registers D and E.

Table 7.11. (*Continued*)

Mnemonic	Bytes	Cycles	Description of Operation
DAA	1	1	Decimal adjust accumulator

The 8-bit value in the accumulator containing the result from an arithmetic operation on decimal operands is adjusted to contain two valid BCD digits by adding a value according to the following rules:

Accumulator

If ($Y \geq 10$) or (carry from bit 3) then $Y = Y + 6$ with carry to X digit. If ($X \geq 10$) or (carry from bit 7) or [($Y \geq 10$) and ($X = 9$)] then $X = X + 6$ (which sets the carry flip-flop).

Two carry flip-flops are used for this instruction: CY, represents the carry from bit 3 (the fourth bit) and is accessible as a fifth flag; CY_2 is the carry from bit 7 and is the usual carry bit.

All condition flip-flops are affected by this instruction.

Mnemonic	Bytes	Cycles	Description of Operation
SHLD $\langle B_2 \rangle$ $\langle B_3 \rangle$	3	5	$[\langle B_3 \rangle \langle B_2 \rangle] \leftarrow (L)$, $[\langle B_3 \rangle \langle B_2 \rangle + 1] \leftarrow (H)$ Store the contents of registers H and L into the memory location addressed by byte two and byte three of the instructions.
LHLD $\langle B_2 \rangle$ $\langle B_3 \rangle$	3	5	$(L) \leftarrow [\langle B_3 \rangle \langle B_2 \rangle]$, $(H) \leftarrow [\langle B_3 \rangle \langle B_2 \rangle + 1]$ Load registers H and L with the contents of the memory location addressed by byte two and byte three of the instruction.
HLT	1	1	On receipt of the HALT Instruction, the activity of the processor is immediately suspended in the STOPPED state. The content of all registers and memory is unchanged, and the PC has been updated.

7.5. PROGRAMMING EXAMPLES

Accumulator Loading

One of the most frequent programming tasks is to bring the data into the accumulator. Table 7.12 shows eight different examples for accumulator loading. Each line presents one independent example.

Table 7.12. Accumulator Loading

Mnemonic	Operand	Explanation	Bytes
MOV	A, B	Load A with register B	1
MVI	A, 23	Load A with data Immediate "23"	2
LDA	4098	Load A with contents of memory LOC 4098	3
MOV	A, M	Load A using H and L as address	1
LDAX	B	Load A using B and C as address	1
LDAX	D	Load A using D and E as address	1
LHLD	4098	Load A indirectly using LOC 4098	4
MOV	A, M		
POP	A	Load A with data from stack	1
IN	10	Load A with data from device 10	2

MOV A, B. This is a one-byte instruction (Table 7.6). The instruction specifies register B as a source of data and accumulator A as a destination for data.

MOVI A, 23. This is a two-byte instruction (Table 7.6). The second byte keeps the data, in this example 23. This second byte is loaded into the accumulator.

LDA 4098. This is a three-byte instruction (Table 7.2). The second and third bytes are used to specify the memory address, in this example 4098.

MOV A, M. This is a one-byte instruction (Table 7.6). This instruction must be preceded by another one that will load the 16-bit memory address into the register pair *H-L*. The MOV instruction will then take the data from their memory location as specified by the *H-L* registers and move them into the accumulator.

LDAX B. This is a one-byte instruction (Table 7.11). This instruction must be preceded by another one that will load the 16-bit memory address into the register pair *B-C*. The LDAX instruction will take the data from their memory location as specified by the *B-C* registers and move them into the accumulator.

LDAX D. This is a one-byte instruction (Table 7.11), which operates in the same way as the LDAX B instruction, except that here register pair *D-E* is used to specify the memory address.

LHLD 4098 and MOV A, M. These two instructions take four bytes (Table 7.11). The LHLD instruction will load the information from memory address 4098 into the register pair *H-L*. The MOV instruction will use the register pair *H-L* to address the memory, and to move the data from the memory location in the accumulator. Hence these two instructions will load *A* indirectly, using location 4098.

IN 10. This is a two-byte instruction (Table 7.10). The second byte is used as the I/O device selection code. The accumulator is loaded from the selected I/O device, through the data bus.

Multibyte Addition

The carry bit and the ADC (add with carry) instructions may be used to add unsigned data quantities of arbitrary length. Consider the following addition of two three-byte unsigned hexadecimal numbers (Table 7.13):

$$\begin{array}{r} 32AF8A \\ +\,84BA90 \\ \hline B76A1A \end{array}$$

This addition may be performed on the 8080 by adding the two low-order bytes of the numbers, then adding the resulting carry to the two next-higher-order bytes, and so on:

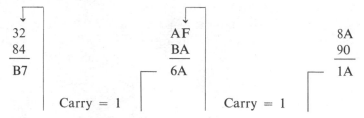

The following routine will perform this multibyte addition, making these assumptions (Table 7.14).

The *C* register holds the length of each number to be added (in this case, 3). The numbers to be added are stored from low-order byte to high-order byte, beginning at memory locations FIRST and SECND, respectively.

Table 7.13

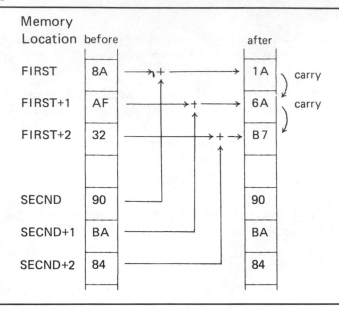

The result will be stored from low-order byte to high-order byte, beginning at memory location FIRST, replacing the original contents of these locations.

Since none of the instructions in the program loop affects the carry bit except ADC, the addition with carry will proceed correctly.

When location DONE is reached, bytes FIRST through FIRST+2 will contain 1A6AB7, which is the sum shown at the beginning of this section arranged from low-order to high-order byte.

The carry (or borrow) bit and the SBB (subtract with borrow) instruction may be used to subtract unsigned data quantities of arbitrary length. Consider the following subtraction of two two-byte unsigned hexadecimal numbers:

$$\begin{array}{r} 1301 \\ -0503 \\ \hline 0DFE \end{array}$$

This subtraction may be performed on the 8080 by subtracting the two low-order bytes of the numbers, and then using the resulting carry bit to adjust the difference of the two higher-order bytes if a borrow occurred (by using the SBB instruction).

Table 7.14

Label	Code	Operand	Comment
MADD:	LXI	B,FIRST	; B and C address FIRST
	LXI	H,SECND	; H and L address SECND
	XRA	A	; Clear carry bit
LOOP:	LDAX	B	; Load byte of FIRST
	ADC	M	; Add byte of SECND ; with carry
	STAX	B	; Store result at FIRST
	DCR	C	; Done if C = 0
	JZ	DONE	
	INX	B	; Point to next byte of ; FIRST
	INX	H	; Point to next byte of ; SECND
	JMP	LOOP	; Add next two bytes
DONE:	——		
	——		
FIRST:	DB	90H	
	DB	0BAH	
	DB	84H	
SECND:	DB	8AH	
	DB	0AFH	
	DB	32H	

Low-order subtraction (carry bit = 0, indicating no borrow):

$$00000001 = 01H$$
$$\underline{11111101 = -(03H + \text{carry})}$$
$$11111110 = 0FEH, \text{ the low-order result}$$

Carry out = 0, setting the carry bit = 1, indicating a borrow

High-order subtraction:

$$00010011 = 13H$$
$$\underline{11111010 = -(05H + \text{carry})}$$
$$00001101$$

Carry out = 1, resetting the carry bit, indicating no borrow

Whenever a borrow has occurred, the SBB instruction increments the subtrahend by 1, which is equivalent to borrowing 1 from the minuend.

To create a multibyte subtraction routine, it is necessary only to duplicate the multibyte addition routine of this section, changing the ADC instruction to an SBB instruction. The program will then subtract the number beginning at SECND from the number beginning at FIRST, placing the result at FIRST.

Decimal Addition

Any 4-bit data quantity may be treated as a decimal number as long as it represents one of the decimal digits from 0 through 9, and does not contain any of the bit patterns representing the hexadecimal digits A through F. To preserve this decimal interpretation when performing addition, the value 6 must be added to the 4-bit quantity whenever the addition produces a result between 10 and 15. This is necessary because each 4-bit data quantity can hold 6 more combinations of bits than there are decimal digits.

Decimal addition is performed on the 8080 by letting each 8-bit byte represent two 4-bit decimal digits. The bytes are summed in the accumulator in standard fashion, and the DAA (decimal adjust accumulator) instruction is then used to convert the 8-bit binary result to the correct representation of two decimal digits. The settings of the carry and auxiliary carry bits also affect the operation of the DAA, permitting the addition of decimal numbers longer than two digits (Table 7.11).

To perform the decimal addition:

$$\begin{array}{r} 2985 \\ + \ 4936 \\ \hline 7921 \end{array}$$

the process works as follows.

1. Clear the carry and add the two lowest-order digits of each number (remember that each two decimal digits are represented by one byte).

$$\begin{array}{r} 85 = 10000101\text{B} \\ 36 = 00110110\text{B} \\ \text{Carry} = \underline{\qquad 0} \\ 0] \ 10111011\text{B} \end{array}$$

Carry = 0   Auxiliary carry = 0

The accumulator now contains BBH.
Reminder: 10111011B = 10111011 Binary

2. Perform a DAA operation. Since the right-most 4 bits are $\geqslant 10D$, 6 will be added to the accumulator.

$$
\begin{array}{r}
\text{Accumulator} = 10111011\text{B} \\
6 = 0110\text{B} \\
\hline
11000001\text{B}
\end{array}
$$

Since the left-most 4 bits are now 910, 6 will be added to these bits, setting the carry bit.

$$
\begin{array}{r}
\text{Accumulator} = 11000001\text{B} \\
6 = 0110\text{B} \\
\hline
1] \ 00100001\text{B}
\end{array}
$$

Carry bit = 1

The accumulator now contains 21H. Store these two digits.

3. Add the next group of two digits:

$$
\begin{array}{r}
29 = 00101001\text{B} \\
49 = 01001001\text{B} \\
\text{Carry} = 1 \\
\hline
0] \ 01110011\text{B}
\end{array}
$$

Carry = 0 \qquad Auxiliary carry = 1

The accumulator now contains 72H.

4. Perform a DAA operation. Since the auxiliary carry bit is set, 6 will be added to the accumulator.

$$
\begin{array}{r}
\text{Accumulator} = 01110011\text{B} \\
6 = 0110\text{B} \\
\hline
0] \ 01111001\text{B}
\end{array}
$$

Carry bit = 0

Since the left-most 4 bits are <10 and the carry bit is reset, no further action occurs.

Thus the correct decimal result 7921 is generated in two bytes.

A routine which adds decimal numbers, then, is exactly analogous to the multibyte addition routine MADD of the preceding section, and may be produced by inserting the instruction DAA after the ADC M instruction of that example.

Subroutines

A subroutine is coded like any other group of assembly language statements and is referred to by its name, which is the label of the first instruction. The programmer references a subroutine by writing its name in the operand field of a CALL instruction. When the CALL is executed, the address of the next sequential instruction after the CALL is pushed onto the stack and program execution proceeds with the first instruction of the subroutine. When the subroutine has completed its work, a RETURN instruction is executed, which causes the top address in the stack to be popped into the program counter, so that program execution continues with the instruction following the CALL. Thus one copy of a subroutine may be called from many different points in memory, preventing duplication of code.

Example (Fig. 7.12): Subroutine MINC increments a 16-bit number held least-significant-byte first in two consecutive memory locations, and then returns to the instruction following the last CALL statement executed. The address of the number to be incremented is passed in the H and L registers.

When the first call is executed, address 2C03H is pushed onto the stack indicated by the stack pointer, and control is transferred to 3C00H. Execution of either RETURN statement in MINC will cause the top entry to be popped off the stack into the program counter, causing execution to continue at 2C03H (since the CALL statement is three bytes long).

When the second call is executed, address 2EF3H is pushed onto the stack, and control is again transferred to MINC. This time, either RETURN instruction will cause execution to resume at 2EF3H.

Note that MINC could have called another subroutine during its execution, causing another address to be pushed onto the stack. This can occur as many times as necessary, limited only by the size of memory available for the stack.

Note also that any subroutine could push data onto the stack for temporary storage without affecting the call and return sequences as long as the same number of data are popped off the stack before executing a RETURN statement.

Transferring Data to Subroutine

A subroutine often requires data to perform its operations. In the simplest case, these data may be transferred in one or more registers. Subroutine MINC in the preceding example, receives the memory address which it requires in the H and L registers.

Label	Code	Operand	Comment
MINC:	INR	M	; Increment low-order byte
	RNZ		; If non-zero, return to
			; calling routine
	INX	H	; Address high-order byte
	INR	M	; Increment high-order byte
	RET		; Return unconditionally

Assume MINC appears in the following program:

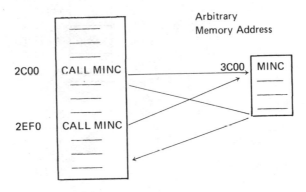

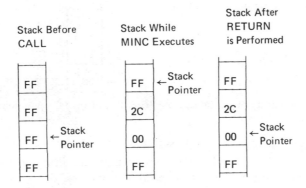

Figure 7.12. Subroutine calls and stack. (Courtesy of Intel Corporation).

287

Sometimes it is more convenient and economical to let the subroutine load its own registers. One way to do this is to place a list of the required data (called a *parameter list*) in some data area of memory, and to pass the address of this list to the subroutine in the *H* and *L* registers (Table 7.15 and Fig. 7.13).

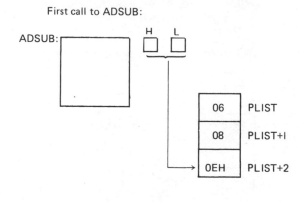

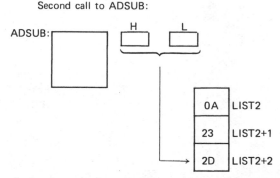

Figure 7.13. Transferring data to subroutine. (Courtesy of Intel Corporation).

For example, the subroutine ADSUB expects the address of a three-byte parameter list in the *H* and *L* registers. It adds the first and second bytes of the list, and stores the result in the third byte.

The first time ADSUB is called, it loads the *A* and *B* registers from PLIST and PLIST+1 respectively, adds them, and stores the result in PLIST+2. Return is then made to the instruction at RET1.

The second time ADSUB is called, the *H* and *L* registers point to the parameter list LIST2. The *A* and *B* registers are loaded with 10 and 35,

Table 7.15

Label	Code	Operand	Comment
	LXI	H, PLIST	; Load H and L with addresses
			; of the parameter list
	CALL	ADSUB	; Call the subroutine
RET1:	———		
PLIST:	DB	6	; First number to be added
	DB	8	; Second number to be added
	DS	1	; Result will be stored here
	LXI	H, LIST2	; Load H and L registers
	CALL	ADSUB	; for another call to ADSUB
RET2:	———		
LIST2:	DB	10	
	DB	35	
	DS	1	
ADSUB:	MOV	A, M	; Get first parameter
	INX	H	; Increment memory address
	MOV	B, M	; Get second parameter
	ADD	B	; Add first to second
	INX	H	; Increment memory address
	MOV	M, A	; Store result at third parameter
			; store
	RET		; Return unconditionally

respectively, and the sum is stored at LIST2+2. Return is then made to the instruction at RET2.

Note that the parameter lists PLIST and LIST2 could appear anywhere in memory without altering the results produced by ADSUB.

This approach has its limitations, however. As coded, ADSUB must receive a list of two and only two numbers to be added, and they must be contiguous in memory. Suppose that we wanted a subroutine (GENAD) which would add an arbitrary number of bytes, located anywhere in memory, and leave the sum in the accumulator (Table 7.16 and Fig. 7.14).

This can be done by passing the subroutine a parameter list that is a list of *addresses* of parameters, rather than the parameters themselves, and signifying the end of the parameter list by a number whose first byte is FFH (assuming that no parameters will be stored above address FF00H).

Table 7.16

Label	Code	Operand	Comment
	LXI	H, PLIST	; Calling program
	CALL	GENAD	
	——		
	——		
PLIST:	DW	PARM1	; List of parameter addresses
	DW	PARM2	
	DW	PARM3	
	DW	PARM4	
	DW	0FFFFH	; Terminator
	——		
	——		
PARM1:	DB	6	
PARM4:	DB	16	
	——		
	——		
PARM3:	DB	13	
	——		
	——		
PARM2:	DB	82	
	——		
	——		
GENAD:	XRA	A	; Clear accumulator
LOOP:	MOV	C, A	; Save current total in C
	MOV	E, M	; Get low order address byte
			; of first parameter
	INX	H	
	MOV	A, M	; Get high order address byte
			; of first parameter
	CPI	0FFH	; Compare to FFH
	JZ	BACK	; If equal, routine is complete
	MOV	D, A	; D and E now address parameter
	LDAX	D	; Load accumulator with parameter
	ADD	C	; Add previous total
	INX	H	; Increment H and L to point
			; to next parameter address
	JMP	LOOP	; Get next parameter
BACK:	MOV	A, C	; Routine done—restore total
	RET		; Return to calling routine

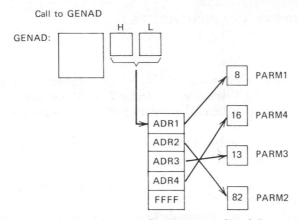

Figure 7.14. General subroutine data transfer. (Courtesy of Intel Corporation).

As implemented below, GENAD saves the current sum (beginning with zero) in the C register. It then loads the address of the first parameter into the D and E registers. If this address is greater than or equal to FF00H, it reloads the accumulator with the sum held in the C register and returns to the calling routine. Otherwise, it loads the parameter into the accumulator and adds the sum in the C register to the accumulator. The routine then loops back to pick up the remaining parameters.

Note that GENAD could add any combination of the parameters with no change to the parameters themselves. The sequence:

```
            LXI         H, PLIST
            CALL        GENAD
            ———
            ———
            ———

PLIST:      DW          PARM4
            DW          PARM1
            DW          0FFFFH
```

would cause PARM1 and PARM4 to be added, no matter where in memory they might be located (excluding addresses above FF00H).

Many variations of parameter passing are possible. For example, if it was necessary to allow parameters to be stored at any address, a calling program could pass the total number of parameters as the first parameter; the subroutine would load this first parameter into a register and use it as a counter to determine when all parameters had been accepted.

7.6. INTERRUPTS AND INPUT/OUTPUT

Interrupts

The 8080 contains a bit named INTE which may be set or reset by the instructions EI and DI described in Table 7.10. Whenever INTE is equal to 0, the entire interrupt handling system is disabled, and no interrupts will be accepted.

When the *CPU* recognizes an interrupt request from an external device, the following actions occur:

1. The instruction currently being executed is completed.
2. The interrupt enable bit, INTE, is reset = 0.
3. The interrupting device supplies, via hardware, one instruction which the *CPU* executes. This instruction does not appear anywhere in memory, and the programmer has no control over it, since it is a function of the interrupting device's controller design. The program counter is not incremented before this instruction.

The instruction supplied by the interrupting device is normally an RST instruction (see Table 7.9), since this is an efficient one-byte call to one of 8 eight-byte subroutines located in the first 64 words of memory. For instance, the Teletype may supply the instruction (Fig. 7.15):

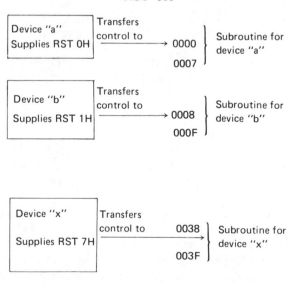

RST 0H

Device "a"
Supplies RST 0H

Transfers control to → 0000
0007
Subroutine for device "a"

Device "b"
Supplies RST 1H

Transfers control to → 0008
000F
Subroutine for device "b"

Device "x"
Supplies RST 7H

Transfers control to 0038
003F
Subroutine for device "x"

Figure 7.15. Interrupt operation. (Courtesy of Intel Corporation).

with each Teletype input interrupt. Then the subroutine that processes data transmitted from the Teletype to the *CPU* will be called into execution via an eight-byte instruction sequence at memory locations 0000H to 0007H.

A digital input device may supply the instruction:

RST 1H

Then the subroutine that processes the digital input signals will be called via a sequence of instructions occupying memory locations 0008H to 000FH.

Note that any of these eight-byte subroutines may in turn call longer subroutines to process the interrupt, if necessary.

Any device may supply an RST instruction (and indeed may supply any 8080 instruction).

The following is an example of an interrupt sequence (Fig. 7.16). Device 1 signals an interrupt as the *CPU* is executing the instruction at 3C0B. This instruction is completed. The program counter remains set to 3C0C, and the instruction RST 0H supplied by device 1 is executed. Since this is a call to location zero, 3C0C is pushed onto the stack and program control is transferred to location 0000H. (This subroutine may perform jumps, calls, or any other operation.) When the RETURN is executed, address 3C0C is popped off the stack and replaces the contents of the program counter, causing execution to continue at the instruction following the point where the interrupt occurred.

In general, any registers or condition bits changed by an interrupt sub-routine must be restored before returning to the interrupted program, or errors will occur. For example, suppose that a program is interrupted just before the instruction:

JC LOC

and the carry bit equals 1. If the interrupt subroutine happens to zero the carry bit just before returning to the interrupted program, the jump to LOC which should have occurred will not take place, causing the interrupted program to produce erroneous results.

Like any other subroutine, then, any interrupt subroutine should save at least the condition bits and restore them before performing a RETURN operation. (The obvious and most convenient way to do this is to save the data in the stack, using push and pop operations.)

Furthermore, the interrupt enable system is automatically disabled when-ever an interrupt is acknowledged. Except in special cases, therefore, an interrupt subroutine should include an EI instruction somewhere to permit detection and handling of future interrupts. Any time after an EI is exe-

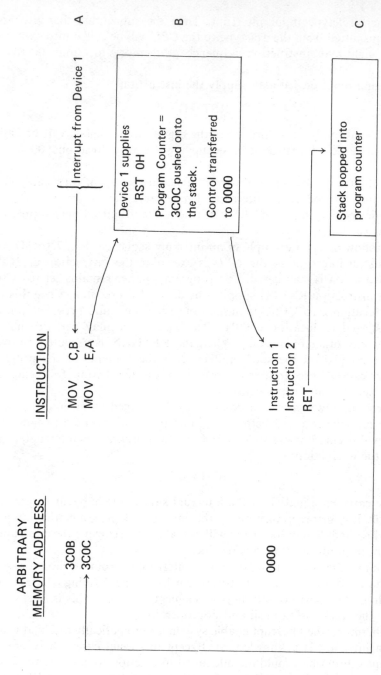

Figure 7.16. Interrupt sequence. (Courtesy of Intel Corporation).

cuted, the interrupt subroutine may itself be interrupted. This process may continue to any level, but as long as all pertinent data are saved and restored, correct program execution will continue automatically.

A typical interrupt subroutine, then, could appear as shown in Table 7.17.

Table 7.17

Code	Operand	Comment
PUSH	PSW	; Save condition bits and accumulator
EI		; Re-enable interrupts
.		;
.		; Perform necessary actions to service
.		; the interrupt
.		
.		
POP	PSW	; Restore machine status
RET		; Return to interrupted program

Priority Interrupt Control Unit (*PICU*)

The system design with multiple interrupt inputs can be simplified by using a special chip called the priority interrupt control unit (*PICU*). The *PICU* is shown in Fig. 7.17.

The 8214 is an eight-level *PICU* designed to simplify interrupt-driven microcomputer systems. The *PICU* can accept eight requesting levels, determine the highest priority, compare this priority to a software-controlled current status register, and issue an interrupt to the system, along with vector information to identify the service routine.

The 8214 is fully expandable by the use of open collector interrupt output and vector information. Control signals are also provided to simplify this function. The *PICU* is designed to support a wide variety of vectored interrupt structures and to reduce package count in interrupt-driven microcomputer systems.

The interrupt vector is described with bits A_0, A_1, and A_2, which are used to set the program counter through the wired-in instruction RST (see Table 7.9).

Input/Output Port

The 8212 is a multimode latch/buffer device designed for use in microcomputer systems. The device consists of an 8-bit latch with tristate output

PIN CONFIGURATION   LOGIC DIAGRAM

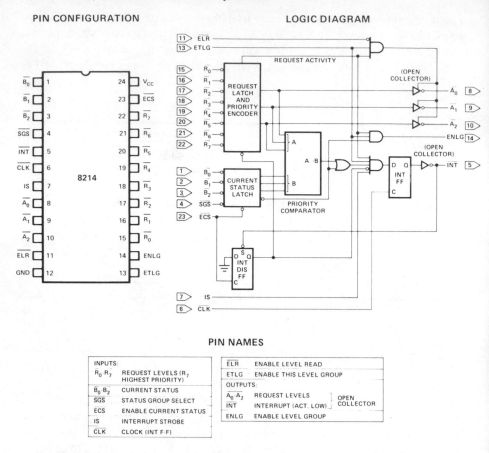

PIN NAMES

INPUTS:			
$R_0 \cdot R_7$	REQUEST LEVELS (R_7 HIGHEST PRIORITY)		
$B_0 \cdot B_2$	CURRENT STATUS		
SGS	STATUS GROUP SELECT		
ECS	ENABLE CURRENT STATUS		
IS	INTERRUPT STROBE		
CLK	CLOCK (INT F·F)		

ELR	ENABLE LEVEL READ	
ETLG	ENABLE THIS LEVEL GROUP	
OUTPUTS:		
$A_0 \cdot A_2$	REQUEST LEVELS	OPEN COLLECTOR
INT	INTERRUPT (ACT. LOW)	
ENLG	ENABLE LEVEL GROUP	

Figure 7.17. Priority interrupt control unit. (Courtesy of Intel Corporation).

buffers, along with control logic and a service request flip-flop. All of the principal peripheral and input/output functions of a microcomputer system can be implemented with this device, Fig 7.18

Many I/O ports can be connected to the same I/O bus, and I/O device selection can be accomplished with a special chip called a *binary decoder*.

Binary Decoder

The binary decoder is shown in Fig. 7.19. The 8205 decoder can be used for the expansion of systems which utilize input ports, output ports, and memory components with active low chip-select input. When the 8205 is

PIN CONFIGURATION

LOGIC DIAGRAM

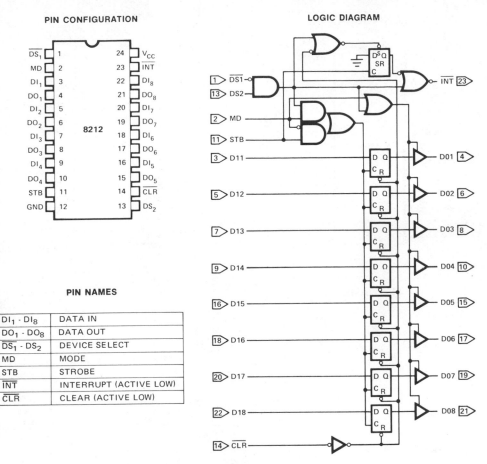

PIN NAMES

DI₁ - DI₈	DATA IN
DO₁ - DO₈	DATA OUT
$\overline{DS_1}$ - DS₂	DEVICE SELECT
MD	MODE
STB	STROBE
$\overline{INT}$	INTERRUPT (ACTIVE LOW)
$\overline{CLR}$	CLEAR (ACTIVE LOW)

Figure 7.18. An 8-bit input/output port. (Courtesy of Intel Corporation).

enabled, one of its eight outputs goes "low"; thus a single row of a memory system is selected. The three-chip enable inputs on the 8205 allow easy system expansion. For very large systems, 8205 decoders can be cascaded so that each decoder can drive eight other decoders for arbitrary memory expansions.

The Intel 8205 is packaged in a standard 16-pin dual-in-line package, and its performance is specified over a temperature range of 0 to +75°C, ambient. The use of Schottky barrier diode clamped transistors to obtain fast switching speeds results in higher performance than is offered by equivalent devices made with a gold diffusion process.

PIN CONFIGURATION   LOGIC SYMBOL

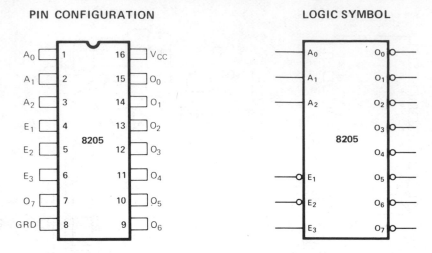

PIN NAMES

$A_0 \cdot A_2$	ADDRESS INPUTS
$\bar{E}_1 \cdot \bar{E}_3$	ENABLE INPUTS
$\bar{O}_0 \cdot \bar{O}_7$	DECODED OUTPUTS

ADDRESS			ENABLE			OUTPUTS							
A_0	A_1	A_2	E_1	E_2	E_3	0	1	2	3	4	5	6	7
L	L	L	L	L	H	L	H	H	H	H	H	H	H
H	L	L	L	L	H	H	L	H	H	H	H	H	H
L	H	L	L	L	H	H	H	L	H	H	H	H	H
H	H	L	L	L	H	H	H	H	L	H	H	H	H
L	L	H	L	L	H	H	H	H	H	L	H	H	H
H	L	H	L	L	H	H	H	H	H	H	L	H	H
L	H	H	L	L	H	H	H	H	H	H	H	L	H
H	H	H	L	L	H	H	H	H	H	H	H	H	L
X	X	X	L	L	L	H	H	H	H	H	H	H	H
X	X	X	H	L	L	H	H	H	H	H	H	H	H
X	X	X	L	H	L	H	H	H	H	H	H	H	H
X	X	X	H	H	L	H	H	H	H	H	H	H	H
X	X	X	H	L	H	H	H	H	H	H	H	H	H
X	X	X	L	H	H	H	H	H	H	H	H	H	H
X	X	X	H	H	H	H	H	H	H	H	H	H	H

Figure 7.19. A one-out-of-eight decoder. (Courtesy of Intel Corporation).

REFERENCES

1. 8080 Microcomputer System Manual, Intel Corp., Santa Clara, Ca., 1975.
2. 8080 Assembly Language Programming Manual, Intel Corp., Santa Clara, Ca., 1974.
3. Brewer, M.: *The Designers Guide to Programmed Logic, for MPS 800 Systems*, Pro–Log Corp., Monterey, Ca., 1974.
4. MCS–8 Microcomputer Set, Users Manual, Intel Corp., Santa Clara, Ca., 1973.

8

M6800 MICROPROCESSOR

Chapter 8 presents 8-bit microprocessor Motorola M6800, which has an 8-bit data bus, a 16-bit address bus, and a control bus. Seven modes of addressing are described: accumulator, immediate, direct, extended, indexed, implied, and relative. The instruction repertoire includes binary and decimal arithmetic, logical, shift, rotate, load, store, conditional or unconditional branch, interrupt, and stack manipulation instructions. The M6800 system is centered on the MicroBus structure, in which both memory and I/O interfaces exist in the same address space. No special instructions are needed for I/O transfer. Supporting I/O chips that simplify the system design are described.

The material* in this chapter has been adapted in part from a publication of Motorola Semiconductor Products Inc. The material so published herein is the full responsibility of the author.

8.1 GENERAL DESCRIPTION

The M6800 family of parts has been designed to achieve several goals in microcomputer architecture. Primarily, these are as follows:

- Minimization of required components
- Minimization of required support packages
- Simplicity of interface
- Simplicity of power requirements
- System throughput

This discussion is intended to demonstrate how these goals have been accomplished by examining the construction and operation of a small microcomputer using M6800 components. Simple examples will also be presented to clarify the operating principles of the system.

Figure 8.1 shows an M6800 microcomputer system with 1024 bytes of read only memory (ROM) for the storage of instructions and permanent data tables, 128 bytes of random access memory (RAM) for the storage of

* Programs, figures, and tables are courtesy and copyright © 1975 by Motorola Semiconductor Products Inc. All rights reserved.

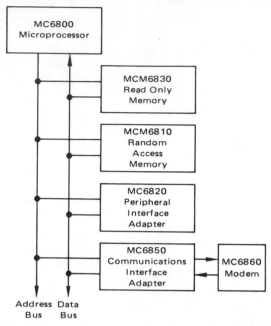

Figure 8.1. A small M6800 microcomputer system. (Courtesy of Motorola Semiconductor Products, Inc.).

temporary data, and two I/O interfaces. Note that the entire system has been implemented with six NMOS packages from the M6800 family.

Figure 8.2 is a symbolic representation of the MC6800 microprocessor, showing its controls and its MicroBus interface. The data and address busses of the processor operate at standard TTL levels and can drive on standard TTL load plus 130 pF. In this application, that drive is sufficient to run with all the other M6800 parts included with no buffers. All the MicroBus parts have this same drive capability and operate at the same standard TTL levels.

The M6800 system has a single address space. The processor references all other bus components as memory locations. Selection of the various memory or I/O packages is accomplished by the state of the address bus alone. This results in considerable simplification of the required bus controls.

Microprocessing Unit (*MPU*)

The MC6800 is a monolithic 8-bit microprocessor forming the central control function for the Motorola M6800 family. Compatible with TTL,

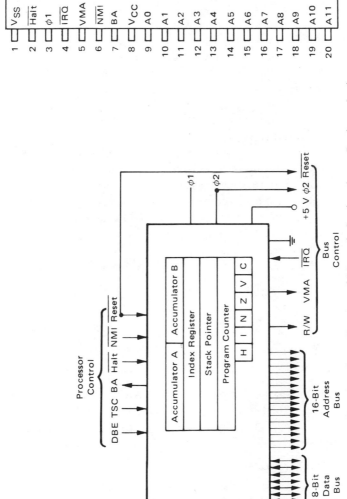

Figure 8.2. Processor bus interface. (Courtesy of Motorola Semiconductor Products, Inc.).

the MC6800, like all M6800 system parts, requires only one +5.0-V power supply, and no external TTL devices for bus interface.

The MC6800 is capable of addressing 65K bytes of memory with its 16-bit address lines. The 8-bit data bus is bidirectional as well as three-state, making direct memory addressing and multiprocessing applications realizable.

- Eight-bit parallel processing
- Bidirectional data bus
- Sixteen-bit address bus—65K bytes of addressing
- Seventy-two Instructions—variable length
- Seven addressing modes—direct, relative, immediate, indexed, extended, implied, and accumulator
- Variable-length stack
- Vectored restart
- Maskable interrupt vector
- Separate nonmaskable interrupt—internal registers saved in stack
- Six internal registers—two accumulators, index register, program counter, stack pointer, and condition code register
- Direct memory addressing (*DMA*) and multiple processor capability
- Clock rates as high as 1 MHz
- Simple bus interface without TTL
- HALT and single-instruction execution capability

Proper operation of the *MPU* requires that certain control and timing signals be provided to accomplish specific functions and that other signal lines be monitored to determine the state of the processor.

Clocks Phase One and Phase Two (*ϕ1, ϕ2*). Two pins are used for a two-phase nonoverlapping clock that runs at the V_{CC} voltage level.

Address Bus (*A0–A15*). Sixteen pins are used for the address bus. The outputs are three-state bus drivers capable of driving one standard TTL load and 130 pF. When the output is turned off, there is essentially an open circuit. This permits the *MPU* to be used in *DMA* applications.

Data Bus (*D0–D7*). Eight pins are used for the data bus. It is bidirectional, transferring data to and from the memory and peripheral devices. It also has three-state output buffers capable of driving one standard TTL load and 130 pF.

Halt. When this input is in the low state, all activity in the machine will be halted. This input is level sensitive. In the HALT mode, the machine will stop at the end of an instruction, bus available will be at a one level, valid memory address will be at a zero level, and all other three-state lines will be in the three-state mode.

Transition of the $\overline{\text{halt}}$ line must not occur during the last 250 nsec of phase one. To ensure single-instruction operation, the $\overline{\text{halt}}$ line must go high for one $\phi 1$ clock cycle.

Three-State Control (TSC). This input causes all of the address lines and the read/write line to go into the off or high-impedance state. This state will occur 500 nsec after TSC $= 2.4$ V. The valid memory address and bus available signals will be forced low. The data bus is not affected by TSC and has its own enable (data bus enable). In *DMA* applications, the three-state control line should be brought high on the leading edge of the phase one clock. The $\phi 1$ clock must be held in the high state and the $\phi 2$ in the low state for this function to operate properly. The address bus will then be available for other devices to directly address memory. Since the *MPU* is a dynamic device, it can be held in this state for only 5.0 μsec or destruction of data will occur in the *MPU*.

Read/Write (R/W). This TTL compatible output signals the peripherals and memory devices whether the *MPU* is in a READ (high) or WRITE (low) state. The normal standby state of this signal is READ (high). Three-state control going high will turn read/write to the off (high impedance) state. Also, when the processor is halted, it will be in the off state. This output is capable of driving one standard TTL load and 130 pF.

Valid Memory Address (VMA). This output indicates to peripheral devices that there is a valid address on the address bus. In normal operation, this signal should be utilized for enabling peripheral interfaces such as the PIA and ACIA. This signal is not three-state. One standard TTL load and 30 pF may be directly driven by this active high signal.

Data Bus Enable (DBE). This input is the three-state control signal for the *MPU* data bus and will enable the bus drivers when in the high state. This input is TTL compatible; however, in normal operation, it would be driven by the $\phi 2$ clock. During an *MPU* read cycle, the data bus drivers will be disabled internally. When it is desired that another device control the data bus, as in direct memory access (*DMA*) applications, DBE should be held low.

Bus Available (BA). The bus available signal will normally be in the low state; when activated, it will go to the high state, indicating that the microprocessor has stopped and that the address bus is available. This will occur if the $\overline{\text{halt}}$ line is in the low state or the processor is in the WAIT state as a result of the execution of a WAIT instruction. At such time, all three-state output drivers will go to their off state and other outputs to their normally inactive level. The processor is removed from the WAIT state by the occurrence of a maskable (mask bit $1 = 0$) or nonmaskable interrupt. This output is capable of driving one standard TTL load and 30 pF.

Interrupt Request $(\overline{IRQ})$. This level-sensitive input requests that an interrupt sequence be generated within the machine. The processor will wait until it completes the current instruction that is being executed before it recognizes the request. At that time, if the interrupt mask bit in the condition code register is not set, the machine will begin an interrupt sequence. The index register, program counter, accumulators, and condition code register are stored away on the stack. Next the *MPU* will respond to the interrupt request by setting the interrupt mask bit high so that no further interrupts can occur. At the end of the cycle, a 16-bit address will be loaded that points to a vectoring address located in memory locations FFF8 and FFF9. An address loaded at these locations causes the *MPU* to branch to an interrupt routine in memory.

The $\overline{\text{halt}}$ line must be in the high state for interrupts to be recognized.

The $\overline{IRQ}$ has a high impedance pull-up device internal to the chip; however, a 3-kΩ external resistor to V_{CC} should be used for wire-OR and optimum control of interrupts.

Reset. This input is used to reset and start the *MPU* from a power-down condition, resulting from a power failure or an initial start-up of the processor. If a positive edge is detected on the input, this will signal the *MPU* to begin the restart sequence. This will start execution of a routine to initialize the processor from its reset condition. All the higher-order address lines will be forced high. For the restart, the last two (FFFE, FFFF) locations in memory will be used to load the program that is addressed by the program counter. During the restart routine, the interrupt mask bit is set and must be reset before the *MPU* can be interrupted by $\overline{IRQ}$.

The clock for the system will operate at a maximum frequency of 1 MHz. The two phases are nonoverlapping square wave complements. At this clock frequency, the MC6800 processor achieves a minimum instruction time of 2 μsec. The two clocks are the only inputs to the processor that do not operate at standard TTL levels.

All of the MicroBus components will operate on the same +5 V power supply and ground.

Figure 8.2 shows all the signals necessary to control the processor and all the pins on the processor package. Note that each signal is on a separate pin. The simplicity of the processor controls results directly from the simplicity of the M6800 MicroBus architecture.

Figure 8.3 shows the initialization of the microprocessor after restart. Reset must be held low for at least eight clock periods after V_{CC} reaches 4.75 V. If reset goes high before the leading edge of $\phi2$, on the next $\phi1$ the first restart memory vector address (FFFE) will appear on the address lines. This location should contain the higher-order 8 bits to be stored into the program counter. The next address (FFFF) should contain the lower-order 8 bits to be stored into the program counter (Table 8.1).

Table 8.1.   Memory Map for Interrupt Vectors

Vector		Description
MS	LS	
FFFE	FFFF	Restart
FFFC	FFFD	Non-maskable Interrupt
FFFA	FFFB	Software Interrupt
FFF8	FFF9	Interrupt Request

Nonmaskable Interrupt ($\overline{NMI}$). A low-going edge on this input requests that a nonmask-interrupt sequence be generated within the processor. As with the $\overline{IRQ}$ signal, the processor will complete the current instruction that is being executed before it recognizes the $\overline{NMI}$ signal. The interrupt mask bit in the condition code register has no effect on $\overline{NMI}$.

The index register, program counter, accumulators, and condition code register are stored away on the stack. At the end of the cycle, a 16-bit address will be loaded that points to a vectoring address located in memory locations FFFC and FFFD. An address loaded at these locations causes the *MPU* to branch to a nonmaskable interrupt routine in memory.

The input $\overline{NMI}$ has a high-impedance pull-up resistor internal to the chip; however, a 3-kΩ external resistor to V_{CC} should be used for wire-OR and optimum control of interrupts.

Inputs $\overline{IRQ}$ and $\overline{NMI}$ are hardware interrupt lines that are sampled during $\phi2$ and will start the interrupt routine on the $\phi1$ after the completion of an instruction.

Figure 8.4 is a flow chart describing the major decision paths and interrupt vectors of the microprocessor. Table 8.1 gives the memory map for interrupt vectors.

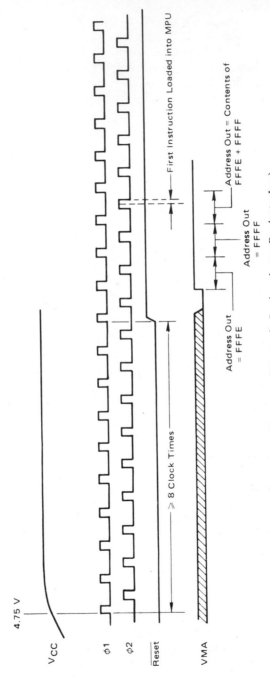

Figure 8.3. Initialization of *MPU* after restart. (Courtesy of Motorola Semiconductor Products, Inc.).

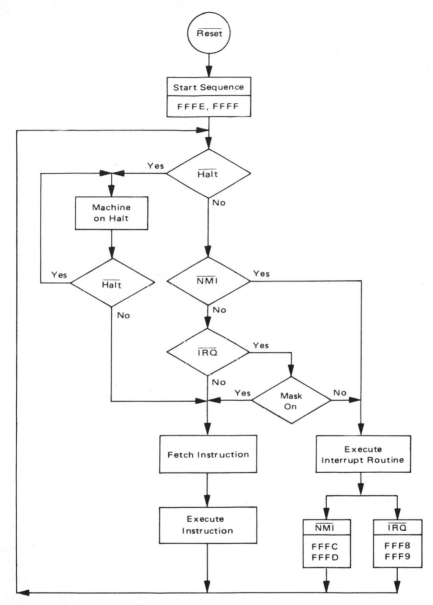

Figure 8.4. *MPU* flow chart. (Courtesy of Motorola Semiconductor Products, Inc.).

Microprocessing Unit Registers

The *MPU* has three 16-bit registers and three 8-bit registers available for use by the programmer (Fig. 8.5).

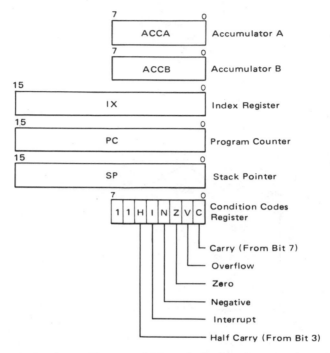

Figure 8.5. *MPU* registers. (Courtesy of Motorola Semiconductor Products, Inc.).

Program Counter. The program counter is a two-byte (16-bit) register that points to the current program address.

Stack Pointer. The stack pointer is a two-byte register that contains the address of the next available location in an external push-down/pop-up stack. This stack is normally a random access read/write memory that may have any convenient location (address). For applications that require storage of information in the stack when power is lost, the stack must be nonvolatile.

Index Register. The index register is a two-byte register used to store data or a 16-bit memory address for the indexed mode of memory addressing.

Accumulators. The *MPU* contains two 8-bit accumulators that are used to hold operands and results from an arithmetic logic unit (*ALU*).

Condition Code Register. The condition code register indicates the results of an arithmetic logic unit operation: negative (N), zero (Z), overflow (V), carry from bit 7 (C), and half-carry from bit 3 (H). These bits of the condition code register are used as testable conditions for the conditional branch instructions. Bit 4 is the interrupt mask bit (1). The unused bits of the condition code register (b6 and b7) are ones.

Figure 8.6 shows the order of saving the microprocessor status within the stack.

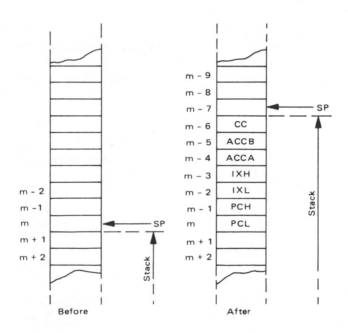

SP = Stack Pointer
CC = Condition Codes (Also called the Processor Status Byte)
ACCB = Accumulator B
ACCA = Accumulator A
IXH = Index Register, Higher Order 8 Bits
IXL = Index Register, Lower Order 8 Bits
PCH = Program Counter, Higher Order 8 Bits
PCL = Program Counter, Lower Order 8 Bits

Figure 8.6. Saving the status of the microprocessor in the stack. (Courtesy of Motorola Semiconductor Products, Inc.).

8.2.   ADDRESSING MODES

The MC6800 8-bit microprocessing unit has seven address modes that can be used by a programmer, with the addressing mode a function of both the type of instruction and the coding within the instruction.

Accumulator (ACCX) Addressing

In accumulator-only addressing, either accumulator A or accumulator B is specified. These are one-byte instructions.

Immediate Addressing

In immediate addressing, the operand is contained in the second byte of the instruction except for LDS and LDX, which have the operand in the second and third bytes of the instruction. The MPU addresses this location when it fetches the immediate instruction for execution. These are two- or three-byte instructions.

Direct Addressing

In direct addressing, the address of the operand is contained in the second byte of the instruction. Direct addressing allows the user to directly address the lowest 256 bytes in the machine, that is, locations 0–255. Enhanced execution times are achieved by storing data in these locations. In most configurations, it should be a random access memory. These are two-byte instructions.

Extended Addressing

In extended addressing, the address contained in the second byte of the instruction is used as the higher 8 bits of the address of the operand. The third byte of the instruction serves as the lower 8 bits of the address for the operand. This is an absolute address in memory. These are three-byte instructions.

Indexed Addressing

In indexed addressing, the address contained in the second byte of the instruction is added to the index register's lowest 8 bits in the MPU. The carry is then added to the higher-order 8 bits of the index register. This result is then used to address memory. The modified address is held in a temporary address register so there is no change to the index register. These are two-byte instructions.

Implied Addressing

In implied addressing, the instruction gives the address (i.e., stack pointer, index register, etc.). These are one-byte instructions.

Relative Addressing

In relative addressing, the address contained in the second byte of the instruction is added to the program counter's lowest 8 bits plus two. The carry or borrow is then added to the high 8 bits. This allows the user to address data within a range of -125 to $+129$ bytes of the present instruction. These are two-byte instructions.

8.3. INSTRUCTION SET

The MC6800 has a set of 72 different instructions. Included are binary and decimal arithmetic, logical, shift, rotate, load, store, conditional or unconditional branch, interrupt, and stack manipulation instructions (Tables 8.2 through 8.6 and Fig 8.7).

8.4. PROGRAMMING EXAMPLES

Addition and Subtraction

Most *MPU*-based systems require that the arithmetic instruction set be combined into more complex routines that operate on numbers larger than one byte. If more than one number system is used, routines must be written for each, or conversion routines to some common base must be used. In many cases, however, it is more efficient to write a specialized routine for each system requirement, that is, hexadecimal (HEX) versus unpacked BCD multiplication, and so on. In this section, several algorithms are discussed with specific examples showing their implementation with the MC6800 instruction set.

The basic arithmetic operations are binary addition and subtraction:

ALPHA + BETA = GAMMA		ALPHA − BETA = GAMMA	
LDAA	ALPHA	LDAA	ALPHA
ADDA	BETA	SUBA	BETA
STAA	GAMMA	STAA	GAMMA

Table 8.2. Microprocessor Instruction Set—Alphabetic Sequence

ABA	Add Accumulators	CLR	Clear	PSH	Push Data
ADC	Add with Carry	CLV	Clear Overflow	PUL	Pull Data
ADD	Add	CMP	Compare		
AND	Logical AND	COM	Complement	ROL	Rotate Left
ASL	Arithmetic Shift Left	CPX	Compare Index Register	ROR	Rotate Right
ASR	Arithmetic Shift Right			RTI	Return from Interrupt
		DAA	Decimal Adjust	RTS	Return from Subroutine
BCC	Branch if Carry Clear	DEC	Decrement		
BCS	Branch if Carry Set	DES	Decrement Stack Pointer	SBA	Subtract Accumulators
BEQ	Branch if Equal to Zero	DEX	Decrement Index Register	SBC	Subtract with Carry
BGE	Branch if Greater than or			SEC	Set Carry
	Equal to Zero	EOR	Exclusive OR	SEI	Set Interrupt Mask
BGT	Branch if Greater than Zero			SEV	Set Overflow
BHI	Branch if Higher	INC	Increment	STA	Store Accumulator
BIT	Bit Test	INS	Increment Stack Pointer	STS	Store Stack Register
BLE	Branch if Less or Equal	INX	Increment Index Register	STX	Store Index Register
BLS	Branch if Lower or Same			SUB	Subtract
BLT	Branch if Less than Zero	JMP	Jump	SWI	Software Interrupt
BMI	Branch if Minus	JSR	Jump to Subroutine		
BNE	Branch if Not Equal to Zero			TAB	Transfer Accumulators
BPL	Branch if Plus	LDA	Load Accumulator	TAP	Transfer Accumulators to Condition
BRA	Branch Always	LDS	Load Stack Pointer		Code Register
BSR	Branch to Subroutine	LDX	Load Index Register	TBA	Transfer Accumulators
BVC	Branch if Overflow Clear	LSR	Logical Shift Right	TPA	Transfer Condition Code Register to
BVS	Branch if Overflow Set				Accumulator
		NEG	Negate	TST	Test
CBA	Compare Accumulators	NOP	No Operation	TSX	Transfer Stack Pointer to Index Register
CLC	Clear Carry			TXS	Transfer Index Register to Stack Pointer
CLI	Clear Interrupt Mask	ORA	Inclusive OR Accumulator	WAI	Wait for Interrupt

These operations are so short that they are usually programmed in line with the main flow. Addition of single-packed BCD bytes requires only one more instruction. The DAA instruction is used immediately after the ADD, ADC, or ABA instruction to adjust the binary generated in accumulator A (ACCA) to the correct BCD value:

```
        LDAA        ALPHA
        ADDA        BETA
        DAA
        STAA        GAMMA
```

Carry	ACCA
X	67	0110 0111 = ACCA
X	+79	carry 0111 1001 = MEMORY
O	146	0 1110 0000 = ACCA	Binary result
	46	1 0100 0110 = ACCA	After DAA; the carry bit will also be set because of the BCD carry

Since no similar instruction is available for BCD subtraction, ten's complement arithmetic may be used to generate the difference. The following routine performs a BCD subtraction of two-digit BCD numbers:

```
LDAA        # $99
SUBA        BETA        (99-BETA) = ACCA
SEC                     Carry = 1
ADCA        ALPHA       ACCA + ALPHA + C = ACCA
DAA                     DECIMAL ADJUST (−100)
STAA        GAMMA       ALPHA-BETA = GAMMA
```

The routine implements the algorithm defined by the following equations:

ALPHA − BETA = GAMMA

ALPHA + (99-BETA) − 99 = GAMMA   9's COMPLEMENT OF BETA

ALPHA + (99-BETA+1) − 100 = GAMMA   10's COMPLEMENT OF BETA

One is added to the nine's complement of the subtrahend by setting the carry bit to find the ten's complement of BETA, which is then added to the minuend ALPHA and saved in ACCA. The DAA instruction adjusts the result in ACCA to the proper BCD values before storing the difference in GAMMA. Since 100 has been added (99 + 1) to the subtrahend by finding the ten's complement, 100 must also be subtracted. This is accomplished by the DAA instruction since the resulting carry is discarded.

Table 8.3. Accumulator and Memory Instructions

OPERATIONS	MNEMONIC	IMMED OP	IMMED ~	IMMED #	DIRECT OP	DIRECT ~	DIRECT #	INDEX OP	INDEX ~	INDEX #	EXTND OP	EXTND ~	EXTND #	IMPLIED OP	IMPLIED ~	IMPLIED #	BOOLEAN/ARITHMETIC OPERATION (All register labels refer to contents)	H (5)	I (4)	N (3)	Z (2)	V (1)	C (0)
Add	ADDA	8B	2	2	9B	3	2	AB	5	2	BB	4	3				A + M → A	●	•	●	●	●	●
	ADDB	CB	2	2	DB	3	2	EB	5	2	FB	4	3				B + M → B	●	•	●	●	●	●
Add Acmltrs	ABA													1B	2	1	A + B → A	●	•	●	●	●	●
Add with Carry	ADCA	89	2	2	99	3	2	A9	5	2	B9	4	3				A + M + C → A	●	•	●	●	●	●
	ADCB	C9	2	2	D9	3	2	E9	5	2	F9	4	3				B + M + C → B	●	•	●	●	●	●
And	ANDA	84	2	2	94	3	2	A4	5	2	B4	4	3				A · M → A	•	•	●	●	R	•
	ANDB	C4	2	2	D4	3	2	E4	5	2	F4	4	3				B · M → B	•	•	●	●	R	•
Bit Test	BITA	85	2	2	95	3	2	A5	5	2	B5	4	3				A · M	•	•	●	●	R	•
	BITB	C5	2	2	D5	3	2	E5	5	2	F5	4	3				B · M	•	•	●	●	R	•
Clear	CLR							6F	7	2	7F	6	3				00 → M	•	•	R	S	R	R
	CLRA													4F	2	1	00 → A	•	•	R	S	R	R
	CLRB													5F	2	1	00 → B	•	•	R	S	R	R
Compare	CMPA	81	2	2	91	3	2	A1	5	2	B1	4	3				A - M	•	•	●	●	●	●
	CMPB	C1	2	2	D1	3	2	E1	5	2	F1	4	3				B - M	•	•	●	●	●	●
Compare Acmltrs	CBA													11	2	1	A - B	•	•	●	●	●	●
Complement, 1's	COM							63	7	2	73	6	3				M̄ → M	•	•	●	●	R	S
	COMA													43	2	1	Ā → A	•	•	●	●	R	S
	COMB													53	2	1	B̄ → B	•	•	●	●	R	S
Complement, 2's (Negate)	NEG							60	7	2	70	6	3				00 - M → M	•	•	●	●	①	②
	NEGA													40	2	1	00 - A → A	•	•	●	●	①	②
	NEGB													50	2	1	00 - B → B	•	•	●	●	①	②
Decimal Adjust, A	DAA													19	2	1	Converts Binary Add of BCD Characters into BCD Format	•	•	●	●	●	③
Decrement	DEC							6A	7	2	7A	6	3				M - 1 → M	•	•	●	●	④	•
	DECA													4A	2	1	A - 1 → A	•	•	●	●	④	•
	DECB													5A	2	1	B - 1 → B	•	•	●	●	④	•
Exclusive OR	EORA	88	2	2	98	3	2	A8	5	2	B8	4	3				A ⊕ M → A	•	•	●	●	R	•
	EORB	C8	2	2	D8	3	2	E8	5	2	F8	4	3				B ⊕ M → B	•	•	●	●	R	•
Increment	INC							6C	7	2	7C	6	3				M + 1 → M	•	•	●	●	⑤	•
	INCA													4C	2	1	A + 1 → A	•	•	●	●	⑤	•
	INCB													5C	2	1	B + 1 → B	•	•	●	●	⑤	•
Load Acmltr	LDAA	86	2	2	96	3	2	A6	5	2	B6	4	3				M → A	•	•	●	●	R	•
	LDAB	C6	2	2	D6	3	2	E6	5	2	F6	4	3				M → B	•	•	●	●	R	•
Or, Inclusive	ORAA	8A	2	2	9A	3	2	AA	5	2	BA	4	3				A + M → A	•	•	●	●	R	•
	ORAB	CA	2	2	DA	3	2	EA	5	2	FA	4	3				B + M → B	•	•	●	●	R	•
Push Data	PSHA													36	4	1	A → Msp, SP - 1 → SP	•	•	•	•	•	•
	PSHB													37	4	1	B → Msp, SP - 1 → SP	•	•	•	•	•	•
Pull Data	PULA													32	4	1	SP + 1 → SP, Msp → A	•	•	•	•	•	•

314

Operations	Mnemonic	IMMED (OP ~ #)	DIRECT (OP ~ #)	INDEX (OP ~ #)	EXTND (OP ~ #)	IMPLIED (OP ~ #)	Boolean/Arithmetic Operation	H	I	N	Z	V	C
	PULB					33 4 1	SP + 1 → SP, MSP → B	•	•	•	•	•	•
Rotate Left	ROL			69 7 2	79 6 3		M ⎫ A ⎬ C ←[b7…b0] B ⎭	•	•	↕	↕	⑥	↕
	ROLA					49 2 1		•	•	↕	↕	⑥	↕
	ROLB					59 2 1		•	•	↕	↕	⑥	↕
Rotate Right	ROR			66 7 2	76 6 3		M ⎫ A ⎬ [b7…b0]→ C B ⎭	•	•	↕	↕	⑥	↕
	RORA					46 2 1		•	•	↕	↕	⑥	↕
	RORB					56 2 1		•	•	↕	↕	⑥	↕
Shift Left, Arithmetic	ASL			68 7 2	78 6 3		M ⎫ A ⎬ C ←[b7…b0]← 0 B ⎭	•	•	↕	↕	⑥	↕
	ASLA					48 2 1		•	•	↕	↕	⑥	↕
	ASLB					58 2 1		•	•	↕	↕	⑥	↕
Shift Right, Arithmetic	ASR			67 7 2	77 6 3		M ⎫ A ⎬ [b7…b0]→ C B ⎭	•	•	↕	↕	⑥	↕
	ASRA					47 2 1		•	•	↕	↕	⑥	↕
	ASRB					57 2 1		•	•	↕	↕	⑥	↕
Shift Right, Logic	LSR			64 7 2	74 6 3		M ⎫ A ⎬ 0 →[b7…b0]→ C B ⎭	•	•	R	↕	⑥	↕
	LSRA					44 2 1		•	•	R	↕	⑥	↕
	LSRB					54 2 1		•	•	R	↕	⑥	↕
Store Acmltr.	STAA		97 4 2	A7 6 2	B7 5 3		A → M	•	•	↕	↕	R	•
	STAB		D7 4 2	E7 6 2	F7 5 3		B → M	•	•	↕	↕	R	•
Subtract	SUBA	80 2 2	90 3 2	A0 5 2	B0 4 3		A − M → A	•	•	↕	↕	↕	↕
	SUBB	C0 2 2	D0 3 2	E0 5 2	F0 4 3		B − M → B	•	•	↕	↕	↕	↕
Subtract Acmltrs.	SBA					10 2 1	A − B → A	•	•	↕	↕	↕	↕
Subtr. with Carry	SBCA	82 2 2	92 3 2	A2 5 2	B2 4 3		A − M − C → A	•	•	↕	↕	↕	↕
	SBCB	C2 2 2	D2 3 2	E2 5 2	F2 4 3		B − M − C → B	•	•	↕	↕	↕	↕
Transfer Acmltrs.	TAB					16 2 1	A → B	•	•	↕	↕	R	•
	TBA					17 2 1	B → A	•	•	↕	↕	R	•
Test, Zero or Minus	TST			6D 7 2	7D 6 3		M − 00	•	•	↕	↕	R	R
	TSTA					4D 2 1	A − 00	•	•	↕	↕	R	R
	TSTB					5D 2 1	B − 00	•	•	↕	↕	R	R

LEGEND:

OP   Operation Code (Hexadecimal);
~   Number of MPU Cycles;
=   Number of Program Bytes;
+   Arithmetic Plus;
−   Arithmetic Minus;
•   Boolean AND;
MSP Contents of memory location pointed to be Stack Pointer.

+   Boolean Inclusive OR;
⊙   Boolean Exclusive OR;
$\overline{M}$ Complement of M;
→   Transfer Into;
0   Bit = Zero;
00   Byte = Zero;

Note — Accumulator addressing mode instructions are included in the column for IMPLIED addressing

CONDITION CODE SYMBOLS:

H   Half carry from bit 3;
I   Interrupt mask
N   Negative (sign bit)
Z   Zero (byte)
V   Overflow, 2's complement
C   Carry from bit 7
R   Reset Always
S   Set Always
:   Test and set if true, cleared otherwise
•   Not Affected

Table 8.4. Index Register and Stack Manipulation Instructions

POINTER OPERATIONS	MNEMONIC	IMMED OP	~	#	DIRECT OP	~	#	INDEX OP	~	#	EXTND OP	~	#	IMPLIED OP	~	#	BOOLEAN/ARITHMETIC OPERATION	H 5	I 4	N 3	Z 2	V 1	C 0
Compare Index Reg	CPX	8C	3	3	9C	4	2	AC	6	2	BC	5	3				$X_H - M, X_L - (M+1)$	•	•	⑦	↕	⑦	•
Decrement Index Reg	DEX													09	4	1	$X - 1 \to X$	•	•	↕	↕	•	•
Decrement Stack Pntr	DES													34	4	1	$SP - 1 \to SP$	•	•	•	•	•	•
Increment Index Reg	INX													08	4	1	$X + 1 \to X$	•	•	↕	↕	•	•
Increment Stack Pntr	INS													31	4	1	$SP + 1 \to SP$	•	•	•	•	•	•
Load Index Reg	LDX	CE	3	3	DE	4	2	EE	6	2	FE	5	3				$M \to X_H, (M+1) \to X_L$	•	•	⑨	↕	R	•
Load Stack Pntr	LDS	8E	3	3	9E	4	2	AE	6	2	BE	5	3				$M \to SP_H, (M+1) \to SP_L$	•	•	⑨	↕	R	•
Store Index Reg	STX				DF	5	2	EF	7	2	FF	6	3				$X_H \to M, X_L \to (M+1)$	•	•	⑨	↕	R	•
Store Stack Pntr	STS				9F	5	2	AF	7	2	BF	6	3				$SP_H \to M, SP_L \to (M+1)$	•	•	⑨	↕	R	•
Indx Reg → Stack Pntr	TXS													35	4	1	$X - 1 \to SP$	•	•	•	•	•	•
Stack Pntr → Indx Reg	TSX													30	4	1	$SP + 1 \to X$	•	•	•	•	•	•

Table 8.5. Jump and Branch Instructions

OPERATIONS	MNEMONIC	RELATIVE OP	~	#	INDEX OP	~	#	EXTND OP	~	#	IMPLIED OP	~	#	BRANCH TEST	H (5)	I (4)	N (3)	Z (2)	V (1)	C (0)
Branch Always	BRA	20	4	2										None	•	•	•	•	•	•
Branch If Carry Clear	BCC	24	4	2										C = 0	•	•	•	•	•	•
Branch If Carry Set	BCS	25	4	2										C = 1	•	•	•	•	•	•
Branch If = Zero	BEQ	27	4	2										Z = 1	•	•	•	•	•	•
Branch If ≥ Zero	BGE	2C	4	2										$N \oplus V = 0$	•	•	•	•	•	•
Branch If > Zero	BGT	2E	4	2										$Z + (N \oplus V) = 0$	•	•	•	•	•	•
Branch If Higher	BHI	22	4	2										C + Z = 0	•	•	•	•	•	•
Branch If ≤ Zero	BLE	2F	4	2										$Z + (N \oplus V) = 1$	•	•	•	•	•	•
Branch If Lower Or Same	BLS	23	4	2										C + Z = 1	•	•	•	•	•	•
Branch If < Zero	BLT	2D	4	2										$N \oplus V = 1$	•	•	•	•	•	•
Branch If Minus	BMI	2B	4	2										N = 1	•	•	•	•	•	•
Branch If Not Equal Zero	BNE	26	4	2										Z = 0	•	•	•	•	•	•
Branch If Overflow Clear	BVC	28	4	2										V = 0	•	•	•	•	•	•
Branch If Overflow Set	BVS	29	4	2										V = 1	•	•	•	•	•	•
Branch If Plus	BPL	2A	4	2										N = 0	•	•	•	•	•	•
Branch To Subroutine	BSR	8D	8	2											•	•	•	•	•	•
Jump	JMP				6E	4	2	7E	3	3				} See Special Operations	•	•	•	•	•	•
Jump To Subroutine	JSR				AD	8	2	BD	9	3					•	•	•	•	•	•
No Operation	NOP										02	2	1	Advances Prog. Cntr. Only	•	•	•	•	•	•
Return From Interrupt	RTI										3B	10	1	} See Special Operations	•	• (11)	•	•	•	•
Return From Subroutine	RTS										39	5	1		•	•	•	•	•	•
Software Interrupt	SWI										3F	12	1	} See Special Operations	•	• (10)	•	•	•	•
Wait for Interrupt	WAI										3E	9	1		•	•	•	•	•	•

317

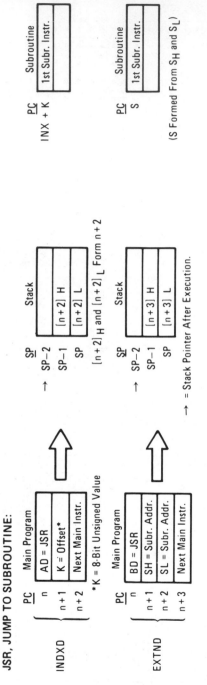
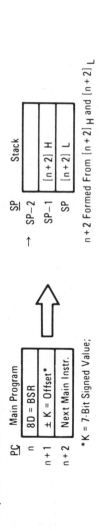

Figure 8.7. Stack, subroutines, and interrupts. (Courtesy of Motorola Semiconductor Products, Inc.).

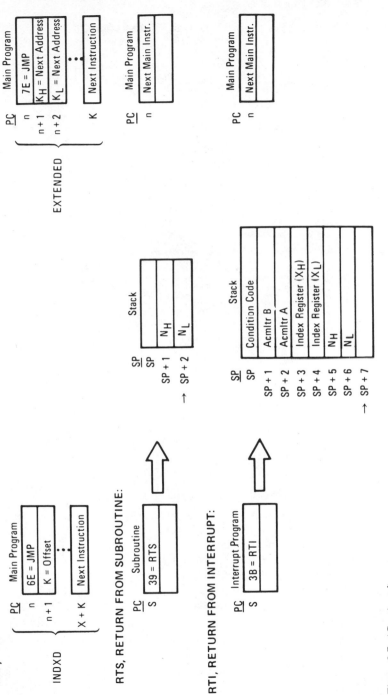

Figure 8.7. (*Continued*)

319

Table 8.6.   Condition Code Register Manipulation Instructions

| OPERATIONS | MNEMONIC | IMPLIED | | | BOOLEAN OPERATION | COND. CODE REG. | | | | | |
		OP	~	#		5 H	4 I	3 N	2 Z	1 V	0 C
Clear Carry	CLC	0C	2	1	$0 \rightarrow C$	•	•	•	•	•	R
Clear Interrupt Mask	CLI	0E	2	1	$0 \rightarrow I$	•	R	•	•	•	•
Clear Overflow	CLV	0A	2	1	$0 \rightarrow V$	•	•	•	•	R	•
Set Carry	SEC	0D	2	1	$1 \rightarrow C$	•	•	•	•	•	S
Set Interrupt Mask	SEI	0F	2	1	$1 \rightarrow I$	•	S	•	•	•	•
Set Overflow	SEV	0B	2	1	$1 \rightarrow V$	•	•	•	•	S	•
Acmltr A → CCR	TAP	06	2	1	$A \rightarrow CCR$	—	—	(12)	—	—	—
CCR → Acmltr A	TPA	07	2	1	$CCR \rightarrow A$	•	•	•	•	•	•

CONDITION CODE REGISTER NOTES:

(Bit set if test is true and cleared otherwise).

1	(Bit V)	Test: Result = 10000000?
2	(Bit C)	Test: Result = 00000000?
3	(Bit C)	Test: Decimal value of most significant BCD Character greater than nine? (Not cleared if previously set.)
4	(Bit V)	Test: Operand = 10000000 prior to execution?
5	(Bit V)	Test: Operand = 01111111 prior to execution?
6	(Bit V)	Test: Set equal to result of N + C after shift has occurred.
7	(Bit N)	Test: Sign bit of most significant (MS) byte = 1?
8	(Bit V)	Test: 2's complement overflow from subtraction of MS bytes?
9	(Bit N)	Test: Result less than zero? (Bit 15 = 1)
10	(All)	Load Condition Code Register from Stack. (See Special Operations)
11	(Bit I)	Set when interrupt occurs. If previously set, a Non—Maskable Interrupt is required to exit the wait state.
12	(All)	Set according to the contents of Accumulator A.

Multiple-precision operations mean that the data and results require more than one byte of memory. The simplest multiple-precision routines are addition and subtraction of 16-bit binary or two's complement numbers. This is often called *double* precision since two consecutive bytes are required to store 16 binary bits of information. The routines shown in Table 8.7 illustrate these functions.

Counting and Delay Generation

When microprocessor systems are initially considered as replacements for conventional logic designs, there is a natural tendency to formulate such questions as the following: What is the program that replaces a flip-flop? A counter? A shift register? A one-shot? The answer to the question then often falls into one of two categories: (1) the number of times something occurs must be determined (counted); (2) a particular time interval must be measured or generated before taking some action.

For applications requiring long counters (up to 16 bits or decimal 65,535) the index register and its full complement of instructions are available.

Table 8.7

LDAA	ALPHA +	
LDAB	ALPHA	
ADDA	BETA +1	ADD LS BYTES
ADCB	BETA	ADD MS BYTES WITH CARRY FROM LS BYTES
STAA	GAMMA +1	
STAB	GAMMA	
LDAA	ALPHA +1	
LDAB	ALPHA	
SUBA	BETA +1	SUBTRACT LS BYTES
SBCB	BETA	SUBTRACT MS BYTES WITH BORROW FROM LS BYTES
STAA	GAMMA +1	
STAB	GAMMA	

When more than one long counter is required simultaneously, a short program can be written that permits two adjacent RAM locations to be used as a 16-bit counter:

	INC	N+1	Increment mem. loc. $N+1$
	BNE	CNTNUE	If result not = 0, continue
	INC	N	
CNTNUE	xxx	xxxxxx	Next program instruction

This sequence effectively increments a 16-bit word located in memory locations N and $N+1$. A similar procedure is available for decrementing a 16-bit word:

	TST	N+1	Mem. loc. $N+1$ = 0?
	BNE	NEXT	No, go decr. $N+1$
	DEC	N	Yes, first decr. N
NEXT	DEC	N+1	Decr. $N=1$

In addition to their use for long counters, these instruction sequences can be used for modifying return addresses. During execution of subroutines and interrupt service routines the program counter containing the return address is stored on the stack, a designated area in RAM. The increment or decrement sequences can be used to change the program counter value on the stack and thus cause the return from subroutine or interrupt to be to a different location in the main program.

It is possible in some cases to use the index register and accumulators for two functions simultaneously when one is a counting function. As an example, assume that data from a peripheral device is to be entered into the *MPU*'s memory via an MC6820 peripheral interface adapter (*PIA*). The peripheral is to indicate the presence of data by setting a flag, bit 7 of the *PIA*'s control register. Each time the flag is set, the *MPU* is to retrieve the data from the *PIA* data register and store them in an internal memory location until a total of eight bytes has been accumulated. Since the *PIA*'s data register and control register look like memory to the *MPU*, a program is required that will cause the *MPU* to monitor one memory location for a change in a flag bit and then fetch the data from another location. This operation is to be repeated the specified number (8) of times.

The sequence of instructions shown in Table 8.8 uses a single register, accumulator *B*, for both the monitoring and counting functions. This program takes advantage of the fact that incrementing an accumulator containing FF causes it to "roll over" to 00. The two's complement of the required count is entered as the byte count. Since this will cause the sign bit (bit 7) of ACCB to be positive, and since the BIT test does not affect ACCB but does update the condition code register, the BIT test followed by the BRANCH ON PLUS instruction can be used to monitor the flag bit. As soon as bit 7 of the control register is set to 1, the BPL test fails and the *MPU* fetches the current data byte by reading the data register (PIADRA) and then pushes the byte onto a stack location in *RAM*. The design of the *PIA* is such that the flag is automatically cleared by the LDAA PIADRA operation. The byte count is then "reduced" by incrementing ACCB and tested by the BRANCH ON NOT EQUAL ZERO instruction. Unless the eighth byte has just been transferred, the program loops back to wait on the next data byte. If the current byte was the eighth, the INCB instruction causes the count to roll over to zero, the branch test fails, and program flow falls through to the next instruction. The other test instructions (TST, CMP, and CBA) can also be used in a similar fashion since they too update the condition code bits but do not affect the register contents. Note also that it was not necessary to bring the contents of the control register into the *MPU* in order to examine the flag.

Table 8.8

:	LDAB	# 08	Put 2's compl. of byte count in ACCB
LOOP1	BITB	PIACRA	Byte available flag set?
	BPL	LOOP1	Not yet, loop back, chk. again.
	LDAA	PIADRA	Yes, fetch byte.
	PSHA		Put byte on stack.
	INCB	.	Eight bytes yet?
	BNE	LOOP1	No, go wait for next byte.
	xxx	xxxxxx	Yes, continue with program.

Delays can be generated in a variety of ways. A typical procedure is shown in the following sequence:

	LDAA #32	Takes 4 cycles to execute
LOOP1	DECA	(2 cycles)
	BNE	(4 cycles)

In this example, the *MPU* will go through LOOP1 32 times so that the total delay introduced by these instructions is, for a 1.0-μsec cycle time:

$$4 + 32\,(2+4) = 196 \ \mu\text{sec}$$

8.5. READ ONLY MEMORY AND RANDOM ACCESS MEMORY BUS INTERFACE

Read Only Memory Bus Interface

The *ROM* bus interface shown in Fig. 8.8 demonstrates the simplicity of interface in the M6800 system. Since all MicroBus components operate at the same TTL levels and with the same drive capability, data, address, and control lines can be connected without buffers. Timing of the memories has been set to permit simple operation at full speed with the processor.

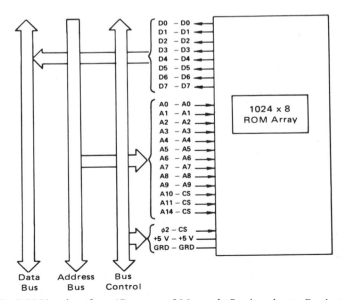

Figure 8.8. *ROM* bus interface. (Courtesy of Motorola Semiconductor Products, Inc.).

The chip selects of the MCM6830 have been used in this example to partially decode the system address lines. In small and medium-sized systems, this partial address decoding will be sufficient to distinguish all packages in the system without using any additional address decoding packages.

Random Access Memory Bus Interface

The *RAM* bus interface (Fig. 8.9) is as straightforward as its *ROM* counterpart. All required outputs may be connected directly without drivers.

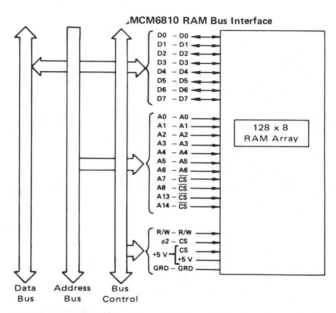

Figure 8.9. *RAM* bus interface. (Courtesy of Motorola Semiconductor Products, Inc.).

The four negative and two positive chip selects on the MCM6810 are used to provide partial address decoding in the system. In this system, the decoding possible with these lines was sufficient to distinguish the *RAM*.

8.6. INPUT/OUTPUT

Concept of the M6800 system

The I/O concepts of a particular microcomputer will determine the control signals required in the system and interface hardware, the extent to which the processor itself acts as the I/O controller, and the software options available for dealing with data at the ports.

Motorola's approach in the M6800 system has centered on the MicroBus structure, in which both memory and I/O interfaces exist in the same address space. The interfaces are individually programmable to provide I/O management. They generate and receive all I/O control signals in the system. They are programmed by control words passed over the system bus. The result is minimization of the hardware controls required on the system bus, together with simplicity and generality of I/O programming.

Peripheral Interface Adapter (*PIA*)

The MC6820 peripheral interface adapter provides a universal means of interfacing peripheral equipment to the MC6800 microprocessing unit. This device is capable of interfacing the *MPU* to peripherals through two 8-bit bidirectional peripheral data buses and four control lines. No external logic is required for interfacing to most peripheral devices.

The functional configuration of the *PIA* is programmed by the *MPU* during system initialization. Each of the peripheral data lines can be programmed to act as an input or output, and each of the four control/ interrupt lines may be programmed for one of several control modes. This allows a high degree of flexibility in the overall operation of the interface.

- Eight-Bit bidirectional data bus for communication with the *MPU*
- Two bidirectional 8-bit buses for interface to peripherals
- Two programmable control registers
- Two programmable data direction registers
- Four individually controlled interrupt input lines, two usable as peripheral control outputs
- Handshake control logic for input and output peripheral operation
- High-impedance three-state and direct transistor drive peripheral lines
- Program-controlled interrupt and interrupt disable capability
- CMOS compatible peripheral lines

Peripheral Interface Adapter Bus Interface

The *PIA* in M6800 systems is used to provide 16 bits of external interface and four control lines at addressable locations in standard system memory. Naturally, the I/O bits are accessed in two words of 8 bits each, but each I/O bit is individually programmable to act as either an input or an output. All operating characteristics of the interface are established by writing from the processor to the data direction and control registers of the *PIA*. This is required at the time of system reset and permitted at any other time.

In the preceding discussion of the system bus, no mention was made of I/O control lines. There are none on the system bus. All devices connected to the processor have the same interface as a memory—a fundamental characteristic of the MicroBus system. The interface for the *PIA* is shown in Fig. 8.10. The register select lines (RS0 and RS1) serve the same purpose in the *PIA* as the address lines do in a memory. For this reason, they are normally connected directly to the low-order address lines of the system. Chip selects are again provided for partial address decoding. In this system, no other decoders are required to distinguish interface packages.

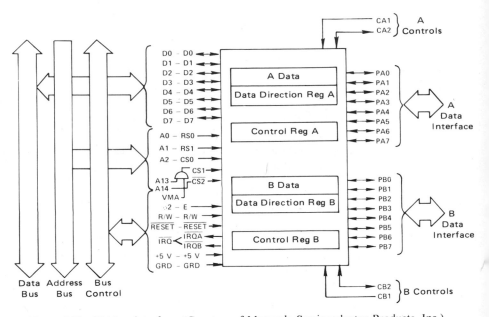

Figure 8.10. *PIA* bus interface. (Courtesy of Motorola Semiconductor Products, Inc.).

Other lines not used in the memory interface are also shown in the *PIA* interface. The VMA is used to protect the device from a spurious read operation during a machine cycle with no intended memory reference. This is necessary, since a read operation can change the state of the *PIA*. The $\overline{IRQA}$ and $\overline{IRQB}$ from the *PIA* are OR-tied to the system $\overline{IRQ}$ line. Since the *PIA* may be used to detect incoming interrupt signals on any of its control lines, this connection must be made in order to initiate the interrupt sequence at the processor. The $\overline{IRQ}$ will be pulled down by the *PIA* after detection of an active transition on any control line which has been enabled as a system interrupt. It will hold $\overline{IRQ}$ down until the interrupt is serviced. Thus no interrupts will ever be lost to the system even if the interrupt mask is set at the processor. Finally, $\overline{reset}$ is used to initialize the interface.

Peripheral Interface Adapter Signals for the Microprocessing Unit

The *PIA* interfaces to the MC6800 *MPU* via an 8-bit bidirectional data bus, three chip-select lines, two register-select lines, two interrupt request lines, a read/write line, an enable line, and a reset line. These signals, in conjunction with the MC6800 VMA output, permit the *MPU* to have complete control over the *PIA*. The VMA may be utilized to gate the input signals to the *PIA*.

PIA Bidirectional Data (D0–D7). The bidirectional data lines (D0–D7) allow the transfer of data between the *MPU* and the *PIA*. The data bus output drivers are three-state devices that remain in the high-impedance (off) state except when the *MPU* performs a *PIA* read operation. The read/write line is in the READ (high) state when the *PIA* is selected for a read operation.

PIA Enable (E). The enable pulse, E, is the only timing signal that is supplied to the *PIA*. Timing of all other signals is referenced to the leading and trailing edges of the E pulse. This signal will normally be a derivative of the MC6800 $\phi 2$ clock.

The E pulse is used to condition the interrupt/control lines CA1, CA2, CB1, and CB2. At least one E pulse must occur from the inactive edge to the active edge of the input signal to set the interrupt flag, when the lines are used as inputs.

PIA Read/Write (R/W). This signal is generated by the *MPU* to control the direction of data transfers on the data bus. A low state on the *PIA* read/write line enables the input buffers, and data are transferred from the *MPU* to the *PIA* on the E signal if the device has been selected. A high on the read/write line sets up the *PIA* for a transfer of data to the bus. The *PIA* output buffers are enabled when the proper address and the enable pulse E are present.

Reset. The active low $\overline{reset}$ line is used to reset all register bits in the *PIA* to a logical zero (low). This line can be used as a power-on reset and as a master reset during system operation.

PIA Chip Select (CS0, CS1, and $\overline{CS2}$). These three input signals are used to select the *PIA*. This CS0 and CS1 must be high and $\overline{CS2}$ must be low for selection of the device. Data transfers are then performed under the control of the enable and read/write signals. The chip-select lines must be stable for the duration of the E pulse.

PIA Register Select (RS0 and RS1). The two register-select lines are used to select the various registers inside the *PIA*. These two lines are used in conjunction with internal control registers to select a particular register that is to be written or read.

The register-select lines should be stable for the duration of the E pulse while in the read or write cycle.

Interrupt Request ($\overline{IRQA}$ and $\overline{IRQB}$). The active low interrupt request lines ($\overline{IRQA}$ and $\overline{IRQB}$) act to interrupt the *MPU* either directly or through interrupt priority circuitry. These lines are "open source" (no load device on the chip) and are capable of sinking a current of 1.6 mA from an external source. This permits all interrupt request lines to be tied together in a wire-OR configuration.

Each interrupt request line has two internal interrupt flag bits that will cause the interrupt request line to go low. Each flag bit is associated with a particular peripheral interrupt line. Also, four interrupt enable bits provided in the *PIA* may be used to inhibit a particular interrupt from a peripheral device.

Servicing an interrupt by the *MPU* may be accomplished by a software routine that, on a priority basis, sequentially reads and tests the two control registers in each *PIA* for interrupt flag bits that are set.

The interrupt flag is cleared (zeroed) as a result of an *MPU* read peripheral data operation.

Peripheral Interface Adapter Lines

The *PIA* provides two 8-bit bidirectional data buses and four interrupt/control lines for interfacing to peripheral devices.

Section A Peripheral Data (PA0–PA7). Each of the peripheral data lines can be programmed to act as an input or output. This is accomplished by setting a 1 in the corresponding data direction register bit for lines which are to be outputs. A 0 in a bit of the data direction register causes the corresponding peripheral data line to act as an input. During an *MPU* read peripheral data operation, the data on peripheral lines programmed to act as inputs appear directly on the corresponding *MPU* data bus lines. In the input mode the internal pull-up resistor on these lines represents a maximum of one standard TTL load.

The data in output register *A* will appear on the data lines that are programmed to be outputs. A logical 1 written into the register will cause a "high" on the corresponding data line, while a 0 results in a "low." Data in output register *A* may be read by an *MPU* read peripheral data *A* operation when the corresponding lines are programmed as outputs. These data will be read properly if the voltage on the peripheral data lines is greater than 2.0 V for a logical 1 output and less than 0.8 V for a logical 0 output. Loading the output lines so that the voltage on these lines does not reach full voltage causes the data transferred into the *MPU* on a read operation to differ from those contained in the respective bit of output register *A*.

Section B Peripheral Data (PB0–PB7). The peripheral data lines in the B section of the *PIA* can be programmed to act as either inputs or outputs in a similar manner to PA0–PA7. However, the output buffers driving these lines differ from those driving lines PA0–PA7. They have three-state capability, allowing them to enter a high-impedance state when the peripheral data line is used as an input. In addition, data on peripheral data lines PB0–PB7 will be read properly from those lines programmed as outputs even if the voltages are below 2.0 V for a "high." As outputs, these lines are compatible with standard TTL and may also be used as a source of up to 1 mA at 1.5 V to directly drive the base of a transistor switch.

Interrupt Input (CA1 and CB1). Peripheral input lines CA1 and CB1 are input-only lines that set the interrupt flags of the control registers. The active transition for these signals is also programmed by the two control registers.

Peripheral Control (CA2). The peripheral control line CA2 can be programmed to act as an interrupt input or as a peripheral control output. As an output, this line is compatible with standard TTL; as an input the internal pull-up resistor on this line represents one standard TTL load. The function of this signal line is programmed with control register *A*.

Peripheral Control (CB2). Peripheral control line CB2 may also be programmed to act as an interrupt input or peripheral control output. As an input this line has high input impedance and is compatible with standard TTL. As an output it is compatible with standard TTL and may also be used as a source of up to 1 mA at 1.5 V to directly drive the base of a transistor switch. This line is programmed by control register *B*.

Internal Controls

Six locations within the *PIA* are accessible to the *MPU* data bus: two peripheral registers, two data direction registers, and two control registers. The selection of these locations is controlled by the RS0 and RS1 inputs, together with bit 2 in the control register, as shown in Table 8.9.

Initialization. A low reset line has the effect of zeroing all *PIA* registers. This will set PA0–PA7, PB0–PB7, CA2, and CB2 as inputs, and all inter-

Table 8.9. Internal Addressing

RS1	RS0	Control Register Bit CRA-2	CRB-2	Location Selected
0	0	1	X	Peripheral Register A
0	0	0	X	Data Direction Register A
0	1	X	X	Control Register A
1	0	X	1	Peripheral Register B
1	0	X	0	Data Direction Register B
1	1	X	X	Control Register B

X = Don't Care

rupts disabled. The *PIA* must be configured during the restart program which follows the reset.

The details of possible configurations of the data direction and control registers are as follows.

Data Direction Registers (DDRA and DDRB). The two data direction registers allow the *MPU* to control the direction of data through each corresponding peripheral data line. A data direction register bit set at 0 configures the corresponding peripheral data line as an input; a 1 results in an output.

Control Registers (CRA and CRB). The two control registers (*CRA* and *CRB*) allow the *MPU* to control the operation of the four peripheral control lines, CA1, CA2, CB1, and CB2. In addition they allow the *MPU* to enable the interrupt lines and monitor the status of the interrupt flags. Bits 0–5 of the two registers may be written or read by the *MPU* when the proper chip-select and register-select signals are applied. Bits 6 and 7 of the two registers are read only and are modified by external interrupts occurring on control line CA1, CA2, CB1, or CB2. The format of the control words is shown in Table 8.10.

Table 8.10. Control Word Format

	7	6	5	4	3	2	1	0
CRA	IRQA1	IRQA2	CA2 Control			DDRA Access	CA1 Control	

	7	6	5	4	3	2	1	0
CRB	IRQB1	IRQB2	CB2 Control			DDRB Access	CB1 Control	

Data Direction Access Control Bit (CRA-2 and CRB-2). Bit 2 in each control register (*CRA* and *CRB*) allows selection of either a peripheral interface register or the data direction register when the proper register select signals are applied to RS0 and RS1.

Interrupt Flags (CRA-6, CRA-7, CRB-6, and CRB-7). The four interrupt flag bits are set by active transitions of signals on the four interrupt and peripheral status lines when those lines are programmed to be inputs. These bits cannot be set directly from the *MPU* data bus and are reset indirectly by a read peripheral data operation on the appropriate section.

Control of CA1 and CB1 Interrupt Input Lines (CRA-0, CRB-0, CRA-1, and CRB-1). The two lowest-order bits of the control registers are used to control the interrupt input lines CA1 and CB1. Bits CRA-0 and CRB-0 serve to enable the *MPU* interrupt signals IRQA and IRQB, respectively. Bits CRA-1 and CRB-1 determine the active transition of the interrupt input signals CA1 and CB1 (Table 8.11).

Table 8.11. Control of Interrupt Inputs CA1 and CB1

CRA-1 (CRB-1)	CRA-0 (CRB-0)	Interrupt Input CA1 (CB1)	Interrupt Flag CRA-7 (CRB-7)	MPU Interrupt Request IRQA (IRQB)
0	0	↓ Active	Set high on ↓ of CA1 (CB1)	Disabled — IRQ remains high
0	1	↓ Active	Set high on ↓ of CA1 (CB1)	Goes low when the interrupt flag bit CRA-7 (CRB-7) goes high
1	0	↑ Active	Set high on ↑ of CA1 (CB1)	Disabled — IRQ remains high
1	1	↑ Active	Set high on ↑ of CA1 (CB1)	Goes low when the interrupt flag bit CRA-7 (CRB-7) goes high

Notes: 1. ↑ indicates positive transition (low to high)

2. ↓ indicates negative transition (high to low)

3. The Interrupt flag bit CRA-7 is cleared by an MPU Read of the A Data Register, and CRB-7 is cleared by an MPU Read of the B Data Register.

4. If CRA-0 (CRB-0) is low when an interrupt occurs (Interrupt disabled) and is later brought high, IRQA (IRQB) occurs on the positive transition of CRA-0 (CRB-0).

Control of CA2 and CB2 Peripheral Control Lines (CRA-3, CRA-4, CRA-5, CRB-3, CRB-4, and CRB-5). Bits 3, 4, and 5 of the two control registers are used to control the CA2 and CB2 peripheral control lines. These bits determine whether the control line will be an interrupt input or an output control signal. If bit CRA-5 (CRB-5) is low, CA2 (CB2) is an interrupt input line similar to CA1 (CB1) (Table 8.12). When CRA-5 (CRB-5) is high, CA2 (CB2) becomes an output signal that may be used to control peripheral data transfers. When in the output mode, CA2 and CB2 have slightly different characteristics (Tables 8.13 and 8.14).

Table 8.12.   Control of CA2 and CB2 as Interrupt Inputs CRA5 (CRB5) is Low

CRA-5 (CRB-5)	CRA-4 (CRB-4)	CRA-3 (CRB-3)	Interrupt Input CA2 (CB2)	Interrupt Flag CRA-6 (CRB-6)	MPU Interrupt Request IRQA (IRQB)
0	0	0	↓ Active	Set high on ↓ of CA2 (CB2)	Disabled — IRQ remains high
0	0	1	↓ Active	Set high on ↓ of CA2 (CB2)	Goes low when the interrupt flag bit CRA-6 (CRB-6) goes high
0	1	0	↑ Active	Set high on ↑ of CA2 (CB2)	Disabled — IRQ remains high
0	1	1	↑ Active	Set high on ↑ of CA2 (CB2)	Goes low when the interrupt flag bit CRA-6 (CRB-6) goes high

Notes: 1.   ↑ indicates positive transition (low to high)

2.   ↓ indicates negative transition (high to low)

3.   The Interrupt flag bit CRA-6 is cleared by an MPU Read of the A Data Register and CRB-6 is cleared by an MPU Read of the B Data Register.

4.   If CRA-3 (CRB-3) is low when an interrupt occurs (Interrupt disabled) and is later brought high, IRQA (IRQB) occurs on the positive transition of CRA-3 (CRB-3).

Table 8.13.   Control of CB2 as an Output CRB-5 is High

CRB-5	CRB-4	CRB-3	CB2	
			Cleared	Set
1	0	0	Low on the positive transition of the first E pulse following an MPU Write "B" Data Register operation.	High when the interrupt flag bit CRB-7 is set by an active transition of the CB1 signal.
1	0	1	Low on the positive transition of the first E pulse following an MPU Write "B" Data Register operation.	High on the positive transition of the next "E" pulse.
1	1	0	Low when CRB-3 goes low as a result of an MPU Write in Control Register "B".	Always low as long as CRB-3 is low. Will go high on an MPU Write in Control Register "B" that changes CRB-3 to "one".
1	1	1	Always high as long as CRB-3 is high. Will be cleared when an MPU Write Control Register "B" results in clearing CRB-3 to "zero".	High when CRB-3 goes high as a result of an MPU write into control register "B".

Input/Output Example

The *PIA* shown in Fig. 8.11 provides a simple example of the role of the interface in the M6800 system. The 8 bits of the *A* side are used as one parallel byte of input data, while the 8 bits of the *B* side serve as an output byte. These operations are set by placing all zeroes (or ones) in the data direction registers with store operations from the processor. The CA1 line is used as an input data ready signal. An active transition (positive in this example) will set its status bit (CRA7) and pull down $\overline{IRQA}$, which is

Table 8.14.   Control of CA2 as an Output CRA-5 is High

CRA-5	CRA-4	CRA-3	CA2 Cleared	Set
1	0	0	Low on negative transition of E after an MPU Read "A" Data operation.	High on an active transition of the CA1 signal.
1	0	1	Low immediately after an MPU Read "A" Data operation.	High on the negative edge of the next "E" pulse.
1	1	0	Low when CRA-3 goes low as a result of an MPU Write in Control Register "A".	Always low as long as CRA-3 is low.
1	1	1	Always high as long as CRA-3 is high.	High when CRA-3 goes high as a result of a Write in Control Register "A".

OR-tied to the system $\overline{\text{IRQ}}$ line. The CA2 line is programmed to go low on a read of the *A* data and remain low until the next active CA1 transition. Thus it provides a data accepted signal. The CB1 line is used as data request signal. It will also detect a positive transition, set its status bit (CRB7), and pull down $\overline{\text{IRQB}}$, which is OR-tied to the system interrupt request line. The CB2 line is programmed to go low on a write of the *B* data and remain low until the next active transition on CB1. In this manner, it provides an output data ready signal. Again, all control line functions are programmed by establishing the patterns shown in the control registers with store operations from the processor.

Figures 8.12*A*–12*D* show a full sequence of I/O operations. Note that all required handshake signals are generated and received locally at the interface. The processor never has to look at the interface until service is required. It never waits for input data to become valid or for output data

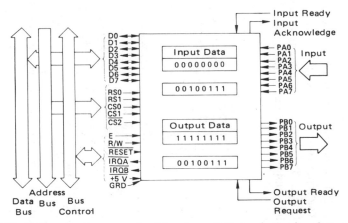

Figure 8.11. *PIA* application example. (Courtesy of Motorola Semiconductor Products, Inc.).

A

Data is presented on the A side by an external device. The Input Ready signal sets a status bit and pulls down $\overline{IRQA}$. The Interrupt response routine will identify this interrupt by polling status bits.

B

The Interrupt Response routine reads the A data. This action automatically clears the interrupt and sends the Input Acknowledge signal.

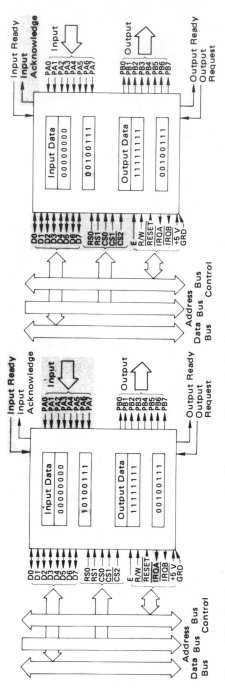

Figure 8.12. *PIA* input/output sequence. (Courtesy of Motorola Semiconductor Products, Inc.).

C

An external device requests data on the B side with Output Request. This sets a status bit and pulls down IRQB.

D

The Interrupt Response routine identifies the interrupt by checking status bits. A read operation is used to clear the interrupt. Writing output data to the B side presents the data to the external device and automatically generates the Output Ready signal.

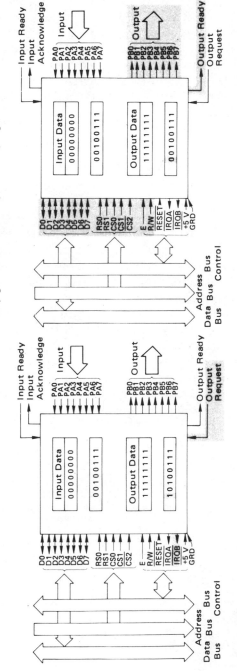

Figure 8.12. (*Continued*)

to be accepted. By reducing processor load in this manner, the *PIA* significantly increases system throughput.

In summary, the MicroBus concept of the M6800 system simplifies both the hardware and the software required in microcomputer applications. Input/output management is provided by individually programmable peripheral interfaces. The processor therefore takes on its appropriate role of system executive—programming the actual operation of the peripheral interfaces and servicing them only when required.

8.7. PROGRAMMING THE PERIPHERALS

Data, Control, and Interrupts

In the preceding example, two distinct functions were relegated to the software: setting the data direction and control register patterns at the time of system initialization, and handling interrupts.

Setting the data direction and control register patterns establishes the operating characteristics of the I/O device. The initialization program for this example is shown in Fig. 8.13. It will establish the patterns shown in Fig. 8.11. Recall that on reset all lines of the *PIA* are initialized as inputs and all interrupts are disabled. Thus the program shown only modifies the registers from these states.

Handling interrupts in a system such as has been described is a problem of software polling. A polling sequence for this example is shown in Fig. 8.14, and the corresponding program in Fig. 8.15.

```
      .
      .          CONFIGURE PIA AT ADDRESS $2004
      .          TO ACCEPT INPUT ON A SIDE, PRESENT
      .          OUTPUT ON B SIDE, AND HANDLE ALL
      .          CONTROLS.  ALL REGISTERS ARE ZERO ON RESET
      .
RESET  LDA  A  #%00100111    SET CONTROLS
       STA  A  $2005         STORE IN CRA
       COM     $2006         SET B FOR OUTPUT
       STA  A  $2007         STORE CONTROLS IN CRB
       .
       .
       .
```

Figure 8.13. *PIA* initialization program. (Courtesy of Motorola Semiconductor Products, Inc.).

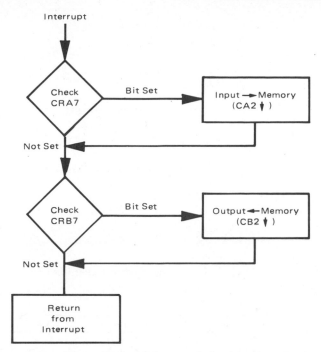

Figure 8.14. Interrupt polling. (Courtesy of Motorola Semiconductor Products, Inc.).

Such a polling approach is usually the lowest-cost alternative for identi-fying interrupts, but may in some instances be too slow. For such applica-tions, hardware may be added to the system to achieve priority encoding of the various interrupt requests. The encoded value of the interrupt request can then be used as a system address to transfer control to the appropriate response routine. This is referred to as "interrupt vectoring."

Partial Address Decoding, Using Chip Select

In any memory system, the chip selects of the memories themselves can be used to achieve a partial decode of the high-order addresses. For small systems this may be sufficient to discriminate among all memory locations. As a simple example, consider the memory system shown in Table 8.15. Each memory section contains 1K bytes and has two chip-select inputs. One of the chip selects will be needed for the $\phi2$ input. The other can be connected to any of the six remaining address lines, permitting six sections of memory to be discriminated as shown in the address table.

```
    •
    •        POLL PIA ON INTERRUPT
    •        AND SERVICE
    •

POLL     LDA  A        $2005
         BPL  POLL2     ˥
         •
         •   (INPUT CHARACTER HANDLING)
         •
POLL2    LDA  A        $2007
         BPL  POLL3
         •
         •   (OUTPUT CHARACTER HANDLING)
         •
POLL3    RTI
```

Figure 8.15. The interrupt polling sequence. (Courtesy of Motorola Semiconductor Products, Inc.).

Table 8.15.   Hypothetical 6K × 8 Memory System Using Chip Selects for Address Decoding

$\overline{CS2}$ = VMA • $\phi2$

Memory Section	Unique Address	CS1
1	1024-2047	A10
2	2048-3072	A11
3	4096-5120	A12
4	8192-9216	A13
5	16384-17408	A14
6	32768-33792	A15

There are, however, some problems of which one should be aware in such systems. First, note that there are several bit patterns which will enable a given section of memory. Section 1, for instance, could be enabled by any of the patterns:

$$0000\ 01XX\ XXXX\ XXXX$$
$$0000\ 11XX\ XXXX\ XXXX$$
$$0001\ 01XX\ XXXX\ XXXX$$
etc.

However, only the first of these discriminates between Section 1 and all other sections. The others are redundant and should be avoided since they enable two bus components simultaneously. In programming, of course, it is possible to avoid references to redundant addresses. During non-memory reference cycles of the processor, though, the state of the address line is not known. For this reason, when redundancy in addressing is possible, VMA should be gated with one of the enable inputs. In Table 8.15 it is shown gated with $\phi 2$.

Another approach to redundancy is to provide sufficient chip-select lines to permit full decoding of a subset of the high-order address lines. This is the approach taken for the memories in the M6800 system, as shown in Table 8.16. Consider the *ROM*'s, for instance. One chip select is used for the $\phi 2$ signal, and another for address line A14, which discriminates *ROM* from other classes of memory. Lines A10 and A11 are fully decoded using the remaining chip selects. Although there are still several bit patterns which might enable a given *ROM* location, <u>none is redundant</u>. This means that it is impossible, either by the chance state of the address lines in a nonmemory reference cycle or by a programming error, to enable two *ROM* packages simultaneously.

Table 8.16. Expanded M6800 System Using Chip Selects for Address Decoding

RAMs

Address	CS	CS	$\overline{CS}$	$\overline{CS}$	$\overline{CS}$	$\overline{CS}$
0-127	$\phi 2$	+5 V	A14	A13	A7	A8
128-255	$\phi 2$	A7	A14	A13	Gnd	A8
256-383	$\phi 2$	A8	A14	A13	A7	Gnd

ROMs

Address	CS	CS	$\overline{CS}$ or CS		$\overline{CS}$ or CS	
7000-73FF	$\phi 2$	A14	A9	—	A10	—
7400-77FF	$\phi 2$	A14	—	A9	A10	—
7800-7BFF	$\phi 2$	A14	A9	—	—	A10
7C00-7FFF	$\phi 2$	A14	—	A9	—	A10

INTERFACES

Address	E	$\overline{CS2}$	CS1	CS0
2004-2007	$\phi 2$	A14	A13 • VMA	A2
2008-200B	$\phi 2$	A14	A13 • VMA	A3

In the *RAM*'s, line A14 is connected to a negative enable, thus discriminating between *RAM* and *ROM*; that is, *RAM* and *ROM* addresses will never be redundant. Line A13 is also connected to a negative enable and is used to provide the same discrimination between *RAM* and I/O devices that line A14 provides between *ROM* and other classes of memory. Lines A7 and A8 are fully decoded using the remaining enables. Again, despite the fact that there are several bit patterns which may enable a given *RAM*, none is redundant.

Finally, the I/O devices are selected with line A14 (connected to $\overline{CS2}$) in its low state, line A13 (connected to CS1) in its high state, and one of the set A2–A12 connected to CS0. The I/O devices are always discriminated from other classes of memory using this system, but among themselves their addresses are potentially redundant. For this reason VMA is shown gated with line A13 to protect against redundant addresses, which may appear in nonmemory reference cycles. Care should also be taken in programming to avoid the redundant bit patterns.

Serial Interface for Asynchronous Communication (*ACIA*)

The *ACIA* provides a special-purpose serial interface for asynchronous communications. It handles all formatting tasks, such as insertion and detection of start, stop, and parity bits, and may be programmed for all common serial formats. These operating characteristics are established by writing the appropriate control pattern to the *ACIA* control register. Register status and all error conditions are indicated in a separate status register.

The bus interface of the *ACIA* (Fig. 8.16) is the same as that for the *PIA*. No unique controls are required. The interface itself manages the serial communications lines and modem control lines. The $\overline{\text{IRQ}}$ output of the *ACIA* may be used to request service from the processor on the input-register-full or output-register-empty conditions. Since both registers are double-buffered, the processor will have a full word time (33 msec at 300 bps) to respond to these conditions.

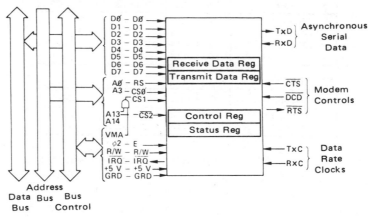

Figure 8.16. Asynchronous communication interface. (Courtesy of Motorola Semiconductor Products, Inc.).

REFERENCES

1. M6800 Systems References and Data Sheets, Motorola Semiconductor Products Inc. Phoenix, Ariz., 1975.
2. Programming Manual M6800 Micro Processor, Motorola Semiconductor Products Inc., Phoenix, Ariz., 1975.

9

PPS-4 MICROPROCESSOR

Chapter 9 presents the 4-bit microprocessor Rockwell PPS-4. This processor has a 12-bit parallel address bus, and an 8-bit instruction/data bus, which is used to form the party line. The instruction repertoire includes data transfer, arithmetic, logical, control, input/output, and special instructions. Programming examples dealing with the blocks of data are presented. The family of *ROM*, *RAM*, and I/O chips is described. Special attention is focused on the general-purpose input/output chips, which are used for direct data exchange or status and control functions with an external peripheral device. Hardware/software subroutine stacking permits unlimited nesting.

The material* in this chapter has been adapted in part from a publication of Rockwell International Corporation. The material so published herein is the full responsibility of the author.

9.1. GENERAL DESCRIPTION

The PPS-4 system is a set of modular MOS/LSI circuits which provides equipment designers with a low-cost means of developing a range of versatile, powerful, custom-programmed microcomputer systems.

A minimum PPS-4 system can be made from only two MOS/LI circuits and a clock circuit. The modular design of the PPS-4 circuits allows designers to create very powerful systems by simply incorporating additional Rockwell memory and/or I/O circuits. The typical system shown in Fig. 9.1 delineates these expansion parameters. The many different types of I/O and memory circuits available enhances the economics and versatility of the PPS-4.

High throughput and fast execution speed enable the PPS-4 to economically implement many functions normally thought to require 8-bit or

---

* Programs, figures, and tables are courtesy and copyright © 1975 by Rockwell International Corporation. All rights reserved.

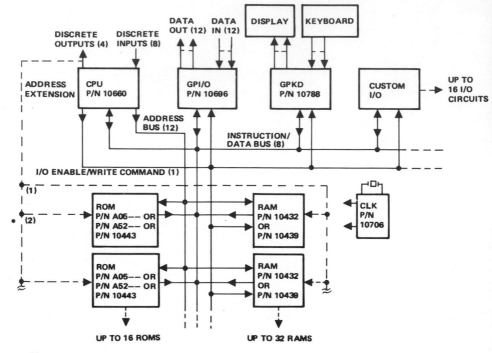

Figure 9.1. Typical system block diagram. (Courtesy of Rockwell International Corporation).

larger processors. High throughput is demonstrated by the PPS-4's strobing and transferring data from the I/O to *RAM* at a rate of 36 μsec per 8-bit byte, and fast execution is demonstrated by the addition of two 8-bit decimal numbers in 240 μsec.

Other design advantages include simpler programming with fewer steps, quicker turn-around in system prototyping, the use of fewer components to implement systems, and the capability of Rockwell to design and produce custom I/O devices to suit a user's unique requirements.

Functional Power

- Fifty instructions, which include—
    Arithmetic and logic operations.
    Conditional and unconditional transfers.
    Direct and indirect subroutine calls.
    Direct and indirect *RAM* addressing.
    Input/output commands.

- Four-bit data words/8-bit instruction words.
- Hardware/software subroutine stacking—unlimited nesting.
- Implementable interrupt.

Performance Power

- Twenty-one line parallel bus structure.
- Fast execution time—adds two 8-digit decimal numbers in 240 μsec.
- High throughout—parallel data transfer RAM to I/O or I/O to RAM:
  4-bit byte/28 μsec.
  8-bit byte/36 μsec.
  12-bit byte/56 μsec.
- Decimal and binary arithmetic modes.
- Directly addressable up to 16   1K $\times$ 8 ROM's or 16   2K $\times$ 8 ROM's, and 32   256 $\times$ 4 RAM's (294,912-bit memory capacity).
- Directly addresses up to 16 I/O circuits.
- Advanced MOS/LSI nonvolatile RAM and electrically alterable ROM circuits.

Design/Production Economics

- No external interface circuitry required between CPU, memories, and I/O circuits.
- Eight LSI interface/control circuits, including a direct bus-to-TTL memory circuit, direct keyboard and display control circuit, and a MODEM/UART circuit on a single chip.
- Custom-designed I/O devices for special applications.
- All I/O circuits TTL compatible.
- Single power supply.
- ROM/RAM (one chip) for production of two-chip (plus clock) minimum systems.
- Four-phase dynamic operation for low power and high speed.
- No memory refresh circuitry required.
- Complete software and hardware development support.

Each of the PPS-4 circuits (except the clock) is packaged in a 42-pin flat pack to provide maximum interfacing capability. A complete system can consist of only two 42-pin packages (the CPU and a ROM or combination

ROM/RAM) plus the four-phase clock generator. The PPS-4 circuits have been designed as a compatible group, and each has been configured to maximize circuit density and processing speed and to minimize power consumption. The *CPU*, with its 12-bit parallel address bus and 8-bit parallel instruction/data bus, directly addresses 4K of 8-bit instruction (*ROM*) words and 4K of 4-bit data (*RAM*) words, while simultaneously the *ROM* outputs instruction words to the *CPU* in the form of 8-bit parallel information and the *RAM* transmits and receives 4 bits of data in parallel during the same one-cycle time.

Central Processing Unit (*CPU*)

The central processing unit (*CPU*) shown in Fig. 9.2 is a 4-bit parallel processor. The *CPU*, through time sharing, utilizes an 8-bit parallel I/D bus to transfer 8-bit word instructions from *ROM* to *CPU* and I/O and also uses it as a dual bidirectional 4-bit parallel data bus to transfer data between the *CPU* and *RAM*'s and I/O's, Fig. 9.3.

For memory expansion, software interrupt, or direct access with peripheral equipment, the *CPU* includes eight discrete input and four discrete output lines.

The *CPU* contains (*a*) microinstruction decoding necessary to receive and decode 50 basic instructions, (*b*) a 4-bit parallel adder/accumulator for arithmetic and logic operations, (*c*) a 12-bit (*B*) register for creating and storing addresses for *RAM*, (*d*) a 12-bit (*P*) register and two 12-bit "save" registers for creating and storing addresses for *ROM*, (*e*) eight discrete input synchronizers, (*f*) four discrete output static drivers, (*g*) two individual-control flip-flops, and (*h*) multiplexed receivers and drivers for interfacing with the 12-bit parallel address bus, the 8-bit parallel data/instruction bus, and the W/IO control line.

Microinstruction Decode. The decode portion of the chip interprets the instructions to control data transfers, arithmetic operations, and set up logical sequences. Instructions are coded in one byte (8 bits) and grouped as arithmetic, logical, data transfer, control transfer, input/output, and special instructions. Direct subroutine calls, unconditional transfers, direct *RAM* address modifications, and the I/O command are considered long instructions because they require two bytes of *ROM* storage. However, the indirect subroutine call and indirect *RAM* address modification require only one byte of *ROM* storage. All instructions are executed in one cycle time of the A clock except long and indirect instructions and the I/O instruction, which are executed in two cycle times.

Adder/Accumulator. The adder is a 4-bit parallel binary adder with an internally connected carry flip-flop for implementing precision arithmetic operations. The adder, together with the 4-bit accumulator, forms the arithmetic logic unit (*ALU*) section of the *CPU*. Functionally, the *CPU* has 10 microinstructions dedicated to arithmetic and logical operations. All are one-cycle instructions and enable direct arithmetic operation between the accumulator and the data stored in *RAM* or *ROM* memory.

In addition to its arithmetic functions, the accumulator is the primary working register in the *CPU* and is the central data interchange point for almost all data transfer operations occurring in the parallel processing system.

During internal data transfer the accumulator is the interfacing data register for both *RAM* and *ROM*. For external data exchanges (input/output) the accumulator is the source of the output data and the receiver register for the input data.

Because of the high usage of the accumulator, a secondary (extra) X register has been included in the *CPU*. The X register is a 4-bit register and is used in conjunction with the accumulator for temporary storage of data.

RAM Address Register. This 12-bit B register consists of three 4-bit registers (*BU*, *BM*, and *BL*), which contain the address location to be accessed in *RAM*. Register *BL* is a counter and can be incremented or decremented by 1 through program control, providing the ability to sequence through *RAM* registers serially by 4-bit character. The upper 8-bits (*BU* and *BM*) of *RAM* address can be set to special values by program control during a transfer operation of data to or from a distant *RAM* location into the working storage area indicated by the 4 bits of *BL*. During *RAM* address modification operations it is also possible to use accumulator A and register X for temporary storage of the upper 8 bits of the new address retrieval from *RAM* without destroying the current *RAM* address pointer.

Program Counter and Save Register. The 12-bit P register and counter contains the address of the next program instruction. The lower 6 bits is a counter which is automatically incremented each cycle time during normal operation. The most significant 6 bits give the *ROM* number and page location. These six bits are modified only by the unconditional transfer (TL) or subroutine call (TML and TM) instructions. The *SA* and *SB* registers are two "save" registers which provide a two-level stack for holding instruction addresses during branching. This gives a direct two-level nesting capability for storing program subroutine addresses in hardware; however, unlimited nesting is available via instruction CYS. This instruc-

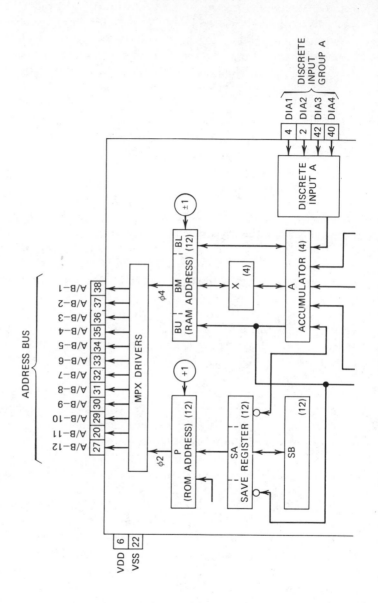

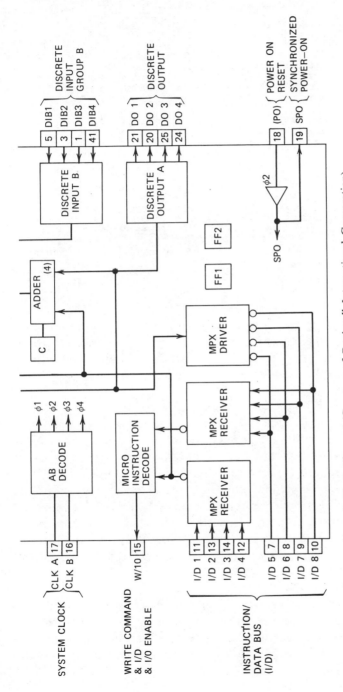

Figure 9.2. Central processing unit block diagram (Courtesy of Rockwell International Corporation).

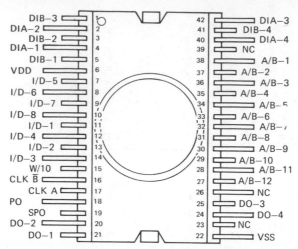

Figure 9.3. *CPU* pin configuration. (Courtesy of Rockwell International Corporation).

tion recirculates register *SA* and accumulator *A* and therefore provides for saving *ROM* program addresses in *RAM*. Since *RAM* can be used for storing program addresses, subroutine nesting becomes limited only by the amount of dedicated storage allocated for this purpose.

Control Flip-Flop (FF) and Discrete Input/Output (I/O). The two control flip-flops, FF1 and FF2, can be set, reset, and tested by program control. There are also eight discrete inputs, which can be copied directly into the accumulator as two separate 4-bit groups. These groups are identified as discrete input group A (DIA) and discrete input group B (DIB). These inputs are intended to be used for inputting special signals, switch position flags, or interrupt lines from circuitry external to the PPS. The contents of the accumulator can be outputted directly to circuits external to the PPS via a special 4-bit parallel output register (DOA) with individual output drivers. These outputs can be used to extend the *ROM* and *RAM* addressing beyond 4K.

Multiplex Drivers and Receivers. The multiplex driver and receiver circuits in the *CPU* provide direct interfacing with the system address and instruction data bus. The bus is time multiplexed and uses a unique precharge technique to achieve an unusually high system fan-out. Systems containing up to 30 circuits can be mechanized without the need for external drivers.

Power-On Reset. During power turn-on it is necessary to initialize the *CPU P* counter to a known state so that the proper sequence of events can occur. This initialization is accomplished by inputting a negative pulse for a time duration of 10 msec or greater. This pulse is generated externally to the PPS, and as long as the pulse is a logic 1, the *P* counter is held reset. The *CPU*, at the same time, generates a synchronized power-on output signal which can be used to initialize other circuits.

Multiplex System Data Transfer. In addition to the power and clock signals 21 multiplexed lines interconnect the *CPU* with *ROM*, *RAM*, and I/O circuits. These lines are functionally grouped as follows:

Twelve parallel address lines
Eight parallel data lines
One WRITE command and I/O enable line

The 12 address lines originate at the *CPU* and are time multiplexed within it to provide direct addressing capability for up to 4096, locations on both the *ROM* and the *RAM*. In addition to the 12 direct address lines, the *ROM* P/N A05__ circuit has two chip-select inputs, and the *RAM* P/N 10432 circuit has one chip-select input. These chip-select lines may be directly controlled by discrete outputs from *CPU* or I/O circuits for memory expansion without the need for auxiliary circuitry. Memory expansion is more fully explained in the description of the *ROM* and *RAM*.

Like the address lines, the eight data bus lines are time-shared lines from the *CPU*. During $\phi 2$ a logical 1 on the write enable line is interpreted by the *RAM*'s as a WRITE enable command, and data on the bus will be written into the *RAM*. The *RAM* is a nondestructive read-out device and therefore is always programmed to read; however, it must be instructed to "write." Because the eight data lines are functioning as a dual 4-bit bi-direction data bus during $\phi 2$, it is possible for the *RAM* to read 4 bits from the designated address out to the data bus and, during the same cycle time, write 4 bits from the data bus into the designated *RAM* address location.

The same line providing the WRITE command to the *RAM* during $\phi 2$ time serves as an I/O enable signal during $\phi 4$ time of the input/output instruction (IOL). If the I/O enable is on (logical 1) at $\phi 4$, the *RAM* will be disabled during the next $\phi2$ time, and the data bus will be used to transfer information between the accumulator in the *CPU* and I/O circuits.

The input/output instruction (IOL) is a special application of the bus timing and requires two clock cycles and two successive *ROM* memory locations. During the first clock cycle the IOL instruction is received from the *ROM* and decoded in the *CPU*. During the second clock cycle the I/O enable line alerts all the I/O circuits, and at the same time an I/O address and command is transmitted from the *ROM* turning on the selected I/O circuit. Data transfer between the selected I/O circuit and the accumulator in the *CPU* will occur during $\phi2$ of the next clock cycle.

A timing diagram of the IOL instruction is shown in Fig. 9.4.

9.2.   INSTRUCTION LIST

Definition of Symbolic Notation

The following pages provide a listing of the 50 instructions which can be used to control generation of *ROM* and *RAM* address, as well as manipulation and transfer of data between the *CPU* and *RAM* and I/O. Definitions of symbols used in the instruction list are also provided, so that a programmer can easily understand the list and begin to visualize how the PPS may be used for a given application.

The definition list is shown in Table 9.1, and the instruction set in Tables 9.2–9.6.

9.3.   ADDRESSING AND PROGRAMMING

Data Address

The four basic data transfer instructions are shown in Table 9.2. These instructions have been designed to provide great flexibility in loading the *CPU* accumulator with data from memory or constants and in exchanging information between the accumulator and memory. The LD, EX, and EXD instructions all have the capability of modifying the data address register, *B*, for the next instruction if this is desired by the programmer. This feature eliminates the need, in many cases, for writing additional instructions to modify register *B*.

The data address word in the PPS-4 is shown in Fig. 9.5; bits b1 through b12 come from the data address register in the *CPU*, which is organized

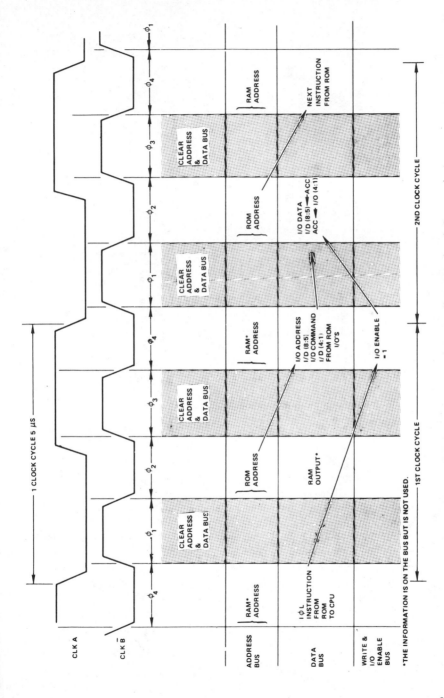

Figure 9.4. Input/output instruction PPS timing. (Courtesy of Rockwell International Corporation).

351

Table 9.1

(Reproduced with permission of Rockwell International, Anaheim, California)

Symbols	Definition
A	Accumulator Register, $A(4:1)$
A/Bn	Line n of Address Bus
B	RAM Address Register, $B(12:1)$
C	Carry Link Flip-Flop
FF_1, FF_2	General Flip-Flop 1, General Flip-Flop 2
I	Instruction (Typically 8-bit Field)
I/Dn	Line n of Instruction/Data Bus
In	Byte n of Long Instruction (i.e., I_1 = 1st byte, I_2 = 2nd byte)
M	RAM Memory Contents Designated by Register B
m	General Numeric Designator, $m = 1, 2, 3, \ldots$
n	General Numeric Designator, $n = 1, 2, 3, \ldots$
P	ROM Program Counter Register, $P(12:1)$
BL	Lower Field of B Register, $B(14:1)$
BM	Middle Field of B Register, $B(8:5)$
BU	Upper Field of B Register, $B(12:9)$
R(n)	Bit n of General Register R
R(m:n)	Bits m through n of General Register R [e.g., $R(12:7)$]
SA	Upper Stack of Save Registers, $SA(12:1)$
SB	Lower Stack of Save Registers, $SB(12:1)$
W/IO	WRITE Command and I/O Enable Line
X	Secondary Accumulator Register, $X(4:1)$
Digit	Four-Bit Field (sometimes referred to as Data or Character)
Byte	Eight-Bit Field
Page	ROM Block of 64 Bytes[a]
← →	Replaces
↔	Exchange
—	One's Complement (e.g., $\overline{A}$ is one's complement of A)
∨	Logical Inclusive OR
⊻	Logical Exclusive OR
∧	Logical And
+	Algebraic Add
−	Algebraic Subtract

[a] A page is defined in the PPS as 64 ROM address locations. The page number is specified by the 6 most significant bits of the 12-bit P register. The locations within a page are defined by the 6 least significant bits.

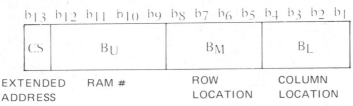

Figure 9.5. Data address word. (Courtesy of Rockwell International Corporation).

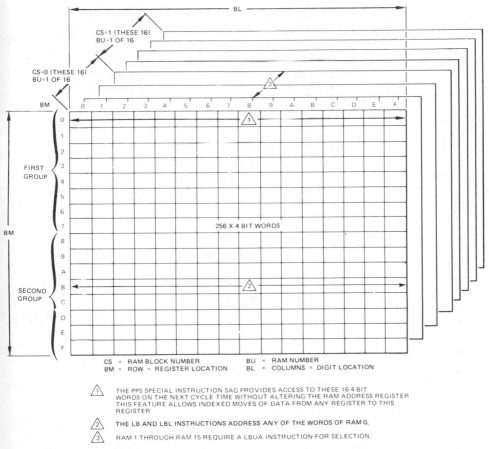

CS = RAM BLOCK NUMBER BU = RAM NUMBER
BM = ROW = REGISTER LOCATION BL = COLUMNS = DIGIT LOCATION

1. THE PPS SPECIAL INSTRUCTION SAG PROVIDES ACCESS TO THESE 16 4-BIT WORDS ON THE NEXT CYCLE TIME WITHOUT ALTERING THE RAM ADDRESS REGISTER. THIS FEATURE ALLOWS INDEXED MOVES OF DATA FROM ANY REGISTER TO THIS REGISTER.

2. THE LB AND LBL INSTRUCTIONS ADDRESS ANY OF THE WORDS OF RAM 0.

3. RAM 1 THROUGH RAM 15 REQUIRE A LBUA INSTRUCTION FOR SELECTION.

Figure 9.6. Data memory organization—hexadecimal addresses. (Courtesy of Rockwell International Corporation).

Table 9.2. Data Transfer Instructions
(Reproduced with permission of Rockwell International, Anaheim, California)

Mnemonics	I/D Bus OP Code Hex & Binary	Name	Description	Symbolic Equation
SC	20 / 0010 0000	Set Carry flip-flop (1 cycle)	The C flip-flop is set to 1.	$C \leftarrow 1$
RC	24 / 0010 0100	Reset Carry flip-flop (1 cycle)	The C flip-flop is set to 0.	$C \leftarrow 0$
SF1	22 / 0010 0010	Set FF1 (1 cycle)	Flip-flop 1 is set to 1.	$FF1 \leftarrow 1$
RF1	26 / 0010 0110	Reset FF1 (1 cycle)	Flip-flop 1 is set to 0.	$FF1 \leftarrow 0$
SF2	21 / 0010 0001	Set FF2 (1 cycle)	Flip-flop 2 is set to 1.	$FF2 \leftarrow 1$
RF2	25 / 0010 0101	Reset FF2 (1 cycle)	Flip-flop 2 is set to 0.	$FF2 \leftarrow 0$
LD	30-37 / 0011 0...	Load Accumulator from Memory (1 cycle)	The 4-bit contents of RAM currently addressed by B register are placed in the accumulator. The RAM address in the B register is then modified by the result of an exclusive-OR of the 3-bit immediate field I(3:1) and B(7:5).	$A \leftarrow M;$ $B(7:5) \leftarrow B(7:5) \forall$ $\lfloor I(3:1) \rfloor$ See Note 3
EX	38-3F / 0011 1...	Exchange Accumulator and Memory (1 cycle)	Same as LD except the contents of accumulator are also placed in currently addressed RAM location.	$A \leftrightarrow M$ $B(7:5) \leftarrow B(7:5) \forall$ $\lfloor I(3:1) \rfloor$ See Note 3

EXD	28-2F 0010 1 _ _ _	Exchange Accumulator and Memory and decrement BL (1 cycle) See Note 3	Same as EX except RAM address in B register is further modified by decrementing BL by 1. If the new contents of BL is 1111, the next ROM word will be ignored.	A ↔ M B(7:5) ← B(7:5) ∀ |I(3:1)|; BL ← BL-1 Skip on BL=1111
LDI	70-7F 0111 _ _ _ _	Load Accumulator Immediate (1 cycle)	The 4-bit contents, immediate field I(4:1), of the instruction are placed in accumulator. (See Note below)	A ← |I(4:1)| See Note 3
LAX	12 0001 0010	Load Accumulator from X register (1 cycle)	The 4-bit contents of the X register are placed in the accumulator.	A ← X
LXA	1B 0001 1011	Load X Register from Accumulator (1 cycle)	The contents of the accumulator are transferred to the X register.	X ← A
LABL	11 0001 0001	Load Accumulator with BL (1 cycle)	The contents of BL register are transferred to the accumulator.	A ← BL
LBMX	10 0001 0000	Load BM with X (1 cycle)	The contents of X register are transferred to BM register.	BM ← X
LBUA	04 0000 0100	Load BU with A (1 cycle)	The contents of accumulator are transferred to BU register. Also, the contents of currently addressed RAM are transferred to accumulator.	BU ← A, A ← M

NOTE
Only the first occurrence of an LDI in a consecutive string of LDI's will be executed. The program will ignore the remaining LDI's and execute next valid instruction.

Table 9.3. Data Transfer Instructions (*Cont'd*)
(Reproduced with permission of Rockwell International, Anaheim, California)

Mnemonics	I/D Bus OP Code Hex & Binary	Name	Description	Symbolic Equation
XABL	19 0001 1001	Exchange Accumulator and BL (1 cycle)	The contents of accumulator and BL register are exchanged.	$A \leftrightarrow BL$
XBMX	18 0001 1000	Exchange BM and X (1 cycle)	The contents of BM register and X register are exchanged.	$X \leftrightarrow BM$
XAX	1A 0001 1010	Exchange Accumulator and X (1 cycle)	The contents of accumulator and X register are exchanged.	$A \leftrightarrow X$
XS	06 0000 0110	Exchange SA and SB (1 cycle)	The 12-bit contents of SA register and SB register are exchanged.	$SA \leftrightarrow SB$
CYS	6F 0110 1111	Cycle SA register and accumulator. (1 cycle)	A 4-bit right shift of the SA register takes place with the four bits which are shifted off the end of SA being transferred into the accumulator. The contents of the accumulator are placed in the left end of SA register.	$A \leftarrow SA(4{:}1)$ $SA(4{:}1) \leftarrow SA(8{:}5)$ $SA(8{:}5) \leftarrow SA(12{:}9)$ $SA(12{:}9) \leftarrow A$
LB **	C0-CF 1st word 1100 ---- 2nd word from page 3 ----	Load B Indirect (2 cycles)	Sixteen consecutive locations on ROM page 3 (I2) contain data which can be loaded into the eight least significant bits of the B register by use of any LB instruction. The four most significant bits of B register will be loaded with zeros. The contents of the SB	$SB \leftarrow SA, SA \leftarrow P$ $P(12{:}5) \leftarrow 0000\,1100$ $P(4{:}1) \leftarrow I1(4{:}1)$ $BU \leftarrow 0000$ $B(8{:}1) \leftarrow [I2(8{:}1)]$ $P \leftarrow SA, SA \leftrightarrow SB$ See Notes 3 and 4

LBL	00 1st word 0000 0000 2nd word ---- ----	Load B Long (2 cycles)	register will be destroyed. This instruction takes two cycles to execute but occupies only one ROM word. (Automatic return) (See Note below.) This instruction occupies two ROM words, the second of which will be loaded into the eight least significant bits of the B register. The four most significant bits of B (BU) will be loaded with zeros. (See Note below)	BU ← 0000 B(8:1) ← [I2(8:1)] See Note 3
INCB	17 0001 0111	Increment BL (1 cycle)	BL register (least significant four bits of B register) is incremented by 1. If the new contents of BL is 0000, then the next ROM word will be ignored.	BL ← BL+1 Skip on BL=0000
DECB	1F 0001 1111	Decrement BL (1 cycle)	BL register is decremented by 1. If the new contents of BL is 1111, then the next ROM word will be ignored.	BL ← BL-1 Skip on BL = 1111

NOTE

Only the first occurrence of an LB or LBL instruction in a consecutive string of LB or LBL will be executed. The program will ignore the remaining LB or LBL and execute the next valid instruction. Within subroutines the LB instruction must be used with caution because the contents of SB have been modified.

357

Table 9.4. Arithmetic Instructions
(Reproduced with permission of Rockwell International, Anaheim, California)

Mnemonics	I/D Bus OP Code Hex & Binary	Name	Description	Symbolic Equation
AD	0B 0000 1011	Add (1 cycle)	The result of binary addition of contents of accumulator and 4-bit contents of the RAM currently addressed by B register, replaces the contents of accumulator. The resulting carry-out is loaded into C flip-flop.	C, A ← A+M
ADC	0A 0000 1010	Add with carry-in (1 cycle)	Same as AD except the C flip-flop serves as a carry-in to the adder.	C,A ← A+M+C
ADSK	09 0000 1001	Add and skip on carry-out (1 cycle)	Same as AD except the next ROM word will be skipped (ignored) if a carry-out is generated.	C, A ← A+M Skip if C = 1
ADCSK	08 0000 1000	Add with carry-in and skip on carry-out (1 cycle)	Same as ADSK except the C flip-flop serves as a carry-in to the adder.	C, A ← A+M+C Skip if C = 1
ADI	60-6E *0110 xxxx Except 65	Add immediate and skip on carry-out (1 cycle)	The result of binary addition of contents of accumulator and 4-bit immediate field of instruction word replaces the contents of accumulator. The next ROM word will be skipped (ignored) if a carry-out is generated. This instruction does not use or change the C flip-flop. The immediate field I(4:1) of this	A ← A+[I(4:1)] Skip if carry-out = one I(4:1) ≠ ´0000 I(4:1) ≠ 1010 See Note 3

358

	Code	Instruction (cycle)	Description	Symbolic Equation
			instruction may not be equal to binary 0000 or 1010 (See CYS and DC)	
DC	65 0110 0101	Decimal Correction (1 cycle)	Binary 1010 is added to contents of accumulator. Result is stored in accumulator. Instruction does not use or change carry flip-flop or skip.	$A \leftarrow A+1010$

LOGICAL INSTRUCTIONS

	Code	Instruction (cycle)	Description	Symbolic Equation
AND	OD 0000 1101	Logical AND (1 cycle)	The result of logical AND of accumulator and 4-bit contents of RAM currently addressed by B register replaces contents of accumulator.	$A \leftarrow A \wedge M$
OR	OF 0000 1111	Logical OR (1 cycle)	The result of logic OR of accumulator and 4-bit contents of RAM currently addressed by B register replaces contents of accumulator.	$A \leftarrow A \vee M$
EOR	OC 0000 1100	Logical Exclusive-OR (1 cycle)	The result of logic exclusive-OR of accumulator and 4-bit contents of RAM currently addressed by B register replaces contents of accumulator.	$A \leftarrow A \forall M$
COMP	OE 0000 1110	Complement (1 cycle)	Each bit of the accumulator is logically complemented and placed in accumulator.	$A \leftarrow \bar{A}$

*xxxx Indicates restrictions on bit patterns allowable in immediate field as specified in the symbolic equation description.

359

Table 9.5. Control Transfer Instructions
(Reproduced with permission of Rockwell International, Anaheim, California)

Mnemonics	I/D Bus OP Code Hex & Binary	Name	Description	Symbolic Equation
T *	80-BF 10-- ----	Transfer (1 cycle)	An unconditional transfer to a ROM word on the current page takes place. The least significant 6-bits of P register P(6:1) are replaced by six bit immediate field I(6:1).	$P(6:1) \leftarrow I(6:1)$
TM**	DO-FF * 1st word 11xx ---- 2nd word from page 3 ---- ----	Transfer and Mark Indirect (2 cycles)	48 Consecutive locations on ROM page 3 contains pointer data which identify subroutine entry addresses. These subroutine entry addresses are limited to pages 4 through 7. This TM instruction will save the address of the next ROM word in the SA register after loading the original contents of SA into SB. A transfer then occurs to one of the subroutine entry addresses. This instruction occupies one ROM word but takes two cycles for execution.	$SB \leftarrow SA,\ SA \leftarrow P$ $P(12:7) \leftarrow 000011$ $P(6:1) \leftarrow I1(6:1)$ $P(12:9) \leftarrow 0001$ $P(8:1) \leftarrow I2(8:1)$ See Note 4 Note: $I1(6:5) \neq 00$
TL	50-5F 1st word 0101 ---- 2nd word ---- ----	Transfer Long (2 cycles)	This instruction executes a transfer to any ROM word on any page. It occupies two ROM words and requires two cycles for execution. The first byte loads P(12:9) with field I1(4:1) and then the second byte I2(8:1) is placed in P(8:1).	$P(12:9) \leftarrow I1(4:1)$; $P(8:1) \leftarrow I2(8:1)$

Mnemonic	Code	Operation	Description	Equation
TML	01-03 * 1st word 0000 00xx 2nd word ---- ----	Transfer and Mark Long (2 cycles)	This instruction executes a transfer and mark to any location on ROM pages 4 through 15. It occupies two ROM words and requires two cycle times for execution.	See Note 4 $SB \leftarrow SA$, $SA \leftarrow P$ $P(12:9) \leftarrow I1(4:1)$ $P(8:1) \leftarrow I2(8:1)$ Note $I1(2:1) \neq 00$
SKC	15 0001 0101	Skip on Carry flip-flop (1 cycle)	The next ROM word will be ignored if C flip-flop is 1.	Skip if $C = 1$
SKZ	1E 0001 1110	Skip on Accumulator Zero (1 cycle)	The next ROM word will be ignored if accumulator is zero.	Skip if $A = 0$
SKBI	40-4F 0100 ----	Skip if BL Equal to Immediate (cycle)	The next ROM word will be ignored if the least significant four bits of B register (BL) is equal to the 4-bit immediate field $I(4:1)$ of instruction.	Skip if $BL = I(4:1)$
SKF1	16 0001 0110	Skip if FF1 Equals 1 (1 cycle)	The next ROM word will be ignored if FF2 is 1.	Skip if $FF1 = 1$
SKF2	14 0001 0100	Skip if FF2 Equals 1 (1 cycle)	The next ROM word will be ignored if FF1 is 1.	Skip if $FF2 = 1$
RTN **	05 0000 0101	Return (1 cycle)	This instruction executes a return from subroutine by loading contents of SA register into P register and interchanges the SB and SA registers.	$P \leftarrow SA$, $SA \leftrightarrow SB$

*xx   Indicates restrictions on bit patterns allowable in the designated bit positions in the instruction field as specified in the symbolic equation description.

**   These instructions, with the exception of T * +1, cannot be used in ROM location 0000.

Table 9.6. Control Transfer Instructions (*Con'd*)
(Reproduced with permission of Rockwell International, Anaheim, California)

Mnemonics	I/D Bus OP Code Hex & Binary	Name	Description	Symbolic Equation
RTNSK **	07 0000 0111	Return and Skip (1 cycle)	Same as RTN except the first ROM word encountered after the return from subroutine is skipped.	P ← SA , SA→SB P ← P+1

INPUT/OUTPUT INSTRUCTIONS

Mnemonics	I/D Bus OP Code Hex & Binary	Name	Description	Symbolic Equation
IOL	1C 1st word 0001 1100 2nd word - - - - - - - -	Input/Output Long (2 cycles)	This instruction occupies two ROM words and requires two cycles for execution. The first ROM word is received by the CPU and sets up the I/O Enable signal. The second ROM word is then received by the I/O devices and decoded for address and command. The contents of the accumulator inverted are placed on the data lines for acceptance by the I/O. At the same time, input data received by the I/O device is transferred to the accumulator inverted.	$\overline{A}$ → Data Bus A ← $\overline{\text{Data Bus}}$ I2 → I/O Device
DIA	27 0010 0111	Discrete Input Group A (1 cycle)	Data at the inputs to discrete. Group A is transferred to the accumulator.	A ← DIA

362

DIB	23 0010 0011	Data at the inputs to discrete Group B is transferred to the accumulator.	A ← DIB
DOA	1D 0001 1101	The contents of the accumulator are transferred to the discrete output register.	DO A ← A

SPECIAL INSTRUCTION

SAG	13 0001 0011	Special Address Generation (1 cycle) — This instruction causes the eight most significant bits of the RAM address output to be zeroed during the next cycle only. Note that this instruction does not alter the contents of the B register.	A/B Bus (12:5) ← 0000 0000 A/B Bus (4:1) ← BL(4:1) Contents of "B" remain unchanged

(Row labels for DIB: Discrete Input Group B (1 cycle); DOA: Discrete Output (1 cycle).)

GENERAL NOTES

(1) The word "skip" or "ignore" as used in this instruction set means the instruction will be read from memory but not executed. Each skipped or ignored word will require one clock cycle time.

(2) The reference to ROM pages and locations are defined as the ROM address appearing on the A/B bus. During initial Power On the starting address is Page 0 Location 0 and is automatically incremented each clock cycle.

(3) Instruction ADI, LD, EX, EXD, LDI, LB and LBL have a numeric value coded as part of the instruction in the immediate field. This numeric value must be in complementary form as seen on the bus. All of these immediate fields which are inverted are shown in brackets.

For example: ADI 1, as written by the programmer who wishes to add one to the value in the accumulator, is converted to 6E$_{(16)}$=0110 [1110]; the bracketed binary value is the value as seen on the data bus.

If the programmer is using the Rockwell Assembler he does not have to manually determine the proper inverted value as the assembler does this for him.

On all instructions which transfer the contents of P into SA, the P register has already been advanced to the next instruction location.

363

into three 4-bit segments, *B* upper (*BU*), *B* middle (*BM*), and *B* lower (*BL*). Bit b13 is used only in very large systems to expand the capacity beyond the 4096 data words that can be addressed directly from the *B* register. The *CS* (chip-select) signal would be normally generated under program control from one of the discrete outputs from the CPU, although a general-purpose I/O device or external switch could also be used.

The data memory organization, showing how each segment of the data address word is used in the addressing scheme, is shown in Fig. 9.6. The *CS* may be thought of as selecting blocks of *RAM* circuits, *BU* as identifying the particular 256 by 4-bit *RAM* memory circuit, *BM* as designating a row of data 16 words long, and *BL* as defining the particular word within that row.

The address modification in the LD, EX, and EXD instructions allow the programmer to modify the row designation portion of the address register (*BM*). The next instruction which uses data memory then may refer to a different row within a group of rows in the same half of the selected *RAM* for the next desired data. For this reason, registers within memory which consist of more than one 4-bit word as usually arranged so that the complete register is organized along a row using the same columns whenever possible. With this organization of memory the PPS-4 programs for manipulations between registers can be very efficient.

Examples

For the following examples, two instructions which will be discussed in detail later need to be introduced. The first of these is LBL (load B long), which presets the *B* register to an address within the first 256 words of data memory, and the second is T (transfer), which causes the program counter to be set to a new value. The actual operation of these instructions is more flexible than has been indicated, but these definitions will suffice to explain the examples.

The first set of examples consists of a series of short programs which set various areas in *RAM* 0 to zero. The programs are shown in Table 9.7.

The symbol # identifies the argument as an absolute hexadecimal address, not an alphanumeric symbol address. The A1 through A4 symbols in the label and argument fields are interpreted as labels since they are not preceded by the # symbol.

Both the initial contents of *RAM* 0 and the contents after executing the above program are shown in Fig. 9.7.

The first example loads the data address register with 007 (in hex), sets the accumulator to zero, and exchanges the accumulator with the addressed

Table 9.7
(Reproduced with permission of Rockwell International, Anaheim, California)

Label	Mnemonic	Immediate Field Argument	Comment
	LBL	# 07	Example 1
A1	LDI	0	
	EXD		
	T	A1	
	LBL	# 7F	Example 2
A2	LDI	0	
	EXD		
	T	A2	
	LBL	# AF	Example 3
A3	LDI	0	
	EXD	3	
	T	A3	
	LBL	# DA	Example 4
A4	LDI	0	
	EX	3	
	LDI	0	
	EXD	3	
	T	A4	

memory cell. Since the value of BL is then set to 6, the program does not skip an instruction, and a transfer to the load immediate zero instruction causes the process to repeat. This process is automatically terminated after the last zero is transferred. The result of this sequence is identified by (1) in Fig. 9.7.

The second example is identical except that the initial address is set to 07F (in hex) so that a complete row is cleared to zero. The result of this sequence is shown as (2) in Fig. 9.7.

The third example also is identical except that the starting address is 0AF (hex) and the capability of modifying BM is demonstrated. When the immediate field value of 3 (011) is exclusively ORed with the corresponding bits in BM, which in this example are equal to A, (1010), the result is 1001 or 9 for the next digit in sequence. On the next digit BM is restored to A, so that the zigzag pattern of zeros results.

RAM NØ. 0

INITIAL CONTENTS OF RAM

RAM NØ. 0

RAM CONTENTS AFTER EXAMPLES 1 THROUGH 4

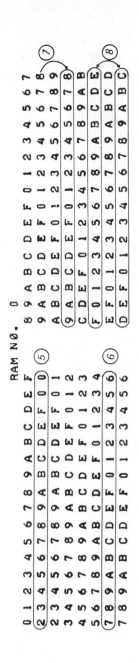

RAM NO. 0

Figure 9.7. *RAM* 0 print-out before and after executing example programs. (Courtesy of Rockwell International Corporation).

RAM CONTENTS AFTER EXAMPLES 5 THROUGH 8

367

In example 4 the initial zero is loaded into ODA (hex) and then the *BM* value is changed to *E* by the 3 in the EX 3 instruction. Zero is again loaded into the accumulator because the latter has the value 6 in it (the original contents of ODA). The zero is then transferred to OEA, and the address modified to OD9 by the EXD 3 instruction. Again the process is repeated until the EXD causes a skip out of the transfer sequence.

Table 9.8 shows a few more examples. The results of these examples are shown in Fig. 9.7.

Example 5 causes a 16-word register to be shifted left by one word, with the least significant word left unchanged.

Table 9.8.
(Reproduced with permission of Rockwell International, Anaheim, California)

LABEL	MNEMONIC	IMMEDIATE FIELD ARGUMENT	COMMENT
	LBL	#1F	Example 5
	LD		LEFT SHIFT
A1	EXD		
	T	A1	
	LBL	# 60	Example 6
	EXD		END AROUND LEFT SHIFT
	T	*+1	
A2	EXD		
	T	A2	
	LBL	#9F	Example 7
A3	LD	2	MOVE
	EXD	2	
	T	A3	
	LBL	#DF	Example 8
A4	LD	2	EXCHANGE
	EX	2	
	EXD		
	T	A4	
	.	.	
	.	.	
	.	.	

Example 6 causes an end-around or circular left shift of a 16-word register. The T *+1 instruction is interpreted as a transfer to this location plus 1 instruction (* means this location) and consequently is effectively a NO OP (no operation) instruction.

Example 7 merely replaces the contents of row B with the contents of row 9.

Example 8 causes the contents of rows D and F to be exchanged.

Binary and Decimal Arithmetic Programs

Table 9.9 shows few examples dealing with binary and decimal arithmetic. The results are shown in Fig. 9.8.

In example 9, two 24-bit binary words are added together and the contents replace the contents of one of the original 24-bit registers.

Similarly, example 10 works with two 32-bit registers, subtracts the register in row 4 from that in row 3, and stores the result back into row 3.

Examples 11 and 12 work with seven-decimal digits to add two decimal numbers and nine-decimal digits to subtract two decimal numbers, respectively. In both of these cases the results of the computation replace the contents of one of the original registers.

Example 13 is similar to example 9 except that the register length is 28 bits and the results of the computation are placed into a third register in *RAM* 0. This is accomplished in the following manner.

Initially, the *B* register is loaded with the location 0C6, the contents of the accumulator are loaded with the memory cell contents in that location, and the *B* middle value is converted to *D* by the argument (1) of a load instruction, so that the address counter now points to *D*6. The contents of that memory cell are added to the accumulator with the ADC instruction. The next three steps accomplish the storage operation in a third register. The first exchange instruction interchanges the original value in register *D*6 with the accumulator. The second exchange instruction re-exchanges them, so that the original value of *D*6 is back in *D*6 and the resulting sum is back in the accumulator, except that, on completion, the second exchange instruction modifies the *B* middle value with 2, so that the address register now points to memory cell *F*6.

Finally, the exchange and decrement instruction stores the 4-bit result in the designated third memory register, and argument 3 translates the *F* in the *B* middle address back to a *C* and decrements *BL* so that the process is ready to be repeated, beginning with the word located in memory cell *C*5.

Table 9.9.
(Reproduced with permission of Rockwell International, Anaheim, California)

LABEL	MNEMONIC	IMMEDIATE FIELD ARGUMENT	COMMENT
	RC		Example 9
	LBL	#05	ADD BINARY
A1	LD	1	
	ADC		
	EXD	1	
	T	A1	
	SC		Example 10
	LBL	#47	SUB (BINARY)
A2	LD	7	
	COMP		
	ADC		
	EXD	7	
	T	A2	
	RC		Example 11
	LBL	#66	ADD (DECIMAL)
A3	LD	1	
	ADI	6	
	ADCSK		
	DC		
	EXD	1	
	T	A3	
	SC		Example 12
	LBL	#A8	SUB (DECIMAL)
A4	LD	2	
	COMP		
	ADCSK		
	DC		
	EXD	2	
	T	A4	
	RC		Example 13
	LBL	#C6	ADD (BINARY) FROM TWO REGISTERS
A5	LD	1	& STORE RESULT IN A THIRD REGISTER
	ADC		
	EX		
	EX	2	
	EXD	3	
	T	A5	
	.		
	.		
	.		

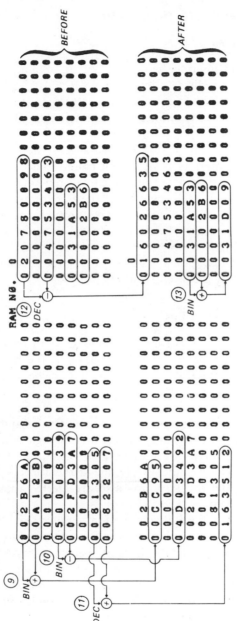

Figure 9.8. Examples of binary and decimal add and subtract operations. (Courtesy of Rockwell International Corporation).

371

9.4. INPUT/OUTPUT AND INTERRUPT

Discrete Input/Output

Direct input/output interface with the *CPU* is obtained through discrete input group A (DIA), discrete input group B (DIB), and discrete output (DOA). The two discrete input instructions sample the inputs on the selected group of 4 bits and load the information directly into the accumulator (Fig. 9.2, Table 9.6).

The discrete output instruction (DOA) causes the contents of the accumulator to be transferred to an output buffer register. The 4 bits in this register supply a continuous output which will remain until another DOA instruction is executed and a new bit pattern is transmitted out, or until power is turned off the *CPU*. If a discrete output bit is coupled back through a discrete input, two cycles should be allowed between issuing the output and sampling the input.

There is no inversion of the data bits between the accumulator and either the discrete output or the discrete inputs.

Input/Output via the Data Bus

The input/output long (IOL) instruction is used to transfer information between the accumulator and the data bus. It is the primary instruction used for communicating with the standard I/O devices used in the PPS-4 system.

The IOL instruction is a two-cycle instruction and uses two successive words from the program memory. The first word signifies to the *CPU* that this is an I/O instruction and sets up internal logic which will cause the second word to be ignored by the *CPU*. This word also sets up logic to provide the proper signal over the WI/O line at the appropriate time so that the data memory and the IO chips also are alerted that this is an I/O instruction.

The second word of the IOL instruction is put on the bus from the selected program memory location, where it is interpreted by all of the I/O devices to determine which I/O device is being addressed, so that it can interpret the command. On all of the standard PPS I/O devices, bits 5 through 8 identify the specific I/O device selected, so that the device having the appropriate chip selection code wired will respond, and bits 1 through 4 provide the specific operation code for that external device (ID bus = party-line bus).

Bits 1 through 4 on the ID bus contain the operation code, which directs the chip selected by the 4 bits on ID bus lines 5 through 8 to perform the desired I/O function.

During the normal data transfer time, the contents of the accumulator are placed on ID bus lines 5 through 8, and whatever is on ID bus lines 1 through 4 is loaded into the accumulator. In both cases—data going to the accumulator from the ID bus and data coming from the accumulator to the ID bus—the information is inverted so that the one's complement of the data is transmitted.

Depending on the 4-bit operation code transmitted to the I/O device, the I/O device will either receive control information (which, for instance, in the printer controller circuit might be used to control the starting or stopping of the printer motor), or it will set up the I/O device to receive or transmit data in inverted form with the accumulator.

The *CPU* does not decode the 4-bit I/O operation code, so that the *CPU*, in effect, is always set up to exchange data. Consequently, if the I/O device is commanded to receive data outputted from the accumulator, the data will be sent out, and whatever is on the ID bus in lines 1 through 4 will be loaded into the accumulator. Depending on the specific I/O device, this may or may not be useful information. The key point here is that the programmer must assume after an output operation that the contents of the accumulator have been changed.

Input/Output Using the General-Purpose I/O Device

The general-purpose input/output (GP I/O) device P/N 10696, shown in Fig. 9.9, provides 12 discrete inputs and 12 discrete static outputs. This device is used for direct data exchange or for status and control functions with an external peripheral device. The GP I/O circuit uses special interface circuitry to directly interface with TTL circuitry. Direct addressing for up to 16 of these circuits is possible by the use of four chip address straps that can be terminated, by the user, to create each chip address. The I/O is accessed with an I/O enable signal from the *CPU* and a simultaneous 8-bit instruction from the *ROM*. Four bits of the instruction are used to address the particular I/O chip; the other 4 bits define the I/O operation.

The 4-bit operation code is interpreted by the I/O to either copy the contents of the accumulator into one of the three 4-bit parallel output registers (*A, B,* or *C*) or transfer data from one of the 4-bit parallel input receivers (*A, B,* or *C*) into the accumulator of the *CPU*. The output drivers are static outputs, and data remain in the output registers until altered. Bits 1 through 4 of the instruction word are commands to the I/O, while bits 5 through 8 are used to address 1 of 16 possible I/O chips. The four I/O select inputs terminated by the user create the addresses for each I/O circuit.

Data are transferred through the GP I/O from input group A, B, or C to I/D 1–4 and from output group A, B, or C to I/D 5–8, most significant to most significant and least significant to least significant.

The general purpose input/output device provides a capability of strobing selected 4-bit groups of data of the 12 bits available for input or transmitting the inverted contents of the accumulator to selected 4-bit groups of output buffers within the GP I/O device. The operation codes for this device are shown in Table 9.10. Note that the groups of input or output bits can be controlled one at a time, two at a time, or all three simultaneously. For instance, the following program may be used to set all 12 outputs of I/O device 6 to zero:

```
CLEAR6    LDI    15        ZERO COMPLEMENT
          IOL    #64
```

The PPS-4 can be very efficient in transferring data to or from external systems, as can be seen from the next program. This program loads data inputted from group A of device 9 into row D, group B into row E, and group C into row F of *RAM* 0. The strobe portion of this program tells the equipment interfacing with the GP I/O device to load the data for sampling. This sequence could have been placed after the data transfer to tell the external equipment that the data have been accepted.

The program is shown in Table 9.11.

Interrupts

The interrupt function causes the main program to be interrupted upon detection of a signal from outside the *CPU*. Control of the microcomputer then jumps to a special program to perform the desired high-priority function and, upon completion, returns control to the main routine.

This interrupt function can be accommodated in the PPS-4 by several methods. By using care in the design of the interfacing hardware and of the program, it may be possible to use the power-on reset signal to the *CPU* to force the program address register to location 0. The action initiated causes the program to determine which external device generated the interrupt and to service it; then, by using prestored information in data memory which identifies which sequence of the program was interrupted, the program can return to an appropriate starting point to continue the routine.

Another interrupt procedure could use a block of external logic which modifies the address on the address bus when the interrupt is accepted. This causes the main program memory to ignore the instruction and sends the address to a special program memory. (This modification of the address

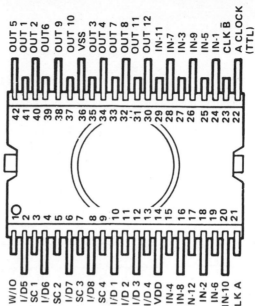

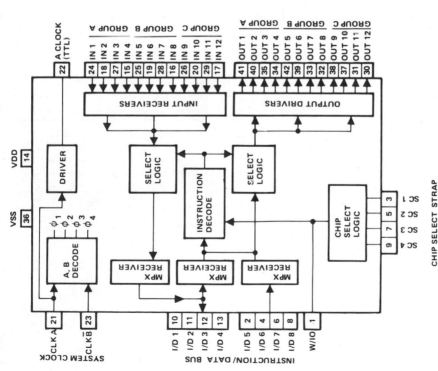

Figure 9.9. General-purpose input/output. (Courtesy of Rockwell International Corporation).

375

Table 9.10. General-Purpose I/O Device Instruction Format
(Reproduced with permission of Rockwell International, Anaheim, California)

I/O CHIP ADDRESSING — CHIP ADDRESS

I/O GROUP SELECTION — SELECT CODE

I/D BUS → CHIP SELECT STRAPS →

CHIP NO.	HEX CODE	CHIP ADDRESS (SC1 SC2 SC3 SC4)
0	0	0 0 0 0
1	1	0 0 0 1
2	2	0 0 1 0
3	3	0 0 1 1
4	4	0 1 0 0
5	5	0 1 0 1
6	6	0 1 1 0
7	7	0 1 1 1
8	8	1 0 0 0
9	9	1 0 0 1
10	A	1 0 1 0
11	B	1 0 1 1
12	C	1 1 0 0
13	D	1 1 0 1
14	E	1 1 1 0
15	F	1 1 1 1

SELECT CODE / I/O GROUP SELECTION

HEX	SELECT CODE	GROUP C	B	A	COMMAND
	READ →				
A	1 0 1 0	–	–	X	Read Group A
9	1 0 0 1	–	X	–	Read Group B
3	0 0 1 1	X	–	–	Read Group C
0	0 0 0 0	X	X	X	If two or three groups are selected the accumulator will copy the logical "OR" value of the selected groups
1	0 0 0 1	X	X	–	
2	0 0 1 0	X	–	X	
8	1 0 0 0	–	X	X	
	SET →				
E	1 1 1 0	–	–	X	Set Group A
D	1 1 0 1	–	X	–	Set Group B
7	0 1 1 1	X	–	–	Set Group C
4	0 1 0 0	X	X	X	If two or three groups are selected the accumulator contents will be copied to each group selected
5	0 1 0 1	X	X	–	
6	0 1 1 0	X	–	X	
C	1 1 0 0	–	X	X	

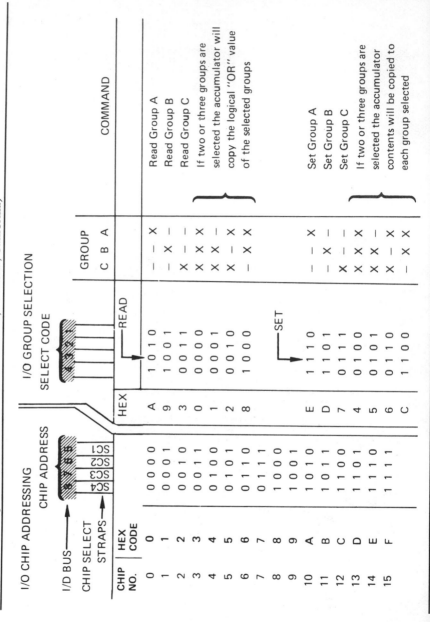

Table 9.11.
(Reproduced with permission of Rockwell International, Anaheim, California)

LOADBLK	LBL	#DF	SET BLOCK ORIGIN
STROBE	LDI	1	OUTPUT 2 CYCLE PULSE
	DOA		
	LDI	0	
	DOA		
	IOL	#9A	LOAD GROUP A
	EX	3	STORE (ROW D)
	IOL	#99	LOAD GROUP B
	EX	1	STORE (ROW E)
	IOL	#93	LOAD GROUP C
	EXD	2	STORE (ROW F) & SET NEXT COL
	T	STROBE	REPEAT 15 TIMES
	•		
	•		

bus could be accomplished most easily by using one of the extended address bits.) The special program memory would automatically send back a TM instruction, which then directs the program into the interrupt servicing routine and saves the program counter. At the conclusion of the interrupt servicing routine, when everything has been restored to the condition it was in at the time of interrupt, a return instruction will restart the main program at the appropriate point. The simplest form of interrupt in the PPS-4 system is a software interrupt. In this case, the programmer writes the program so that the *CPU* periodically looks for the interrupt signal by way of a discrete input or an input from an I/O circuit.

If the signal is present, the *CPU* transfers to the interrupt servicing routine; if no signal is present, it continues with the main routine and periodically examines the appropriate input signal for an interrupt. The interrupt interrogations can be located in the program in situations where a minimum amount of status storing must be accomplished, so that the interrupt program can be very efficient. With this technique, an interrupt interrogation can be as short as 15 μsecs. In some other microprocessors, the bookkeeping associated with a hardware interrupt may take as long as 20 msec and also require a significant amount of external hardware to implement.

The software interrupt procedure is the recommended procedure for interrupts on the PPS-4.

REFERENCES

1. Data Sheet, Parallel Processing System (PPS-4) Microcomputer, Rockwell International Corp., Anaheim, Ca., 1973.
2. PPS-4 Microcomputer Program Library, Rockwell International Corp., Anaheim, Ca., 1973.
3. PPS-4 Bus Interface Circuit, Rockwell International Corp., Anaheim, Ca., 1973.

10

PPS-8 MICROPROCESSOR

Chapter 10 presents the 8-bit microprocessor Rockwell PPS-8. This processor has a 14-bit multiplexed address bus and an 8-bit bidirectional data/instruction bus. The PPS-8 has an extensive instruction repertoire for performing a variety of arithmetic, logical, and data manipulation functions. Programming examples show the power of these instructions, especially when dealing with blocks of data. Special attention is focused on the parallel data controller chip, which is a flexible device to interface the PPS-8 to external devices. This device operates on the principle of control/status word. Another chip, the *DMA* controller, provides all the parts necessary for up to 8 *DMA* channels.

The material* in this chapter has been adapted in part from a publication of Rockwell International Corporation. The material so published herein is the full responsibility of the author.

10.1. GENERAL DESCRIPTION

The Rockwell 8-bit parallel processing system (PPS-8) is an advanced-design, modular, microcomputer system which uses a unique four-phase clock timing system for logic functions and control. Proven P-channel MOS technology is used to implement the PPS-8 system byte (8-bit)-oriented architecture. Rockwell MOS technology and the unique design of the PPS-8 offer superior performance for less cost over a wide range of applications, including point-of-sale equipment, data entry terminals, and peripheral/process control. The wide range of applications and performance is achieved by high system throughput, efficient character-oriented instructions, flexible input/output capabilities, and system modularity/expandability.

The standard PPS-8 system, shown in Fig. 10.1, consists of a central processor unit (*CPU*) device, random access memory (*RAM*) device(s), read only memory (*ROM*) device(s), multiphase clock generator, direct

* Programs, figures, and tables are courtesy and copyright © 1975 by Rockwell International Corporation. All rights reserved.

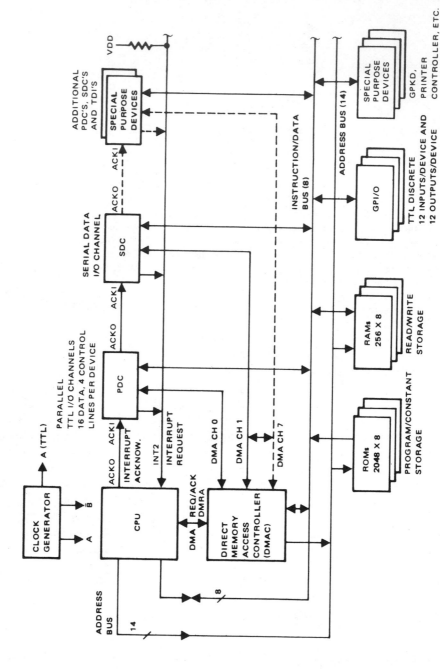

Figure 10.1. PPS-8 microcomputer system. (Courtesy of Rockwell International Corporation).

memory access controller (*DMAC*) device, parallel data controller (*PDC*) device, and serial data controller (*SDC*) device.

The basic system can be supplemented with special-purpose and custom I/O devices as required for specific applications. For example, a 1200-band telecommunications data interface device, a printer controller device, a bus-interface device, and a keyboard/display controller device are available.

All of the various MOS devices that make up the PPS-8 are packaged in identical standard 42-lead plastic packages with the exception of the clock generator, which is in a TO 100 package. The overall dimensions of the body of the plastic package, exclusive of the leads, are 0.640 in. in width, 1.060 in. in length, and 0.15 in. in thickness. This standardization in packaging provides optimum flexibility when designing and packaging a specific PPS-8 System.

PPS-8 Basic Devices and Throughput

Central processor unit (*CPU*)
Read only memory (*ROM*)
Clock generator
General-purpose input/output (GP I/O)
Parallel data controller (*PDC*)
Direct memory access controller (*DMAC*)
Random access memory (*RAM*)

Instruction access:	2 μsec
Operand access:	2 μsec
Complete instruction cycle:	4 μsec
Decimal addition:	12 μsec/digit
Decimal subtraction:	12 μsec/digit
Block data moving:	12 μsec/byte
Table search:	12 μsec/byte
Digit (4-bit) string shifting:	8 μsec/digit

Central Processing Unit (*CPU*)

The PPS-8 central processor unit, shown in Fig. 10.2, is a complete 8-bit parallel processor implemented on a single MOS chip. The *CPU* uses four-phase dynamic logic for operation, and all power requirements are met from a single 17-V power supply.

The *CPU* contains the following:

(*a*) Logic necessary to receive and decode the instructions.

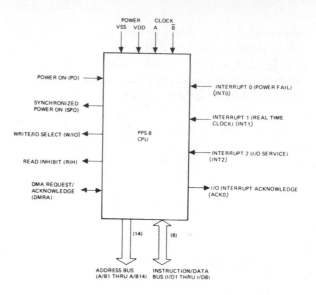

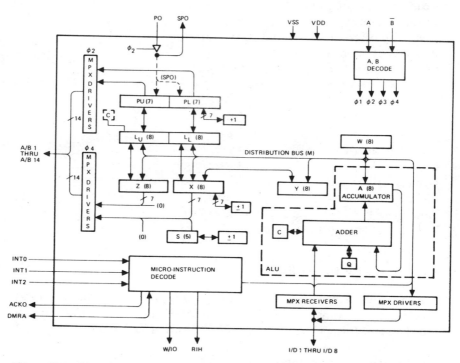

Figure 10.2. Central processing unit block diagram. (Courtesy of Rockwell International Corporation).

(*b*) An 8-bit parallel adder/accumulator for arithmetic and logical operations.

(*c*) A 14-bit *P* register for sequencing through the *ROM* program.

(*d*) A 16-bit *L* register for subroutine linkage, *RAM* operand addressing, and *ROM* indirect addressing.

(*e*) Three 8-bit registers (*X*, *Y*, and *Z*) for *RAM* operand addressing.

(*f*) A 5-bit stack pointer *S* for addressing a dedicated *RAM* area.

(*g*) Logic for processing a priority interrupt structure.

(*h*) Direct memory access (*DMA*) mode.

(*i*) Multiplexed receivers and drivers for interfacing with the 14-bit multiplexed address bus and the 8-bit bidirectional data/instruction bus.

The *CPU*, through time multiplexing, utilizes an 8-bit bidirectional bus to transfer instructions from the *ROM* to the *CPU* (and I/O) during $\phi 4$, and to transfer data between the *CPU*, *RAM*'s and I/O devices during $\phi 2$.

Instruction Decode. The decode portion of the chip contains logic to decode the instructions, sense interrupt or *DMA* requests, and provide signals to control data transfer, arithmetic, logical, and indexing operations. Instructions are either one, two, or three bytes in length and require from one to three cycles for execution.

Accumulator Register and Arithmetic Logic Unit (ALU). The adder is an 8-bit parallel binary adder with an internally connected carry flip-flop (*C*) for implementing extended precision arithmetic operations. In addition, the adder has built-in capability to facilitate packed BCD (decimal) arithmetic and the manipulation of hexadecimal data. Circular shifting of the accumulator contents right and left with carry linkage is also provided. The adder, with the 8-bit accumulator register (*A*) and associated logic circuits, forms the arithmetic and logical unit (*ALU*) section of the *CPU*.

In addition to its arithmetic functions, the *A* register is the primary working register in the *CPU* and is the central data interchange point for most data transfer operations.

P Register (14 bits). The *P* register contains the address of the instruction currently being executed, and automatically increments (least significant 7 bits) to fetch the next byte from instruction memory (*ROM*). It may be altered during the execution of BRANCH, RETURN, or SKIP instructions.

L Register (16 bits). The *L* register is used to save the return address after a subroutine call or an interrupt. It also serves as an address register for indirect *ROM* operands and can be used as an alternative *RAM* address register or as a general-purpose programming register.

Z Register (8 bits). This register holds the 7 most significant bits of the 14-bit *RAM* operand address or may be used as a general-purpose programming register.

X Register (8 bits). The *X* register holds the 7 least significant bits of the 14-bit *RAM* operand address. The most significant bit (8th bit) is used as an upper *RAM* address control bit. If the upper address control bit is:

Logical 1: the *Z* register contents are output for the most significant 7 bits of the *RAM* address.

Logical 0: logic 0 is output for the most significant 7 bits of the *RAM* address.

This register may be loaded, stored, autoincremented, or autodecremented under program control.

Y Register (8 bits). The *Y* register is used as an alternative lower *RAM* address register and as a "loop counter," or it may serve as a general-purpose programming register.

S Register (5 bits). The 5-bit up-down counter register *S* is used as an address pointer to a 32-byte "stack" in *RAM*. This stack pointer is automatically incremented each time a byte is "pushed" into the stack and decremented each time a byte is "popped" from the stack.

W Register (8 bits). The *W* register serves primarily as an internal buffer register. Additionally, it is used in conjunction with the LAL and PSHL instructions.

Power-On Reset (PO). The power-on input signal is used to initialize the *CPU* to a known starting address and state during a power-on sequence. The power-on (PO) signal is generated externally to the *CPU*. The *CPU* receives this signal, initializes the internal logic states, and, at the same time, generates a synchronized power-on output (SPO) signal, which serves to initialize other circuits of the PPS-8.

Multiplex System Data Transfer

During each program counter bit time, the *CPU* will address the instruction memory (*ROM*), read and decode the instruction, execute the instruction, and increment (or load) the program counter in preparation for the next instruction. This bit time or a single-cycle instruction execution time is 4 μsec at 250-kHz frequency. The proprietary instruction architecture and multiphase clocking scheme of the 8-bit *CPU* result in unusually high data handling rates for a relatively slow external clocking system.

The PPS circuits are controlled from a crystal controlled clock generator, which provides two synchronized and phased clock signals. These signals, designated A and $\overline{\text{B}}$, are received by the *CPU* and are logically divided into four phases, so that the internal signals are being manipulated at four times the frequency of the external A clock. For example, if the A clock is 250 kHz, logic signal flow within the *CPU* will occur at 1 MHz. The basic clock timing is shown in Fig. 10.3.

The PPS parallel bus transfer lines are synchronized by the A and $\overline{\text{B}}$ clock signals so that data transfer occurs only during $\phi2$ and $\phi4$ time, as depicted in Fig. 10.3.

In addition to the power and clock signals, 24 multiplexed lines interconnect the *CPU* with *ROM*, *RAM*, and I/O devices. These lines are functionally grouped as follows:

Fourteen parallel address lines (A/B 1 through 14)
Eight parallel bidirectional data lines (I/D 1 through 8)
One WRITE command/I/O enable (W/I/O) line
One READ INHIBIT (RIH) command line

The fourteen address lines originate from the *CPU* and are time multiplexed within it to provide direct addressing capability for up to 16,384 8-bit bytes of *ROM* and 16,384 bytes of *RAM*.

Like the address lines, the eight data bus lines are time shared between the *CPU*, *ROM*, *RAM*, and I/O's.

During $\phi2$, a logical 1 on the write enable line is interpreted by the *RAM*'s as a WRITE enable command, and the data on the bus will be written into the *RAM*, using the preceding $\phi4$ address. During the preceding $\phi1$, the *RAM* would be commanded not to read via the RIH command (logical 1). The *RAM* is a nondestructive read-out device and is always programmed to read unless instructed not to by the RIH command.

The same line providing the WRITE command to the *RAM* during $\phi2$ time serves as an I/O enable signal during $\phi4$ time when communication is desired to (or from) an I/O device addressed on the data bus. If the I/O enable is on (logical 1) at $\phi4$, the read inhibit line will be used to disable the *RAM* during the $\phi2$ transmittal of information between the *CPU* and the addressed I/O device.

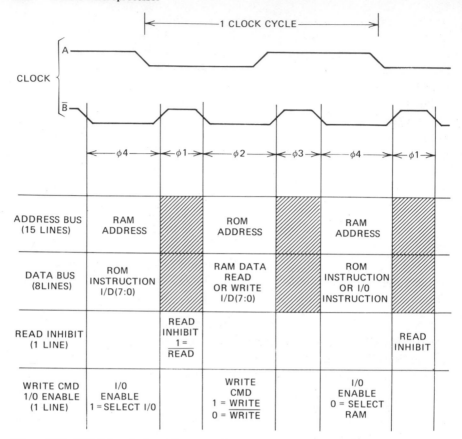

Figure 10.3. PPS-8 bus timing. (Courtesy of Rockwell International Corporation).

10.2. INSTRUCTION SET

The definition of symbolic notation is given in Table 10.1, and the PPS-8 instructions are described in Tables 10.2–10.10. The PPS-8 has an extensive instruction repertoire for performing a variety of arithmetic, logical, and data manipulation functions in a manner that is efficient in both instruction memory required and speed of execution. Most instruction types require only a single 8-bit byte, but two- and three-byte formats are also included to provide extended addressing/functional capability. In the tables, reference is made to notes, which are listed after Table 10.10.

Table 10.1.
(Reproduced with permission of Rockwell International, Anaheim, California)

Symbol	Symbolic Notation Item or Function
A	Accumulator Register $A(1:8)$
X	RAM Address Register and Index, $X(1:8)$
Y	RAM Address Register $Y(1:8)$
Z	RAM Address Register $Z(1:8)$
L	Link Register $L(1:16)$
P	Program Counter Register $P(1:14)$
S	Stack Pointer Register
W	The W Register
C	Carry Flip-Flop
IC	Intermediate state of Carry Flip-Flop
Q	Intermediate Carry Flip-Flop
I	Instruction $I(1:8)$
I1	First byte of multiple byte instruction $I1(1:8)$
I2	Second byte of multiple byte instruction $I2(1:8)$
I3	Third byte of multiple byte instruction $I3(1:8)$
M	RAM memory contents
R(n)	Bit n of Register R
R(n:m)	Bit n through m of R, inclusively
W/IO	Write and I/O Enable Control Line
RIH	Read Inhibit Control Line
Byte	Eight-bit Data Field
Digit	Four-bit Data Field
Page	Block of 128 bytes
$\longrightarrow$	Replaces (or $\longleftarrow$)
$\longleftrightarrow$	Exchange
$\overline{R}$	1's complement of state R.
$\wedge$	Logical Product (AND)
$\vee$	Logical Sum (Inclusive OR)
$\veebar$	Logical (Exclusive OR)
$-$	Algebraic Subtract
$+$	Algebraic Add
$>$	Greater than
$<$	Less than
$=$	Equal to
I/D(8:1)	Instruction/Data Bus (lines 1 through 8)
(L)	ROM memory contents addressed by L
SP_u	Byte from upper address portion of Subroutine Entry Pool
SP_1	Byte from lower address portion of Subroutine Entry Pool

Table 10.2. List of Instructions
(Reproduced with permission of Rockwell International, Anaheim, California)

MNEMONIC	NAME	BYTES	CYCLES	DESCRIPTION VERBAL	DESCRIPTION SYMBOLIC	NOTES
L	Load A	1	1	The current RAM operand is placed in the accumulator	A ← M	1
LN	Load A, Increment Address	1	1	Same as L. Additionally, the X register is incremented	A ← M X ← X+1, skip if X=0	1,2,8
LD	Load A, Decrement Address	1	1	Same as L. Additionally, the X register is decremented	A ← M X ← X-1, skip if X=127	1,2,8
LNXL	Load A, Increment Address, Exchange L	1	1	Same as LN. Additionally, the contents of the L register and the Z & X registers are exchanged	A ← M X ← X+1, skip if X=0 Z, X ↔ L	1,2,8
LDXL	Load A, Decrement Address, Exchange L	1	1	Same as LD. Additionally, the contents of the L register and the Z & X registers are exchanged	A ← M X ← X-1, skip if X=127 Z, X ↔ L	1,2,8
LNCX	Load A, Increment & Compare Address, Exchange L	1	1	Same as LNXL. Additionally, the next instruction is skipped if X = Y	A ← M X ← X+1 Skip if X=0 or X=Y Z, X ↔ L	1,2,8, 19

Mnemonic	Name		Description		Operation	Notes
LDCX	Load A, Decrement & Compare Address, Exchange L	1	Same as LDXL. Additionally, the next instruction is skipped if X = Y	1	A←M X←X-1 Skip if X=127 or X=Y Z,X↔L	1,2,8, 19
LNXY	Load A, Increment Address, Exchange Y	1	Same as LN. Additionally, the contents of the X & Y registers are exchanged	1	A←M X←X+1, skip if X=0 X↔Y	1,2,8
S	Store A	1	The contents of the accumulator are stored in the current RAM operand address	1	M←A	1
SN	Store A, Increment Address	1	Same as S. Additionally, the X register is incremented	1	M←A X←X+1, skip if X=0	1,2,8
SD	Store A, Decrement Address	1	Same as S. Additionally, the X register is decremented	1	M←A X←X-1, skip if X=127	1,2,8
SNXL	Store A, Increment Address, Exchange L	1	Same as SN. Additionally, the contents of the L register and the Z & X registers are exchanged	1	M←A X←X+1, skip if X=0 Z,X↔L	1,2,8
SDXL	Store A, Decrement Address, Exchange L	1	Same as SD. Additionally, the contents of the L register and the Z & X registers are exchanged	1	M←A X←X-1, skip if X=127 Z,X↔L	1,2,8

Table 10.3. List of Instructions (*Cont'd*)
(Reproduced with permission of Rockwell International, Anaheim, California)

MNEMONIC	NAME	BYTES	CYCLES	DESCRIPTION		NOTES
				VERBAL	SYMBOLIC	
SNCX	Store A, Increment & Compare Address, Exchange L	1	1	Same as SNXL. Additionally, the next instruction is skipped if X = Y	M←A $\quad$ X←X+1 $\quad$ Skip if X=0 or X=Y $\quad$ Z,X↔L	1,2,8, 19
SDCX	Store A, Decrement & Compare Address, Exchange L	1	1	Same as SDXL. Additionally, the next instruction is skipped if X = Y	M←A $\quad$ X←X-1 $\quad$ Skip if X=127 or X=Y $\quad$ Z,X↔L	1,2,8, 19
SNXY	Store A, Increment Address, Exchange Y	1	1	Same as SN. Additionally, the contents of the X and Y registers are exchanged	M←A $\quad$ X←X+1, skip if X=0 $\quad$ X↔Y	1,2,8
X	Exchange	2	2	These instructions are identical to the corresponding store instructions except that the accumulator and the current RAM operand are exchanged	A↔M	1,6
XN	Exchange, Increment Address	2	2	←	A↔M $\quad$ X←X+1, skip if X=0	1,2,6,8

390

Mnemonic	Description				Operation	
XD	Exchange, Decrement Address	2	2		$A \leftrightarrow M$ $X \leftarrow X-1$, skip if X=127	1,2,6,8
XNXL	Exchange, Increment Address, Exchange L	2	2		$A \leftrightarrow M$ $X \leftarrow X+1$, skip if X=0 $Z, X \leftrightarrow L$	1,2,6,8
XDXL	Exchange, Decrement Address, Exchange L	2	2		$A \leftrightarrow M$ $X \leftarrow X-1$, skip if X=127 $Z, X \leftrightarrow L$	1,2,6,8
XNCX	Exchange, Increment & Compare Address, Exchange L	2	2		$A \leftrightarrow M$ $X \leftarrow X+1$ Skip if X=0 or X=Y $Z, X \leftrightarrow L$	1,2,6,8, 19
XDCX	Exchange, Decrement & Compare Address, Exchange L	2	2	These instructions are identical to the corresponding store instructions except that the accumulator and the current RAM operand are exchanged	$A \leftrightarrow M$ $X \leftarrow X-1$ Skip if X=127 or X=Y $Z, X \leftrightarrow L$	1,2,6,8, 19

Table 10.4. List of Instructions (*Cont'd*)
(Reproduced with permission of Rockwell International, Anaheim, California)

MNEMONIC	NAME	BYTES	CYCLES	DESCRIPTION		NOTES
				VERBAL	SYMBOLIC	
XNXY	Exchange, Increment Address, Excahnge Y	2	2	These instructions are identical to the corresponding store instructions except that the accumulator and the current RAM operand are exchanged	A ⟷ M X ⟵ X+1, skip if X=0 X ⟷ Y	1,2,6,8
LX	Load X	1,2	2	The current RAM operand is placed in the X register	X ⟵ M	4
LY	Load Y	1,2	2	The current RAM operand is placed in the Y register	Y ⟵ M	4
LZ	Load Z	1,2	2	The current RAM operand is placed in the Z register	Z ⟵ M	4
LAI	Load A Immediate	1-3	3	The specified literal operand is placed in the accumulator	A ⟵ I3	3,4
LXI	Load X Immediate	1-3	3	The specified literal operand is placed in the X register	X ⟵ I3	3,4
LYI	Load Y Immediate	1-3	3	The specified literal operand is placed in the Y register	Y ⟵ I3	3,4

LZI	Load Z Immediate	1-3	3	The specified literal operand is placed in the Z register	$Z \leftarrow 13$	3,4
LAL	Load A through Link	1,2	3	The ROM operand addressed by the L register is placed in the accumulator	$W \leftarrow A,$ $A \leftarrow (L)$ $L \leftarrow L+1$	4,5,14
LXL	Load X through Link	1,2	3	The ROM operand addressed by the L register is placed in the X register	$X \leftarrow (L)$ $L \leftarrow L+1$	4,5
LYL	Load Y through Link	1,2	3	The ROM operand addressed by the L register is placed in the Y register	$Y \leftarrow (L)$ $L \leftarrow L+1$	4,5
LZL	Load Z through Link	1,2	3	The ROM operand addressed by the L register is placed in the Z register	$Z \leftarrow (L)$ $L \leftarrow L+1$	4,5
LXA	Load X from A	1	1	The contents of the accumulator are placed in the X register	$X \leftarrow A$	16
LYA	Load Y from A	1	1	The contents of the accumulator are placed in the Y register	$Y \leftarrow A$	16
LZA	Load Z from A	1	1	The contents of the accumulator are placed in the Z register	$Z \leftarrow A$	16

Table 10.5. List of Instructions (*Cont'd*)
(Reproduced with permission of Rockwell International, Anaheim, California)

MNEMONIC	NAME	BYTES	CYCLES	DESCRIPTION			NOTES
				VERBAL	SYMBOLIC		
LLA	Load L from A	1	1	The contents of the accumulator are placed in the upper 8 bits of the L register	$L(16:9) \leftarrow A$		16
XY	Exchange Y	1	1	The contents of the X and Y register are exchanged	$X \leftrightarrow Y$		
XL	Exchange L	1	1	The contents of the L register and the Z & X registers are exchanged	$L \leftrightarrow Z,X$		
XAX	Exchange A and X	1	1	The contents of the X register and the accumulator are exchanged	$A \leftrightarrow X$		
XAY	Exchange A and Y	1	1	The contents of the Y register and the accumulator are exchanged	$A \leftrightarrow Y$		
XAZ	Exchange A and Z	1	1	The contents of the Z register and the accumulator are exchanged	$A \leftrightarrow Z$		
XAL	Exchange A and L	1	1	The contents of the upper half of the L register and the accumulator are exchanged	$A \leftrightarrow L(16:9)$		
INCX	Increment X	1	1	The X register is incremented by one	$X \leftarrow X+1$ Skip if X=0		2

Mnemonic	Operation			Description	Function	Notes
DECX	Decrement X	1,2	1	The X register is decremented by one	X ← X-1 Skip if X=127	2
INXY	Increment X, Exchange Y	1,2	1	The X register is incremented and the contents of the X and Y registers are exchanged	X ← X+1, skip if X=0 X ↔ Y	2
DEXY	Decrement X, Exchange Y	1,2	1	The X register is decremented and the contents of the X and Y registers are exchanged	X ← X-1, skip if X=127 X ↔ Y	2
INCY	Increment Y	2	2	The Y register is incremented by one	Y ← Y+1 Skip if Y=0	2,7,8
DECY	Decrement Y	2	2	The Y register is decremented by one	Y ← Y-1 Skip if Y=127	2,7,8
PSHA	Push A	1,2	2	The contents of the accumulator are pushed into the stack	A → (S) S ← S+1	4,13
PSHX	Push X	1,2	2	The contents of the X register pushed into the stack	X → (S) S ← S+1	4,13
PSHY	Push Y	1,2	2	The contents of the Y register are pushed into the stack	Y → (S) S ← S+1	4,13
PSHZ	Push Z	1,2	2	The contents of the Z register are pushed into the stack	Z → (S) S ← S+1	4,13

Table 10.6. List of Instructions (*Cont'd*)
(Reproduced with permission of Rockwell International, Anaheim, California)

MNEMONIC	NAME	BYTES	CYCLES	DESCRIPTION		NOTES
				VERBAL	SYMBOLIC	
PSHL	Push L	1	3	The contents of the L register are pushed into the stack and replaced by the contents of the A and W registers	L → (S+1,S) A,W → L S ← S+2	13,14
POPA	Pop A	1,2	2	The uppermost byte is popped from the stack and placed in the accumulator	S ← S-1 A ← (S) Skip if S=31	4,13
POPX	Pop X	1,2	2	The uppermost byte is popped from the stack and placed in the X register	S ← S-1 X ← (S) Skip if S=31	4,13
POPY	Pop Y	1,2	2	The uppermost byte is popped from the stack and placed in the Y register	S ← S-1 Y ← (S) Skip if S=31	4,13
POPZ	Pop Z	1,2	2	The uppermost byte is popped from the stack and placed in the Z register	S ← S-1 Z ← (S) Skip if S=31	4,13
POPL	Pop L	1	3	The uppermost 2 bytes are popped from the stack and placed in the L register	S ← S-2 L ← (S+1,S)	13

Mnemonic			Description	Operation	
A	1	1	The sum of the accumulator and the current RAM operand are placed in the accumulator	$C,A \leftarrow A+M$ $Q \leftarrow IC$	10,1
AC	1	1	Same as A except the carry flip-flop, C, is used as a carry-in	$C,A \leftarrow A+M+C$ $Q \leftarrow IC$	10,1
ASK	1	1	Same as A. Additionally, the next instruction is skipped if a carry-out is generated	$C,A \leftarrow A+M$ $Q \leftarrow IC$ Skip if C=1	10,1
ACSK	1	1	Same as AC. Additionally, the next instruction is skipped if a carryout is generated	$C,A \leftarrow A+M+C$ Skip if C=1	10,1
AISK	1-3	3	The sum of the accumulator and the specified literal operand is placed in the accumulator	$A \leftarrow A+I3$ $Q \leftarrow IC$ Skip if carry-out	3,4,10
INCA	1	1	The accumulator is incremented by one	$A \leftarrow A+1$ $Q \leftarrow IC$	10
DC	1	1	The hexadecimal value 66 is added to the accumulator	$A \leftarrow A+66_{16}$ $Q \leftarrow IC$	10,16
DCC	1	1	The accumulator is modified based on the states of the C&Q flip-flops	$\begin{array}{ll} C,Q & \\ 0,0 & A \leftarrow A+(9A)_{16} \\ 0,1 & A \leftarrow A+(A0)_{16} \\ 1,0 & A \leftarrow A+(FA)_{16} \\ 1,1 & \text{No change} \end{array}$	10,16

Table 10.7. List of Instructions (*Cont'd*)
(Reproduced with permission of Rockwell International, Anaheim, California)

MNEMONIC	NAME	BYTES	CYCLES	DESCRIPTION		NOTES
				VERBAL	SYMBOLIC	
AN	Logical AND	1	1	The logical product of the accumulator and the current RAM operand is placed in the accumulator	$A \leftarrow A \wedge M$	1
ANI	Logical AND Immediate	1-3	3	The logical product of the accumulator and the specified literal operand is placed in the accumulator	$A \leftarrow A \wedge I3$	3,4
OR	Logical OR	1	1	The logical sum of the accumulator and the current RAM operand is placed in the accumulator	$A \leftarrow A \vee M$	1
EOR	Logical Exclusive OR	1	1	The logical exclusive or (addition without carry) of the accumulator and the current RAM operand is placed in the accumulator	$A \leftarrow A \triangledown M$	1
COM	Complement.	1	1	The one's complement of the accumulator is placed in the accumulator	$A \leftarrow \overline{A}$	16
SC	Set Carry	1	1	The carry flip-flop, C, is set (1)	$C \leftarrow 1$	10
RC	Reset Carry	1	1	The carry flip-flop, C, is reset (0)	$C \leftarrow 0$	10

RAR	Rotate A Right	1	1	The accumulator and C flip-flop are circular shifted one bit to the right	$A(8:1) \rightarrow \boxed{C}$	16
RAL	Rotate A Left	1	1	The accumulator and C flip-flop are circular shifted one bit to the left	$A(8:1) \leftarrow \boxed{C}$	16
MDR	Move Digit Right	1	1	The accumulator is shifted right 4 bits and the least significant 4 bits of the current RAM operand are placed in the vacated accumulator positions	$A(8:5) \rightarrow A(4:1)$ $M(4:1) \rightarrow A(8:5)$	16,18
MDL	Move Digit Left	1	1	The accumulator is shifted left 4 bits and the most significant 4 bits of the current RAM operand are placed in the vacated accumulator positions	$A(8:5) \leftarrow A(4:1)$ $A(4:1) \leftarrow M(8:5)$	16,18
SB	Set Bit (n)	1,2	2	The specified bit of the current RAM operand is set (1)	$M \leftarrow M \vee 2^{(n-1)}$	4
RB	Reset Bit (n)	1,2	2	The specified bit of the current RAM operand is reset (0)	$M \leftarrow M \wedge \overline{2^{(n-1)}}$	4
B	Branch	1,2	1,2	The specified address is placed in the P-register	$P(7:1) \leftarrow I1(7:1)$ If $I1(8)=1$, $P(14:8) \leftarrow I2(7:1)$	12,16

Table 10.8. List of Instructions (*Cont'd*)
(Reproduced with permission of Rockwell International, Anaheim, California)

MNEMONIC	NAME	BYTES	CYCLES	DESCRIPTION		NOTES
				VERBAL	SYMBOLIC	
BDI	Branch, Disable Interrupts	2	2	Same as B. Additionally, the interrupts are disabled	$P(7:1) \leftarrow I1(7:1)$ $P(14:8) \leftarrow I2(7:1)$ Disable Interrupts	12,16
BL	Branch and Link	1,2	3	The specified address is placed in the P-register. The previous contents of the P-register (incremented) are saved in the L register together with the state of the C flip-flop. The previous contents of the L register are pushed into the stack	$L \leftarrow (S+1,S)$ $S \leftarrow S+2$ $P \leftarrow L(15:9,7:1)$ $C \leftarrow L(16)$ If $I1(6)=1$ $P(14:8) \leftarrow SP_u(7:1)$ $P(7:1) \leftarrow SP_1(7:1)$ If $I1(6)=0$ $P(12:8) \leftarrow I1(5:1)$ $P(7:1) \leftarrow I2(7:1)$ $P(13) \leftarrow I2(8)$ $P(14) \leftarrow 0$	15,16
RT	Return	1	3	The P-register and C flip-flop are loaded from the L-register. The uppermost 2 bytes are popped from the stack and placed in the L-register	$P \leftarrow L(15:9,7:1)$ $C \leftarrow L(16)$ $S \leftarrow S-2$ $L \leftarrow (S+1,S)$	11

Mnemonic	Name			Description	Operation	
RSK	Return & Skip	1	3	Same as RT except that the next instruction (i.e., the instruction at the "return" location) is skipped	$P \leftarrow L(15:9,7:1)$ $C \leftarrow L(16)$ $S \leftarrow S-2, L \leftarrow (S+1,S)$ Skip next instruction	11
RTI	Return, Enable Interrupts	1	3	Same as RT. Additionally, the interrupts are enabled	$P \leftarrow L(15:9,7:1)$ $C \leftarrow L(16)$ $S \leftarrow S-2, L \leftarrow (S+1,S)$ Enable interrupts	
NOP	No Operation	1	1	No function is performed. The branch condition tag is used		
SKC	Skip if Carry	1	1	The next instruction is skipped if the carry flip-flop, C, is set	Skip if $C=1$	8
SKNC	Skip if No Carry	1	1	The next instruction is skipped if the carry flip-flop, C, is reset	Skip if $C=0$	8
SKZ	Skip if Zero	1	1	The next instruction is skipped if the accumulator equals zero	Skip if $A=0$	8
SKNZ	Skip if Non-Zero	1	1	The next instruction is skipped if the accumulator does not equal zero	Skip if $A \neq 0$	8
SKP	Skip if Positive	1	1	The next instruction is skipped if the most significant bit of the accumulator is zero	Skip if $A(8)=0$	8

Table 10.9. List of Instructions (*Cont'd*)
(Reproduced with permission of Rockwell International, Anaheim, California)

MNEMONIC	NAME	BYTES	CYCLES	DESCRIPTION		NOTES
				VERBAL	SYMBOLIC	
SKN	Skip if Negative	1	1	The next instruction is skipped if the most significant bit of the accumulator is one	Skip if $A(8)=1$	8
SKE	Skip if Equal	1	1	The next instruction is skipped if the accumulator and the current RAM operand are equal	Skip if $A=M$	8
BBT	Branch if Bit (n) True	2,3	2,3	A program branch is executed if the specified bit of the current RAM operand is true (1)	If $M \wedge 2^{(n-1)}=1$, then $P(7:1) \leftarrow I2(7:1)$ & if $I2(8)=1$, $P(14:8) \leftarrow I3(7:1)$	9,12,16
BBF	Branch if Bit (n) False	2,3	2,3	A program branch is executed if the specified bit of the current RAM operand is false (0)	If $M \wedge 2^{(n-1)}=0$, then $P(7:1) \leftarrow I2(7:1)$ & if $I2(8)=1$, $P(14:8) \leftarrow I3(7:1)$	9,12,16
BC	Branch if Carry	2,3	2,3	A program branch is executed if the carry flip-flop, C, is set (1)	If $C=1$, then $P(7:1) \leftarrow I2(7:1)$ & if $I2(8)=1$, $P(14:8) \leftarrow I3(7:1)$	9,12,16, 8

BNC	Branch if No Carry	2,3	2,3	A program branch is executed if the carry flip-flop, C, is reset (0)	If C=0, then P(7:1) ← I2(7:1) & if I2(8)=1, P(14:8) ← I3(7:1)	9,12,16, 8
BZ	Branch if Zero	2,3	2,3	A program branch is executed if the accumulator equals zero	If A=0, then P(7:1) ← I2(7:1) & if I2(8)=1, P(14:8) ← I3(7:1)	9,12,16, 8
BNZ	Branch if Non-Zero	2,3	2,3	A program branch is executed if the accumulator does not equal zero	If A≠0, then P(7:1) ← I2(7:1) & if I2(8)=1, P(14:8) ← I3(7:1)	9,12,16, 8
BP	Branch if Positive	2,3	2,3	A program branch is executed if the most significant bit of the accumulator is zero	If A(8)=0, then P(7:1) ← I2(7:1) & if I2(8)=1, P(14:8) ← I3(7:1)	9,12,16, 8
BN	Branch if Negative	2,3	2,3	A program branch is executed if the most significant bit of the accumulator is one	If A(8)=1, then P(7:1) ← I2(7:1) & if I2(8)=1, P(14:8) ← I3(7:1)	9,12,16, 8
BNE	Branch if Not Equal	2,3	2,3	A program branch is executed if the accumulator is not equal to the current RAM operand	If A≠M, then P(7:1) ← I2(7:1) & if I2(8)=1, P(14:8) ← I3(7:1)	9,12,16, 8

Table 10.10. List of Instructions (*Cont'd*)
(Reproduced with permission of Rockwell International, Anaheim, California)

MNEMONIC	NAME	BYTES	CYCLES	DESCRIPTION		NOTES
				VERBAL	SYMBOLIC	
IO4	Digit I/O (C, D)	2	2	Command C is transmitted to I/O device D. Bits 8-5 of the accumulator are transmitted to the device and bits 1-4 are received from the device	I2 → I/D(8:1) A(8:5) → I/D(8:5) A(4:1) ← I/D(4:1)	16,17
IN	Input (C, D)	2	2	Command C is transmitted to I/O device D. The accumulator is loaded with a data byte transmitted by the device. If D is omitted, a zero (all-call) device address is transmitted	I2 → I/D(8:1) A ← I/D(8:1)	16,17
OUT	Output (C, D)	2	2	Same as IN except the accumulator contents are transmitted to the device	I2 → I/D(8:1) A → I/D(8:1)	16,17
RIS	Read Interrupt Status	2	2	The accumulator is loaded with the interrupt status word from the highest priority I/O device currently requesting service.	I2 → I/D(8:1) A ← I/D(8:1)	16,17

Notes for Instructions Listed in Tables 10.2–10.10

1. The address (14 bits) for RAM operands is specified by the Z and X registers. The lower 7 bits of X specify the byte address (least significant 7 bits). If bit 8 of the X register is 1, the high-order 7 bits of RAM address (the page address) are specified by the least significant 7 bits of the Z register. Otherwise, the page address is set to 0.

2. All instructions that increment or decrement the X or Y register will automatically skip the next sequential instruction in the event of an overflow, $X/Y(7:1) = 0$, or underflow, $X/Y(7:1) = 127$, respectively.

3. Immediate or "literal" operands are stored in ROM (instruction memory) as the third byte of the instruction. However, a single literal can be shared by multiple instructions by placing it in the literal pool. See the discussion headed "Data Pools."

4. These instructions can utilize the command pool to "share" the second instruction byte. See the discussion headed "Data Pools."

5. All instructions which load registers using the ROM address in the L register also automatically increment the L register by 1.

6. The instructions which exchange a RAM operand with the accumulator are all two-byte instructions. The second byte is actually the corresponding one-byte STORE instruction. The first byte essentially "conditions" the store operation for an exchange. For this reason, the second byte of these instructions can be executed individually (by branching to it) if advantageous to the programmer.

7. Each of the instructions INCY and DECY is made up of two individual instructions (XY and INXY or DEXY).

8. When a SKIP command is executed, the next sequential instruction (not just the next byte) is ignored. One cycle is required for each byte which is skipped. The only deviation from this rule occurs when the skip is followed by one of the composite instructions: memory exchange (Note 6), conditional branches (Note 9), or increment/decrement Y (Note 7). In these cases only one byte is skipped.

9. Conditional BRANCH instructions require two or three bytes. The first byte is actually the corresponding SKIP instruction, and the second (and third, if required) byte is a BRANCH instruction. If this type of instruction were preceded by another conditional SKIP instruction, only the first byte of the conditional branch would be skipped.

10. The DC and DCC instructions are provided to facilitate decimal arithmetic mechanizations in which two decimal digits are packed in one 8-bit byte. The C flip-flop is used to save the carry-out from the 8-bit adder and thus facilitate software mechanizations for extended precision arithmetic. In addition, an intermediate state of the carry propagation logic, i.e., the carry from the fourth bit position, is saved in the Q flip-flop for use by the DCC instruction. Instruction sequences for decimal addition and subtraction are illustrated below.

Addition			Subtraction	
LZI	PAGE	Load addresses	LZI	PAGE
LXI	OP1	of operands	LXI	OP1
LYI	OP2		LYI	OP2

	Addition				**Subtraction**	
	RC		Initialize carry/borrow		SC	

LOOP	LNXY			LOOP	LNXY
	DC		Add/subtract two		COM
	AC		digits with carry/		AC
	DCC		borrow from pre-		DCC
	SNXY		vious result		SNXY
	B	LOOP			B	LOOP

11. If the next instruction to be executed or skipped after a RT or RSK instruction is a BRANCH, B or BDI, the branch tag (bit 7) must be set in the RT or RSK instruction. This is accomplished by coding RT$ or RSK$.

12. BRANCH instructions are provided in two formats. The one-byte format modifies only the low-order 7 bits of the P register, allowing a branch within the current 128-byte page. The two-byte format modifies the entire 14 bits of the P register and allows a branch anywhere in memory (16K). The two formats are distinguished by bit 8 of the first byte (0) = long format, 1 = short format). If bit 8 of the second byte of the two-byte format is 0 (the BDI instruction), the interrupts are disabled. Note that the PPS-8 assembler selects the optimum format automatically for all branch-type instruction. See Section 10.3.

13. See discussion headed "Data Stack."

14. The LAL and PSHL instructions provide a unique capability to reduce overhead in subroutines which require two full addresses* as part of their calling sequence. An efficient software mechanization for this type of subroutine is to use the Z and X registers for one address and the L register for the other, leaving the Y register for a block-size parameter, for instance. The following example illustrates the use of the LAL and PSHL instructions in such a subroutine.

	BL	SUBR	
Calling	DW*	N	Block size
Sequence	DWA*	SOURCE	Two-byte source address
	DWA*	DEST	Two-byte destination address
SUBR	LYL		Block size $\rightarrow Y$
	LXL		Source address $\rightarrow Z, X$
	LZL		
	LAL		Destination address $\rightarrow A, W$
	LAL		
	PSHL		$A, W \rightarrow L$, return address $\rightarrow$ stack
	•		
	•		
	POPL		Return address $\rightarrow L$
	RT		Exit from subroutine

* DW and DWA are assembler pseudo-op codes. DW is a one-byte data word. DWA is a two-byte data word address, assembled with the least significant 7 bits in the first byte and the most significant 7 bits in the second byte.

15. BRANCH AND LINK instructions (subroutine calls) are provided in two formats. The one-byte format uses shared addresses from the subroutine entry pool (see discussion headed "Data Pools") and allows a branch anywhere in memory (16K). The two-byte format does not use the subroutine entry pool. It allows a branch within the lower half (8K) of memory. Note that the PPS-8 assembler selects the optimum format automatically for all branch-type instructions. See Section 10.3.

16. These instructions may not be followed immediately by a BRANCH (B) instruction. However, the PPS-8 assembler will automatically insert a one-byte NOP with a branch tag in this case.

17. All input/output instructions require two bytes. The second byte is gated to the I/O devices with the W/IO signal. See Section 10.4.

18. The MDR and MDL instructions can be used to efficiently shift a string of BCD (decimal) digits, as would be required for normalizing a number in packed decimal format, for instance. An example is shown below.

```
LEFT    LXI     BOTTOM
        LZI     BOTTOM
        LAI     NEWDATA

LOOP    MDR
        XD
        B       LOOP
```

Timing: 4 cycles/2 digits
          8 μsec/digit

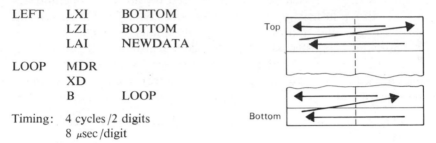

19. Comparison of X and Y registers is for least significant 7 bits only.

10.3. ADDRESSING AND PROGRAMMING

Data Stack

The first 32 bytes of *RAM* (addresses 0–31) are organized as a push-down stack to facilitate the processing of external interrupts and subroutine "nesting." The stack operates on a last-in first-out (LIFO) basis, and instructions are provided to push (store) the contents of any register into the stack or to pop (load) registers from the stack. In addition, return addresses are automatically saved in the stack when normal or interrupt subroutines are entered, and restored from the stack when subroutines are exited. The current "level" of subroutine linkage is saved in the L (link) register, and the previous L register contents are pushed into the stack.

The 5-bit S register is used as a stack pointer. It is incremented after each byte is pushed into the stack and decremented before each byte is popped from the stack. The pointer thus specifies the last byte popped from (or the next byte to be pushed into) the stack. If the stack pointer is popped to a value of 31 with a POPX, POPY, POPZ, or POPA instruction, the next instruction will be skipped. This feature is provided so that the value of the stack pointer can be determined under program control for use in a power failure recovery routine.

Random Access Memory Operands

All dynamically variable data for PPS-8 programs are stored in 2048-bit (256-byte) *RAM* devices. Up to 16K bytes of *RAM* are directly addressable.

The byte address (lower 7 address bits) of *RAM* operands is specified by the X register. The page address (upper 7 address bits) of *RAM* operands is specified by the Z register or is set equal to page 0, depending on bit 8 of the byte address register ($1 = Z$ register, $0 =$ page 0).

Although a single register pair (Z, X) is used for all *RAM* operand addresses, the PPS-8 instruction repertoire provides considerable power and efficiency for operand addressing. Using the ability to exchange the Y register and the L register with the Z and X registers, two full (14-bit) addresses and one byte (7-bit) address are directly available, selected in conjunction with normal data transfer (load/store) operations. A single, one-byte instruction can perform all of the following functions in one cycle:

1. Transfer an 8-bit operand from the accumulator to the *RAM* or vice versa.
2. Increment or decrement the operand address.
3. Test for a page boundary and skip if one is encountered.
4. Test for completion of a program loop (byte addresses equal), and skip if completed.
5. Select another byte address to be used for a subsequent *RAM* operand, that is, exchange X with Y or Z, X, and L.

This organization is particularly efficient when dealing with blocks of data, that is, program loops. This efficiency is demonstrated in the example shown in Table 10.11.

Read Only Memory Operands

The PPS-8 provides the capability to store constant data in *ROM* devices together with the PPS-8 instructions. This type of data is important for two reasons:

1. *ROM* storage is significantly less expensive than *RAM* storage.
2. All data which are to be permanently retained (preserved during power-off) must be stored in *ROM* devices.

Therefore considerable flexibility is provided for storing and accessing program data (operands) from ROM. In particular, the PPS-8 is designed to accommodate three types of ROM operands:

1. Immediate (literal) operands. This type of operand is stored either in-line with the instruction sequence or in the literal pool. These operands are accessed by "immediate" type instructions (LAI, LXI, AISK, ANI, etc.).

2. Subroutine parameters. This type of ROM operand is stored in-line with the instruction sequence immediately after a subroutine call (BL instruction) and represents data to be "passed" to a subroutine. These operands are accessed by "load through link" type instructions (LAL, LXL, LYL, etc.).

3. Constant tables. This type of operand need not be stored in-line with the instruction sequence and can be placed wherever convenient for the programmer. Tables of constants, such as character codes or data look-up tables, can be stored in this manner and accessed by "load through link" type instructions (LAL, LXL, LYL, etc.). Note that a table of branch addresses can be constructed in ROM and accessed using the subroutine RETURN instruction (RT). The following example illustrates this capability.

Problem: One of N possible control characters has been received from some input device. Select the appropriate processing routine corresponding to the particular character.

Sample Program: Two tables are stored in ROM, aligned with respect to page boundaries (Fig. 10.4).

First, the character is "looked up" in the character code table, CHAR, which will contain all functionally legitimate characters. Assume that the character to be processed is stored initially in location TEMP in RAM page 0.

```
      LZI    CHAR  ⎫
      LXI    CHAR  ⎬   Load address of character table into L.
      XL           ⎭

      LXI    TEMP      Address of character → X

LOOP  LAL              Get character from CHAR ⎫ 5 cycles/
      BNE    LOOP      Compare characters      ⎬ character
```

The index of the character (its position in CHAR) is now in the L register. This value is used as an index to select the address of the processing routine from CHARLOC. The RETURN (RT) instruction is then used to branch to the routine.

Table 10.11

(Reproduced with permission of Rockwell International, Anaheim, California)

Example 1:   Move a Block of Data

(*a*) One data block must be in page 0, aligned on page boundary:

```
        LZI       SOURCE
        LXI       SOURCE
        LYI       DEST

LOOP    LNXY                        ⎫   3 cycles/byte
        SNXY                        ⎬   (up to 128 bytes)
        B         LOOP              ⎭
```

(*b*) Data blocks can be anywhere in memory:

```
        LZI       DEST
        LXI       DEST
        XL
        LZI       SOURCE
        LXI       SOURCE
        LYI       END

LOOP    LNXL                        ⎫
        SNCX                        ⎬   3 cycles/byte
        B         LOOP              ⎭
```

Example 2:   Clear or Initialize a Block of Data

(*a*) Block must be in page 0, aligned on page boundary:

```
        LXI       BLOCK
        LAI       0 (or initialization constant)

LOOP    SN                          ⎫
        B         LOOP              ⎬   2 cycles/byte
```

(*b*) Data block can be anywhere in memory:

```
        LZI       BLOCK
        LXI       BLOCK
        LYI       COUNT
        LAI       0 (or initialization constant)

LOOP    SNXY                        ⎫
        DEXY                        ⎬   3 cycles/byte
        B         LOOP              ⎭
```

Table 10.11   (*Continued*)

Example 3:   Decimal Addition

(*a*) Augend in page 0 (aligned); addend anywhere:

```
          LZI       ADDEND
          LXI       ADDEND
          LYI       AUGEND
          RC

LOOP  LNXY
          DC
          AC                              6 cycles/2 digits
          DCC
          SNXY
          B         LOOP
```

(*b*) Augend and addend anywhere, not aligned on page boundary:

```
          LZI       AUGEND
          LXI       AUGEND
          XL
          LZI       ADDEND
          LXI       ADDEND
          LYI       END
          RC

LOOP  LNXL
          DC
          AC                              6 cycles/2 digits
          DCC
          SNCX
          B         LOOP
```

The value in L is actually the character's index plus 1. Therefore the CHARLOC table is displaced by 1 relative to the CHAR table.

```
     LAI      CHARLOC, U       Page address of CHARLOC into L
     LLA
     LXL                       Address from CHARLOC → X
     LZI      PROCESS          Page address → Z
     XL                        Routine address → L
     RT                        Branch to processing routine
```

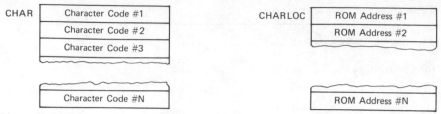

Figure 10.4. Character look-up table. (Courtesy of Rockwell International Corporation).

Data Pools

The PPS-8 has a unique feature designed to minimize instruction storage for multibyte instructions. This feature allows certain data to be "shared" by multiple instructions through access to common data pools stored in a dedicated portion of *ROM*. Three separate pools are provided: the command pool, the literal pool, and the subroutine entry pool. Figure 10.5 shows the location of these pools in *ROM*.

10.4. INPUT/OUTPUT

Digital Input/Output (IO4)

The PPS-8 system is designed to interface with the external environment via both general-purpose and special-purpose input/output devices. The I/O devices communicate with the *CPU* or *RAM* over the system data bus, I/D1 through I/D8.

Two basic types of I/O commands are available in the PPS-8 *CPU*. The I/O instructions are all two-byte, two-cycle instructions. The second instruction byte is interpreted by the I/O devices. The presence of this byte on the I/D bus is indicated by the W/IO signal set by the *CPU*. The specific function of a particular I/O command is dependent on the type of I/O device being addressed. The two I/O command types are shown in Fig. 10.6.

Digital command is provided for compatibility between the PPS-8 system and the PPS-4 I/O devices. One of 16 I/O devices can be addressed, and up to 16 unique commands can be selected. A bidirectional transfer of 4-bit digits is performed. Bits 5–8 of the PPS-8 accumulator are driven over the I/D bus to the I/O device, and bits 1–4 of the accumulator are loaded with data driven from the I/O device.

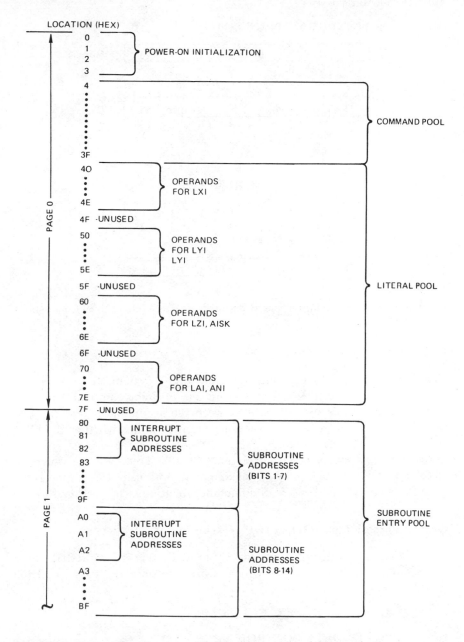

Figure 10.5. Data pools. (Courtesy of Rockwell International Corporation).

413

DIGIT INPUT/OUTPUT (IO4)

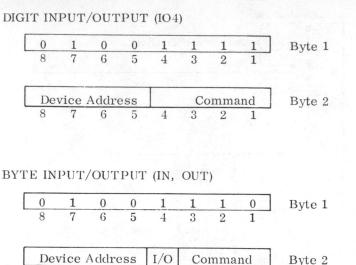

0	1	0	0	1	1	1	1	Byte 1
8	7	6	5	4	3	2	1	

Device Address				Command				Byte 2
8	7	6	5	4	3	2	1	

BYTE INPUT/OUTPUT (IN, OUT)

0	1	0	0	1	1	1	0	Byte 1
8	7	6	5	4	3	2	1	

Device Address				I/O	Command			Byte 2
8	7	6	5	4	3	2	1	

Figure 10.6. Input/output instructions. (Courtesy of Rockwell International Corporation).

Byte Input/Output (In, Out)

This is the primary I/O command in the PPS-8 system. It provides for addressing one of 16 devices, specifying one of eight command options, and transferring one byte of data between the accumulator and the I/O device. Bit 4 of the second instruction byte determines whether the *CPU* is to transmit or receive the data.

A device address of 0 is used as an "all-call" command to which all PPS-8 I/O devices react. (One of the command options in this format is the READ INTERRUPT STATUS command, mentioned in Section 10.7.)

General-Purpose Input/Output (GP I/O)

This is a basic I/O device providing 12 static discrete inputs and 12 static discrete outputs. The GP I/O, which is used by both the PPS-4 and the PPS-8, is shown in Fig. 9.9.

10.5. PARALLEL DATA CONTROLLER (*PDC*)

The parallel data controller (*PDC*), shown in Fig. 10.7, is a flexible parallel input/output device for interfacing the PPS-8 system to external devices or

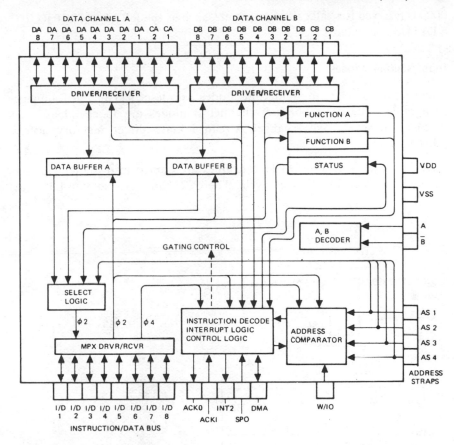

Figure 10.7. Parallel data controller block diagram. (Courtesy of Rockwell International Corporation).

for interfacing between multiple PPS systems. The device provides two independent, bidirectional I/O channels, each of which operates in a variety of parallel data transfer modes. Each channel consists of 10 TTL-compatible lines: 8 data lines and 2 control lines (DA1–DA8, CA1 and CA2; DB1–DB8, CB1 and CB2). Each channel has its own data buffer (8 bits) and function register (8 bits); the two channels share a common status register (5 bits). The function (mode) of each channel is programmable and is selected by control data loaded into the associated function register under *CPU* program control. Direct addressing for up to 15 *PDC*'s is possible through the use of four chip-select address straps (AS1–AS4), which can be user-terminated to create each device address. (Address

0000 is reserved for "all call" commands, such as the READ INTERRUPT STATUS command.)

Input/Output Modes

The *PDC* channel A input/output modes are described in the following paragraphs. The corresponding channel B modes are independently selectable; however, only channel A can initiate direct memory access (*DMA*) requests.

Static Input (Fig. 10.8). The data lines are copied into the data buffer during $\phi2$ of each PPS-8 clock cycle. The *CPU* can read the data buffer at

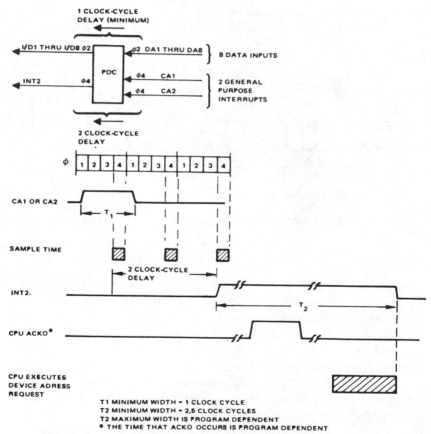

Figure 10.8. Static input. (Courtesy of Rockwell International Corporation).

any time. Both control lines are individually selectable as *CPU* interrupts, that is, an interrupt request is generated by a TTL false-to-true transition of either CA1 or CA2. Interrupt timing is shown in Fig. 10.8.

Static Output (Fig. 10.9). The data lines are driven continuously from the data buffer, which the *CPU* can load at any time. Both control lines are individually selectable as *CPU* interrupts. Interrupt timing is identical to that for static input (Fig. 10.8).

Static Input/Output (Fig. 10.10). Data lines DA5–DA8 are copied into the high-order 4 bits of the data buffer during $\phi2$ of each PPS-8 clock cycle. Data lines DA1–DA4 are driven continuously from the low-order 4 bits of the data buffer. The *CPU* can load or read the data buffer at any time. When the *CPU* loads the data buffer, only the low-order 4 bits are modified. Both control lines are individually selectable as *CPU* interrupts. Interrupt timing is identical to that for static input (Fig. 10.8).

Clocked Input The data lines are copied into the data buffer on a TTL false-to-true transition of CA2. The *CPU* can read the data buffer at any time. Both control lines are individually selectable as *CPU* interrupts. Interrupt timing for CA1 is identical to that for static input (Fig. 10.8); Control line CA2 is also selectable as a *DMA* request (channel A only).

Clocked Output. The data lines are driven continuously from the data buffer, which the *CPU* can load at any time. A positive pulse is generated on CA1 each time the data buffer is loaded by the *CPU* or (channel A only)

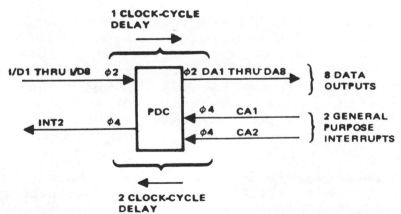

Figure 10.9. Static output. (Courtesy of Rockwell International Corporation).

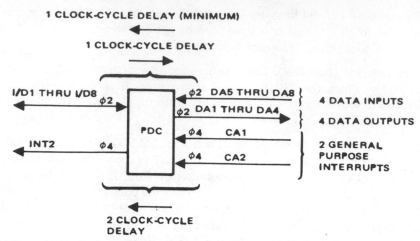

Figure 10.10. Static input/output. (Courtesy of Rockwell International Corporation).

via *DMA*. Control line CA2 is selectable as a *CPU* interrupt. Interrupt timing for CA2 is identical to that for static input (Fig. 10.8).

Clocked Input/Output. Data lines DA5–DA8 are copied into the high-order 4 bits of the data buffer on a TTL false-to-true transition of CA2 (same as for clocked input, Fig. 10.11). Data lines DA1–DA4 are driven continuously from the low-order 4 bits of the data buffer. A positive pulse is generated on CA1 each time the data buffer is loaded by the *CPU* (same as for clocked output). The *CPU* can load or read the data buffer at any time. When the data buffer is loaded, only the low-order 4 bits are modified. Control line CA2 is selectable as a *CPU* interrupt.

Handshake Input. Control lines CA1 and CA2 are both initially at a TTL false level. The data lines are then copied into the data buffer on a TTL false-to-true transition of CA2. Control line CA1 is set to a TTL true level immediately after loading the input data into the data buffer. The *CPU* may read the data buffer at any time after CA2 has made the false-to-true transition. CA1 is set to a TTL false level when the data buffer is read by the *CPU* (or stored in the *RAM* via *DMA*), provided that CA2 has returned to a TTL false level. Control line CA2 is selectable as a *CPU* interrupt and/or (channel A only) a *DMA* request.

Handshake Output. The data lines are driven continuously from the data buffer. Control lines CA1 and CA2 are both initially at a TTL false level. Control line CA1 is then set to a TTL true level when the data buffer is loaded by the *CPU* or (channel A only) via *DMA*. CA1 is set false on a

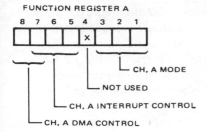
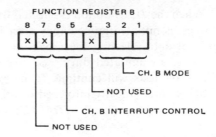

BIT	FUNCTION REGISTER A	FUNCTION REGISTER B
1 - 3	ESTABLISHES 1 OF 8 BASIC I/O MODES	ESTABLISHES 1 OF 8 BASIC I/O MODES
4	NOT USED	NOT USED
5	CA1 INTERRUPT CONTROL	CB1 INTERRUPT CONTROL
6	CA2 INTERRUPT CONTROL	CB2 INTERRUPT CONTROL
7	DMA END-OF-BLOCK INTERRUPT CONTROL	NOT USED
8	DMA ENABLE	NOT USED

Figure 10.11. Function register fields (control word). (Courtesy of Rockwell International Corporation).

TTL false-to-true transition of CA2. The data buffer may be reloaded any time after CA2 has returned false. Control line CA2 is selectable as a *CPU* interrupt and/or (channel A only) a *DMA* request.

Direct Memory Access

Four of the modes (clocked input, clocked output, handshake input, and handshake output) allow optional *DMA* operation on channel A.

When the *DMA* option is selected for the clocked input mode or the handshake input mode, each *DMA* request is initiated 1.5 clock cycles after detection of the false-to-true transition of CA2.

When the DMA option is selected for the clocked output mode, the initial request is initiated immediately after function register A is loaded with the control data selecting the mode and option. The second and subsequent requests are initiated during $\phi2$ preceding the TTL true period of CA1. These requests will continue to be generated with each output until the PDC is automatically informed of an end-of-block condition by the direct memory access controller ($DMAC$).

Function Registers

The functions (modes) of each channel are programmable and are controlled by the associated function register. Each register is loaded with a control word under CPU program control. Fig. 10.11 shows the fields in each of the function registers. As indicated in Fig. 10.11, each channel provides eight basic I/O modes; different modes can be programmed and operated simultaneously on the two channels.

Status Register

The contents of the status register can be copied into the CPU accumulator under program control. Figure 10.12 shows the format of the information contained in the status register.

Parallel Data Controller Instruction Set

The PDC responds to eight commands from the PPS-8 CPU. Four of these are of the output (OUT) type and are described below.

1. LFRA—Load Function Register A. This command loads function register A with the contents of the CPU accumulator and resets bits 4, 7, and 8 of the status register.

2. LFRB—Load Function Register B. This command loads function register B with the contents of the CPU accumulator and resets bits 5 and 6 of the status register.

3. LBRA—Load Buffer Register A. This command loads buffer register A with the contents of the CPU accumulator and resets bit 8 of the status register.

4. LBRB—Load Buffer Register B. This command loads buffer register B with the contents of the CPU accumulator and resets bit 6 of the status register.

The remaining four commands are of the input (IN) type and are described below.

5. RBRA—Read Buffer Register A. The contents of buffer register A are placed in the CPU accumulator, and bit 8 of the status register is reset.

STATUS REGISTER

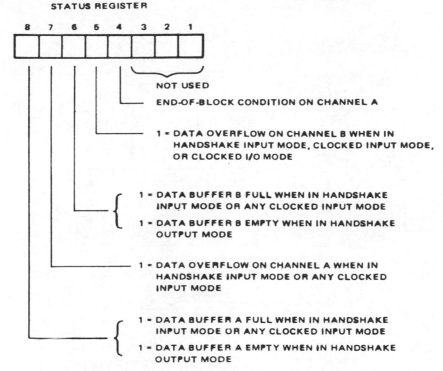

Figure 10.12. Status register format. (Courtesy of Rockwell International Corporation).

6. RBRB—Read Buffer Register B. The contents of buffer register *B* are placed in the *CPU* accumulator, and bit 6 of the status register is reset.

7. RSR—Read Status Register. The contents of the status register are placed in the *CPU* accumulator, and bits 5 and 7 of the status register are reset.

8. RIS—Read Interrupt Status. If the appropriate conditions are met (see Section 10.7: Interrupts), the contents of the interrupt status word are placed in the *CPU* accumulator. (This command is unique in that it always contains a device address of 0.)

10.6. DIRECT MEMORY ACCESS CONTROLLER (*DMAC*)

The direct memory access controller (*DMAC*) allows PPS-8 I/O devices to access *RAM* on a cycle-steal basis without disturbing *CPU* program execution. The *DMAC* (Fig. 10.13) provides control of the address bus (A /B1– A /B14) and two memory control signals (RIH and W /IO) during direct memory access (*DMA*) operations. Control for eight separate *DMA* channels is provided by a single *DMAC*.

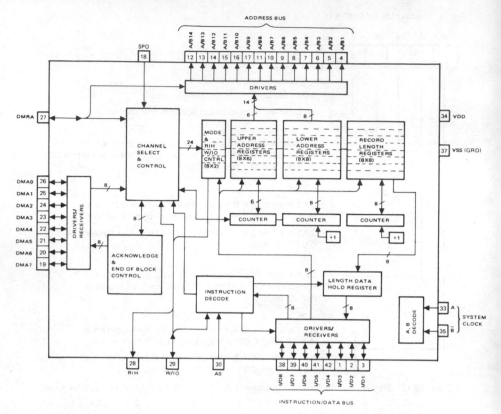

Figure 10.13. Direct memory access controller. (Courtesy of Rockwell International Corporation).

Eight *DMA* request/acknowledge lines (*DMA0–DMA7*) provide bi-directional communication between the I/O devices and the *DMAC*. Bi-directional communication over a single line is accomplished through the use of time multiplexing and pulse coding techniques. Each *DMA* line (channel) has a fixed position in a priority structure used to resolve simultaneous requests. The channels are numbered in order of priority, with *DMA0* having the highest priority. An additional *DMA* request/acknowledge line (*DMRA*) provides bidirectional communication between the *DMAC* and the *CPU*.

Eight 14-bit address registers and eight 8-bit record length registers are included in the *DMAC*; one address register and one record length register are associated with each of the eight *DMA* channels. Each register can be loaded under *CPU* program control. Two additional control bits are provided for each *DMA* line. One of these control bits specifies whether the *RAM* is to read or to write when a *DMA* request occurs on the associated *DMA* line. The other control bit is used to select a special cycle mode.

A holding register, associated with the record length registers, allows the *CPU* to sample the contents of any record length register. When any record length register is loaded by the *CPU*, its previous contents are transferred to the holding register. The contents of the holding register may be read under *CPU* program control.

Figure 10.14 shows a typical *DMAC* application. For simplicity, only a single I/O device, a parallel data controller (*PDC*), is shown connected to the *DMAC*. When the *PDC* requires *DMA* service, it transmits a pulsed *DMA* request over *DMA*0. The *DMAC* forwards the *DMA* request to the *CPU* over *DMRA*. The *CPU* acknowledges the *DMA* request at the completion of the current instruction, provided that the instruction is a non-I/O type. If the *CPU* is executing an I/O instruction, it will continue program execution until it has completed a non-I/O instruction, at which time it will acknowledge the *DMA* request. The *CPU* then enters a "wait" mode, during which it floats its address bus drivers, data bus drivers, R1H,

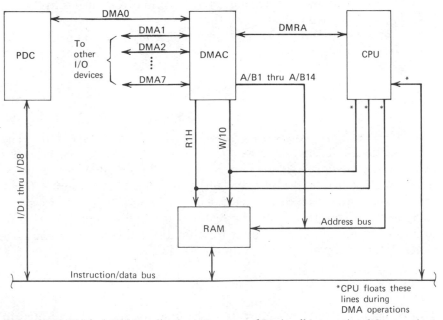

Figure 10.14. Typical *DMA* application. (Courtesy of Rockwell International Corporation).

and W/IO. This wait mode is retained until completion of the *DMA* operations.

When the *DMAC* receives the *CPU* acknowledge signal, the following operations occur:

1. The *DMAC* drives an acknowledge signal over the highest priority line currently requesting service.
2. The *DMAC* drives the address bus with the contents of the appropriate address register.
3. The *DMAC* drives RIH and W/IO false or true, depending on whether the addressed *RAM* is to read or write.
4. The I/O device either drives data onto or captures data from the I/D bus.

After each byte is transferred, the *DMAC* increments the appropriate address register and record length register. The *DMA* operations continue until one of the following events occurs:

1. The I/O device ceases to request *DMA* service.
2. The record length register makes a transition from 255 to 0.
3. The lower address register makes a transition from all 1's to 0's.
4. The *CPU* interrupt 0 is triggered.
5. The *DMAC* receives a request on a higher priority channel than the one currently being serviced.

10.7. INTERRUPTS

The PPS-8 system provides a multilevel priority interrupt structure. The *CPU* has three interrupt input signals (INT0, INT1, INT2), which have a fixed priority relationship with respect to resolving simultaneous requests. Interrupt 0 has highest priority, and interrupt 2 has lowest priority. Interrupts 0 and 1 are designed for dedicated special-purpose functions, nominally power failure detection and a real-time clock. Interrupt 2 is designed to operate as a single request input for a multisource priority system constructed "externally" in the input/output devices.

Interrupt 0

This is the highest priority interrupt and would normally be dedicated to a function requiring rapid response, such as power failure detection. This level cannot be disabled under program control and will be honored at the completion of the current instruction.* The program interrupt is triggered by a false-to-true transition of the INT0 input signal.

Interrupt 1

This interrupt has priority over interrupt 2 if they occur simultaneously, and is honored at the completion of the current instruction provided that (*a*) interrupt 0 is not pending, and (*b*) the interrupts are enabled.* This interrupt, which is triggered by a false-to-true transition of the INT1 input signal, is intended as a real-time clock.

Interrupt 2

This is the primary PPS-8 interrupt and is used for servicing all I/O device interrupt requests. It is honored at the completion of the current instruction provided that (*a*) interrupt 0 or 1 is not pending, and (*b*) the interrupts are enabled.* The interrupt is triggered by a true state on the INT2 input signal. An acknowledge signal (ACKO) is provided and is designed to allow a multilevel priority interrupt structure to be constructed externally to the *CPU*. Logic for this interrupt structure is included in the I/O devices that require access to the *CPU* interrupt (e.g., the *PDC* and *SDC*).

The system interconnection for the interrupt structure is shown in Fig. 10.1 and is described below.

1. Each device interrupt source to be included in the interrupt structure has an interrupt request (INT2) output signal. The INT2 output signals from all the devices are OR-tied to form the INT2 input to the *CPU*.

2. In addition, each device has an acknowledge input (ACKI) and an acknowledge output (ACKO). These signals are interconnected to form a priority "chain." The ACKO signal from one device is connected to the ACKI signal of the next-lower-priority device. The ACKI signal of the highest-priority device is connected to the interrupt acknowledge (ACKO) output of the *CPU*.

3. When a device wants interrupt service, it sets its INT2 output true. Any number of devices can simultaneously request interrupt service.

4. When an interrupt request is honored, the *CPU* transmits a one-cycle pulse on the ACKO output. This pulse is propagated, one-cycle device, down the priority chain until it reaches the first device (i.e., the highest-priority device) currently requesting service. This device does not propagate the acknowledge signal any further, thus breaking the priority chain.

* Interrupts are not honored under the following conditions: (*a*) just before a BRANCH (B) instruction, (*b*) immediately after a SKIP-type or ADD instruction, and (*c*) (INT1 and INT2 only) during a direct memory access (*DMA*) operation.

5. After a time delay sufficient to allow the acknowledge to be propagated completely through the priority chain, the *CPU* program executes a READ INTERRUPT STATUS (RIS) command (a specific command code in the "all-call" format). The requesting device which has received the acknowledge pulse transmits its device address (1–15) and interrupt status information over the I/D bus to the *CPU*. This address is decoded under *CPU* software control and used to identify the proper interrupt processing routine.

6. Receipt of the device address request is also used by the I/O device to reset its INT2 output (however, the INT2 input to the *CPU* may still be true because of other requests).

Processing a PPS-8 interrupt involves the following steps:

1. The *CPU* "honors" the interrupt request by disabling the interrupt system and executing a BRANCH AND LINK (BL) instruction. The BL instruction is "created" by the *CPU* logic and requires no additional data other than the interrupt request signal. The operand (i.e., subroutine entry address) for the BL instruction is taken from one of the first three locations in the subroutine entry pool, depending on which interrupt is being processed.

2. If interrupt 2 is being honored, the interrupt acknowledge (ACKO) pulse is automatically transmitted.

3. The interrupt processing subroutine will normally first save the contents of any *CPU* registers necessary in processing the interrupt by pushing them into the data stack. Note that the acknowledge pulse for interrupt 2 will be propagated down the priority chain while the *CPU* is performing this function.

4. If interrupt 2 is being processed, the interrupt processing subroutine will execute a READ INTERRUPT STATUS (RIS) instruction to determine which I/O device caused the interrupt.

5. At the completion of the interrupt processing routine, the *CPU* registers will be restored by popping their original contents from the stack.

6. Execution of the interrupted program can be resumed by executing an RTI instruction, which also reenables the interrupt system.

REFERENCES

1. Product Description. Parallel Processing System (PPS–8) Microcomputer. Rockwell International Corp., Anaheim, Ca., 1974.
2. Display Controller Circuit, Data Sheet. Rockwell International Corp., Anaheim, Ca., 1974.
3. 1200 bps Telecommunications Data Interface, Data Sheet, Rockwell International Corp., Anaheim, Ca., 1974.

11

IMP 4/8/16 AND PACE MICROPROCESSORS

Chapter 11 presents the slice-oriented microprocessors National IMP 4/8/16. The basic slice in this family is the 4-bit register and arithmetic and logic unit (*RALU*). Combining the *RALU*'s in parallel network, one can build 4-, 8-, or 16-bit microsystems. The 16-bit system, IMP 16, is formed by connecting four *RALU*'s in parallel. The heart of the system is the control read only memory (*CROM*). The *CROM* stores the set of microprograms used to implement the IMP 16 instruction set. A large variety of instructions is supported in two *CROM*'s, including multiplication, division, and double-precision instructions. Input/output is performed through a 16-bit data bus and a 16-bit address bus. The microprocessor PACE represents an upgraded version of the IMP 16, with the *CPU* on a single chip.

The material* in this chapter has been adapted in part from a publication of National Semiconductor Corporation. The material so published herein is the full responsibility of the author.

11.1 IMP-16 MICROCOMPUTER AND REGISTER AND ARITHMETIC LOGIC UNIT (*RALU*)

General Description

The IMP-16C is a 16-bit parallel processor. It is packaged on an $8\frac{1}{2} \times$ 11-in. printed wiring card. A 144-pin connector is located on the edge of the card for connecting the IMP-16C circuits to interfacing units.

The major functional units of the IMP-16C, shown in Fig. 11.1, are as follows:

- Central processing unit (*CPU*)
- Clock generators
- Input multiplexer
- Data buffer

- Control flags
- Conditional jump multiplexer
- On-card memory
- Address latches

* Programs, figures, and tables are courtesy and copyright © 1975 by National Semiconductor Corporation. All rights reserved.

427

428

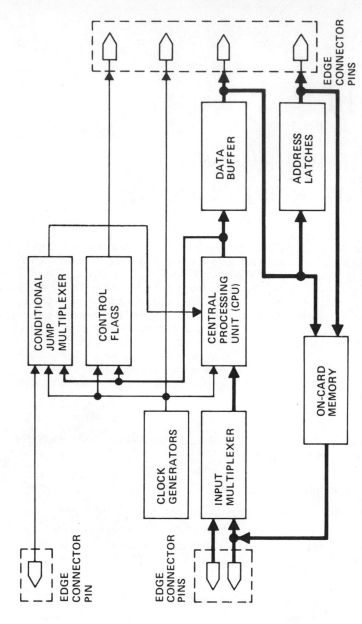

Figure 11.1. IMP-16C major functional units. (Courtesy of National Semiconductor Corporation).

The *CPU* is configured around the National Semiconductor general-purpose controller/processor (GP C/P) MOS/LSI devices, as shown in the simplified block diagram of Fig. 11.2. The MOS/LSI devices consist of one control read only memory (*ROM*) and four register and arithmetic logic units (*RALU*'s). Each *RALU* handles 4 bits, and a 16-bit unit is formed by connecting four *RALU*'s in parallel. A 4-bit-wide control bus is used by the *CROM* to communicate most of the control information to the *RALU*'s. The *CPU* includes provision for adding a second *CROM* for an optional extended instruction set.

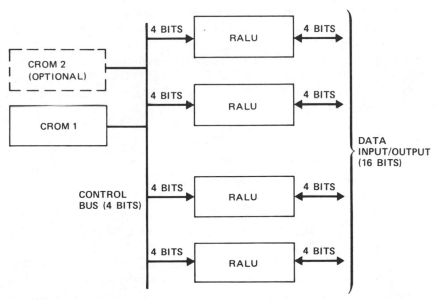

Figure 11.2. IMP-16C *CPU* components. (Courtesy of National Semiconductor Corporation).

The clock generator provides the MOS clock drivers and *CPU* timing signals. The system clock is distributed outside of the IMP-16C for synchronization of peripheral units with the IMP-16C.

External to the MOS/LSI circuits but still within the IMP-16C are control flags for both the IMP-16C, and external interfacing circuits. These control flags are in addition to the status flags that are internal to the *RALU*'s.

Data from the user's peripheral devices and add-on memory are received by the input multiplexer. Data from the on-card memory are also processed through the input multiplexer en route to the central processing unit.

Output data are made available from the 16-bit data buffer via the card-edge connector to the user's peripheral devices and add-on memory. A 16-bit address bus is also brought out to the card-edge connector for addressing both add-on memory and peripheral devices.

The memory on the IMP-16C card consists of 256 words of read/write memory and sockets for 512 words of *PROM* or *ROM*. A maximum of 65,536 words may be addressed.

IMP-16 Operational Features

Word length: 16 bits.

Instruction set: 43 in basic instruction set; 17 optional instructions available with extended set (macroinstructions implemented by *CPU*-resident microprogram).

Arithmetic: Parallel, binary, fixed point, two's complement.

Memory: 256 16-bit words of semiconductor read/write memory; sockets for 512 16-bit words of semiconductor read only memory. Capable of addressing 65,536 16-bit words.

Addressing: Page size of 256 words. For direct and indirect modes:

- Absolute.
- Relative to program counter.
- Relative to accumulator 2 (indexed).
- Relative to accumulator 3 (indexed).

Typical instruction-execution speeds: Register-to-register addition—4.55 μsec; memory-to-register addition—7.7 μsec; register input/output—10.15 μsec.

Input/output and control: 16-bit data-input port, 16-bit data-output bus, 16-bit address bus, 6 general-purpose flags, 4 general-purpose jump-condition inputs, 1 general interrupt input, 1 control panel interrupt input.

Register and Arithmetic Logic Unit (*RALU*)

Four 4-bit *RALU*'s constitute the arithmetic section shown in Fig. 11.3. This section includes the following major units:

- Input/output multiplexer.
- Last-in/first-out (LIFO) stack.
- Sixteen status flags, storable and retrievable as a 16-bit register:

    Link flag (L).
    Carry flag (CY).
    Overflow flag (OV).
    13 general-purpose flags (2 of which are directly accessible to user at the edge connector).

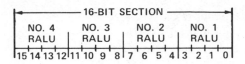

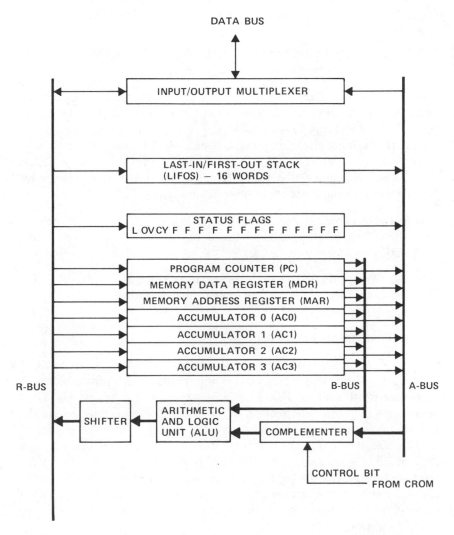

Figure 11.3. IMP-16C-bit arithmetic section. (Courtesy of National Semiconductor Corporation).

431

- Program counter (PC).
- Memory data register (MDR).
- Memory address register (MAR).
- Four accumulators ($AC0$, $AC1$, $AC2$, and $AC3$).
- Arithmetic and logic unit (ALU).
- Shifter.
- Buses.

Three buses are internal to the $RALU$: A bus, B bus, and R bus. These buses are described below.

A Bus (Operand Bus). The contents of all $RALU$ registers may be loaded onto the A bus; data from the top of the last-in/first-out (LIFO) stack and from the $RALU$ status flags (combined as a 16-bit word) may be loaded as operands. During such loading on the A bus, the data may be complemented under control of the $CROM$. The contents of the A bus may be gated through the ALU and shifter to the R bus or out of the $RALU$ to the IMP-16C data bus through the input/output multiplexer.

B Bus (Operand Bus). The contents of all $RALU$ registers may be loaded onto the B bus. The contents of the B bus may be loaded only into the arithmetic and logic unit (ALU).

R Bus (Result Bus). The R bus serves to transfer the results of ALU operations to any $RALU$ register, the LIFO stacks, and the $RALU$ flags.

Last-in/First-Out (LIFO) Stack

Each $RALU$ has a stack that operates on a last-in/first-out basis. The stack is 16 words high and is accessible through the top location. The 16-bit-per-word stack of Fig. 11.3 is contained in the four 4-bit $RALU$'s comprising the arithmetic section. A 16-bit data word is entered via the R bus and retrieved via the A bus. As a word is entered into the top location of the stack, the 16 bits in the top location are pushed down one level, and the entered bits occupy the top location. In turn, the contents of each lower level are replaced by the contents of the next higher location, and the contents of the bottom location are lost. The reverse process occurs when a word is retrieved from the stack; in this case, zeros are entered into the bottom location.

The stack is used primarily for the saving of status during interrupts and for temporary storage of subroutine return addresses. It may also serve to temporarily store data, using the appropriate instructions.

RALU Flags

There are 16 *RALU* status flags. These flags may be pushed onto the stack for temporary storage during interrupt processing and transferred back into their respective flag flip-flops after completion of the interrupt service. Whenever the status flags are manipulated, the entire complement of flags is configured as a 16-bit register; the L (link), CY (carry), and OV (overflow) flags are the first, second, and third most significant bits, respectively, and the remaining general-purpose flags comprise the 13 less significant bits. The CY or the OV flag may be selected for output on the CYOV line from the *RALU*'s, under control of the SEL control flag.

Program Counter (PC)

The program counter (*PC*) holds the address of the next instruction to be executed. It is incremented by 1 immediately after the fetching of each instruction during execution of the current instruction. When there is a branch to another address in the main memory, the branch address is set into the *PC*. A SKIP instruction merely increments the *PC* by 1, thus causing one instruction to be skipped.

Memory Data Register (MDR) and Memory Address Register (MAR)

The memory data register (*MDR*) holds data transferred from the main memory to the processor, or vice versa. When fetching data, the effective address is placed in the memory address register (*MAR*), and the FETCH instruction causes the data word to be transferred from the designated main-memory location to the *MDR*. Conversely, when storing data in the main memory, the data word is placed in the *MDR*, the effective address is placed in the *MAR*, and the STORE instruction causes the data word to be transferred to the designated memory location.

Accumulators (AC0-AC3)

The accumulators hold operands for data manipulation during arithmetic and logical operations. Also, the result of an operation is usually stored temporarily in one of the four accumulators. Data words may be fetched from memory to the accumulator or stored from the accumulator into memory. The particular accumulator to take part in an operation is specified by the programmer in the appropriate instruction.

Arithmetic and Logic Unit (ALU)

The arithmetic and logic unit (*ALU*) performs both arithmetic and logical operations: binary addition, AND, OR, and exclusive OR. Arithmetic and logical operations are effected by the microprogram that is part of the *CROM*. The IMP-16C performs arithmetic, using the two's complement technique. The contents of the A bus may be selectively complemented under the control of control bits from the *CROM*.

The output of the *ALU* is transferred to the R bus through the shifter and may then be stored in the stack or in any of the *RALU* registers. The shifter is capable of performing a single-position shift, either to the left or to the right, during each basic machine cycle.

Input/Output Multiplexer

The input/output multiplexer handles data, address, and instruction transfers into and out of the *RALU* from or into the main memory and peripheral devices on a time-multiplexed basis. As shown in Fig. 11.3, output data (to a data bus) must be received from the A bus, and input data pass from the In/Out multiplexer to the R bus.

11.2. CONTROL READ ONLY MEMORY (*CROM*)

All the processors described so far have been built on the principle of fixed wired instructions. Each instruction, or a group of instructions, is supported with a piece of hardware in the *CPU*.

The IMP-16 system is designed on a different principle, called *microprogramming*. The heart of the microsystem is another, still simpler computing system. One could speak of the computer within the computer. The built-in computer is supported with the control read only memory (*CROM*), which stores the set of microprograms used to implement the IMP-16 instruction set.

Figure 11.4 is a simplified block diagram emphasizing the role of the *CROM* and four *RALU*'s as part of the IMP-16C. Data buffers are provided between the *CPU* MOS/LSI devices and other parts of the equipment that have been implemented with TTL logic. These buffers are TRI-STATE® logic elements that permit bus-connected inputs.

The primary control of the *RALU* devices is accomplished via the 4-bit control bus, which is time-multiplexed to transfer four 4-bit words of control information per machine cycle. The functions effected by the control bits are indicated in Fig. 11.5.

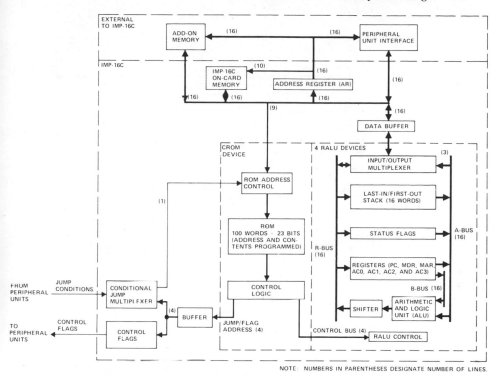

Figure 11.4. *CROM* and *RALU* interrelations. (Courtesy of National Semiconductor Corporation).

The *CROM* contains a microprogram that implements the standard instruction set. This microprogram resides in a 100×23 bit *ROM*. During an instruction fetch, the 9 most significant bits of the instruction word are transferred to the *CROM*; these 9 bits comprise the op code and other pertinent control fields of an instruction word. The instruction bits are decoded, and then the *ROM* address control in the *CROM* directs the control sequence to an entry point in the microprogram. The sequence continues until execution of the fetched instruction is completed. Then the *CROM* goes through another fetch cycle to fetch the next instruction from memory. This process is continuously repeated.

11.3. MEMORY ADDRESSING

The IMP-16C instruction set provides for direct and indirect memory addressing. For direct addressing, three distinct modes are available: base

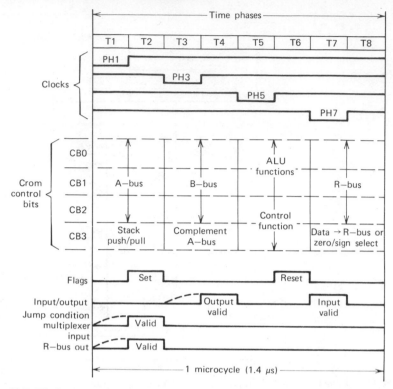

Figure 11.5. Timing control. (Courtesy of National Serviceconductor Corporation).

page (or absolute), program-counter relative, and indexed. The mode of addressing is specified by the XR field of the simplified instruction word format shown in Fig. 11.6.

Base Page Addressing

When the XR field is 00, it specifies base page addressing. Base page is directly accessible from any location in the address space of the memory. In this mode, the effective address is formed by setting bits 8–15 to zero and using the value of the 8-bit displacement field as an absolute address. Up to 256 words (locations 0–255) may be addressed in this way.

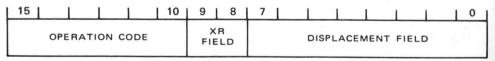

Figure 11.6. Memory reference instruction format. Courtesy of National Semiconductor Corporation).

Program Counter Relative Addressing

Program counter relative addressing is specified when the XR field is 01. The displacement is treated as a signed number so that its sign bit (bit 7) is propagated to bits 8–15, and the effective address is formed by adding the contents of the PC to the resulting number. This permits PC relative addressing -128 and $+127$ locations from the PC value; however, at the time of formation of the address, the PC has already been incremented in the microprogram and is pointing to the next macroinstruction. For this reason, the actual addressing range is from -127 to $+128$ from the current instruction.

Indexed Addressing

Indexed addressing is done with reference to accumulator 2 or 3 ($AC2$ or $AC3$). In this mode, the displacement field is again interpreted as a signed 8-bit number from -128 to $+127$ with the sign (bit 7) extended through bits 8–15. The contents of the chosen index register ($AC2$ when $XR = 10_2$ and $AC3$ when $XR = 11_2$) are added to the number formed from the displacement value to yield an effective address that can reach any location in 65,536 words of memory.

Indirect Addressing

Indirect addressing is accomplished by first calculating the effective address (EA), using the same method as for direct addressing; the memory location at this address contains a number that then serves as the address of the operand. The following instructions employ indirect addressing:

- LOAD INDIRECT
- STORE INDIRECT
- JUMP INDIRECT
- JUMP TO SUBROUTINE INDIRECT

A summary of addressing modes is presented in Table 11.1.

11.4. INSTRUCTION SET

Notation and Symbols

Table 11.2 lists definitions of the notation and symbols used in the IMP-16C instruction descriptions. The notations are given first in alphabetical

Table 11.1

XR Field	Addressing Mode	Effective Address	Range
00	Base	EA = disp	$0 \leqslant disp \leqslant 255$
01	Relative to Program Counter	EA = disp + (PC)	$-128 \leqslant disp \leqslant 127$
10	Relative to AC2	EA = disp + (AC2)	$-128 \leqslant disp \leqslant 127$
11	Relative to AC3	EA = disp + (AC3)	$-128 \leqslant disp \leqslant 127$

order, followed by the symbols. Upper-case mnemonics refer to fields in the instruction word; lower-case mnemonics refer to the numerical values of the corresponding fields. In cases where both lower- and upper-case mnemonics are composed of the same letters, only the lower-case mnemonic is given in Table 11.2. The use of lower-case notation designates variables.

Instruction Description

Eight functional types of instructions comprise the basic IMP-16C instruction set:

- LOAD and STORE
- Arithmetic
- Logical
- SKIP
- Shifts
- Transfer of control
- Register
- Input/output and miscellaneous

An extended instruction set is available for the IMP-16C in the form of a second *CROM*. This set consists of 17 instructions divided into five categories:

- Double-word arithmetic
- Load and store byte
- Bit operations
- Interrupt handling operations
- Transfer of control operations

The basic instruction set is shown in Tables 11.3 to 11.11.

Table 11.2. Notation Used in Instruction Descriptions

Notation	Meaning
ACr	Denotes a specific working register (AC0, AC1, AC2, or AC3), where r is the number of the accumulator referenced in the instruction.
AR	Denotes the address register used for addressing memory or peripheral devices.
cc	Denotes the 4-bit condition code value for conditional branch instructions.
ctl	Denotes the 7-bit control-field value for flag, input/output, and miscellaneous instructions.
CY	Indicates that the Carry flag is set if there is a carry due to the instruction (either an addition or a subtraction).
disp	Stands for displacement value and it represents an operand in a nonmemory reference instruction or an address field in a memory reference instruction. It is an 8-bit, signed twos-complement number except when base page is referenced; in the latter case, it is unsigned.
dr	Denotes the number of a destination working register that is specified in the instruction-word field. The working register is limited to one of four: AC0, AC1, AC2, or AC3.
EA	Denotes the effective address specified by the instruction directly, indirectly, or by indexing. The contents of the effective address are used during execution of an instruction. See Table 11–1.
fc	Denotes the number of the referenced flag See Table 11–13.

Table 11.2 (Continued).

Notation	Meaning
INTEN	Denotes the Interrupt Enable control flag.
IOREG	Denotes an input/output register in a peripheral device.
L	Denotes 1-bit link (L) flag.
OV	Indicates that the overflow flag is set if there is an overflow due to the instruction (either an addition or a subtraction).
PC	Denotes the program counter. During address formation, it is incremented by 1 to contain an address 1 greater than that of the instruction being executed.
r	Denotes the number of a working register that is specified in the instruction-word field. The working register is limited to one of four: AC0, AC1, AC2, or AC3.
SEL	Denotes the Select control flag. It is used to select the carry or overflow for output on the carry and overflow (CYOV) line of the CPU, and to include the link bit (L) in shift operations.
sr	Denotes the number of a source working register that is specified in the instruction-word field. The working register is limited to one of four: AC0, AC1, AC2, or AC3.
xr	When not zero, this value designates the number of the register to be used in the indexed and relative memory-addressing modes. See Table 11-1.

( )	Denotes the contents of the item within the parentheses. (ACr) is read as "the contents of ACr." (EA) is read as "the contents of EA."
[ ]	Denotes "the result of."
~	Indicates the logical complement (ones complement) of the value on the right-hand side of ~.
↑	Means "replaces."
↓	Means "is replaced by."
@	Appearing in the operand field of an instruction, denotes indirect addressing.
<	Denotes an AND operation.
>	Denotes an OR operation.
▷	Denotes an exclusive OR operation.

Table 11.3. Load and Store Instructions

Instruction	OpCode	Operation	Assembler Format
LOAD	1000	$(ACr) \leftarrow (EA)$	LD r, disp(xr)
LOAD INDIRECT	1001	$(ACr) \leftarrow ((EA))$	LD r, @disp(xr)
STORE	1010	$(EA) \leftarrow (ACr)$	ST r, disp(xr)
STORE INDIRECT	1011	$((EA)) \leftarrow (ACr)$	ST r, @disp(xr)

Table 11.4. Arithmetic Instructions

Instruction	OpCode	Operation	Assembler Format
ADD (ADD)	1100	$(ACr) \leftarrow (ACr) + (EA), OV, CY$	ADD r, disp(xr)
SUBTRACT (SUB)	1101	$(ACr) \leftarrow (ACr) + \sim (EA) + 1, OV, CY$	SUB r, disp(xr)

Table 11.5. Logical Instructions

Instruction	OpCode	Operation	Assembler Format
AND	01100	$(ACr) \leftarrow (ACr) \wedge (EA)$	AND r, disp(xr)
OR	01101	$(ACr) \leftarrow (ACr) \vee (EA)$	OR r, disp(xr)

442

Table 11.6. Skip Instructions

Instruction	Operation Code	Operation	Assembler Format
Memory References			
INCREMENT AND SKIP IF ZERO	011110	$(EA) \leftarrow (EA) + 1;$ IF $(EA) = 0$, $(PC) \leftarrow (PC) + 1$	ISZ disp(xr)
DECREMENT AND SKIP IF ZERO	011111	$(EA) \leftarrow (EA) - 1;$ IF $(EA) = 0$, $(PC) \leftarrow (PC) + 1$	DSZ disp(xr)
Register References			
SKIP IF GREATER	1110	IF $(AC_r) > (EA)$, $(PC) \leftarrow (PC) + 1$	SKG r, disp(xr)
SKIP IF NOT EQUAL	1111	IF $(AC_r) \neq (EA)$, $(PC) \leftarrow (PC) + 1$	SKNE r, disp(xr)
Limited Register Reference			
SKIP IF AND IS ZERO	01110	IF $[(AC_r) \wedge (EA)] = 0$, $(PC) \leftarrow (PC) + 1$	SKAZ r, disp(xr)

Table 11.7. Transfer-of-Control Instructions

Instruction	Operation Code	Operation	Assembler Format
Jumps			
JUMP	001000	$(PC) \leftarrow EA$	JMP disp(xr)
JUMP INDIRECT	001001	$(PC) \leftarrow (EA)$	JMP @disp(xr)
JUMP TO SUBROUTINE	001010	$(STK) \leftarrow (PC); (PC) \leftarrow EA$	JSR disp(xr)
JUMP TO SUBROUTINE INDIRECT	001011	$(STK) \leftarrow (PC); (PC) \leftarrow (EA)$	JSR @disp(xr)
Branch			
BRANCH-ON CONDITION	0001	IF CC IS TRUE $(PC) \leftarrow (PC) + disp$	BOC cc, disp
Returns			
RETURN FROM INTERRUPT	000000010	$(PC) \leftarrow (STK) + ctl$; INTEN FLAG SET	RTI ctl
RETURN FROM SUBROUTINE	000000100	$(PC) \leftarrow (STK) + ctl$	RTS ctl
JUMP TO SUBROUTINE IMPLIED	000000111	$(STK) \leftarrow (PC); (PC) \leftarrow FF80_{16} + ctl$	JSRI ctl

Table 11.8. Branch-On Condition Codes

Condition Code	Condition Tested	Remarks
0000	Interrupt Line = 1	Interrupt need not be tested by macroprogram
0001	(AC0) = 0	
0010	(AC0) $\geqslant$ 0	
0011	Bit 0 of AC0 = 1	
0100	Bit 1 of AC0 = 1	
0101	(AC0) $\neq$ 0	
0110	CONTROL PANEL INTERRUPT LINE = 1	
0111	CONTROL PANEL START = 1	
1000	STACK FULL LINE = 1	
1001	INTERRUPT ENABLE = 1	
1010	CARRY/OVERFLOW = 1	Carry if SEL = 0; overflow if SEL = 1
1011	(AC0) $\leqslant$ 0	
1100	User	
1101	User	Available for general-purpose use
1110	User	
1111	User	

Table 11.9. Shift Instructions

Instruction	Operation Code	Operation SEL = 0	Operation SEL = 1	Assembler Format
ROTATE LEFT (disp > 0)	010110	$(ACr_0) \leftarrow (ACr_{15})$, $(ACr_n) \leftarrow (ACr_{n-1})$	$(ACr_0) \leftarrow (L)$, $(L) \leftarrow (ACr_{15})$, $(ACr_n) \leftarrow (ACr_{n-1})$	ROL r, m
ROTATE RIGHT (disp < 0)	010110	$(ACr_{15}) \leftarrow (ACr_0)$, $(ACr_n) \leftarrow (ACr_{n+1})$	$(ACr_{15}) \leftarrow (L)$, $(L) \leftarrow (ACr_0)$, $(ACr_n) \leftarrow (ACr_{n+1})$	ROR r, m
SHIFT LEFT (disp > 0)	010111	$(ACr_n) \leftarrow (ACr_{n-1})$, $(ACr_0) \leftarrow 0$	$(L) \leftarrow (ACr_{15})$, $(ACr_n) \leftarrow (ACr_{n-1})$, $(ACr_0) \leftarrow 0$	SHL r, m
SHIFT RIGHT (disp < 0)	010111	$(ACr_{15}) \leftarrow 0$, $(ACr_n) \leftarrow (ACr_{n+1})$	$(ACr_{15}) \leftarrow (L)$, $(L) \leftarrow 0$, $(ACr_n) \leftarrow (ACr_{n+1})$	SHR r, m

NOTE: For all shift and rotate instructions, "m" denotes the number of positions to be shifted or rotated, and is equal to the absolute value of disp.

Table 11.10. Register Instructions

Instruction	Operation Code	Operation	Assembler Format
Register and Stack			
PUSH ONTO STACK	010000	(STK) ← (ACr)	PUSH r
PULL FROM STACK	010001	(ACr) ← (STK)	PULL r
EXCHANGE REGISTER AND STACK	010101	(STK) ← (ACr), (ACr) ← (STK)	XCHRS r
Register and Immediate			
LOAD IMMEDIATE	010011	(ACr) ← disp (sign extended)	LI r, disp
ADD IMMEDIATE, SKIP IF ZERO	010010	(ACr) ← (ACr) + disp (sign extended), OV,CY; if (ACr) = 0, (PC) ← (PC) + 1	AISZ r, disp
COMPLEMENT AND ADD IMMEDIATE	010100	(ACr) ← ~ (ACr) + disp (sign extended)	CAI r, disp

Instruction	Operation Code			Operation	Assembler Format
	OP1	OP2	OP3		
Register to Register					
REGISTER ADD	0011	0	00	(ACdr) ← (ACsr) + (ACdr), OV,CY	RADD sr, dr
REGISTER EXCHANGE	0011	1	00	(ACsr) ← (ACdr), (ACdr) ← (ACsr)	RXCH sr, dr
REGISTER COPY	0011	1	01	(ACdr) ← (ACsr)	RCPY sr, dr
REGISTER EXCLUSIVE-OR	0011	1	10	(ACdr) ← (ACsr) ∇ (ACdr)	RXOR sr, dr
REGISTER AND	0011	1	11	(ACdr) ← (ACsr) $\wedge$ (ACdr)	RAND sr, dr

Table 11.11. Input/Output, Halt, and Flag Instructions

Instruction	Operation Code	Operation	Assembler Format
Input/Output			
REGISTER IN	000001000	(AR) ← ctl + (AC3); (AC0) ← (IOREG)	RIN ctl
REGISTER OUT	000001100	(AR) ← ctl + (AC3); (IOREG) ← (AC0)	ROUT ctl
Halt			
HALT	000000000	Processor halts.	HALT
Status Flags			
PUSH STATUS FLAGS ONTO STACK	000000001	(STK) ← (STATUS FLAGS)	PUSHF
PULL STATUS FLAGS FROM STACK	000000101	(STATUS FLAGS) ← (STK)	PULLF

Instruction	Operation Code		Operation	Assembler Format
	OP1	OP2		
Control Flags				
SET FLAG	00001	0	fc set; (AR) ← ctl	SFLG fc
PULSE FLAG	00001	1	fc pulsed; (AR) ← ctl	PFLG fc

11.5. INPUT/OUTPUT OPERATIONS

Input/Output Instructions

Input/output operations are carried out with the RIN (register in) and ROUT (register out) macroinstructions. Functionally, they are similar to the LOAD and STORE instructions in that they address a particular device and initiate data exchanges. The effective address of an I/O device is determined by the sum of the contents of accumulator 3 ($AC3$) and the 7-bit control field of the RIN or ROUT instruction. The timing for these instructions is shown in Fig. 11.7.

Sixteen bits are available for address and command codes. Although a number of schemes are possible, the one described here has proved useful for many applications. The low-order 3 bits may be used to define an I/O "order," and bits 3–6 are the device addresses (Fig. 11.8). Each peripheral device decodes the address field of the I/O instruction command, and if the read peripheral or the write peripheral flag is active, the device will respond. The 3 "order" bits permit eight possible auxiliary operations for each I/O class; for example, these orders may be read data, read status, reset device, rewind tape, backspace, or write data. The assignment of the various orders is left to the systems programmer.

The 4 bits of the device address field permit direct addressing of 16 devices; however, by loading accumulator 3 (which is added to bits 0–6 of the instruction) with a 16-bit value before executing a RIN or ROUT instruction, up to 65,536 addresses may be specified.

Data Transfer to Peripheral Devices

Peripheral device data may be accessed by the read peripheral and write peripheral control flags in conjunction with the peripheral device address. The actual transfer of data is effected by the RIN and ROUT instructions during T7 (input) and T4 (output), respectively (Fig. 11.5). Peripheral device control may be achieved by using the order field of the instruction (Fig. 11.8) or by dedicating a general-purpose control flag to a peripheral device control function, which can then be controlled by use of the SFLG and PFLG instructions. Similarly, peripheral device status can be sensed by issuing an order to read status over the data bus, or by dedicating one of the general-purpose user jump conditions to this function and using the BRANCH ON CONDITION (BOC) instruction. (The control flags and jump condition inputs can actually serve to implement a very low-cost serial-data interface without using the data bus at all.)

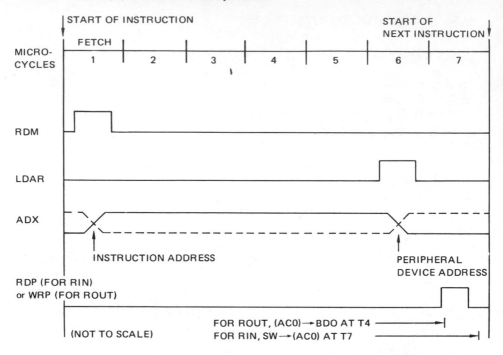

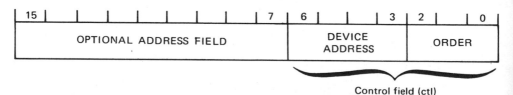

Figure 11.7. Timing sequence for RIN and ROUT instructions. (Courtesy of National Semiconductor Corporation).

The functions performed as a result of an I/O command vary. For example, a READ PERIPHERAL order to a magnetic disk typically initiates a block transfer of information. In contrast, a similar order to a Teletype typically executes the transfer of a single character.

The use of I/O instructions is best illustrated by an example. Consider the case of reading in characters from a serial Teletype unit and transmitting them back immediately (echoing). The program segment shown in Table 11.12 will do this effectively. The first few comment lines define the I/O orders for the Teletype unit. It is assumed that the Teletype is sending data serially over the line corresponding to bit 15.

15							7	6			3	2			0
OPTIONAL ADDRESS FIELD								DEVICE ADDRESS				ORDER			

Control field (ctl)

Figure 11.8. Input/output word format. (Courtesy of National Semiconductor Corporation).

Table 11.12

Instruction	Comment
;	DEFINE I/O ORDERS
;	5 = RESET
;	2 = READ DATA
;	4 = ENABLE TTY PAPER TAPE READER
;	3 = WRITE DATA
;	TTYAD = TTY ADDRESS IN BIT 3–6
;	C1 = 1 (BRANCH IF AC0 = 0)
START: LI 3, TTYAD	LOAD AC3 WITH ADDRESS OF TTY
ROUT 5;	RESET TELETYPE (ORDER FIELD = 5)
LI 2, 8	SET COUNT FOR 8 BITS
READ: ROUT 4;	ENABLE TTY READER
RIN 2;	READ IN TTY DATA
BOC C2, .+2;	TEST FOR START BIT; C2 REFERS TO AC0 = 0
JUMP READ;	READ DATA AGAIN (UNTIL START BIT FOUND)
JSR DELAY;	START BIT FOUND; DELAY FOR PROPER TIMING
INPUT: ROUT 3;	SEND BIT TO PRINTER
JSR DELAY;	DELAY ROUTINE TO TIME OUT 1 BIT
RIN 2;	READ TTY DATA
SHR 0, 1;	SHIFT DATA ONE POSITION
AISZ 2, −1;	TEST TO SEE IF DONE
JMP INPUT;	NOT DONE; READ MORE DATA
DELAY: .;	START OF DELAY SUBROUTINE

11.6.   INTERRUPT SYSTEM

General Features

The IMP-16C system recognizes one level of interrupt in its present configuration. A general interrupt request is initiated by the interrupt request signal (INTRA) to the interrupt handler. Also provided is a control panel interrupt input (CPINT). The workings of both types are described below.

A peripheral device (or any external condition) may send an interrupt request to the IMP-16C over the INTRA line. If the interrupt enable flag is set (i.e., no other interrupt currently being serviced), the interrupt request is latched in a flip-flop and awaits service. During the next instruction fetch cycle, the processor resets the interrupt enable flag (INTEN) and transfers control to location 1 in main memory. At the same time, the *PC* value is saved on the stack.

The instruction in location 1 of main memory typically will be the start of an interrupt service routine or a jump to service routine. In the IMP-16C, the stack overflow condition causes an interrupt on the same line. The interrupt service routine can detect this type of interrupt by using a BRANCH ON CONDITION (BOC) instruction with cc = 8 (stack full). The interrupt sequence is best illustrated by an example.

Example of Interrupt Request and Service. The case considered here is that of a real-time clock that provides interval timing by sending timed interrupts to the processor. The hardware for this feature would consist of a presettable counter that raises a status signal after it has counted through its sequence. This signal can be used as an interrupt request.

As an example of the use of this timer, consider an application in which it is desired to sample a waveform at regular intervals. The real-time clock can be used to generate interrupts at these intervals, and a processing subroutine can read the contents of an analog-to-digital converter driven by the waveform under test. The program segment in Table 11.13 shows how this can be done. The clock is assumed to use bit 0 on the data bus to signal its status. This signal is also wired to the general interrupt request line. The interrupt status of the clock is read over bit 0 of the data bus by issuing a READ STATUS order. (Note that other devices could use other bits of the data bus to respond to this order simultaneously. The data bits may then be tested to determine devices that are requesting interrupt service.)

The first few lines of the program are comments that describe the various order codes and addresses assigned to the real-time clock and the A /D converter. The remaining lines of the program segment perform operations according to the requirements above; the comments serve to annotate the program.

11.7. PACE MICROPROCESSOR

General Features

PACE (processing and control element) is a single-chip, 16-bit microprocessor packaged in a standard, hermetically sealed, 40-pin ceramic dual-in-line package.

Silicon gate, P-channel enhancement mode standard process technology ensures high performance, high reliability, and high producibility.

- 16-bit instruction word: Provides addressing flexibility and speed.
- 8- or 16-bit data word: Ensures wide application.
- Powerful instruction set: Facilitates efficient programming.
- Common memory and peripheral addressing: Provides powerful I /O instructions.

- Shares instructions with National's IMP-16 basic set: Allows software compatibility.
- Four general-purpose accumulators: Reduce memory data transfers.
- 10-word stack: Provides interrupt processing/data storage.
- Six vectored priority interrupt levels: Simplify interrupt service and hardware.
- Programmer-accessible status register: May be preserved, tested, or modified.
- 2-μsec microcycle: Provides fast instruction execution.
- Can utilize DM8531 1K $\times$ 16 *ROM*: Provides single memory package.
- Two clock inputs: Minimize external components.

A connection diagram of a typical PACE system is shown in Fig. 11.9, and the *CPU* in Fig. 11.10.

Seven data registers are provided, four of which are directly available to the programmer (as accumulators $AC0$ to $AC3$) for data storage and address formation. $AC0$ is the principal working register, $AC1$ is the secondary working register, and $AC2$ and $AC3$ are page pointers or auxiliary data registers. The other three registers serve as a program counter, and two temporary registers are used by the control section to effect the PACE instruction set. Additional data storage is provided for up to 10 words by a last-in first-out or push-pull stack.

A unique feature of the PACE *ALU* is the ability to operate on either 8- or 16-bit data, as specified by the programmer through the use of a status flag. This feature allows character-oriented and other 8-bit applications to use the system in the optimal way.

Status

All status and control bits for PACE are provided in a single status flag register, whose contents may be loaded from or to any accumulator or the stack. This allows convenient testing, masking, and storage of status. In addition, a number of status bits may be tested directly by the conditional BRANCH instruction, and any bit may be individually set or reset. The function of each bit in the status flag register is listed in Table 11.14 and described briefly below. The carry flag is set to the state of the carry output resulting from binary and BCD arithmetic instructions, and serves as a carry input for some of these instructions. The overflow flag is set true if an arithmetic overflow results from a binary arithmetic instruction.

The link flag serves as a 1-bit extension for certain shift and rotate instructions. The byte flag is used to specify an 8-bit data length for data processing instructions, while arithmetic operations for address formation remain at

Table 11.13

Label	Instruction	Comment
;		INTERRUPT SEQUENCE FOR REAL-TIME
;		CLOCK AND WAVEFORM SAMPLER
;		RTC = ADDRESS OF REAL-TIME CLOCK
;		ADC = ADDRESS OF A/D CONVERTER
;		2 = START CLOCK (I/O ORDER)
;		1 = READ DATA ORDER
;		0 = READ INTERRUPT STATUS ORDER
;		C3 = 3; CC FOR BIT 0 OF AC0 = 1
;		CLOCK INTERRUPT STATUS HAS BEEN ASSIGNED BIT 0 ON BUS
LOC1:	JMP INTR:	THIS INSTRUCTION IS IN LOCATION X'0001
; MAIN PROGRAM FOLLOWS:		
	SFLG 1; ...	ENABLE INTERRUPT SYSTEM
	LI 3, RTC;	LOAD AC3 WITH CLOCK ADDRESS
	ROUT 2; ...	START TIMER ON CLOCK

```
; SERVICE ROUTINE FOLLOWS:
INTR:           LI      3, 0;           CLEAR AC3 BEFORE EXECUTING RIN
                RIN     0;              READ DATA BUS TO CHECK INTERRUPTING DEVICE.
                BOC     C3, CLKINT;     BRANCH TO CLOCK SERVICE IF BIT 0 = 1.
                 . . .

; CLOCK SERVICE ROUTINE FOLLOWS:
CLKINT:         LI      3, RTC;         LOAD AC3 WITH CLOCK ADDRESS
                ROUT    2;              RESTART TIMER
                LI      3, ADC;         LOAD ADDRESS OF A/D CONVERTER
                RIN     1;              READ ADC DATA.
                JSR     SAMPLE;         GO TO DATA SAMPLE PROCESSING SUBROUTINE.
                RTI     ;               RETURN FROM INTERRUPT.
                 . . .

; CONTINUE PROCESSING OF OTHER INTERRUPTS.
                 . . .

SAMPLE: . . . . . . . . . . . .;        START OF ROUTINE TO PROCESS DATA FROM A/D CONVERTER.
```

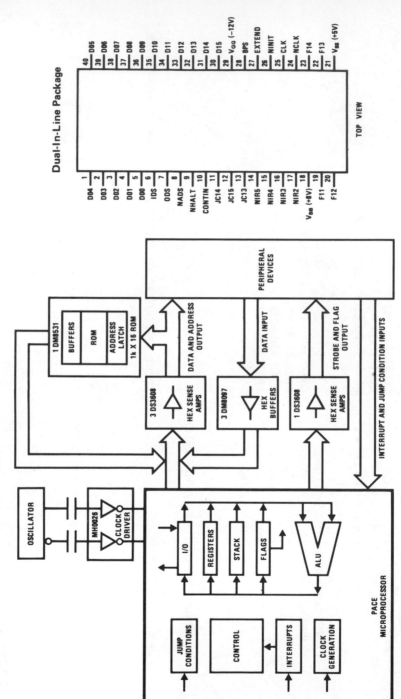

Figure 11.9. PACE block and connection diagrams. (Courtesy of National Semiconductor Corporation).

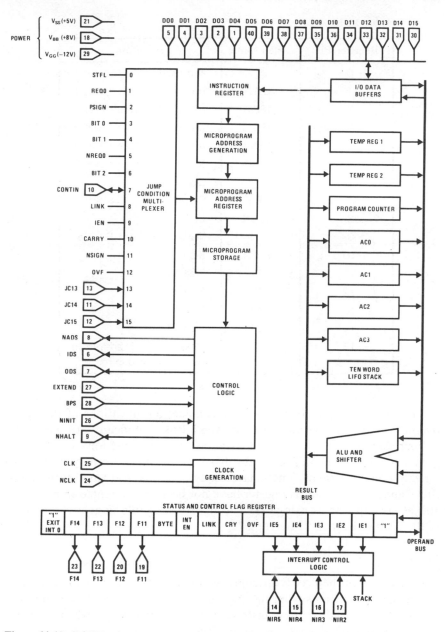

Figure 11.10. PACE microprocessor. (Courtesy of National Semiconductor Corporation).

Table 11.14

Register Bit	Flag Name	Function
0	"1"	Not used—always logic 1
1	IE1	Interrupt Enable Level 1
2	IE2	Interrupt Enable Level 2
3	IE3	Interrupt Enable Level 3
4	IE4	Interrupt Enable Level 4
5	IE5	Interrupt Enable Level 5
6	OVF	Overflow
7	CRY	Carry
8	LINK	Link
9	IEN	Master Interrupt Enable
10	BYTE	8-bit data length
11	F11	Flag 11
12	F12	Flag 12
13	F13	Flag 13
14	F14	Flag 14
15	"1"	Always logic 1, addressed for Interrupt 0 exit

the 16-bit data length. In the 8-bit data mode, modifications of the carry, overflow, and link flags are based on the 8 least significant data bits only.

Four flags (bits 10–14) which may be assigned functions by the programmer are provided. These flags drive output pins and may be used to directly control system functions or may serve as software status flags. Bits 0 and 15 of the status register have not been implemented in hardware and always appear as a logic 1. The interrupt enable flags are explained in the Section headed "Interrupts".

Control

The operation of the PACE microprocessor consists of repeatedly accessing or fetching instructions from the external program store and executing the operations specified by these instructions. These two steps are carried out under the control of a microprogram (the microprocessor is not designed for user microprogramming). The microprogram is similar to a state table specifying the series of states of system control signals necessary to carry out each instruction. Microprogram storage is provided by a programmable logic array, and microprogram routines are implemented to fetch and execute instructions.

The fetch routine causes an instruction address to be transferred from the program counter register to the I/O bus and initiates an input data operation. When the instruction is provided on the data bus, the fetch routine causes it to be loaded into the instruction register. The instruction-operation code is transformed into the address of the appropriate instruction-execution routine by the address generation logic. As the last step of the fetch routine, this address is loaded into the microprogram address register, causing a branch to the appropriate instruction-execution routine.

The execution routine consists of one or more microinstructions to implement the functions required by the instruction. For example, the routine for a register ADD instruction would access the two accumulators to be added over the operand bus, cause the *ALU* to perform an ADD operation, load the carry and overflow flags from the *ALU*, and store the result in the specified accumulator. The control logic interprets the microinstructions to carry out these operations. The final step of the execution routine is a jump back to the fetch routine to access the next instruction. Each microcycle requires 2 μsec and 4 or 5 microcycles are typically required to fetch and execute a machine instruction.

Other routines implemented by the microprogram include interrupt servicing and system initialization. The microprogram controls the operation of a conditional jump multiplexer, which is used to specify 16 conditions for the conditional BRANCH instruction. The conditions that may be tested are indicated in Table 11.15 and include four signal inputs to the chip, which may be used to test external system conditions.

The control circuitry may be initialized at any time by use of the NINIT input signal. This will cause the stack addressing circuitry, all flags, and the program counter to be set to zero, the strobes to go false, and level zero interrupt enable to go true. This signal should always be used to initialize the processor after applying power. The first instruction after initialization is accessed from location zero.

Interrupts

The PACE microprocessor provides a six-level, vectored, priority interrupt structure. This permits automatic identification of an interrupting device's level and allows all devices on an interrupt level to be enabled or disabled as a group, independently of other interrupt levels. An individual interrupt enable is provided in the status register for each level, as shown in Fig. 11.11, and a master interrupt enable (IEN) is provided for all five lower-priority levels as a group. Negative true interrupt request inputs are pro-

Table 11.15

Number	Mnemonic	Condition
0	STFL	Stack full
1	REQ0	(AC0) equal to zero[1]
2	PSIGN	(AC0) has positive sign[2]
3	BIT 0	Bit 0 of AC0 true
4	BIT 1	Bit 1 of AC0 true
5	NREQ0	(AC0) is non-zero[1]
6	BIT 2	Bit 2 of AC0 is true
7	CONTIN	CONTIN (continue) input is true
8	LINK	LINK is true
9	IEN	IEN is true
10	CARRY	CARRY is true
11	NSIGN	(AC0) has negative sign[2]
12	OVF	OVF is true
13	JC13	JC13 input is true
14	JC14	JC14 input is true
15	JC15	JC15 input is true

Note 1: If the selected data length is 8 bits, only bits 0-7 of AC0 are tested.

Note 2: Bit 7 is the sign bit (instead of bit 15) if the selected data length is 8 bits.

vided to allow several interrupts to be wire-ORed on each input. When an interrupt request occurs, it will set the interrupt request latch if the corresponding interrupt enable is true. The latch will be set by any pulse exceeding one clock period in duration, a feature which is useful for capturing narrow timing or control pulses. If the master interrupt enable (IEN) is true, an interrupt will be generated. During the interrupt sequence an address is provided by the output of the priority encoder and is used to access the pointer for the highest-priority interrupt request (IR0 is highest priority, IR5 is lowest priority). The pointers are stored in locations 2–7 (see Table 11.16) for interrupt requests 1–5 and 0, respectively. The pointer specifies the starting address of the interrupt service routine for the particular interrupt level. Before executing the interrupt service routine, the program counter is pushed on the stack and IEN is set false. The interrupt service routine may set IEN true after turning off the interrupt enable for the level currently being serviced (or resetting the interrupt request). (The interrupt enables may be set and reset, using the SFLG and PFLG instructions.)

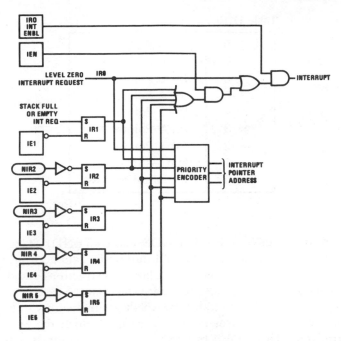

Figure 11.11. Interrupt logic. (Courtesy of National Semiconductor Corporation).

The nonmaskable level-zero interrupt (IR0) is an exception to this interrupt procedure. It has a program counter storage location pointer (the program counter is not stored on the stack for this particular interrupt in order to preserve the processor state), which is followed by the level-zero interrupt service routine. The IR0 interrupt enable is cleared when a level-zero interrupt occurs (IEN is unaffected) and may be set true by addressing (nonexistent) status flag 15. This allows execution of one more instruction (typically JMP@) to return from the IR0 interrupt routine before another interrupt will be acknowledged. This interrupt level is typically used by the control panel, which then can always interrupt the application program and does not affect system status. The control panel service routine interprets and executes the functions specified by the control panel switches and displays selected data on the panel lights. Level-zero interrupts are generated by driving the NHALT signal line low.

Data Input and Output

All data transfers between PACE and external memories or peripheral devices take place over the 16 data lines (D00–D15) and are synchronized by

Table 11.16

8	Int 0 Program
7	Int 0 PC Pointer
6	Int 5 Pointer
5	Int 4 Pointer
4	Int 3 Pointer
3	Int 2 Pointer
2	Int 1 Pointer
1	Not Assigned
Loc 0	Initialization Inst

the four control signals (NADS, IDS, ODS, and EXTEND). Data transfers occur during each instruction access and during the data accesses required by memory reference instructions. This class of instructions could perhaps more properly be called the "I/O reference class" in the case of the PACE microprocessor, since all data transfers, whether with memory or peripheral devices or a central processor data bus, occur through the execution of these instructions. This unified bus architecture is in contrast with the arrangement of many other microprocessors and minicomputers that have one instruction type (I/O class) for communication with peripheral devices and another instruction type (memory reference class) for communication with memories. The advantage of the approach used by PACE is that a wider variety of instructions (the entire memory reference class) is available for communication with peripherals. Thus the DSZ (DECREMENT AND SKIP IF ZERO) instruction can be used to decrement a peripheral device register, or the SKAZ (SKIP if AND is ZERO) instruction can be used to test the contents of a peripheral device status register. The LD (LOAD) and ST (STORE) instructions serve for simple data transfers.

All I/O transactions consist of an address output interval followed by a data transfer interval. The address specifies a memory location or peripheral device. The allocation is entirely up to the user (within the requirements for interrupt pointers). A straightforward allocation is to assign all addresses from 0000_{16} to $7FFF_{16}$ as memory addresses and all addresses from 8000_{16} to $FFFF_{16}$ as peripheral device addresses. In this case, the most significant address bit specifies whether the transaction is with memory or a peripheral device. A variety of easily decoded address allocation schemes may be used, depending on the amount of *ROM*, *RAM*, and peripheral devices and the particular application. Both address and data words are transmitted or received as 16-bit parallel data over the data lines (D00–D15). If 8-bit data are being transferred, the unused bits can be treated as "don't care" bits by the hardware and the 8-bit data length selected by the software.

Data transfer operations are synchronized by the NADS (address data strobe), IDS (input data strobe), ODS (output data strobe), and EXTEND signals as shown in Fig. 11.12. Address data are provided on the 16 data lines. An NADS is provided in the center of the address data and may be used to strobe the address into an address latch. A number of memory products provide address latches on the chip, thus avoiding the need for implementing this function externally. The input data strobe and output data strobe indicate the type of data transfer and may be used to enable TRI-STATE® I/O buffers and gate data into registers or memories as required by the system design. The EXTEND input allows the I/O cycle time to be extended by multiples of the clock cycle to adapt to a variety of memory and peripheral devices or for *DMA* bus interfacing.

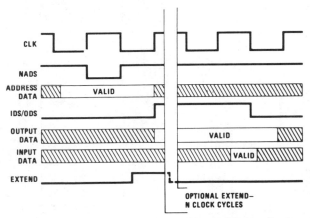

Figure. 11.12. PACE timing. (Courtesy of National Semiconductor Corporation).

Instructions

PACE shares instructions with the IMP-16 basic set. The PACE instruction set is shown in Table 11.17. Compare with the IMP-16 instructions (Tables 11.3–11.11).

A simple example program is provided by the binary multiply routine shown in Table 11.18. This program multiplies the 16-bit value in $AC2$ by the 16-bit value in $AC1$ and provides a 32-bit result in $AC0$ (high order) and $AC1$ (low order). Worst-case execution time is under 1 msec.

Table 11.17

Mnemonic	Meaning	Operation	Assembler Format	Instruction Format (bits 15→00)
Branch Instructions				
BOC	Branch On Condition	$(PC) \leftarrow (PC) + disp$ if cc true	BOC cc, disp	0 1 0 0 | cc | disp
JMP	Jump	$(PC) \leftarrow EA$	JMP disp (xr)	1 0 0 0 1 0 | xr | disp
JMP@	Jump Indirect	$(PC) \leftarrow (EA)$	JMP @disp (xr)	1 0 0 0 1 1 | xr | disp
JSR	Jump to Subroutine	$(STK) \leftarrow (PC),\ (PC) \leftarrow EA$	JSR disp (xr)	0 0 0 1 0 1
JSR@	Jump to Subroutine Indirect	$(STK) \leftarrow (PC),\ (PC) \leftarrow (EA)$	JSR @disp (xr)	1 0 0 1 0 1
RTS	Return from Subroutine	$(PC) \leftarrow (STK) + disp$	RTS disp	1 0 0 0 0 0 0 0 0 | disp
RTI	Return from Interrupt	$(PC) \leftarrow (STK) + disp,\ IEN = 1$	RTI disp	0 1 1 1 1 1 | disp
Skip Instructions				
SKNE	Skip if Not Equal	If $(ACr) \neq (EA),\ (PC) \leftarrow (PC) + 1$	SKNE r, disp (xr)	1 1 1 1 | r | xr | disp
SKG	Skip if Greater	If $(AC0) > (EA),\ (PC) \leftarrow (PC) + 1$	SKG 0, disp (xr)	1 0 0 1 1 | r
SKAZ	Skip if AND is Zero	If $[(AC0) \wedge (EA)] = 0,\ (PC) \leftarrow (PC) + 1$	SKAZ 0, disp (xr)	1 0 1 1 1 0
ISZ	Increment and Skip if Zero	$(EA) \leftarrow (EA) + 1$, if $(EA) = 0,\ (PC) \leftarrow (PC) + 1$	ISZ disp (xr)	1 0 0 0 1 1
DSZ	Decrement and Skip if Zero	$(EA) \leftarrow (EA) - 1$, if $(EA) = 0,\ (PC) \leftarrow (PC) + 1$	DSZ disp (xr)	1 0 1 1 0 1
AISZ	Add Immediate, Skip if Zero	$(ACr) \leftarrow (ACr) + disp$, if $(ACr) = 0,\ (PC) \leftarrow (PC) + 1$	AISZ r, disp	0 1 1 1 1 0 | r | disp
Memory Data-Transfer Instructions				
LD	Load	$(ACr) \leftarrow (EA)$	LD r, disp (xr)	1 1 0 0 | r | xr | disp
LD@	Load Indirect	$(AC0) \leftarrow ((EA))$	LD 0, @disp (xr)	1 0 1 0 0 0
ST	Store	$(EA) \leftarrow (ACr)$	ST r, disp (xr)	1 1 0 1 | r
ST@	Store Indirect	$((EA)) \leftarrow (AC0)$	S1 0, @disp (xr)	1 0 1 1 0 0
LSEX	Load with Sign Extended	$(AC0) \leftarrow (EA)$ bit 7 extended	LSEX 0, disp (xr)	1 0 1 1 1 1
Memory Data-Operate Instructions				
AND	AND	$(AC0) \leftarrow (AC0) \wedge (EA)$	AND 0, disp (xr)	1 0 1 0 1 0 | xr | disp
OR	OR	$(AC0) \leftarrow (AC0) \vee (EA)$	OR 0, disp (xr)	1 0 1 0 0 1
ADD	Add	$(ACr) \leftarrow (ACr) + (EA),\ OV,\ CY$	ADD r, disp (xr)	1 1 1 0 | r
SUBB	Subtract with Borrow	$(AC0) \leftarrow (AC0) + \sim (EA) + (CY),\ OV,\ CY$	SUBB 0, disp (xr)	1 0 0 1 0 0
DECA	Decimal Add	$(AC0) \leftarrow (AC0) +_{10} (EA) +_{10} (CY),\ OV,\ CY$	DECA 0, disp (xr)	1 0 0 0 1 0

Table 11.17 (Continued)

Mnemonic	Meaning	Operation	Assembler Format	Instruction Format (15 14 13 12 11 10 09 08 07 06 05 04 03 02 01 00)
Register Data-Transfer Instructions				
LI	Load Immediate	$(ACr) \leftarrow disp$	r, disp	0 1 0 1 0 0 | r | disp
RCPY	Register Copy	$(ACdr) \leftarrow (ACsr)$	sr, dr	0 1 0 1 1 1 | dr | sr | not used
RXCH	Register Exchange	$(ACdr) \leftarrow (ACsr),\ (ACsr) \leftarrow (ACdr)$	sr, dr	0 1 0 1 0 1 | dr | sr | not used
XCHRS	Exchange Register and Stack	$(STK) \leftarrow (ACr),\ (ACr) \leftarrow (STK)$	r	0 0 0 1 1 1 | r | not used
CFR	Copy Flags into Register	$(ACr) \leftarrow (FR)$	r	0 0 0 0 0 1
CRF	Copy Register into Flags	$(FR) \leftarrow (ACr)$	r	0 0 0 0 1 0
PUSH	Push Register onto Stack	$(STK) \leftarrow (ACr)$	r	0 1 1 0 0 0
PULL	Pull Stack into Register	$(ACr) \leftarrow (STK)$	r	0 1 1 0 0 1
PUSHF	Push Flags onto Stack	$(STK) \leftarrow (FR)$		0 0 0 0 1 1 | not used
PULLF	Pull Stack into Flags	$(FR) \leftarrow (STK)$		0 0 0 1 0 0 | not used
Register Data-Operate Instructions				
RADD	Register Add	$(ACdr) \leftarrow (ACdr) + (ACsr),\ OV,\ CY$	sr, dr	0 1 1 0 1 0 | dr | sr | not used
RADC	Register Add with Carry	$(ACdr) \leftarrow (ACdr) + (ACsr) + (CY),\ OV,\ CY$	sr, dr	0 1 1 1 0 1
RAND	Register AND	$(ACdr) \leftarrow (ACdr) \wedge (ACsr)$	sr, dr	0 1 0 1 0 1
RXOR	Register EXCLUSIVE OR	$(ACdr) \leftarrow (ACdr) \veebar (ACsr)$	sr, dr	0 1 1 0 1 0
CAI	Complement and Add Immediate	$(ACr) \leftarrow \sim (ACr) + disp$	r, disp	0 1 1 1 0 0 | r | disp
Shift And Rotate Instructions				
SHL	Shift Left	$(ACr) \leftarrow (ACr)$ shifted left n places, w/wo link	r, n, ℓ	0 0 1 0 1 0 | r | n | ℓ
SHR	Shift Right	$(ACr) \leftarrow (ACr)$ shifted right n places, w/wo link	r, n, ℓ	0 0 1 0 1 1
ROL	Rotate Left	$(ACr) \leftarrow (ACr)$ rotated left n places, w/wo link	r, n, ℓ	0 0 1 0 0 0
ROR	Rotate Right	$(ACr) \leftarrow (ACr)$ rotated right n places, w/wo link	r, n, ℓ	0 0 1 0 0 1
Miscellaneous Instructions				
HALT	Halt	Halt		0 0 0 0 0 0 | not used
SFLG	Set Flag	$(FR)\ fc \leftarrow 1$	fc	0 0 1 1 | fc | 1
PFLG	Pulse Flag	$(FR)\ fc \leftarrow 1,\ (FR)\ fc \leftarrow 0$	fc	0 0 1 1 | fc | 0

Table 11.18.   Binary Multiply Routine

```
CONST:   WORD  X'FFFF        ; CONSTANT FOR DOUBLE PREC. ADD
START:   LI    R1, 0         ; CLEAR RESULT REGISTER
         LI    R3, 16        ; LOOP COUNT TO AC3
         CAI   R0, 0         ; COMPLEMENT MULTIPLIER
LOOP:    RADD  R1, R1        ; SHIFT RESULT LEFT INTO CARRY
         RADC  R0,R0         ; SHIFT CARRY INTO MULTIPLIER
                             ; AND MULTIPLIER INTO CARRY
         BOC CARRY, TEST     ; TEST FOR ADD
         RADD  R2, R1        ; ADD MULTIPLICAND TO RESULT
         SUBB  R0, CONST     ; ADD CARRY TO H.O. RESULT
TEST:    AISZ  R3, −1        ; DECREMENT LOOP COUNT
         JMP LOOP            ; REPEAT LOOP
```

REFERENCES

1. IMP–16C Application Manual National Semiconductor Corp., Santa Clara, Ca., 1974.
2. PACE Users Manual, National Semiconductor Corp., Santa Clara, Ca., 1975.

PART III

New Microprocessors and Special-Purpose Microsystems

PDP-11 Minicomputer and LSI-11 Microcomputer.
F8 Microprocessor.
SMS Microcontroller.
3000 Bipolar Microcomputer Set.
IM6100 Microprocessor and PDP-8 Minicomputer.

Typical laboratory microcomputer (LSI-11). Such a system could be used for data acquisition, process control, data processing, and simulation. (Courtesy of Digital Equipment Corporation.)

12

PDP-11 MINICOMPUTER
AND LSI-11 MICROCOMPUTER

Chapter 12 presents two software-compatible systems, the PDP-11 minicomputer and the LSI-11 microcomputer. These are 16-bit systems with powerful instruction sets and a large variety of addressing modes. Whereas the PDP-11 is a hard-wired machine, the LSI-11 uses microprograms stored in control read only memory to implement the PDP-11's instruction set. The instruction repertoire, which is the most comprehensive of any microcomputer or minicomputer, consists of over 400 instructions. All operations in the PDP-11 and LSI-11 are accomplished with one set of instructions. Since peripheral device registers can be manipulated as flexibly as necessary by the central processor, instructions that are used to manipulate data in memory can serve equally well for data in peripheral device registers. The system architecture, as well as programming and interfacing examples, is described.

The material* in this chapter has been adapted in part from a publication of Digital Equipment Corporation. The material so published herein is the full responsibility of the author.

12.1. PDP-11 MINICOMPUTER

Operational Features

All PDP-11 computers have the following features:

- 16-bit word (two 8-bit bytes).

---

* Programs, figures, and tables are courtesy and copyright © 1975 by Digital Equipment Corporation. All rights reserved.

- Word or byte processing. There is very efficient handling of 8-bit characters without the need to rotate, swap, or mask.

- Asynchronous operation. The system components run at their highest possible speed; replacement with faster devices means faster operation without other hardware or software changes.

- Modular component design. There is extreme ease and flexibility in configuring systems.

- Stack processing. Hardware sequential memory manipulation makes it easy to handle structured data, subroutines, and interrupts.

- Direct memory access (*DMA*). Inherent in the architecture is direct memory access for multiple devices.

- Eight general-purpose registers. Fast integrated circuits are used for accumulators or address generation.

- Automatic priority interrupt. A four-line, multilevel system permits grouping of interrupt lines according to response requirements.

- Vectored interrupts. Fast interrupt response without device polling is provided.

- Single and double operand instructions. A powerful and convenient set of programming instructions is available.

- Power fail and automatic restart. Hardware detection and software protection for fluctuations in the AC power are provided.

All computer system components and peripherals connect to and communicate with each other on a single high-speed bus known as the *unibus*—the key to the PDP-11's many strengths. Addresses, data, and control information are sent along the 56 lines of the bus.

The form of communication is the same for every device on the unibus. The processor uses the same set of signals to communicate with memory as with peripheral devices. Peripheral devices also use this set of signals when communicating with the processor, memory, or other peripheral devices. Each device, including memory locations, processor registers, and peripheral device registers, is assigned an address on the unibus. Thus peripheral device registers may be manipulated as flexibly as core memory by the central processor. All the instructions that can be applied to data in core memory can be applied equally well to data in peripheral device registers. This is a particularly powerful feature, considering the special capability of PDP-11 instructions to process data in any memory location as though it were an accumulator.

With bidirectional and asynchronous communications on the unibus, devices can send, receive, and exchange data independently without processor intervention. For example, a cathode ray tube display can refresh itself from a disk file while the central processor unit attends to other tasks. Because it is asynchronous, the unibus is compatible with devices operating over a wide range of speeds.

System Introduction

The whole computer is organized around a single bus, called the unibus. The processor, memory, and all peripheral devices share the same high-speed bus. The unibus enables the processor to view peripheral devices as active memory locations which perform special functions. Peripheral devices can thus be addressed as a memory. In other words, memory reference instructions can operate directly on control, status, or data registers in peripheral devices. The computer word is 16 bits.

The computer is equipped with eight general registers, $R0-R7$. All registers are program-accessible and can be used as accumulators, as pointers to memory locations, or as full-word index registers. Registers $R0-R5$ are used for general-purpose access, while the sixth and the seventh registers are used as a stack pointer and a program counter, respectively:

$$R6 \equiv SP \text{ (stack pointer)}$$
$$R7 \equiv PC \text{ (program counter)}.$$

Figure 12.1a shows a simplified block diagram of the processor and is divided into five major functional areas: unibus, interface, data paths, general-purpose registers, and timing state and control logic.

All information transfers are performed through the data paths. The bus interface and general-purpose registers interconnect only through the data

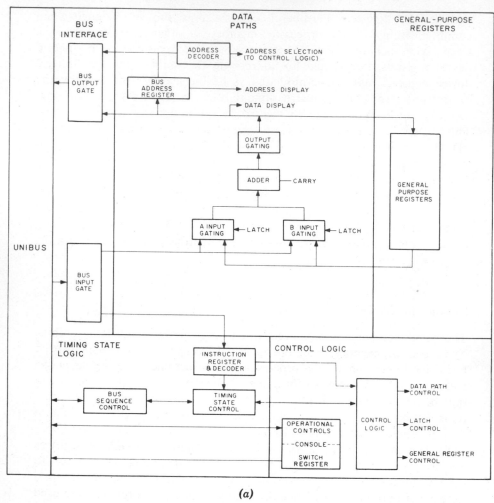

(a)

Figure 12.1. PDP-11 processor block diagram. (*a*) Simplified internal organization; (*b*) data flow (courtesy of Digital Equipment Corporation).

paths, so that frequent transfers of data set up a flow of information in a figure-eight pattern, Fig. 12.1*b*. This flow is from the unibus to the bottom of the data paths, from the top of the data paths to the general-purpose registers, from the general-purpose registers to the bottom of the data paths, and from the top of the data paths to the unibus.

Addressing is performed through the general register. The general

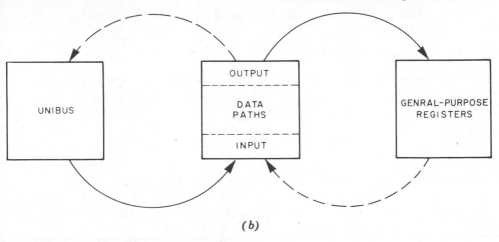

(b)

Figure 12.1. (*Cont'd.*)

registers can be used interchangeably as index registers or as sequential list pointers to gain access to tabular data. Address arithmetic may be performed directly in the general registers.

The general form of a single operand instruction is shown in Fig. 12.2*a*; 3 bits are used to specify the register, and 3 bits are used to specify the addressing mode.

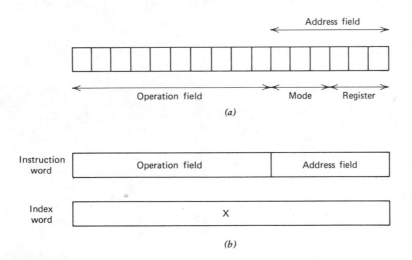

Figure 12.2. Instruction format.

12.2. ADVANCED ADDRESSING MODES

Direct Register Addressing

General registers can be used as simple accumulators for operating on frequently accessed variables. In this mode, the operand is held directly in the
general register. The assembler interprets instructions of the form

OPR R

as general register operations. *R* has been defined as a register name and
OPR is used to represent a general instruction mnemonic.

Example. Complement operation COM R2. The instruction will complement the contents of *R2*. The example is shown in Fig. 12.3. The operand
to be complemented is 014.

Indirect or Deferred Addressing

Operands that are pointed to be addresses (indirect or deferred) are denoted
to the assembler by the symbol @. Thus the instruction of the form

OPR @ R or OPR (R)

specifies deferred register addressing; the contents of the register are the
address of the operand.

Example. COM @ R2. In Fig. 12.3 the operand to be complemented is
1234.

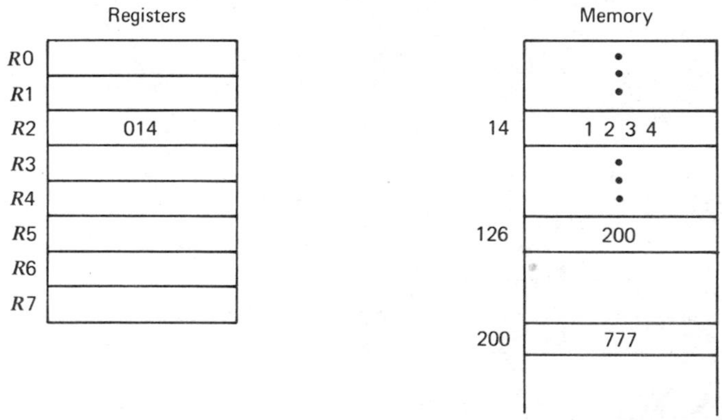

Registers		Memory	
R0			⋮
R1			
R2	014	14	1 2 3 4
R3			⋮
R4			
R5		126	200
R6			
R7		200	777

Figure 12.3. Addressing modes.

Indexed Addressing

General registers may be used as index registers to permit random access of items in tables or stacks of data. The instruction of the form

$$\text{OPR } X(R)$$

specifies the indexed mode addressing. The effective address is the sum of X (address of the memory location) and the contents of the specified general register R.

In this computer the assembler will translate the indexed instruction into two binary words, as shown in Fig. 12.2b.

As an example, let us suppose that the computer is requested to perform the complement instruction, COM 112 (R2). Suppose that the index register $R2$ contains the quantity 014. Then the effective address of the operand is the sum $112 + 014 = 126$. In general

$$\text{M, effective address} = X + (R).$$

This example is shown in Fig. 12.3. The effective address is 126 and the operand to be complemented is 200.

Indexed mode addressing can be deferred or indirect. It is specified by instructions of the form

$$\text{OPR @ } X(R).$$

The effective address is the contents of the indexed address:

$$\text{M, effective address} = (X + (R)).$$

Example. COM @ 112 (R2). The contents of $R2$ are 014, Fig. 12.3. The indexed address is then $112 + 014 = 126$. Hence the effective address is 200, and the operand to be complemented is 777.

Indexing is very useful in operating program loops and in dealing with lists of data. Suppose that the same operation has to be performed in each pass of the loop, but on the next item from the list. To modify the operation, it is enough to increment the contents of the index register every time the program passes through the loop. X presents the starting address of the list (in the first example it is 112).

At the beginning, the contents of the index register can be zero; after the first pass it will be incremented to one, after the second pass it will be two, and so on. This will modify the operation in the following way:

First pass	COM 112
Second pass	COM 113
Third pass	COM 114

Incrementing of the index register is performed automatically, if requested by the instruction, and is called autoincrementing.

Autoincrementing and Autodecrementing

Autoincrement addressing provides for automatic stepping of a pointer through the sequential elements of a table of operands. It can be used in an indexed operation or in a general register addressing operation.

In this mode, the address of the operand is taken from the general register, and then the contents of the register are stepped (incremented) to address the next word. Instructions of the form

$$OPR \ (R)+$$

specify autoincrement addressing.

In the same way, the instruction of the form

$$OPR \ -(R)$$

specifies autodecrement addressing.

These modes can also be indirect or deferred. Instructions are then of the form

$$OPR \ @ \ (R)+$$
$$OPR \ @ \ -(R).$$

Immediate Addressing

Immediate addressing provides time and space improvement for access of constant operands by including the constant in the instruction. In this computer, the assembler recognizes address expressions of the form, $\# n$, as immediate operands:

$$OPR \ \# \ n$$

This instruction is assembled in two computer words, the second word keeping the operand, n.

Absolute, Relative, and Deferred-Relative Addressing

These are standard modes of addressing, and here we shall only define their form.

Absolute addressing:

$$OPR \ @ \ \# \ A$$

Relative addressing (relative to the program counter):

$$\text{OPR @ A}$$

Deferred relative addressing:

$$\text{OPR @ A}$$

These instructions are assembled in two computer words, the second word keeping the displacement A.

12.3. INSTRUCTION SET AND PROGRAMMING EXAMPLES

The Instruction Set

The computer has a processor status register (PS), Fig. 12.4, which contains the information on the current priority of the processor, the results of previous operations and an indication for detecting the execution of an instruction to be trapped during program debugging. Four bits of the PS are assigned to monitoring different results of previous instructions. These bits are as follows:

Z if the result was zero.
N if the result was negative.
C if the operation resulted in a carry from the most significant bit.
V if the operation resulted in an arithmetic overflow.

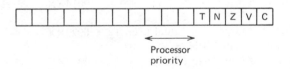

Figure 12.4. Processor status register (PS).

Table 12.1 PDP-11 Instruction Repertoire

Mnemonic	Instruction operation	OP code	Condition codes ZNCV	Timing
DOUBLE OPERAND GROUP: OPR scr, dst				
MOV(B)	MOVe (Byte) (src) → (dst)	.1SSDD	$\sqrt{}\ \sqrt{}\ -0$	2.3
CMP(B)	CoMPare (Byte) (src) − (dst)	.2SSDD	$\sqrt{}\ \sqrt{}\ \sqrt{}\ \sqrt{}$	2.3*
BIT(B)	BIt Test (Byte) (src) ∧ (dst)	.3SSDD	$\sqrt{}\ \sqrt{}\ -0$	2.9*
BIC(B)	BIt Clear (Byte) ~(src) ∧ (dst) → (dst)	.4SSDD	$\sqrt{}\ \sqrt{}\ -0$	2.9
BIS(B)	BIt Set (Byte) (src) ∨ (dst) → (dst)	.5SSDD	$\sqrt{}\ \sqrt{}\ -0$	2.3
ADD	ADD (src) + (dst) → (dst)	06SSDD	$\sqrt{}\ \sqrt{}\ \sqrt{}\ \sqrt{}$	2.3
SUB	SUBtract (dst) − (src) → (dst)	16SSDD	$\sqrt{}\ \sqrt{}\ \sqrt{}\ \sqrt{}$	2.3
CONDITIONAL BRANCHES: Bxx loc				
BR	BRanch (unconditionally) loc → (PC)	0004XX	——	2.6 −
BNE	Branch if Not Equal (Zero) loc → (PC) if Z = 0	0010XX	——	2.6 −
BEQ	Branch if Equal (Zero) loc → (PC) if Z = 1	0014XX	——	2.6 −
BGE	Branch if Greater or Equal (Zero) loc → (PC) if N $\veebar$ V = 0)	0020XX	——	2.6 −
BLT	Branch if Less Than (Zero) loc → (PC) if N $\veebar$ V = 1	0024XX	——	2.6 −
BGT	Branch if Greater Than (Zero) loc → (PC) if Z v (N $\veebar$ V = 0)	0030XX	——	2.6 −
BLE	Branch if Less Than or Equal (Zero) loc → (PC) if Z v (N $\veebar$ V) = 1	0034XX	——	2.6 −
BPL	Branch if Plus loc → (PC) if N = 0	1000XX	——	2.6 −
BMI	Branch if MInus loc → (PC) if N = 1	1004XX	——	2.6 −
BHI	Branch if HIgher loc → (PC) if C v Z = 0	1010XX	——	2.6 −
BLOS	Branch if LOwer or Same loc → (PC) if C v Z = 1	1014XX	——	2.6 −

BVC	Branch if oVerflow Clear loc → (PC) if V = 0	1020XX	——	2.6—
BVS	Branch if oVerflow Set loc → (PC) if V = 1	1024XX	——	2.6—
BCC (or BHIS)	Branch if Carry Clear loc → (PC) if C = 0	1030XX	——	2.6—
BCS (or BLO)	Branch if Carry Set loc → (PC) if C = 1	1034XX	——	2.6—

SUBROUTINE CALL: JSR reg, dst

JSR	Jump to SubRoutine (dst) → (tmp), (reg) ↓ (PC) → (reg), (tmp) → (PC)	004RDD	——	4.4

SUBROUTINE RETURN: RTS reg

RTS	ReTurn from Subroutine (reg) → PC, ↑ (reg)	00020R	——	3.5

SINGLE OPERAND GROUP: OPR dst

CLR(B)	CLeaR (Byte) 0 → (dst)	.050DD	1000	2.3
COM(B)	COMplement (Byte) ~ (dst) → (dst)	.051DD	√ √ 00	2.3
INC(B)	INCrement (Byte) (dst) + 1 → (dst)	.052DD	√ √ −√	2.3
DEC(B)	DECrement (Byte) (dst) − 1 → (dst)	.053DD	√ √ −√	2.3
NEG(B)	NEGate (Byte) ~ (dst) + 1 → (dst)	.054DD	√ √ √ √	2.3
ADC(B)	ADd Carry (Byte) (dst) + (C) → (dst)	.055DD	√ √ √ √	2.3
SBC(B)	SuBtract Carry (Byte) (dst) − (C) → (dst)	.056DD	√ √ √ √	2.3
TST(B)	TeST (Byte) 0 − (dst)	.057DD	√ √ 00	2.3*
ROR(B)	ROtate Right (Byte) rotate right 1 place with C	.060DD	√ √ √ √	2.3°
ROL(B)	ROtate Left (Byte) rotate left 1 place with C	.061DD	√ √ √ √	2.3°
ASR(B)	Arithmetic Shift Right (Byte) shift right with sign extension	.062DD	√ √ √ √	2.3°
ASL(B)	Arithmetic Shift Left (Byte) shift left with lo-order zero	.063DD	√ √ √ √	2.3°
JMP	JuMP (dst) → (PC)	0001DD	——	1.2
SWAB	SWAp Bytes bytes of a word are exchanged	0003DD	√ √ 00	2.3

CONDITION CODE OPERATORS: OPR   1.5

Condition Code Operators set or clear combinations of condition code bits. Selected bits are set if S = 1 and cleared otherwise. Condition code bits corresponding to bits set as marked in the word below are set or cleared.

CONDITION CODE OPERATORS:

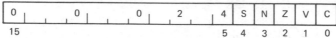

0	0	0	2	4	S	N	Z	V	C
15					5	4	3	2	1	0

Thus SEC = 000261 sets the C bit and has no effect on the other condition code bits (CLC = 000241 clears the C Bit)

OPERATE GROUP: OPR

HALT   HALT   000000   —   1.8
        processor stops; (RO) and the HALT address in lights

WAIT   WAIT   000001   —   1.8
        processor releases bus, waits for interrupt

RTI   ReTurn from Interrupt   000002   √ √ √ √   4.8
        ↑ (PC), ↑ (PS)

IOT   Input/Output Trap   000004   √ √ √ √   9.3
        (PS)↓, (PC)↓, (20) → (PC), (22) → (PS)

RESET   RESET   000005   —   20 ms.
        an INIT pulse is issued by the CP

EMT   EMulator Trap   104000—104377 √ √ √ √   9.3
        (PS)↓, (PC)↓, (30) → (PC), (32) → (PS)

TRAP   TRAP   104400—104777 √ √ √ √   9.3
        (PS)↓, (PC)↓, (34) → (PC), (36) → (PS)

The instruction set is shown in Table 12.1. Note the following details.

1. The computer has a group of double operand instructions. For example, the instruction MOV src, dst will take the operand from the source and will carry it to the destination. The addressing modes for the source and the destination are the same as for single operand instructions:

General register addressing: OPR RX,RY.
Deferred addressing: OPR @ RX, @ RY   or   OPR(RX),(RY).
Indexed addressing: OPR A(RX), B(RY).
Deferred indexed addressing: OPR @ A(RX), @ B(RY).
Autoincrement: OPR (RX)+, (RY)+.
Autoincrement deferred: OPR @ (RX)+, @ (RY)+.
Autodecrement: OPR −(RX), −(RY).

Autodecrement deferred: OPR @ $-$(RX), @ $-$(RY).

Immediate addressing: OPR # C, DEST.

Absolute addressing: OPR @ # A, DEST.

Relative addressing: OPR A, DEST.

Deferred relative addressing: OPR @ A, DEST.

2. The instruction can address the full word or a byte (*B*). For this reason the addresses of the full words are only even addresses.

3. Subroutine linkage instructions, JSR and RTS, and special instructions will be described separately.

Table 12.2

HIST:	MOV # OTABLE, R0	Set up to clear output table
	MOV = # $-$100., R1	100 entries in output table
CLOOP:	CLR(R0)+	Clear next entry
	INC R1	Check if done
	BNE CLOOP	If not, continue clearing
	MOV # ITABLE, R0	Set up input pointer
	MOV # $-$1000.,R1	Length of table
	MOV # 100., R2	Max input value
HLOOP:	MOV (R0) +, R4	Get next input value
	BLE NOCOUNT	Ignore if less than or equal zero
	CMP R4, R2	Check against max value
	BGT NOCOUNT	Ignore if greater
	ASL R4	2 bytes per table entry
	INC OTABLE (R4)	Increment proper element
NOCOUNT:	INC R1	Input done?
	BNE HLOOP	If not, continue scanning
	HALT	Histogram complete

Programming Example

This example demonstrates the generation of a table (histogram) that shows the frequency of occurrence of each value in another table within the range of values 1–100. Values outside the range 1–100 are ignored. The program is shown in Table 12.2. The flow chart is shown in Fig. 12.5. The whole program is split into six parts, *a* to *f*.

(*a*) Initialize the loop for clearing the output table. The instruction MOVE # OTABLE, R0 puts the address OTABLE into the register R0. The instruction MOVE # $-$100., R1 puts the number $-$100 into the register R1.

(*b*) The instruction CLR (R0)+ clears the first location, OTABLE. It

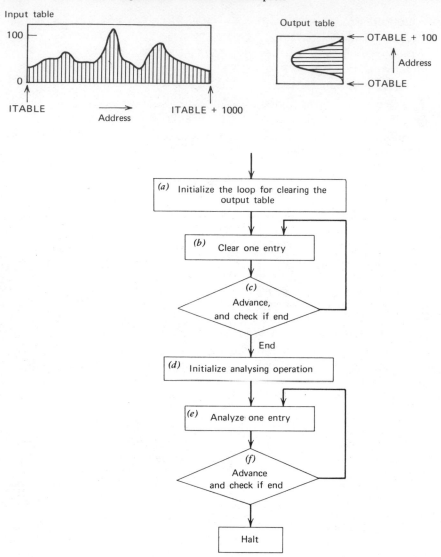

Figure 12.5. Generation of the histogram, flow chart.

also increments the contents of the register R0, so that they are now equal to OTABLE + 1 (preparation for the next entry).

(c) The instructions INC R1, BNE CLOOP perform counting until the contents of R1 change from the original value −100 to the value zero.

(d) The instruction MOV # ITABLE, R0 puts the address ITABLE into the register R0. The next two instructions load the register R1 with −1000 and R2 with 100. In this way the analyzing operation is initialized.

(e) The next four instructions take one item from ITABLE and check if it is in the range 0–100. If it is in this range, the instruction ASL R4 multiplies the value of the item by two (word addresses are only even addresses). The instruction INC OTABLE (R4) adds one to the effective address OTABLE + 2x (ITABLE + i), where i denotes that the ith item from ITABLE is analyzed.

(f) The last three instructions count the number of loops, and when the job is finished, they halt the program.

12.4. STACK, SUBROUTINES, AND INTERRUPTS

Stack

A stack is a dynamic sequential list of data with special provision for access from one end. A stack is also called a push down, or last-in-first-out list. Storage and retrieval from stacks are called *pushing* (↓) and *popping* (↑), respectively. These operations are illustrated in Fig. 12.6.

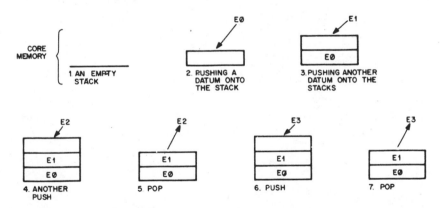

Figure 12.6. Illustration of push and pop operations (courtesy of Digital Equipment Corporation).

The stack has only one entry at the top of the stack. The address of this entry is stored in the general register R6, which is used as a stack pointer (SP). Using the SP, one can use the stack to store the information on it or to take it out.

Example. Saving the registers R0–R4 on the stack. The program segment for this job is shown in Table 12.3. This program will push the registers R0–R4 on the stack. R0 is at the top of the stack.

Table 12.3

SAVE:	MOV R4, −(SP)	R5 was pushed by the JSR
	MOV R3, −(SP	R5 will be at the bottom of the stack
	MOV R2, −(SP)	R4, R3, R2, R1, and R0 in order
	MOV R1, −(SP)	will be aobve it
	MOV R0, −(SP)	R0 is at the top of the stack

Example. Restoring the registers $R0$–$R4$ from the stack. The program segment for this job is shown in Table 12.4. Note that in the first example SP was autodecremented to point every time to one address higher on the stack. In the second example, SP was autoincremented to point every time to one address towards the bottom of the stack.

Table 12.4

MOV (SP) +, R0	The registers are restored
MOV (SP) +, R1	in reverse order to that in
MOV (SP) +, R2	which they were put on
MOV (SP) +, R3	the stack.
MOV (SP) +, R4	

The stack can be used in three ways:

- Through programming (as shown in the examples of Table 12.3 and Table 12.4)
- Automatically, when the subroutine instructions JSR and RTS are used
- Automatically, when interrupt occurs

Subroutines and Stacks

The subroutine call instruction is JSR reg, dst. During the execution of this instruction the computer hardware will automatically perform the following operations:

dst → (tmp)	Where *tmp* is an internal processor register.
reg ↓	Push register contents onto processor stack.
(PC) → (reg)	*PC* holds location following JSR; this address is now stored in register. Is will be used as a return address from the subroutine.
(tmp) → (PC)	Jump to subroutine at the destination address.

Note that the register is used to store the return address. The original contents of this register are automatically saved on the stack.

The return from the subroutine instruction RTS reg performs the following operations:

$(reg) \rightarrow PC$ Return address in the program counter.

$\uparrow (reg)$ Restore the old contents of the register by popping it from the stack.

Table 12.5 shows the example of the 16-bit unsigned integer multiply subroutine. The first instruction is jump to subroutine. It is followed by three locations, keeping the addresses of multiplicand, multiplier, and the product, respectively. In this example the register $R5$ is used to keep the return address.

Table 12.5

	JSR R5, MULT	
	.WORD MCAND	Address of multiplicand
	.WORD MPLIER	Address of multiplier
	.WORD PROD	Address of product
MULT:	CLR R0	
	MOV @ (R5)+, R1	Get multiplier into R1·
	MOV @ (R5)+, R2	Get multiplicand into R2
	MOV # −16., R3	Set counter
MLOOP:	ASL R0	Double prec shift
	ROL R1	Shift and add multiply
	BCC NOADD	Most significant bit governs add
	ADD R2, R0	If set add in multiplicand
	ADC R1	Keep 32-bit product
NOADD:	INC R3	Done?
	BNE MLOOP	If not continue
	MOV (R5)+, R2	Get address to store product
	MOV R0 (R2)+	Put low-order away, move to high
	MOV R1, (R2)	Put high-order away
	RTS R5	Return to calling program

Note the following important features of the subroutine-stack operation:

The subroutine call provides for automatic nesting of subroutines, re-entrancy, and multiple-entry points. Subroutines may call their subroutines (or indeed themselves) to any level of nesting without making special provision for storage of return addresses at each level of subroutine call. The subroutine calling mechanism modifies no fixed location in the memory and thus also provides for reentrancy. This allows one copy of a subroutine to be shared among several interrupting processes.

Interrupt and Stacks

The machine has four priority levels of interrupt. Thus, higher-level requests can interrupt the processing of lower-level interrupt service, and auto-

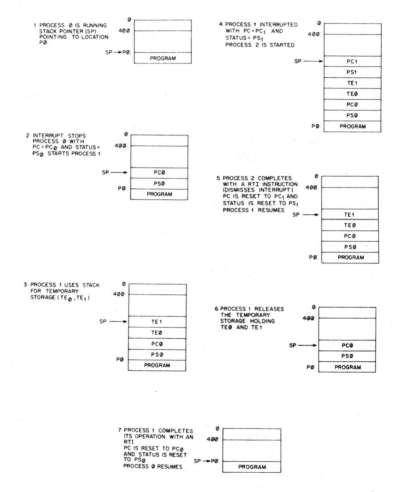

Figure 12.7. Stack and nested device servicing (courtesy of Digital Equipment Corporation).

matically return control to the lower-level interrupt service routine when the higher-level servicing is completed.

Every time an interrupt occurs, the processor automatically pushes the current central processor status (PS) and then the current program counter (PC) onto the stack.

Each interrupt routine is ended with the return from the interrupt instruction, RTI. This instruction performs the following operations:

$SP \uparrow (PC)$ Restore the program counter from the stack
$SP \uparrow (PS)$ Restore the processor status from the stack

An example of the use of the stack for nested servicing of interrupts and for temporary storage of data is shown in Fig. 12.7. Note that the SP always points to the top word of the stack.

12.5 UNIBUS INTERFACING

Unibus Lines

The unibus is the only bus in the PDP-11 that connects all peripheral devices, memories, and the central processor. The processor uses the same set of signals to communicate with all memories and devices. The important point here is that the form of communication used by the processor and peripheral devices is identical. Consequently, the same set of program instructions used to reference the memory is used to reference peripheral devices. Device-status registers, device-control registers and device-data registers are each assigned unique "memory" addresses. For example, the instruction MOVB R0, PUNCH would load the punch-buffer register with an 8-bit character contained in R0. Other instructions would monitor the punch status, and the program could determine when the punching operation was complete.

The unibus consists of 56 signal lines. All devices, including the processor, are connected to these lines in parallel, Fig. 12.8. The bidirectional nature of 51 signal lines permits signals to flow in either direction. The remaining five unidirectional lines are used for priority bus control. All 56 signals and their functions are listed in Table 12.6.

Data Transfer Signals

Address lines are used by the master device to select the slave with which it will communicate. Lines A(17:01) specify a unique 16-bit word. In byte operations, A00 specifies the byte being referenced. Peripheral devices are

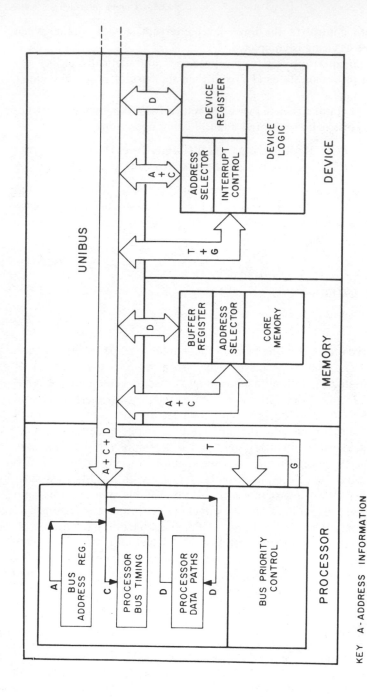

KEY A - ADDRESS INFORMATION
C - CONTROL + TIMING SIGNALS
D - DATA INFORMATION
T - CONTROL TRANSFER SIGNALS
G - BUS GRANT SIGNALS

Figure 12.8. Unibus interface block diagram (courtesy of Digital Equipment Corporation).

Table 12.6. Unibus Signals

Name	Mnemonic	Source	Destination	Timing	Function
Data transfer signals (for transfer of data to or from master)					
Address	A⟨17:00⟩	master	all	MSYN	Selects slave device
Data	D⟨15:00⟩	master	slave	MSYN (DATO, DATOB)	
		slave	master	SSYN (DATI, DATIP)	
Control	C⟨1:0⟩	master	slave	MSYN	Selects transfer operation
Master sync	MSYN	master	slave	Beginning of transfer	Initiates operation and gates A, C and D signals
Slave sync	SSYN	slave	master	Data accepted (DATO, DATOB) Data Available (DATI, DATIP)	Response to MSYN
Parity available	PA	master	slave	Same as Data	Indicates paritied data
Parity bit	PB	master	slave	Same as Data	Transmits parity bit
Priority transfer signals (for transfer of bus control to a priority selected master)					
Nonprocessor request	NPR	any	processor	Asynchronous	Highest priority bus request
Bus request	BR⟨7:4⟩	any	processor	Asynchronous	Requests bus mastership
Nonprocessor grant	NPG	processor	next master	In parallel with data transfer	Transfers bus control
Bus grant	BG⟨7:4⟩	processor	next master	After instruction	Transfers bus control
Selection acknowledge	SACK	next master	processor	Response to NPG or BG	Acknowledges grant and inhibits further grants
Bus busy	BBSY	master	all	Except during transfer of control	Asserts bus mastership
Interrupt	INTR	master	processor	After asserting BBSY (not after NPR) device may perform several transfers before asserting INTR.	Transfers bus control to handling routine in processor

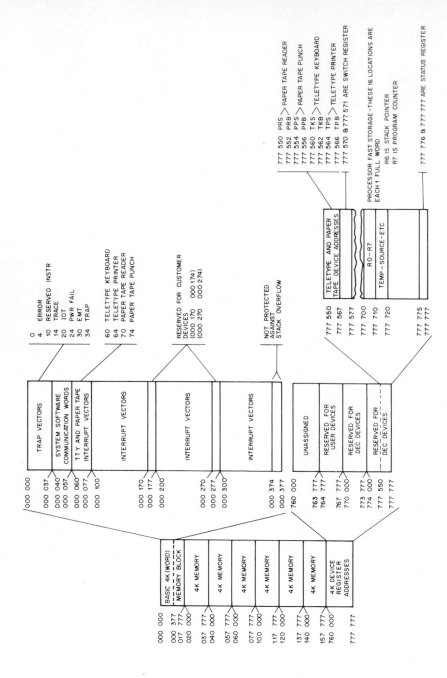

Figure 12.9. PDP-11 Address map (courtesy of Digital Equipment Corporation).

490

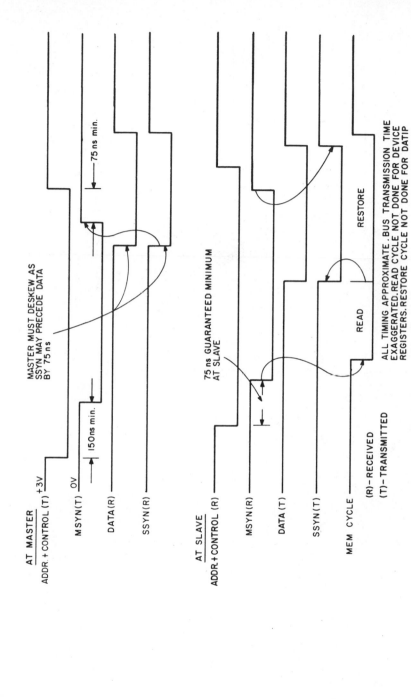

Figure 12.10. Master-slave interlocking. (*a*) DATI timing diagram; (*b*) DATO timing diagram (courtesy of Digital Equipment Corporation).

491

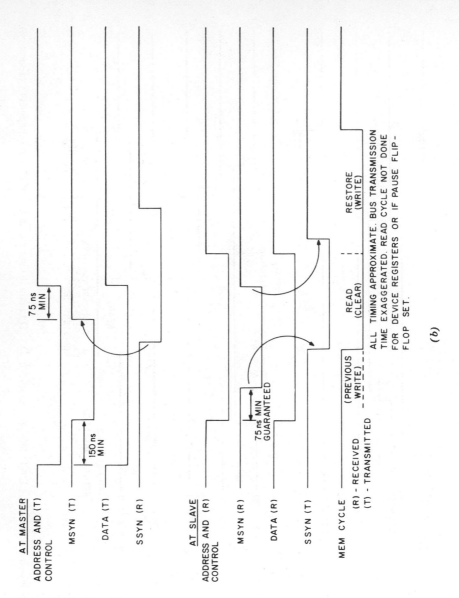

Figure 12.10. (*Cont'd.*)

492

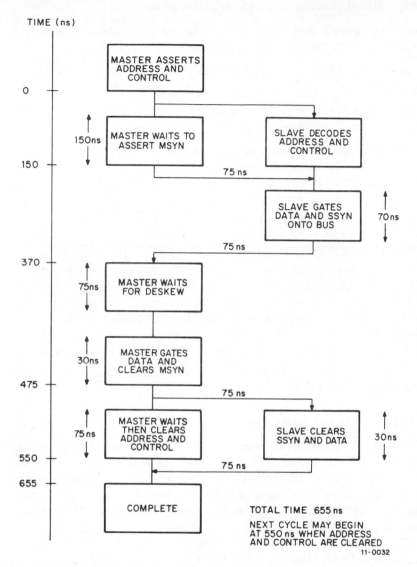

Figure 12.11. Typical DATI timing flow (courtesy of Digital Equipment Corporation).

normally assigned an address from within the bus address allocations from 760000–777777. The address map is shown in Fig. 12.9.

Data lines D(15:00) are used to transfer information between the master and the slave.

Control lines C(1:0) specify one of four possible transfer operations (two input and two output modes).

Master slave Synchronization Lines. All bus activity is asynchronous and depends on interlocking of control signals. In every case the master generates the signal MSYN. The slave responds with SSYN. The master signal is dropped in response to the slave signal. Figure 12.10 shows the timing for two basic operations: DATI (data in, from the slave to the master) and DATO (data out, from the master to the slave).

Example of DATO. The master sets control for DATO, sets address for the unique slave device, and sets data for the information to be transferred. The master then asserts MSYN. This signal is received by the slave that recognizes its address; it responds by accepting the data and asserting SSYN, SSYN is received by the master which then negates control, address, data, and MSYN. The slave sees MSYN negated and negates SSYN. The master device continues its operation when it sees SSYN negated.

Example of DATI. The operation is similar as above, and shown schematically in Fig. 12.11.

Basic Interface and Address Selector

When the basic read/write interface is used, data transfers are under the control of the program, and the register is assigned an address on the unibus. As shown in Fig. 12.12, the basic interface uses an address-selector module to decode the unibus address lines and to control the clocking of information into the register and the gating of output information from the register the the bus data lines.

The address-selector module provides gating signals for up to four device registers. A block diagram of this module is shown in Fig. 12.13. Line A00 is used for byte control.

Lines A01 and A02 are decoded to select one of four addressable device registers (SELECT 0, 2, 4, and 6).

Lines A(12:03) are used to select the device. The device address is determined by jumpers on the module. Address lines A(17:13) must all be ones. This specifies an address within the top 8K byte address bounds for device registers.

Lines C(1:0) determine the input or output operation.

The signal MSYN comes from the master and the slave responds with the SSYN.

The right-hand side of Fig. 12.13 shows the gating of the bit 07 of the device data register to unibus line D07. The gating is identical for the other 15 bits.

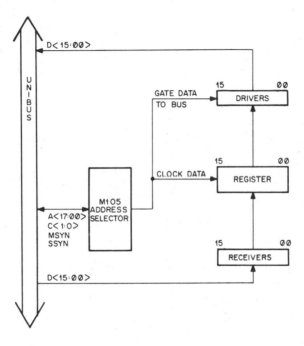

Figure 12.12. Basic interface—block diagram (courtesy of Digital Equipment Corporation).

12.6.   PROGRAMMING OF PERIPHERALS

The actual transfer of data between a device and the unibus takes place through one or more registers in the device. The registers may be the data registers, as in the exampl or control-status registers (CSR).

The control word and the status word are stored in one 16-bit CSR. The preferred bit assignment is given in Fig. 12.14a. The exact nature of register assignments varies with each device. Figure 12.14b shows the control-status register of a high-speed paper-tape reader.

Now we show examples of programmed I/O transfer with the paper tape reader. The device will have the control-status register, to which we give the symbolic name PRS, and the data register, with the symbolic name PRB.

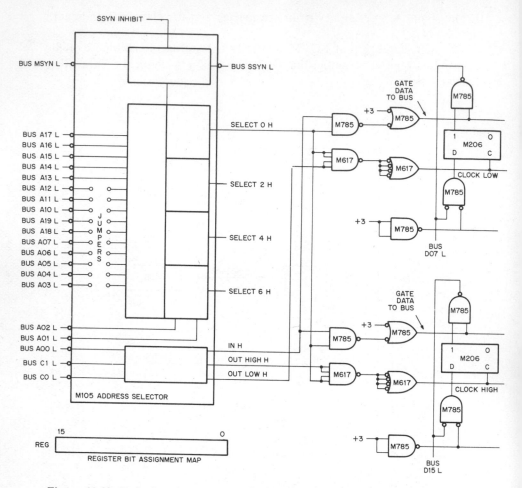

Figure 12.13. Basic interface—circuit schematic (courtesy of Digital Equipment Corporation).

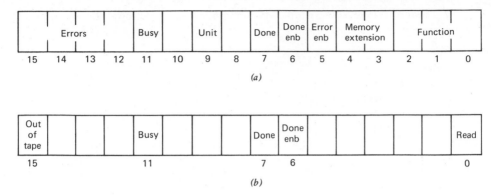

Figure 12.14. Control-status register (CSR). (*a*) Preferred bit assignment; (*b*) CSR of a high-speed paper-tape reader.

Example. Input of characters. The program is shown in Table 12.7. The characters should be stored sequentially in the list with the starting address BUFFER. When the address LIMIT on the list is reached, further inputting of characters should be stopped. Note the following important details:

1. The instruction INC PRS will set bit 0 in the PRS register. This bit instructs the device to read one character.

2. The instruction BIT PRS, # 100200 tests if the contents of the PRS register are equal to 100200. This is the pattern for BUSY and DONE bits.

3. The instruction MOVB PRB, (R)+ moves 1 byte (character) from the reader data register PRB into the location BUFFER. It also increments *R* to prepare the pointer BUFFER + 1 for the next input.

Table 12.7

	MOV R, −(SP)	Save R on the stack
	MOV # BUFFER, R	Pointer to input buffer into register R
START:	INC PRS	Start up reader
LOOP:	BIT PRS, #100200	Test DONE and ERROR bits
	BEQ LOOP	Branch back if none on yet
	BMI ERROR	Branch to error routine if minus
	MOVB PRB, (R)+	Move byte from device buffer register to user's buffer and increment pointer
	CMP #LIMIT, R	Check for end of buffer
	BGE START	Get next character
	MOV (SP)+, R	Restore R

Example. Character output to the paper tape punch. The program is shown in Table 12.8. The operation is similar to previous example.

Table 12.8

	MOV	R0, −(SP)	Save R0
	MOVE	R1, −(SP)	Save R1
	MOV	NCHAR, R0	Number of characters into R0
	MOV	BUFFER, R1	User buffer address into R1
LOOP:	BIT	PPS, . . 100200	Test device ready and error bits
	BEQ	LOOP	Fall through if on
	BMI	ERROR	Branch on error
	MOVB	(R1) +, PPB	Output character, increment pointer
	DEC	R0	Decrement character counter (and set condition doces
	BGT	LOOP	Repeat if greater than zero
	MOV	(SP) +, R0	Restore R0
	MOV	(SP) +, R1	Restore R1

Programmed Device Interface

Figure 12.15 shows an example of the program controlled interface with an analog-to-digital convertor (ADC). The interface functionally operates with three-bus addresses. One address is assigned for the multiplexer (ADMUX) register, which is used to select one of the 64 analog inputs. The second address is for the converted digital output (ADDBR) register, and the third address is assigned to a 1-bit control and status register (ADSCR).

The program initiates the following tasks: the START CONVERSION signal is generated in this interface by the CLOCK ADMUX signal, which loads the multiplexer register, tests the READY (CONVERSION COMPLETE) bit until the bit is set, and then transfers the data from the digital output lines of the ADC to the processor. The program is shown in Table 12.9. INPUT is a location containing the number of the desired analog input line.

Table 12.9

	MOV INPUT, ADMUX	Select analog input
READY:	TSTB ADCSR	Check for conversion complete
	BPL READY	No, test again
	MOV ADDBR, R4	Yes, obtain data

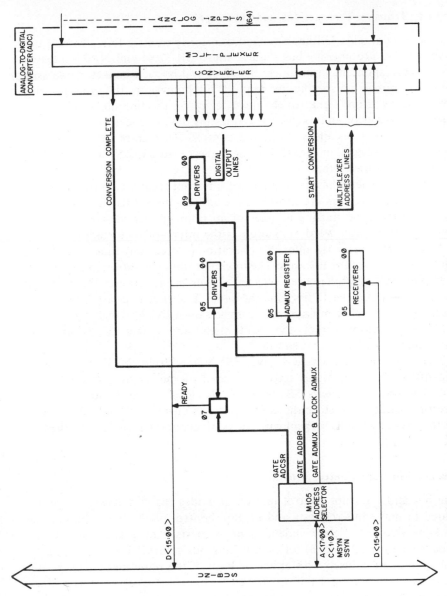

Figure 12.15. Programmed device interface, block diagram (courtesy of Digital Equipment Corporation).

499

Priority Transfer Transactions and Interrupts

The unibus contains 13 lines classified as priority transfer lines, Table 12.6. Five of these are priority bus request lines, BR (7:4) and NPR, and five are the corresponding grant lines, BG (7:4) and NPG, which the processor uses to respond to a specific bus request. Each device of the same priority level passes a grant signal to the next device on the line unless it has requested bus control; in this case the requesting device blocks the signal from the following devices and assumes bus control. An example of this priority chaining is illustrated in Fig. 12.16. The highest priority is NPR, and then in order are priorities 7 to 4.

Each priority level has its own pair of interrupt locations in the memory. These interrupt vectors are shown in the address map, Fig. 12.9. Two consecutive words, the starting address of an interrupt service routine and a new processor status word are stored at the interrupt vector address.

A device may cause the interrupt operation to occur any time it gains bus control with one of the BR lines. The interrupt timing is shown in Fig. 12.17.

1. A device which has been selected as bus master asserts INTR and a vector address on the D lines, at the same time that is clears SACK and asserts BBSY. SACK must remain asserted until INTR is asserted.

2. The processor receives the INTR signal and asserts SSYN when the data (interrupt vector) are read in.

3. The interrupting device receives SSYN and clears INTR, the D lines, and BBSY. This constitutes active release of the bus to the processor.

4. The processor clears SSYN when INTR is cleared, and enters the interrupt sequence to store the contents of the current *PC* and *PS* registers on the stack, and replace them with the contents of the location specified by the vector address.

Bus and Interrupt Control Module

The bus and interrupt control module provides the circuits and logic required to make bus requests and to gain control of the bus. The module contains two completely independent requests and grant-acknowledge circuits (channels A and B) for establishing bus control. The interrupt control circuit can be used with either or both of the requested channels and provides a unique vector address for each channel. Figure 12.18 is a block diagram of the module interconnection for two-channel interrupt.

Interrupt Serviced Interface

Figure 12.19 shows an example of the interrupt serviced interface for an analog-to-digital converter (ADC). The main difference between this interface

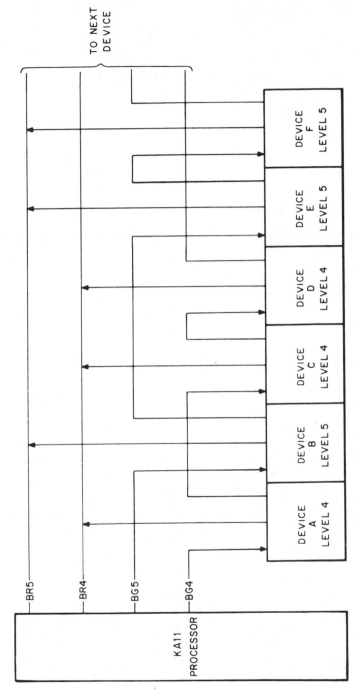

Figure 12.16. Priority-chaining example (courtesy of Digital Equipment Corporation).

501

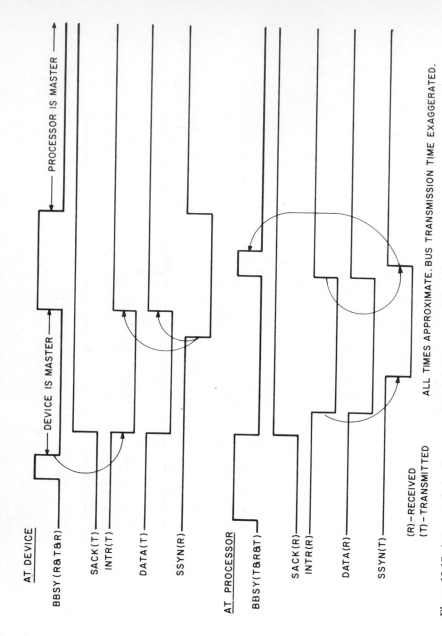

AT DEVICE

BBSY(R&T&R)

SACK(T)
INTR(T)

DATA(T)

SSYN(R)

AT PROCESSOR

BBSY(T&R&T)

SACK(R)
INTR(R)

DATA(R)

SSYN(T)

DEVICE IS MASTER — PROCESSOR IS MASTER —

(R) – RECEIVED
(T) – TRANSMITTED   ALL TIMES APPROXIMATE. BUS TRANSMISSION TIME EXAGGERATED.

Figure 12.17. Interrupt timing (courtesy of Digital Equipment Corporation).

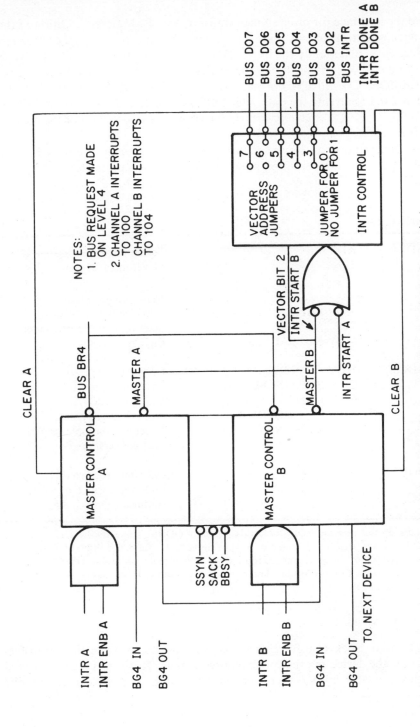

Figure 12.18. Bus and interrupt control module (courtesy of Digital Equipment Corporation).

503

and the interface for programmed transfer, Fig. 12.15, is the addition of the interrupt control module. The interrupt serviced interface allows the processor to execute concurrently the instructions of another program while the ADC performs a cycle of operation. The processor responds to a READY (CONVERSION COMPLETE) signal from the ADC by interacting with the device and analyzing the data after they have been collected. An additional flip-flop is used to enable or disable interrupt operation (bit 6 of the control status register).

A typical interrupt service routine that collects data from the ADC and enters an evaluation routine after the final conversion cycle is shown in Table 12.10.

Table 12.10[a]

ADCVEC:	ADCSER	Set up ADC vector area
	240	Status includes priority level 5
	⋮	
	⋮	Main program follows
	MOV BUFSTRT,BUFADR	Initialize buffer pointer
	CLR ADMUX	Start multiplexer at channel 0
	MOV # 100, ADCSR	Enable interrupt
	⋮	
ADCSER:	MOV ADDBR, @ BUFADR	Collect data
	CMP BUFADR,BUFSTRT+174	Last one?
	BEQ DONE	Yes, go to DONE
	ADD # 2, BUFADR	No, increment pointer
	INC ADMUX	Increment multiplexer and start conversion
	RTI	
DONE:	CLR ADCSR	Clear interrupt enable
	⋮	Follow this with the evaluation routines

[a] The addresses used are ADCSR, ADMUX, and ADDBR. These are the device registers in the interface. BUFSTRT contains the starting address of a buffer. BUFADR is a location to be used by the device service routine. ADCVEC is the address specified by jumpers on the Interrupt Control Module and contains the address of the device service routine tagged ADCSER.

Block Transfer

High-speed block transfer devices use the unibus to make data transfers between the device and the core memory (*DMA*). These devices are provided with addressible registers that control the flow of data. A typical set might be

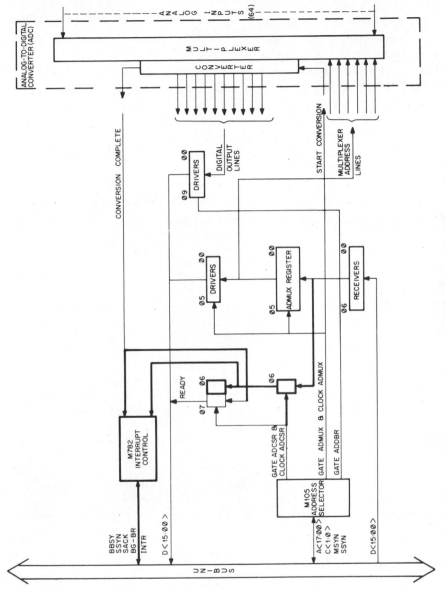

Figure 12.19. Interrupt serviced interface (courtesy of Digital Equipment Corporation).

505

Control and status register (DKS)
Memory-address register (DKMA)
Word-count register (DKWC)
Device address register (DKDA)

Loading the device-address register would in general initiate the transfer, which then will proceed without processor intervention. The device issues nonprocessor requests for the unibus. These requests, when granted, allow direct data transfer between the device and the memory. These requests are interleaved with processor requests for the bus.

The DONE or appropriate error bits are set in the CSR with completion of the transfer or when an error occurs. These can cause an interrupt or can be tested to determine when the device needs assistance.

The program is shown in Table 12.11. The first half initializes the DMA transfer. The second part is a loop which tests to see if the transfer is performed. The transfer itself is performed without program intervention as a job parallel with the loop.

Table 12.11

MOV #401, DKS	Read block of data (function 1) from unit 1
MOV #BUFARD, DKMA	Buffer address to memory-address register
MOV #BUFCNT, DKWC	Word count to word-count register
MOV #BLKNO, DKDA	Block number to device-address register, which starts the transfer; when data is needed.
⋮	
LOOP: BIT #DKMSK, DKS	Test done bit and error bits
BEQ LOOP	Branch back if none on
BIT #DKEMSK, DKS	Test for any error bits
BNE ERROR	Branch if any on; data is now in buffer at BUFADR

12.7. LSI-11 MICROCOMPUTER

Basic Chips

Large-scale integration (LSI) technology has made it possible to achieve high performance and reliability in smaller packages and at lower costs. Digital Equipment Corporation has taken advantage of this technology by developing a chip set in the form and function of a PDP-11. This set consists of four distinct chips, each a 40-pin, dual-in-line package. The four chips are the control chip, the data chip, and two microm (microcode read only memory) chips.

Control Chip. This chip provides the microinstruction address sequence for the microm and control for the data access port. It contains the following features:

• Programmable translation array (PTA): provides a decoding mechanism for generating microinstruction addresses from macroinstructions.
• Location counter (LC): used to store the location in the microm from which accesses are being made.
• Return register (RR): used to hold a subroutine return address.
• Data access control logic: provides control and timing signals for the data access port.
• Interrupt logic: provides control over three internal flags for the processor and four external flags for the system.

Data Chip. The data chip incorporates the paths, registers, and logic to execute microinstructions. It offers the following features:

• Register file: provides multiple registers for storage of frequently required data.
• Arithmetic and logic unit (ALU): performs the arithmetic and logic operations necessary for instruction execution.
• Condition flags logic: monitors the status of the result from the ALU section.
• Data access port: provides access to the data address lines.

Microm Chips. The microm chips provide storage of the microcode of the basic PDP-11/35, 11/40 instruction set, resident ODT (octal debugging technique) firm ware, resident ASCII/console routine, and bootstrap.

An additional fifth chip (third microm) can be added to the LSI-11 processor to extend the instruction set to include fixed- and floating-point arithmetic functions.

LSI-11 Bus Concept

The bus is a simple, fast, easy-to-use interface between LSI-11 modules. All LSI-11 modules connected to this common bidirectional bus structure receive the same interface signal lines. A typical system application in which the processor module, memory modules, and peripheral device interface modules are connected to the bus is shown in Fig. 12.20.

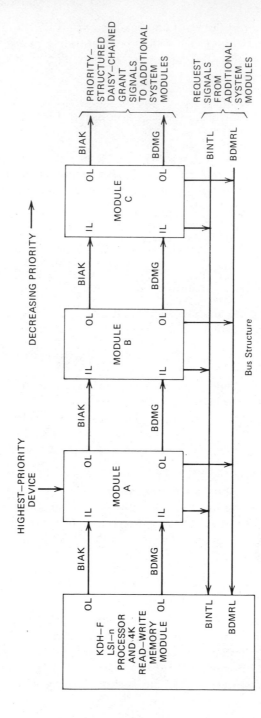

Figure 12.20. LSI-11 bus and priority structure. (Courtesy of Digital Equipment Corporation).

Bus data and control lines are bidirectional open collector lines that are asserted low. The bus is composed of 16 data/address lines, 18 control/synchronization signal lines, and maintenance lines. Control signal lines include two daisy-chained grant signals (four signal pins), which provide a priority-structured I/O system. The highest-priority device is the module electrically located closest to the microcomputer module. Higher-priority devices pass a grant signal to lower-priority devices only when not requesting service. For example, "module A," shown in Fig. 12.20, is the highest-priority device and is capable of interrupting processor operation (when interrupts are enabled) or executing *DMA* transfers at any time. Modules B and C have lower and still lower priorities, respectively, and can receive a grant signal when module A is not requesting service. Similarly, module C can receive a grant signal when neither module A nor module B is requesting service.

Both address and data words (or bytes) are multiplexed over the 16-bit bus. For example, during a programmed data transfer, the processor first asserts an address on the bus for a fixed time. After the address time has been completed, the processor executes the programmed input or output data transfer; the actual data transfer is asynchronous and requires a reply from the addressed device. Bus synchronization and control signals provide this function.

The processor module is capable of driving six device slots (double-height) along the bus, as supplied. Devices or memory can be installed in any location along this bus; however, special memory control signals for memory bank selects cannot extend beyond the first six slots.

The processor's on-board memory address latch and address decoder addresses both the processor module's 4K *RAM* and generates bank-select signals on the bus. Bank-select signals can select 4K memory banks up to a maximum of 32K.

The bus provides a vectored interrupt interface for any device. Hence device polling is not required in interrupt processing routines. This results in a considerable savings in processing time when many devices requiring interrupt service are interfaced along the bus. When a device receives an interrupt grant signal, the processor inputs the device's interrupt vector. The vector points to two addresses which contain a new processor status word and the starting address of the interrupt service routine for the device.

One input signal line functions as an external event interrupt line via a Schmitt trigger circuit on the processor module. This signal line can be connected to a frequency source, such as a line frequency, and used as a real-time interrupt. A switch on the processor module enables or inhibits this function. When enabled, the device connected to this line has the highest interrupt priority external to the processor. Interrupt vector 100_8 is reserved for this function, and an interrupt request via the external event line causes new *PC* and *PS* words to be loaded from locations 100_8 and 102_8.

Input/Output Operations

Every processor instruction requires one or more I/O operations. The first operation required is a data input transfer (DATI), which fetches an instruction from the location addressed by the program counter (*PC* or *R7*). This operation is called a DATI bus cycle. If no operands are referred to in memory or in an I/O device, no additional bus cycles are required for instruction execution. However, if memory or a device is referred to, additional DATI, data input pause [DATIO(B)], or data output transfer (DATO) bus cycles are required. Between these bus cycles, the processor can service *DMA* requests. In addition, the processor can service interrupt requests only before instruction FETCH DATI bus cycles when the *PS* word bit 7 is 0.

The following paragraphs describe the types of bus cycles. Note that the sequences for I/O operations between processor and memory or between processor and I/O device are identical. DATO (or DATOB) cycles are equivalent to write operations, and DATI cycles are equivalent to read operations. In addition, DATIO(B) cycles provide an efficient means of executing an equivalent read/modify/write operation by making it unnecessary to assert an address a second time.

Input Operations. The sequence for a DATI operation is illustrated in Fig. 12.21 and Table 12.12. These operations are asynchronous and depend on the previous operation being successfully completed. The processor waits for the addressed memory or device to assert BREPLY L in response to its input request (BDIN L), for 10 μsec (normal response). However, if

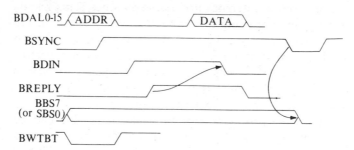

Note: Actual LSI-11 bus signals are asserted low (L)

Figure 12.21. Input cycle signal sequence. (Courtesy of Digital Equipment Corporation).

Table 12.12

Bus Signal	Signal Function
BDA L 0-15 L	Buffered Data/Address Lines. Addresses and data are multiplexed over this 16-line bus.
BWTBT L	Write/Byte, control signal. When asserted at address time, it signals a write transaction; at data time, a byte output.
BHALT L	Run/Halt line. Devices can assert this line to halt processor operation.
BBS7 L	I/O select signal–upper 4K addresses
BREF L	Refresh Select. This signal overrides SBS0-6L when doing a memory refresh operation.
BDIN L	Data input transfer control signal.
BDOUT L	Data output transfer control signal.
BSYNC L	Synchronize control signal. The microcomputer or a DMA module asserts this signal during all addressing and data I/O operations.
BREPLY L	Reply control signal. This signal is a response to BDIN L or BDOUT L.
BINT L	Interrupt request.
BIAK I L	Interrupt Grant In. ⎱ Daisy-chained signal generated in response to BINT L.
BIAK O L	Interrupt Grant Out. ⎰
BINIT L	Initialize. This signal is asserted by the processor to clear or initialize all system devices.
BDMR L	Direct Memory Access Request.
BDMG I L	Direct Memory Access Grant In. ⎱ Daisy-chained signal generated in response to BDMR L.
BDMG O L	Direct Memory Access Grant Out. ⎰
BEVNT L	External Event Line input to processor.
BPOKH	Power Okay. This input signal is asserted when system ac power is normal.
BDCOK H	DC Power Okay. This input signal is asserted by the power supply when there is sufficient dc voltage available to sustain reliable system operation.

BREPLY is not asserted during that time (error condition), the processor traps through location 4 and clears the bus signals. Figure 12.21 shows relative signal timing.

Observe that BWTBT L is not asserted during the address time; this always indicates that an input data transfer is to be executed.

DATIP cycles are the DATI portion of the read/modify/write operation. An address and an input word are first executed in a manner similar to the DATI cycle; however, BSYNC L remains in the active state after completing the input data transfer. This causes the addressed device to remain selected, and an output transfer follows without any further device addressing. After completing the output transfer, the device terminates BSYNC L, completing the DATIP cycle.

Output Operations. The sequence required for a DATO or DATOB bus cycle is shown in Fig. 12.22. Like the input operations, failure to receive BREPLY L within 10 μsec after asserting BDOUT L is an error, resulting in a time-out trap through location 4. Relative timing is shown in the output cycle signal diagram (Fig. 12.22).

Observe that BWTBT L will be asserted during the address time to indicate that an output data transfer is to follow. If a DATOB is to be executed, BWTBT L remains active for the duration of the bus cycle; however, if a DATO (word transfer) is to be executed, BWTBT L goes passive during the remainder of the cycle.

Direct Memory Access Operations

Direct memory access I/O operations involve a peripheral device and system memory. A device can transfer data to or from the 4K memory on the processor module or any read/write memory module along the bus. The actual sequence of operations for executing the data transfer, once a device has been granted *DMA* bus control, is as already described for I/O bus cycles, except that the device, not the processor, controls the operation. Memory addressing, timing, and control signal generation/response are provided by logic contained on the device's *DMA* interface module; the processor is not involved with address and data transfers during a *DMA* operation.

Interrupts

A device can interrupt the processor only when interrupts are enabled and the device in question is the closest one requesting interrupt service. The

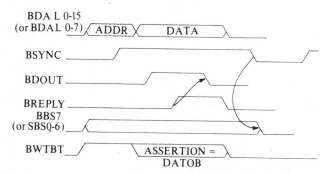

Figure 12.22. Output cycle signal sequence. (Courtesy of Digital Equipment Corporation).

microcomputer *PS* word bit 7 is 1 when external interrupts are disabled. Device priority is highest for devices electrically closest to the processor along the bus. However, the external event line is the highest-priority external interrupt request.

Any device that can interrupt the processor can also interrupt the service routine execution of a lower-priority device if the *PS* word bit 7 is 0; consequently, interrupt nesting to any level is possible with this interrupt structure. Each device normally contains a control status register (*CSR*), which includes an interrupt enable bit. A program must set this bit before an interrupt request can actually be issued by a device.

REFERENCES

1. PDP-11 Handbook, Digital Equipment Corp., Maynard, Mass., 1974.
2. PDP-11 Unibus Interface Manual, Digital Equipment Corp., Maynard, Mass., 1974.
3. LSI-11 Microcomputer, Digital Equipment Corp., Maynard, Mass., 1975.

13

F8 MICROPROCESSOR

Chapter 13 presents the 8-bit Fairchild F-8 microprocessor. The *CPU* contains two I/O ports and 64 general registers and is connected over an 8-bit data bus with *ROM* and memory interface chips. Memory interface provides 16-bit address lines for memory expansion. Each memory circuit has a local timer to generate program-initiated delays. Each *ROM* has an interrupt line, and interrupt requests may be daisy-chained together in any order to form a priority level of interrupts. Within each local interrupt control circuit is a 16-bit interrupt address vector. The instruction set and programming examples are described.

The material* in this chapter has been adapted in part from a publication of Fairchild Camera and Instruments Co. The material so published herein is the full responsibility of the author.

13.1. GENERAL FEATURES

The F8 family of microprocessor circuits is manufactured using N-channel isoplanar MOS technology. Some of the features and characteristics of this microprocessor set are the following:

- Eight-bit data organization.
- Instruction cycle time of 2 μsec
- Over 70 instructions
- Sixty-four general-purpose read/write registers
- Binary and decimal arithmetic and logic functions
- Internal clock generation
- Internal power-on and reset
- Input/output capability included on the circuits
- Multilevel interrupt system
- Programmable interval timers

---

* Programs, figures, and tables are courtesy and copyright © 1975 by Fairchild Camera and Instruments Co. All rights reserved.

A complete microprocessor system constructed with F8 components requires as few as two integrated circuits. Larger, more powerful systems may be built with additional F8 components. The family of F8 parts contains the following:

- 3850 Central processing unit (*CPU*).
- 3851 Read only memory (*ROM*).
- 3852 Dynamic memory interface (*MI*).
- 3853 Static memory interface (*MI*).
- 3854 Direct memory access (*DMA*).

These circuits may be combined to form an 8-bit microprocessor. Additional semiconductor components such as memories can easily be added to expand the full system capability.

Central Processing Unit

The *CPU* contains the following features:

- An accumulator
- Sixty-four scratch-pad registers
- Two I/O ports
- Interrupt control circuitry
- Power-on detect
- Clock circuits that can be operated in one of three modes: an *RC* network, crystal control, external master frequency.

Central Processing Unit Data Busses

Figure 13.1 shows the data path organization of all major fun.   .1 blocks in the *CPU*. Data within this chip are transmitted between blocks via four busses. These are as follows:

The Result Bus. The result bus receives the results of the arithmetic and logic unit (*ALU*) operation and makes them available for storage in one of the receiving registers associated with the system. Data from the result bus are passed on to either the *W* register (status), the accumulator, the scratch-pad register, or the indirect scratch-pad address register, or are gated to the data bus through the transfer gate(s) for availability in the I/O port or for transmission over the external data bus to the rest of the circuits in the F8 system.

Left Multiplexer Bus. The left multiplexer bus gates the accumulator into one of the operand ports in the *ALU*.

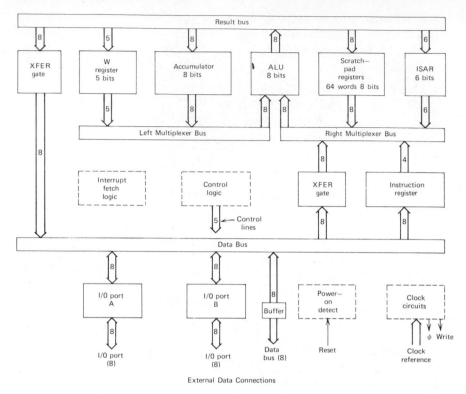

Figure 13.1. F8 *CPU* circuit data path organization: 3850. (Courtesy of Fairchild Camera and Instruments Co.)

When the contents of the status register are transferred, they are gated through the *ALU* from the left multiplexer to the result bus.

Right Multiplexer Bus. The right multiplexer bus transfers the second operand required by the *ALU*. This operand may be taken from the scratch-pad registers, from the scratch-pad address register, from the instruction register (used only when immediate operands are contained in the instruction), or from the data bus via the transfer gates. The data bus permits the operands to be extracted either from other chips associated with the microprocessor system or from the I/O ports contained on the *CPU*.

The Data Bus. The data bus is the principal path for transmitting 8-bit bytes between the *CPU* and other circuits in a microprocessor system. It also transmits data between the *CPU* I/O ports and the accumulator. Data entering the *CPU* may originate from a *ROM*, a *RAM*, or the memory interface circuits. Three types of information are transmitted on the data bus:

- Data (or operands)
- Input/output port addresses used for activating an I/O port designated by an I/O instruction
- Program address transmitted during branch or interrupt functions

Information travels into and out of the *CPU* over the data bus.

Central Processing Unit Registers

Figure 13.1 shows the major *CPU* registers and their relationship with respect to the *CPU* busses. These *CPU* registers are as follows:

- The accumulator
- The *ALU*.
- The *W* (status) register.
- The scratch-pad registers and the indirect scratch-pad address registers (ISARs).
- The I/O ports.

Each of these registers is described below.

The Accumulator. The accumulator is an 8-bit storage register. It retains the result of *ALU* operations and transfers information into and out of the scratch-pad memory, bulk memory, and I/O ports. The contents of the accumulator may be either shifted or complemented.

Arithmetic Logic Unit (ALU). The *ALU* is an 8-bit, parallel logic network used in the execution of the F8 instructions. Binary and decimal ADD operations may be executed. In addition, complement, logical AND, logical OR, logical XOR, increment, compare, and decrement operations may be executed. One operand of the *ALU* is usually supplied by the accumulator. The other operand may be either scratch-pad memory data, bulk memory data, the ISAR, or the instruction register. Outputs from the *ALU* are placed in the accumulator via the result bus.

W (Status) Register. The *W* register stores the status indications resulting from an arithmetic or logic operation (Fig. 13.2).

There are four condition codes in the F8, namely, positive, zero, overflow, and carry. The user can test for any of these four or any combination of them. The logical implications of these 4 bits are as follows:

(*a*) Positive: set by the most significant bit of the result being zero.
(*b*) Zero: set by the result being zero.

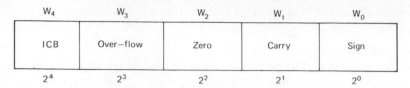

Figure 13.2. W (status) Register. (Courtesy of Fairchild Camera and Instruments Co.).

(*c*) Carry: set by the carry coming out of the most significant bit.

(*d*) Overflow: set by exclusive *OR*, the carry from the 7th and 8th bits. This is an indication of a change of sign in signed arithmetic.

There is also:

(*e*) The interrupt control bit (ICB), used to mask the *CPU* interrupt sequence. If the ICB is set, the *CPU* may be interrupted. However, a zero in the ICB causes interrupts to be ignored.

The Scratch-pad Registers and Indirect Scratch-pad Address Registers *(ISAR).* The *CPU* contains 64 8-bit registers. Systems requiring more than 64 bytes of read/write memory may be expanded with multiple-sourced memories such as the 2102, connected to the *CPU* via an F8 memory interface (*MI*) circuit.

There are two modes of addressing the scratch-pad registers:

- Direct addressing of the lowest-order 12 bytes of scratch pad
- Indirect addressing of any of the 64 bytes of scratch pad

Direct address is performed by a one-byte instruction. The first 4 bits are the op code, while the remaining bits are the scratch-pad memory location. Indirect addressing of scratch-pad memory locations is also performed in one byte. In this case, however, the indirect scratch-pad address register (*ISAR*) points to the desired scratch-pad location.

Figure 13.3 is a diagram of the organization of the scratch-pad registers. Notice that only the lower registers of the scratch pad may be directly addressed. All 64 registers in the scratch pad, however, may be indirectly addressed, using the 6-bit *ISAR*.

Special assignments in the scratch pad are used by specific instructions to link the program counter, the stack register, the status register, and the data counter to the scratch pad. This allows a multiple-level software system under interrupt control. The Q and the K locations are generally used for storing address vectors of 16 bits from either the program counter or the stack register. The Q registers are scratch-pad registers 14 and 15. The K registers are address locations 12 and 13. Scratch-pad locations 10 and 11 are designed as the H registers, while location 9 is the J register.

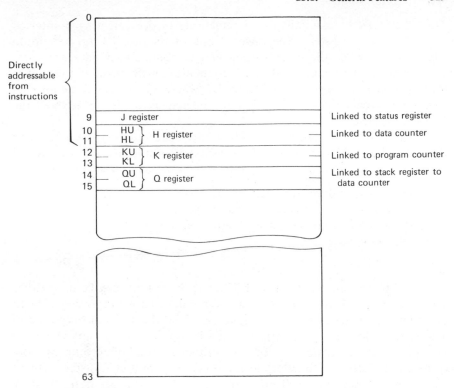

Figure 13.3. Scratch-pad registers. (Courtesy of Fairchild Camera and Instruments Co.).

Memory reference instructions that access information storage some-where in 65,536 bytes of bulk memory use a 16-bit address contained in the data counters in the memory chips. Addresses may be loaded to the 16-bit data counters from one of two memory locations, designated as either *H* or *Q* in the scratch pad.

Scratch-pad location 9 may be used for storing the status register when handling interrupt routines.

Instructions in which the operation code designates that the scratch pad is addressed by the 6-bit content of the *ISAR* have one of three modes of execution:

1. Indirect address by the *ISAR*.
2. Indirect address by the *ISAR*, followed by incrementing the *ISAR* (lower 3 bits) at the conclusion (completion) of the instruction execution.
3. Indirect address by the *ISAR*, followed by decrementing the *ISAR* (lower 3 bits) at the conclusion of the instruction execution.

Thus the *ISAR* is essentially an incrementing or decrementing pointer to the scratch-pad registers. The lower 3 bits of the *ISAR* form a modulo eight counter when the incrementing and decrementing modes are used. Thus, if the *ISAR* contains 30_8, an incrementing instruction will reference this location and increase the *ISAR* to 31_8, whereas a decrementing instruction will reference the same location and decrement the lower 3 bits of the *ISAR*, to yield 37_8.

When the *ISAR* is used to indirectly address a scratch-pad location, one of three addressing modes may be employed. In all instances, the *ISAR* supplies the register address. The three modes are as follows:

S: the *ISAR* contents are unchanged.
I: the *ISAR* is incremented by 1 after execution.
D: the *ISAR* is decremented by 1 after execution.

Input/Output Ports

The *CPU* has two bidirectional I/O ports. Each port may be used either for gathering data from the external electronics or for outputting data to other circuits. Latches in the outbound side hold the 8 bits of output data. The *CPU* I/O ports are directly selected by the control circuits when the OUTS or INS instruction is executed with an operand of zero or one. Because these ports are directly selected, input and output transfer to them are faster than for other I/O ports. The *CPU* I/O ports are designated by the 4-bit addresses 0000 and 0001.

13.2.   READ ONLY MEMORY AND MEMORY INTERFACE (*MI*)

General Features

While the *CPU* carries out the processing, the *ROM* and *MI* circuits supply memory to an F8 system. To do this, several registers are necessary to link onto the F8 data bus. These are as follows:

- Program counter (*PC*0)
- Stack register (*PC*1)
- Data counter (*DC*)
- An incrementer/adder

Each circuit, the 3851 *ROM*, 3852 dynamic memory interface, and the 3853 static memory interface, contains these functional registers. In addition, the 3851 *ROM* and the 3853 static *MI* each contains an interrupt level (Figs. 13.4, 13.5, 13.6).

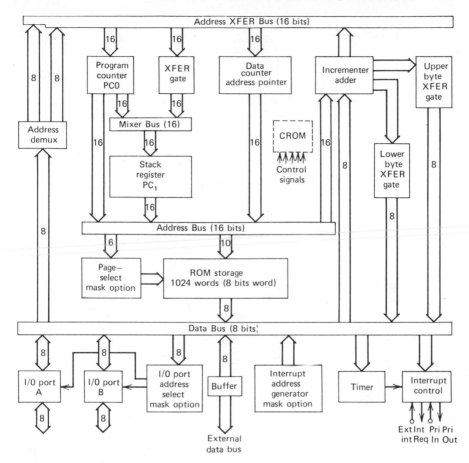

Figure 13.4. Block diagram of *ROM* circuit: 3851. (Courtesy of Fairchild Camera and Instruments Co.).

Data Path Organization

The three circuits (3851 *ROM*, 3852 dynamic *MI*, and 3853 static *MI*) have very similar data path organization, as Figs. 13.4, 13.5, and 13.6 reveal. The major registers of each of these circuits are connected by three 16-bit busses and one 8-bit bus. These busses and the function they perform are as follows.

Address Transfer Bus. This 16-bit bus transfers an address from the data bus to the program counter, stack register, or data counter(s). In addition,

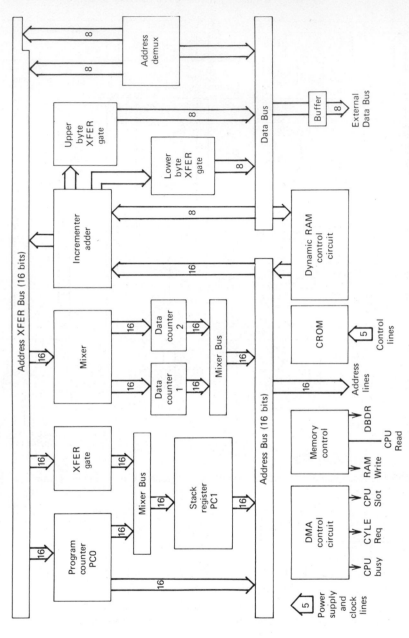

Figure 13.5. F8 memory interface Chip: 3852. (Courtesy of Fairchild Camera and Instruments Co.).

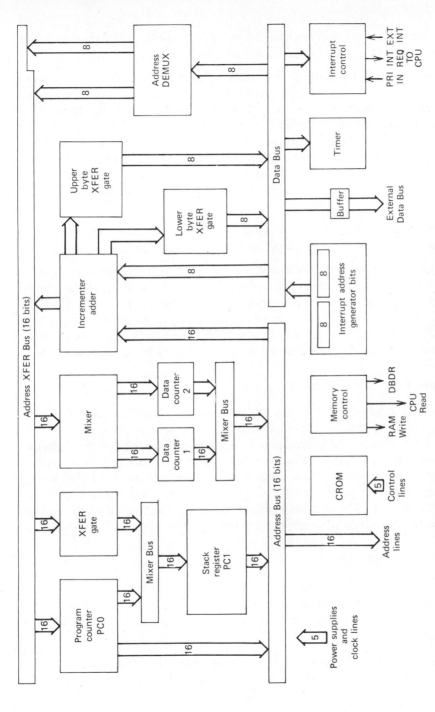

Figure 13.6. F8 memory interface Chip: 3853. (Courtesy of Fairchild Camera and Instruments Co.).

523

the contents of the incrementer/adder and the address bus may be transferred to these registers via the address transfer bus.

Address Bus. The address bus receives the program counter, stack register, and data counter(s) and passes these addresses to the incrementer/adder. In addition, the 16 lines of the address bus are actually used for memory reference from either the program counter or data counter(s). In the *ROM*, the upper 6 bits of the address bus are used for selecting *ROM* pages (one of 64 1024-byte pages). The lower 10 bits serve as the *ROM* address. In the memory interface circuits, the 16-bit address bus is outputted for use by external memory. No paging is performed by the *MI* circuits.

Mixer Bus. The mixer bus selects either the program counter or the address transfer bus to be gated into the stack register.

Data Bus. The 8-bit data bus is the principal path for transmitting 8-bit bytes between the other circuits in the F8 system. Each of the three circuits, 3851, 3852, and 3853, contains four port assignments. These are linked by the data bus to the accumulator of the *CPU*. The data bus also passes 8-bit addresses between F8 circuits in a system. The four busses are gated by signals produced by the control circuitry, discussed in the next section.

Timing and Control Circuitry

The 3851 *ROM*, 3852 *MI*, and 3853 *MI* are sequential circuits. The logic states of these circuits are selected by the five control lines generated by the *CPU*. The central processor also supplies the timing for these circuits (the ϕ and write signals). For each instruction cycle (defined by the period of the write signal) the five control lines select a location of the control *ROM* located in each circuit. The contents of the *CROM* address are the control lines used by internal gating of the logic. The clock lines are used to sequence the circuit through its logic states.

Program Counter (*PC*0)

The program counter contains the address of the next instruction byte to be fetched from memory. After a fetch cycle executes, the program counter is automatically incremented. There are four ways to modify the *PC*0 under program control:

1. From the *CPU* via the data bus, using branch instructions.
2. From a memory address, using JMP or PI instructions.

3. From the stack pointer with a POP instruction.
4. From the scratch-pad memory, using PK or LR instructions.

Stack Register (*PC*1)

The stack register is directly linked to the program counter and receives the latter's contents whenever an interrupt is generated or when the program counter is pushed to the stack register with a PUSH instruction (PI) or PK instruction. It is the function of the stack register to simplify the creation of the address stack.

Two sources of data exist for the stack register. Information is normally pushed from the program counter via the mixer bus to the stack register during the PUSH instruction. The stack register may also be loaded directly from the address transfer bus by a program instruction. This facilitates loading the stack register before executing a POP instruction for returns from subroutines back to the next higher level programs in a multilevel program system. Instructions exist to transfer the stack register to and from scratch pad.

Data Counter (*DC*)

The F8 contains a data counter for referencing memory addresses. Because it is 16 bits long, the *DC* may address up to 64K bytes of memory. A group of instructions exists which use the *DC* to point to their operands in the memory space. The *DC* is incremented by 1 at the conclusion of the memory access cycle; thus it will be pointing to the next location in memory. This is convenient because control loops for transferring data fields need not contain an extra instruction to increment the *DC*. Specific instructions link the *DC* to the two bytes of storage, located in the *CPU* scratch pad, designated as locations *H* and *Q*. Data field locations may be stored in either of these locations and may be transferred to the data counter before initiating a routine that will fetch a field of data from bulk memory.

The 3852 and 3853 memory interface circuits each have two data counters, one active and one inactive. Both are 16 bits wide. The active data counter, which is used to access memory and to communicate to the *CPU*, is loaded directly from an instruction operand, using the DCI instruction. In addition, the data counter may be transferred to and from scratch pad with the LR DC, H, LR DC, Q, LR H, DC, and LR Q, DC instructions. The instruction XDC swaps the contents of the active and inactive *DC*'s. The active data counter is incremented after every memory reference, whereas the inactive data counter is not.

The Incrementer/Adder

Each time the program counter or data counter is used to fetch a byte from storage, it is either incremented or modified, depending on the type of instruction to be executed. The incrementer/adder receives the contents of the counter from the address bus, increments it, and transfers the result back to the appropriate counter. The incrementing is done over a full 16-bit field. During the execution of BRANCH and ADD TO DATA counter instructions, 8 bits (a displacement vector) are added to the present contents of the register in the incrementer/adder and then returned. In both cases the 8-bit vector is in two's complement notation; hence the displacement vector may range from -128 to $+127$.

Addressable Ports

The 3851, 3852, and 3853 each have four addressable ports. These are 8-bit registers connected to the data bus and linked to the accumulator of the *CPU* by the instruction set. Each port is referenced by an 8-bit address. The upper 6 bits of the address refer to the circuit on which the ports are located; the lower 2 bits select one of the four ports. Thus the port addresses are referred to as X0, X1, X2, and X3, where X is a 6-bit binary number. Each port on the circuit may be written into with output instructions. The contents of the I/O ports may be read with input instructions. These instructions transfer contents between ports and the accumulator on the *CPU*. In the *ROM* circuit, two ports are used as 8-bit I/O ports. The remaining two ports are the 8-bit timer and the local interrupt control circuitry. In the 3852, the dynamic memory interface, one port is used to control the dynamic refresh circuitry and to select the state of the *DMA* control circuit. One other port may serve as an 8-bit storage register. The remaining ports are not assigned. In the 3853, the static *MI* circuit, one port is assigned to the timer and another to the local interrupt control circuitry. In addition, two ports are used as a programmable interrupt address vector. Table 13.1 lists the addressable ports and their respective functions.

Page-Select Logic

Page-select logic is required in the memory of an F8 system for memory references and for driving the data bus. The *ROM* circuit performs the page select internally, comparing the upper 6 address bits with a 6-bit page number. This page number is selected by the user; it is a mask option. The

Table 13.1

Port Address	Function
	3851 *ROM*
X00[a]	*ROM* I/O port A
X01[a]	*ROM* I/O port B
X10[a]	*ROM* local interrupt control
X11[a]	*ROM* timer
	3852 Dynamic Memory Interface
0C	8-bit register
0D	Control bits for refresh and *DMA*
0E	Not assigned
0F	Not assigned
	3853 Static Memory Interface
0C	*MI* interrupt vector, upper byte
0D	*MI* interrupt vector, lower byte
0E	*MI* local interrupt control
0F	*MI* timer

[a] X is a 6-bit binary number. It cannot be 0.

most significant six address lines are compared against the *ROM* page number in the page-select block, and a decision is made to activate or deactivate the fetch control signals. The page-select logic is external to the 3852 *MI* and 3853 *MI* circuits, allowing users total flexibility in memory addressing.

The internal logic of the memory interface circuits, however, do require a page-select signal. This is used to drive the data bus whenever the *CPU* requests the contents of the program counter or data counter. Several instructions transfer *PC*1 and *DC* to the scratch-pad memory. If the address in the requested register lies within the memory space of the *MI* (determined by the page-select line), that circuit will respond. This also holds true for the *ROM*; however, the page selection is performed internally. Both the 3852 *MI* and 3853 *MI* have a pin, REGDR. The page-select line should be connected to this pin, which is bidirectional. It may simultaneously be used to control the enabling of a buffer and a driver for the data bus. The *ROM* circuit also has a pin, DBDR, to control the enabling of a buffer / driver for the data bus.

Local Timer

Each memory circuit (*ROM* and *MI*) has a local timer to generate program-initiated delays. To the programmer, the timer is an 8-bit register, addressable via F8 output instructions to the specified timer port address. Delay codes, calculated by the assembler, are loaded into the accumulator and then transferred to the timer (a polynomial shift register). An output instruction to the timer port number performs this function. After it is loaded, the timer counts down.

The timer runs continuously. It signals the interrupt control circuitry after every timer cycle (3.953 msec). However, when an OUTS instruction is executed with the timer port number as the operand, the timer is jammed with a specific count and the local interrupt control logic clears any stored timer interrupt. The timer continues from that count to count down and generate an internal interrupt request. Again, the timer continues to cycle every 3.953 msec (for a 2-MHz system). If the ICB of the *CPU* is not set, or if the local interrupt control logic is not set for timer interrupts, a timer-initiated interrupt will be stored by the local interrupt control circuitry. When the local interrupt control logic is finally set, the memory chip will request interrupt service; the request will be serviced when the ICB of the *CPU* is set.

Time delays between 0 and 254 counts may be chosen. The timer is decremented once every 31 ϕ clock cycles; therefore the counter may count as high as 7905 clock cycles. (For a system at 2 MHz, a ϕ clock cycle occurs every 500 nsec.) Longer durations are achieved by counting multiple interrupts as they occur. The timer may be stopped by loading it with all ones.

13.3. INSTRUCTIONS AND PROGRAMMING

Definitions

Definitions of operand variables are given in Table 13.2, and Table 13.3 lists the formats of constants that are used. An instruction set is presented in Tables 13.4–13.13.

Table 13.2

Operand Variable	Definition
i	Immediate value
rn	Scratch-pad register n; n is between 0 to 63
x	Source register
Y	Destination register
a	Address digit
t	Test condition, used in conditional BRANCH instructions
d	Digit value, used in Table 0.0 format only; Refer to Table 0.0 for acceptable digits

Table 13.3

Operand Constant[a]	Definition	Alternative Form of Operand
H'd'	Hexadecimal digit; d may be one of the digits 0–9, A, B, C, D, E, F	
D'd'	Decimal digit; d may be one of the digits 0–9	d[a]
O'd'	Octal digit; d may be one of the digits 0–7	
C'd'	Character; 8 bits that are one of the ASCII characters	
B'd'	Binary digit; d may be either 1 or 0	
T'd'	Timer counts	

[a] Each character represents 4 binary bits. More than one digit, d, may be used to represent the full value of the operand as required. *Example:* A 16-bit binary number 0110 0011 0100 1001 may be represented in hexadecimal notation as H'6349'.

Table 13.4. Accumulator Group Instructions

Op Code	Operand(s)	Machine Format	Function	Status Bits				Comment
				OVF	Zero	Carry	Sign	
SR	1	12	SHIFT RIGHT ONE	0	1/0	0	1	
SR	4	14	SHIFT RIGHT FOUR	0	1/0	0	1	
SL	1	13	SHIFT LEFT ONE	0	1/0	0	1/0	
SL	4	15	SHIFT LEFT FOUR	0	1/0	0	1/0	
COM	—	18	ACC ← (ACC) ⊕ H'FF'	0	1/0	0	1/0	Complement
LNK	—	19	ACC ← (ACC) + CB	1/0	1/0	1/0	1/0	Link carry to ACC
INC	—	1F	ACC ← (ACC) + 1	1/0	1/0	1/0	1/0	Increment
LIS	i	7i	ACC ← H'i'		—			Load immediate short ($ACC_0 - ACC_3$)
CLR	—	70	ACC ← H'00'			—		Clear
LI	ii	20 ii	ACC ← H'ii'			—		Load immediate
NI	ii	21 ii	ACC ← (ACC) ∧ H'ii'	0	1/0	0	1/0	AND immediate
OI	ii	22 ii	ACC ← (ACC) ∨ H'ii'	0	1/0	0	1/0	OR immediate
XI	ii	23 ii	ACC ← (ACC) ⊕ H'ii'	0	1/0	0	1/0	Exclusive OR immediate
AI	ii	24 ii	ACC ← (ACC) + H'ii' (binary add)	1/0	1/0	1/0	1/0	ADD immediate
CI	ii	25 ii	H'ii' + $\overline{(ACC)}$ + 1	1/0	1/0	1/0	1/0	Compare immediate and set status W

Table 13.5. Scratch-Pad Register Instructions

Op Code	Operand(s)	Machine Format	Function	OVF	Zero	Carry	Sign	Comment
LR	y,x		GENERAL LOAD REGISTER FORMAT ALLOWABLE OPERANDS LISTED BELOW					
	A,r[a]	4r	ACC ← (r)			—		
	A,KU	00	ACC ← (r12)			—		
	A,KL	01	ACC ← (r13)			—		
	A,QU	02	ACC ← (r14)			—		
	A,QL	03	ACC ← (r15)			—		
	r,A	5r	r ← (ACC)			—		
	KU,A	04	r12 ← (ACC)			—		
	KL,A	05	r13 ← (ACC)			—		
	QU,A	06	r14 ← (ACC)			—		
	QL,A	07	r15 ← (ACC)			—		
AS	r	Cr	ACC ← (ACC) + (r)(binary)	1/0	1/0	1/0	1/0	Binary addition
ASD	r	Dr	ACC ← (ACC) + (r)(decimal)	1/0	1/0	1/0	1/0	Decimal addition
NS	r	Fr	ACC ← (ACC) $\wedge$ (r)	0	1/0	0	1/0	Logical AND
XS	r	Er	ACC ← (ACC) $\oplus$ (r)	0	1/0	0	1/0	Exclusive OR
DS	r	3r	r ← (r) + H'FF'(decrement)	1/0	1/0	1/0	1/0	Decrement (-1)

[a] Operand r formats are as follows:

Direct Addressing	Indirect Addressing
0 through 11 (decimal form)	S or 12
	I or 13
H'0' through H'B' (hexadecimal form)	D or 14

Table 13.6. Data Counter Instructions

Op Code	Operand(s)	Machine Format	Function	Status Bits				Comment
				OVF	Zero	Carry	Sign	
LR	Q,DC	0E	r14 ← (DCU); r15 ← (DCL)		—			Load data counter (DC) into Q
LR	H,DC	11	r10 ← (DCU); r11 ← (DCL)		—			Load DC into H
LR	DC,Q	0F	DCU ← (r14); DCL ← (r15)		—			Load Q into DC
LR	DC,H	10	DCU ← (r10); DCL ← (r11)		—			Load H into DC
ADC	—	8E	DC ← (DC) + (ACC)		—			Add ACC to DC
DCI	iiii	2A ii ii	DC ← H'iiii'		—			Load DC immediate
XDC	—	2C	DC ⮂ DC₁ (Memory interface circuit only)		—			Exchange data counters DC_0, DC_1

Table 13.7. Indirect Scratch-Pad Address Register Instructions

Op Code	Operand(s)	Machine Format	Function	Status Bits OVF	Zero	Carry	Sign	Comment
LR	A,IS	0A	ACC ← (ISAR)				—	Load ACC from ISAR
LR	IS,A	0B	ISAR ← (ACC)				—	Load ISAR from ACC
LISU	a	01100a[a]	ISARU ← a				—	Load a to ISAR upper octal digit
LISL	a	01101a[a]	ISARL ← a				—	Load a to ISAR lower octal digit

[a] a is 3 bits.

Table 13.8. Memory Reference Instructions

Op Code	Operand(s)	Machine Format	Function	Status Bits OVF	Zero	Carry	Sign	Comment
LM	—	16	ACC ← ((DC))	—			—	Load ACC
ST	—	17	(DC) ← (ACC)	—			—	Store to memory
AM	—	88	ACC ← (ACC) + ((DC)) {binary}	1/0	1/0	1/0	1/0	Add memory, bin.
AMD	—	89	ACC ← (ACC) + ((DC)) {decimal}	1/0	1/0	1/0	1/0	Add memory, dec.
NM	—	8A	ACC ← (ACC) ∧ ((DC))	0	1/0	0	1/0	AND memory
OM	—	8B	ACC ← (ACC) ∨ ((DC))	0	1/0	0	1/0	OR memory
XM	—	8C	ACC ← (ACC) ⊕ ((DC))	0	1/0	0	1/0	Exclusive OR memory
CM	—	8D	((DC)) + ($\overline{ACC}$) + 1	1/0	1/0	1/0	1/0	Compare memory and set status W

Table 13.9. Status Register Instructions

Op Code	Operand(s)	Machine Format	Function	Status Bits				Comment
				OVF	Zero	Carry	Sign	
LR	W,J	1D	W ← (r9)					Restore status
LR	J,W	1E	r9 ← (W)		—			Save status

Function format for LR W,J:

W_4	W_3	W_2	W_1	W_0
INT	OVF	ZERO	CARRY	SIGN

(Privileged instruction)[a]

[a] Privileged instructions inhibit interrupt service at the end of the instruction.

Table 13.10. Program Counter Instructions

Op Code	Operand(s)	Machine Format	Function	Status Bits OVF	Zero	Carry	Sign	Comment
LR	K,P	08	$r12 \leftarrow (PC_1U)$; $r13 \leftarrow (PC_1L)$		—			Load K register from $PC1$
LR	P,K	09	$PC_1U \leftarrow (r12)$; $PC_1L \leftarrow (r13)$		—			Load $PC1$ from K
LR	P0,Q	0D	$PC_0U \leftarrow (r14)$; $PC_0L \leftarrow (r15)$		—			Load $PC0$ from Q register
PK	—	0C	$PC_0U \leftarrow (r12)$; $PC_0L \leftarrow (r13)$ and $PC_1 \leftarrow (PC_0)$ (Privileged instruction)[a]		—			Call to subroutine direct
PI	aaaa[b]	28 ii ii	$PC_1 \leftarrow (PC_0)$; $PC_0 \leftarrow$ H'aaaa' (Privileged instruction)[a]		—			Call to subroutine immediate
POP	—	1C	$PC_0 \leftarrow (PC_1)$ (Privileged instruction)[a]		—			Return from subroutine

[a] Privileged instructions inhibit interrupt service request at the end of the instruction.
[b] The contents of the accumulator are destroyed.

535

Table 13.11. Branch Instructions

Op Code	Operand(s)	Machine Format	Function	Status Bits OVF	Zero	Carry	Sign	Comment
BR	aa	90 aa	$PC_0 \leftarrow ((PC_0) + 1) + H\text{‘aa’}$				—	Unconditional branch
JMP	aaaa[a]	29 aa aa	$PC_0 \leftarrow H\text{‘aaaa’}$ Privileged instruction[b]				—	Branch immediate
BT	t,aa[c]	8t aa	$PC_0 \leftarrow ((PC_0) + 1) + H\text{‘aa’}$ if any test is true $PC_0 \leftarrow (PC_0) + 2$ if no test is true				—	Conditional branch true
BP	aa	81 aa	$PC_0 \leftarrow ((PC_0) + 1) + H\text{‘aa’}$ if SIGN = 1 $PC_0 \leftarrow (PC_0) + 2$ if SIGN = 0				—	Branch if positive
BC	aa	82 aa	$PC_0 \leftarrow ((PC_0) + 1) + H\text{‘aa’}$ if CARRY = 1 $PC_0 \leftarrow (PC_0) + 2$ if CARRY = 0			—	—	Branch on carry
BZ	aa	84 aa	$PC_0 \leftarrow ((PC_0) + 1) + H\text{‘aa’}$ if ZERO = 1 $PC_0 \leftarrow (PC_0) + 2$ if ZERO = 0		—		—	Branch on zero

STATUS BIT TESTS

2^2	2^1	2^0
ZERO	CARRY	SIGN

536

			Operation	Description
BM	aa	91 aa	$PC_0 \leftarrow ((PC_0) + 1) + H\text{'aa'}$ if SIGN = 0 $PC_0 \leftarrow (PC_0) + 2$ if SIGN = 1	—	Branch on negative
BNC	aa	92 aa	$PC_0 \leftarrow ((PC_0) + 1) + H\text{'aa'}$ if CARRY = 0 $PC_0 \leftarrow (PC_0) + 2$ if CARRY = 1	—	Branch if no carry
BNZ	aa	94 aa	$PC_0 \leftarrow ((PC_0) + 1) + H\text{'aa'}$ if ZERO = 0 $PC_0 \leftarrow (PC_0) + 2$ if ZERO = 1	—	Branch if not zero
BF	t,^{d}aa	9t^d aa	$PC_0 \leftarrow ((PC_0) + 1) + H\text{'aa'}$ if selected status bits are all 0 $PC_0 \leftarrow (PC_0) + 2$ if any status bit is 1	—	Branch if false

TEST CONDITIONS

2^3	2^2	2^1	2^0
OVF	ZERO	CARRY	SIGN

BNO	aa	98 aa	$PC_0 \leftarrow ((PC_0) + 1) + H\text{'aa'}$ if OVF = 0 $PC_0 \leftarrow (PC_0) + 2$ if OVF = 1	—	Branch if no overflow
BR7	aa	8F aa	$PC_0 \leftarrow ((PC_0) + 1) + H\text{'aa'}$ if ISAR $\neq$ 7 $PC_0 \leftarrow (PC_0) + 2$ if ISAR = 7	—	Branch on *ISAR*

[a] The contents of the accumulator are lost.
[b] Privileged instructions inhibit interrupt service request at the end of the instruction.
[c] t is only 3 bits.
[d] t is 4 bits.

537

Table 13.12.   Interrupt Control Instructions

Op Code	Operand(s)	Machine Format	Function	OVF	Zero	Carry	Sign
DI	—	1A	DISABLE INTERRUPT			—	
EI	—	1B	ENABLE INTERRUPT (Privileged instruction)[a]				

(Status Bits: OVF, Zero, Carry, Sign)

[a] Privileged instructions inhibit interrupt service at the completion of execution of the instruction.

Programming Examples

Test for 1 in 6th or 4th bit:
```
LR   A,R
NI   B'00101000'
BNZ
```

Test for 1 in 6th and 4th bits:
```
LR   A, R
NI   B'00101000'
XI   B'00101000'
BZ
```

Test for 6th bit in register being 0:
```
LR   A,R
NI   B'00100000'
BZ
```

Test to see whether register R is greater than B'01110000' ($+$ 112):
```
LR   A,R
CI   B'01110000'
BM   In this case, there is no need for
     testing overflow
```

Comparing $A = B$ (sign or unsigned):

A is in accumulator
```
CI    B        Compare with B
BZ    Equal    If zero flags set, go to equal
- - - - - - - - - -   Unequal
```

Comparing $A > B$ (unsigned):
```
CI    B
BNC   Y1       If A greater than B, go to Y1
- - - - - - - - -   A is either less than or equal to B
```

Table 13.13. Input/Output Instructions

Op Code	Operand(s)	Machine Format	Function	Status Bits				Cycles
				OVF	Zero	Carry	Sign	
INS	a	Aa	ACC ← (INPUT PORT a) Input ports 00 to 0F only	0	1/0	0	1/0	4[a]
IN	aa	26 aa	ACC ← (INPUT PORT aa) Input ports 04 through FF only	0	1/0	0	1/0	4
OUTS	a	Ba	OUTPUT PORT a ← (ACC) Output ports 00 to 0F only			—		4[a]
OUT	aa	27 aa	OUTPUT PORT aa ← (ACC) Output ports 04 through FF only			—		4

[a] Two cycles when I/O port address is 0 or 1.

539

Comparing two numbers algebraically: In accordance with the above procedure to compare two signed numbers, the exclusive OR function of sign and overflow bit is required; one method of performing such a function is shown below.

CI	B	A is in accumulator B is compared with A
BF9	GRT	If both OVF and POS are zero, $A > B$; hence branch to GRT
BNO	Y1	To come to this instruction–either overflow = 1 or positive = 1. If overflow = 0, positive is equal to 1; hence jump to Y1
BN	GRT	Now overflow = 0; if positive = 0, $A > B$
Y1		At this point, either OVF = 1 or POS = 1; hence $A \leq B$

Sixteen-Bit Addition/Subtraction Subroutine

The flow chart is shown in Fig. 13.7, and the program in Table 13.14.

13.4. INTERRUPT AND INPUT/OUTPUT

Interrupt

Figure 13.8 is a block diagram of the interrupt interconnection for a typical F8 system. Both the 3851 *ROM* and 3853 static memory interface have the capability for either of two types of interrupts, internal or external. The internal interrupts may be generated by the programmable timer, whereas the external interrupt is stimulated by the outside world. A local interrupt control circuit containing two latches is built on each chip. These latches are the select bit and the interrupt enable bit. These two bits have four possible states (Table 13.15). These control latches are loaded under program control, using an output instruction. This loading clears the interrupt control logic, except for any pending timer interrupt. The operand for the OUT or OUTS instruction must be the predefined port number of the interrupt control circuit. The two control bits allow each interrupt circuit to have independently controlled enable/disable capability; if enabled, the

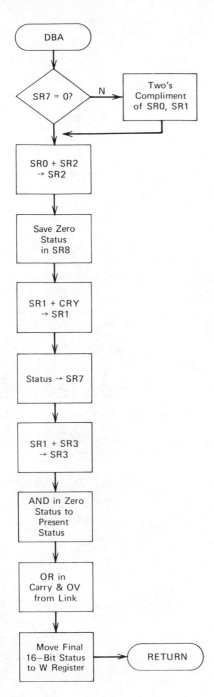

Figure 13.7. Double-precision addition. (Courtesy of Fairchild Camera and Instruments Co).

Table 13.14

LOC	OBJECT CODE	STMT	SOURCE STATEMENT
			* DOUBLE PRECISION BINARY ADD (16 BIT) OR:
			* SUBTRACT SUBROUTINE.
			* UPON ENTRY:
			* IF SR7 = 0 ADD, OTHERWISE SUBTRACT.
			* AUGEND = SCRATCH REGS 0 AND 1(1 MSB).
			* ADDEND = SCRATCH REGS 2 AND 3(3 MSB).
			* (THESE DOUBLE REGISTERS ARE TREATED AS
			* 16 BIT SIGNED NUMBERS WITH BIT 7 OF
			* REGS 1 AND 3 BEING THE SIGN BIT)
			* (IF SUBTRACT, THEN (R2,R3)–(R0,R1).)
			* UPON EXIT:
			* SUM OR DIFF IS CONTAINED IN R2,R3.
			* W-REG CONTAINS THE STATUS OF THE 16
			* BIT ADD.
20D7	70	126	DBA LIS 0
20D8	C7	127	AS 7
20D9	84 B	128	BZ ADD IF SR7 = 0, THEN GO DO ADD.
20DB	40	129	LR A,0
20DC	18	130	COM
20DD	1F	131	INC
20DE	50	132	LR 0,A
20DF	1B	133	LR J,W
20E0	41	134	LR A,1
20E1	18	135	COM COMPLEMENT FOR SUBTRACT.
20E2	1D	136	LR W,J
20E3	19	137	LNK
20E4	51	138	LR 1,A

Address			Label	Op	Operand	Comment
20E5	40		ADD	LR	A,0	GET LSB OF AUGEND.
20E6	C2			AS	2	ADD LSB OF ADDEND.
20E7	52			LR	2,A	SAVE PARTIAL SUM.
20E8	1E			LR	J,W	
20E9	49			LR	A,9	GET STATUS AND OR IN ALL BITS
20EA	22	1B		OI	H'1B'	BUT ZERO.
20EC	58			LR	8,A	SAVE IN SRB FOR CALC OF FINAL.
20ED	1D			LR	W,J	GET ORIG STATUS BACK IN W-REG.
20EE	41			LR	A,1	GET 2ND BYTE OF AUGEND.
20EF	19			LNK		ADD 1 IF CARRY FROM PREV ADD.
20F0	1E			LR	J,W	SAVE STATUS, MAY BE OV OR CARRY.
20F1	C3			AS	3	ADD LSB OF ADDEND.
20F2	53			LR	3,A	SAVE IN REG 1.
20F3	49			LR	A,9	MOVE STATUS SAVED FROM LINK
20F4	57			LR	7,A	ADD TO SR 7.
20F5	1E			LR	J,W	
20F6	49			LR	A,9	GET STATUS FROM FINAL ADD AND
20F7	F8			NS	8	'AND' IN ZERO STATUS FROM
20F8	58			LR	8,A	FIRST ADD.
20F9	47			LR	A,7	
20FA	59			LR	9,A	MOVE STATUS SAVED FROM LINK
20FB	48			LR	A,8	BACK TO W-REG AND 'OR' IN
20FC	1D			LR	W,J	OV AND CARRY BITS TO FINAL
20FD	92	4		BNC	DBA1	STATUS.
20FF	22	2		OI	2	
2101	1D			LR	W,J	
2102	98	3	DBA1	BNO	DBAX	
2104	22	8		OI	8	
2106	59		DBAX	LR	9,A	MOVE FINAL STATUS TO W-REG.
2107	1D			LR	W,J	
2108	1C			POP		RETURN.

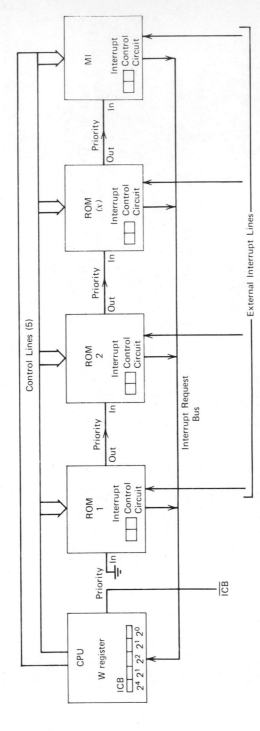

Figure 13.8. F8 interrupt interconnection. (Courtesy of Fairchild Camera and Instruments Co.).

544

Table 13.15

Select Bit	Interrupt Enable Bit	Function
0	0	No interrupt
0	1	External interrupt enabled
1	0	No interrupt
1	1	Timer (internal) interrupt enabled

select bit may choose either internal (timer-generated) interrupts or external interrupts.

Each *ROM* has a priority in and a priority out line so that they may be daisy-chained together, in any order, to form a priority level of interrupts. The first circuit in line should have its priority in line tied to V_{SS} (or tied to the $\overline{ICB}$ pin of the *CPU* chip). Since the *MI* has only a priority in line, it must be at the end of the chain. All memory chips are tied back to the *CPU* chip via the interrupt request bus. When an interrupt requires servicing, the local interrupt logic signals the central processor via the interrupt request bus and does not pass on the priority out signal. If the memory chip has no interrupt, it simply passes the priority out signal on to the next memory chip in line. Again, the same decision is made by that unit.

By daisy-chaining the priority lines, the interrupt levels are set up. The first memory chip in line has the highest interrupt level, and the last units (Fig. 13.8) are the lowest. The *MI* in an F8 system will always be at the lowest priority level.

To generate a timer interrupt, the timer must be set under program control. An interrupt occurs when the timer times out AND the interrupt control has been set (select bit = 1, enable bit = 1) and ICB of the *CPU* is set. The timer may time out before the interrupt control bit is set or the local interrupt control is enabled for internal interrupts; even so, an interrupt will still be initiated after the required conditions have been met. Any pending timer interrupt is cleared whenever the timer of the memory chip is reloaded. The ICB is always cleared after the *CPU* has acknowledged an interrupt request.

The generation of an external interrupt request is also controlled by the local interrupt control circuit. If the select bit is set to 0 and the enable bit is set to 1, the control logic of the memory chip will be responsive to external interrupts. To guarantee an interrupt, the external interrupt line must drop from V_{DD} to V_{SS} (1 to 0), and stay down for a minimum of two write clock times (4 μsec for a 2-μsec system clock). The ICB may or may not be set when this occurs. If it is not set, the request will be stored by the local interrupt control logic until the ICB is re-enabled. However, the stored external interrupt request will be lost whenever the control bits are reloaded. The ICB will be cleared after the *CPU* has acknowledged the interrupt request. The stored external interrupt request will be cleared after the interrupt is serviced. The operation of the local interrupt control circuitry is complex, and the preceding verbal description may be an oversimplification of this crucial function.

Within each local interrupt control circuit is a 16-bit interrupt address vector. This vector is the address to which the program counter will be set after an interrupt is acknowledged. Thus it is the address of the first executable instruction of the interrupt routine. The 3851 *ROM* has a mask-programmed interrupt address, selected by the user. It is another mask option of the *ROM*. Fifteen bits—bits 0–6 and 8–15—are selected by the designer. Bit seven (2^7) is dependent on the type of interrupt. This bit will be 0 for internal-timer-generated interrupts and 1 for external interrupts. The interrupt address vector of the 3853 static *MI* is programmable via output instructions. Port OC of the 3853 *MI* is assigned to hold the upper 8 bits of the 16-bit address (bits 2^8–2^{15}), while port OD holds the lower 7 bits (bits 2^0–2^6). Bit 7 (2^7) of the interrupt address vector (bit 7 of port OD) is controlled by the local interrupt hardware, just as in the F8 *ROM* chip. It will be 0 if timer interrupts are enabled and 1 if external interrupts or no interrupts are enabled. The programmable interrupt address vector of the 3853 *MI* is assigned the bits shown in Fig. 13.9.

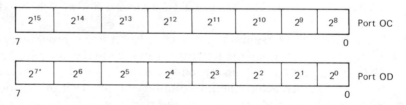

* This bit is controlled by the local interrupt control circuit.

Figure 13.9. Interrupt bit assignment. (Courtesy of Fairchild Camera and Instruments Co.).

The interrupt vector may be loaded by means of an OUT or OUTS instruction. It may be read back into the accumulator using an IN or INS instruction with port OC or OD as operand.

When the interrupt logic sends an interrupt request signal and the *CPU* is enabled to service it, the normal state sequence of the *CPU* is interrupted at the end of an instruction. The *CPU* signals the interrupt circuits via the five control lines. The requesting local interrupt circuit sends a 16-bit interrupt address vector (from the interrupt address generator) onto the data bus in two consecutive bytes. The address is made available to the program counter via the address demultiplexer circuits, and simultaneously it is made available to all other circuits on the data bus. It is the address of the next instruction to be executed. The program counter ($PC0$) of each memory chip is set with this new address, while the stack register ($PC1$) is loaded with the previous contents of the program counter. The information in $PC1$ is lost. Thus the next instruction to be executed is determined by the value of the interrupt address vector.

The interrupt control bit (ICB) of the *CPU* (loaded in the *W* register) allows interrupts to be recognized. Clearing the ICB prevents acknowledgment of interrupts. The ICB is cleared during power-on or external reset, and after an interrupt is acknowledged. The interrupt status of the *ROM* chips is not affected by the execution of the DISABLE INTERRUPT (DI) instruction. At the conclusion of most instructions, the fetch logic checks the state of the interrupt request line. If there is an interrupt, the next instruction fetch cycle is suspended and the system is forced into an interrupt sequence. The *CPU* allows interrupts only after certain instructions. The exceptions are the following F8 instructions:

(PK)	Push *K*
(PI)	Push immediate
(POP)	Pop
(JMP)	Jump
(OUTS)	Output short (excluding OUTS 01 and 02)
(OUT)	Output
(EI)	Set ICB
(LR W,J)	Load the status register from scratch pad
POWER ON	

Therefore it is possible to perform one more instruction after these *CPU* operations without being interrupted. This capability is especially useful during routines that perform interrupt housekeeping operations. For instance, whenever an interrupt occurs, the program counter is pushed into the stack register ($PC1$). Probably this value should be saved for later use. If there were no way to block interrupts, another one could occur before $PC1$ was safely stored into memory. Thus the ability to disable interrupts is essential.

Input/Output

A typical *F8* system has at least one *CPU* with one or more *ROM* memory circuits and perhaps a memory interface circuit connected to the data bus (Fig. 13.10). An F8 I/O operation involves the movement of data between

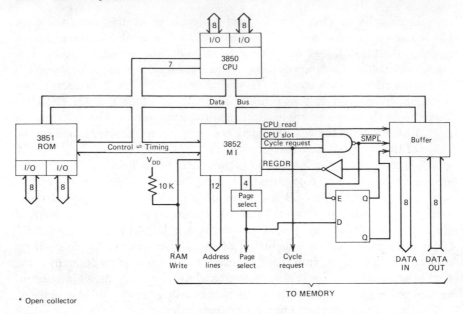

* Open collector

Figure 13.10. 3850, 3851, and 3852 interface in an F8 system. (Courtesy of Fairchild Camera and Instruments Co.).

the accumulator and an I/O port. This may be accomplished with one of four instructions, which are also used to reference the interrupt control blocks and the timer registers (also referred to as "ports"). An example of an output instruction is as follows:

$$\text{OUT} \qquad \text{aa}$$

In this example, byte aa refers to port address aa. Each port (I/O, interrupt control block, timer) in an F8 system has a predefined output port number. The two *CPU* ports are always labeled 00 and 01; they are accessed by the INS and OUTS instruction only.

Port Address
H'00' *CPU* circuit, I/O port 0
H'01' *CPU* circuit, I/O port 1
H'02' not assigned
H'03' not assigned

The selection of the four *ROM* port addresses is a customer's mask option, while the memory interface port numbers are preassigned. Each circuit, *ROM* or *MI*, is given four sequential port addresses.

The transfer of data from the accumulator to the I/O port is completed with an OUT or OUTS instruction. Sampling of the I/O ports may be done with either an IN or INS instruction.

The OUTS and INS instructions are one byte in length; the first 4 bits are the op code, and the remaining 4 bits are the port address. Thus only 16 ports may be referenced with these instructions. These are the lower 16 ports, 00 through 0F. The OUT and IN instructions are two bytes long. The first byte is the op code; the second, the port number. Any one of 256 ports may be referenced by this instruction. Ports 00 and 01 are addressable only with the OUTS and INS instructions.

Each I/O port has an 8-bit latch on the output side; therefore it will retain the data of the last output instruction. Since these ports are bidirectional, data may also be read into the accumulator from the same port. The only restriction is that the output port bit latch must have a zero in it for input data to be valid. This is a consequence of the wired-OR connection of the I/O ports. Therefore, if a full 8-bit byte is to be transferred into the accumulator, the I/O port buffer must have previously been set to all zeros.

REFERENCES

1. F–8 Preliminary Microprocessor User's Manual, Fairchild Camera and Instruments Co., Mountain View, Ca., 1975.

2. F8M Micromodule User's Manual, Fairchild Camera and Instruments Co., Mountain View, Ca., 1975.

3. Application Notes, F8 Microprocessor, Fairchild Camera and Instruments Co., Mountain View, Ca., 1975.

14
SMS MICROCONTROLLER

Chapter 14 presents the Scientific Micro Systems MicroController, specifically designed for control applications. The MicroController is composed of a *CPU* with 8-bit general-purpose registers, 16-bit-word program memory, optional read/write data storage, and a complete input/output system called the interface vectors. The address of an external device is determined via the program within the MicroController. The I/O system appears to the MicroController as a set of internal registers. The system has a repertoire of eight instructions which allow the user to test input status lines, set or reset output control lines, and perform high-speed I/O data transfer. Each instruction is executed completely in 300 nsecs.

The material* in this chapter has been adapted in part from a publication of Scientific Micro Systems. The material so published herein is the full responsibility of the author.

14.1. MICROCONTROLLER SYSTEM

General Features

The SMS MicroController is a microcomputer designed for control. It features the following:

- An instruction execution time of 300 nsec.
- Direct address capability—up to 4096 16-bit words of program memory.
- Eight 8-bit general-purpose registers.
- Simultaneous data transfer and data edit in a single instruction cycle time.
- An *n*-way branch or *n*-entry table look-up in two instruction cycle times.
- Equal speed of instructions operation on 1-, 2-, 3-, 4-, 5-, 6-, 7-, or 8-bit data formats.

* Programs, figures, and tables are courtesy and copyright © 1975 by Scientific Micro Systems. All rights reserved.

The MicroController instruction set features control-oriented instructions which directly access variable-length I/O and internal data fields. These instructions provide very high performance for moving and interpreting data. This feature makes the MicroController ideal for switching, controlling, and editing applications.

Data from external devices may be processed (tested, shifted, added to, etc.) without first moving them to internal storage because the I/O system appears to the MicroController as a set of internal registers. In fact, the entire concept is to treat data at the I/O interface no differently from internal data. This concept extends to the software, which allows variables at the I/O system to be named and treated in the same way as data in storage.

MicroController Functional Components

The MicroController is a complete microcomputer system consisting of the following:

- A central processing unit called the interpreter.
- Read only program storage.
- Optional read/write data storage called working storage with variable field address of 1 to 8 bits.
- A complete input/output system called the interface vector.

Figure 14.1 illustrates the MicroController architecture. The MicroController *CPU* contains an arithmetic logic unit (*ALU*), program counter, interface vector address register (*IVL*), and working storage address register (*IVR*). Eight 8-bit general-purpose registers are provided, including seven working registers and an auxiliary register that performs as a working register and also provides an implied operand for many instructions. The MicroController registers are shown in Fig. 14.1 and are summarized below.

Control Registers

Instruction. A 16-bit register containing the current instruction.

Program Storage Address (AR). A 13-bit register containing the address of the current instruction being accessed from program storage.

Program Counter (PC). A 13-bit register containing the address of the next instruction to be read from program storage.

IV Byte Address (IVL). An 8-bit register containing the address of the current byte being accessed from the interface vector. The *IVL* is under program control.

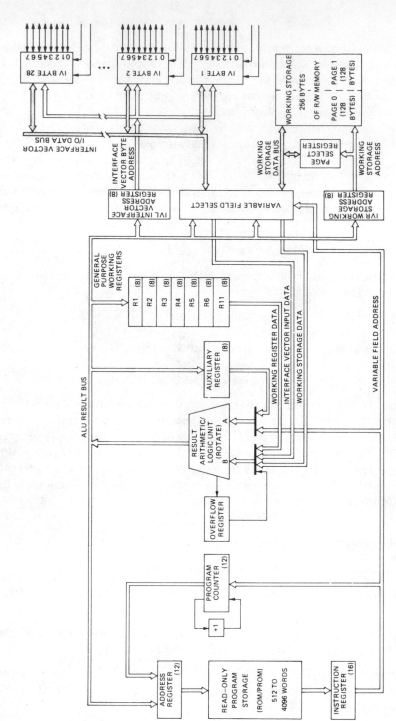

Figure 14.1 Microcontroller architecture. (Courtesy of Scientific Micro Systems).

Working Storage Address (IVR). An 8-bit register containing the address of the current byte being accessed from working storage. The *IVR* is under program control.

Data Registers

Working Registers (WR). Seven 8-bit registers for data storage.

Overflow (OVF). A 1-bit register that retains the most significant bit position carry from *ALU*. Arithmetically treated as $2°$.

Auxiliary (AUX). An 8-bit register. Source of implied operand for arithmetic and logical instructions. May be used as a working register.

A crystal external to the *CPU* is used to generate the *CPU* system clock. The *CPU* provides eight instructions.

The 16-bit MicroController instructions are stored in 512–4096 words of read only program storage. Program storage can be implemented with either mask-coded *ROM*'s or *PROM*'s.

The input/output system, called the interface vector, serves as the data path over which information is transferred into and out of the Micro-Controller. The basic elements of the interface vector are as follows:

- The general purpose 8-bit I/O registers, or interface vector (IV) bytes, whose tristate data path serves as the connection points to the user system.
- The *IVL* register, which contains the address of the IV byte currently being accessed.
- Variable field selection, which permits 1- to 8-bit field access of a selected IV byte in a single instruction.

The interface vector eliminates the need for costly interface logic and provides a simple, well-defined interconnection point to the user system.

Working storage is available as an option that provides 256 bytes of read/write memory for program data or I/O data buffering. Working storage consists of the following:

- 256 8-bit bytes of read/write memory organized as two pages (banks), page 0 and page 1, of 128 bytes each.
- The working storage address register, *IVR*, which holds the address of the byte currently accessed in either page 0 or page 1, depending on the state of the page-select register.
- The page-select register, addressed through *IVR*, is a single-bit register used to select page 0 or page 1 of working storage.
- Variable field select, which permits 1- to 8-bit field transfers to or from an addressed working storage byte in a single instruction.

14.2.   MICROCONTROLLER INSTRUCTION SET

The MicroController has a repertoire of eight instructions which allow the user to test input status lines, set or reset output control lines, and perform high-speed I/O data transfers. All instructions are 16 bits in length. Each instruction is executed completely in 300 nsec.

All instructions are specified by a 3-bit operation (op) code field. The operand may consist of the following fields: source (S) field, destination (D) field, rotate (R) field, length (L) field, immediate (I) operand field, and (program storage) address (A) field (Table 14.1).

Table 14.1

OPERATION	FORMAT	RESULT	NOTES
MOVE	C S L D	Content of data field addressed by S, L replaces data in field specified by D, L.	If S and D both are register addresses then L specifies a right rotate of L places applied to the register specified by S.
ADD		Sum of AUX and data specified by S, L replaces data in field specified by D, L.	
AND		Logical AND of AUX and data specified by S, L replaces data in field specified by D, L.	
XOR		Logical exclusive OR of AUX and data specified by S, L replaces data in field specified by D, L.	
XMIT	C S L I	The literal value I replaces the data in the field specified by S, L.	If S is IV or WS address then I limited to range 00-37. Otherwise I limited to range 000-377.
NZT	C S I	If the data in the field specified by S, L equals zero, perform the next instruction in sequence. If the data specified by S, L is not equal to zero, execute the instruction at address determined by using the literal I as an offset to the Program Counter.	If S specifies an IV or WS address then I is limited to the range 00 - 37. I is limited to the range 000 - 377 otherwise.
XEC	C S L I	Perform the instruction at address determined by applying the sum of the literal I and the data specified by S, L as an offset to the Program Counter. If that instruction does not transfer control, the program sequence will continue from the XEC instruction location.	The offset operation is performed by reducing the value of PC to the nearest multiple of 32 (if I : 00 - 37) or 256 (if I : 000 - 377) and adding the offset.
JMP	C I	The literal value I replaces contents of the Program Counter.	I limited to the range 00000 - 07777.

The op code field is used to specify one of eight MicroController instructions:

Op Code Octal Value	Instruction		Result
0	MOVE	S,L,D	$(S) \rightarrow D$
1	ADD	S,L,D	(S) plus $(AUX) \rightarrow D$
2	AND	S,L,D	$(S) \wedge (AUX) \rightarrow D$
3	XOR	S,L,D	$(S) \oplus (AUX) \rightarrow D$
4	XEC	I,L,S or I,S	Execute instruction at current *PC* offset by $1 + (S)$
5	NZT	I,L,S or I,S	Jump to current *PC* offset by I if $(S) \neq 0$
6	XMIT	I,L,S or I,S	Transmit literal $I \rightarrow S$
7	JMP	A	Jump to program location A

The S and D fields specify the source and destination of the operation defined by the op code field. The auxiliary register is the implied source for the instructions ADD, AND, and XOR, which require two source fields. In other words, instructions of the form:

$$\text{ADD } X,Y$$

imply a third operand, say Z, located in the auxiliary register, so that the operation which takes place is actually $X + Z$, with the result stored in Y. This powerful capability means that three variables are referenced in 300 nsecs.

14.3. PROGRAMMING EXAMPLES

Looping

Looping is terminated by incrementing a counter and testing for zero. Register $R1$ is used as counter register and is loaded with a negative number, so that the program counts up to zero.

	XMIT	NEG, RI	Load negative loop count.
ALPHA:	. . .		Loop start.
	.		
	.		
	.		
	XMIT	I, AUX	Store increment value in *AUX* register, which is an implicit operand of ADD instruction.

ADD	R1, R1	Increment counter register. Add contents of *AUX* to contents of *R*1 and store the sum in *R*1.
NZT	R1, ALPHA	Test contents of *R*1 for zero. If zero, execute next sequential instruction; otherwise, jump to ALPHA and continue execution from there.

.

.

.

Time: 900 nsecs.

Inclusive OR (8 bits)

Generate inclusive OR of the contents of *R*1 and *R*2. Store the logical result in *R*3. Although the MicroController does not have an OR instruction, it can be quickly implemented by making use of the fact that (A $\oplus$ B) $\oplus$ (A $\wedge$ B) is logically equivalent to A $\vee$ B.

MOVE	R2, AUX	Load one of the operands into *AUX* register so that it can be used as the implicit operand of XOR and AND instructions.
XOR	R1, R3	Take exclusive OR of *AUX* and *R*1. Store result in *R*3.
AND	R1, AUX	Take AND of *AUX* and *R*1. Place results in *AUX*.
XOR	R3, R3	Take exclusive OR of *AUX* (A $\vee$ B) and *R*3 (A $\oplus$ S). Store result in *R*3, which now contains inclusive OR of *R*1 and *R*2.

Time: 1.2 μsecs.

16-Bit ADD, Register to Register

Add a 16-bit value stored in *R*1 and *R*2 to a 16-bit value in *R*3 and *R*4. Store the result in *R*1 and *R*2.

MOVE	R2, AUX	Move low-order byte of first operand to *AUX* in preparation for ADD
ADD	R4, R2	Add the low-order bytes of the two operands and store the result in *R2* which contains the low-order byte of the result.

MOVE	R1, AUX	Move high-order byte of first operand to *AUX*.
ADD	OVF, AUX	Add in possible carry from addition of low-order bytes.
ADD	R3, R1	Add the high-order bytes plus carry and place result in *R*1, which contains the high-order byte of the result.

Time· 1.5 μsecs.

16-Bit ADD, Memory to Memory

Add a 16-bit value in working storage, OPERAND1, to a 16-bit value in working storage, OPERAND2, and store result in working storage, OPERAND1. *H*1 and *L*1 represent the high- and low-order of bytes of OPERAND1; *H*2 and *L*2, the high- and low-order bytes of OPERAND2.

XMIT	L2, IVR	Transmit address of low-order byte of second operand to *IVR*.
MOVE	L2, AUX	
XMIT	L1, IVR	
ADD	L1, L1	
MOVE	OVF, AUX	Move possible carry from addition of low-order bytes to *AUX* register.
XMIT	H2, IVR	Add high-order byte of second operand to possible carry. Store result in *AUX*.
ADD	H2, AUX	
XMIT	H1, IVR	
ADD	H1, H1	High=order byte of sum is in H1. Low=order byte of sum is in L1.

Time: 2.7 μsecs.

14.4. INPUT/OUTPUT SYSTEM

Addressing Data on the Interface Vector

As described in preceding sections, the interface vector is the MicroController's input/output system. It provides a simple interconnection to the user status, control, and data lines.

The interface vector is composed of general-purpose I/O registers called interface vector (IV) bytes. In the MicroController described here, the interface vector may consist of up to 28 IV Bytes.

As seen in Fig. 14.1, the *IVL* register serves as the address register to the IV bytes. In order for an instruction access (read or write) to an IV Byte, the address of that byte must first be placed into the *IVL* register. Thus two instructions are required to operate on an interface vector byte:

XMIT   ADDRESS, IVL

MACHINE INSTRUCTION

Once the IV byte is selected (addressed), it will remain selected until the *IVL* register is loaded with another address. From the user's standpoint, however, all IV byte outputs can be read by an external device regardless of whether they are selected or not.

Although the address range of the *IVL* is $0-377_8$, only 28 IV bytes are available on current system offerings. The addressing for the 28 IV bytes is 01_8-34_8.

Each IV byte consists of eight storage latches which hold data transferred between the interpreter and the user system, eight tristate I/O lines, and two I/O control lines, called byte input control (BIC) and byte output control (BOC) (Fig. 14.2). The control lines functions are summarized in Table 14.2.

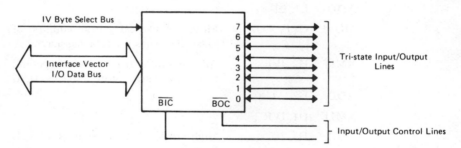

Figure 14.2. Interface vector providing dynamically defined data flow. (Courtesy of Scientific Micro Systems).

Byte Assembly from Bit Serial Input

This is typical of problems associated with interfacing to serial communications lines. An 8-bit byte is assembled from bit inputs that arrive sequentially at the interface vector. A single bit on the interface vector named STROBE is used to define bit timing, and a second bit, named INPBIT, serves as the bit data interface (Fig. 14.3, Table 14.3).

Control Sequence

Output a specific 5-bit pattern in response to a specified 3-bit input field (Fig. 14.4, Table 14.4).

Table 14.2

Control Lines		Function
BOC (low true)	BIC (low true)	
H	H	Eight I/O lines in high-impedance state—disable
L	H	Eight I/O lines in output mode—8-bit storage latch data available in the output lines
X	L	Eight I/O lines in input mode—data can be read by Interpreter

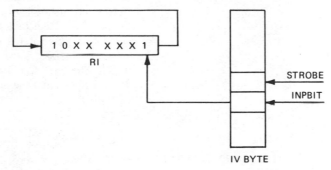

Figure 14.3. Bit serial input. (Courtesy of Scientific Micro Systems).

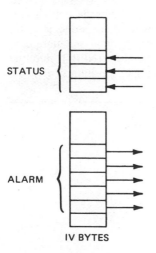

Figure 14.4. Status/alarm control sequence. (Courtesy of Scientific Micro Systems).

559

Table 14.3

	XMIT	0, R1	R1 will be used as a character buffer. It has been cleared.
	XMIT	8, R2	R2 will be used as a bit counter.
	XMIT	INPADR, IVL	Select IV byte that contains INPBIT and STROBE.
NEXTBIT:	NZT	STROBE, *+2	Test STROBE for data ready. The MOVE instruction is executed only when STROBE = 1.
	JMP	*−1	
	MOVE	INPBIT, AUX	
	XOR	R1(1), R1	Rotate R1 one place right. This puts a zero in the least significant bit position. Then take the exclusive OR of this rotated version of R1 and of *AUX*. Place the result in R1. The least significant bit of R1 will then equal the latest value of INPBIT.
	XMIT	−1, AUX	
	ADD	R2, R2	Decrement R2.
	NZT	R2, NEXTBIT	If R2 is not yet zero, more bits must be collected to complete the byte being assembled.
	MOVE	R1(1), R1	This instruction will be executed only when 8 bits have been collected. After this is done, it is still necessary to rotate one more time to get the last INPBIT into the high-order bit position of R1.

Time: 1.8 μsec/bit.

Table 14.4

	XMIT STATUS, IVL	Choose the IV byte, which receives the 3-bit input from user's system.
	MOVE STATUS, R1	Move the 3 bits of interest from the IV byte to register $R1$. The 3 bits are automatically right-justified.
	XMIT ALARM, IVL	Choose the IV byte through which the response is sent to the user's system.
	XEC PATTERN(R1),8	Select specific pattern from PATTERN table.
	JMP *+9	
PATTERN:	XMIT A, ALARM	
	XMIT B, ALARM	
	XMIT C, ALARM	
	. .	Transmit proper pattern to output IV byte subfield by executing just one of these instructions. A–H represent the names associated with eight different control bit patterns.
	. .	
	. .	
	XMIT H, ALARM	
	. .	
	. .	
	. .	

ime: 1.5 μsecs.

REFERENCE

1. The Microcontroller System Description, Scientific Micro Systems, Mountain View, Ca., 1975.

15

3000 BIPOLAR
MICROCOMPUTER SET

Chapter 15 describes Intel bipolar microcomputer set 3000. The set is composed of high-speed bipolar LSI circuits which simplify the construction of microprogrammed central processors and device controllers. The basic cycle time is 85 nsecs. A microprogram control unit controls the sequence in which microinstructions are fetched from the microprogram memory. The central processing element contains all the circuits that represent a 2-bit-wide slice through the data processing section of a digital computer. The look-ahead carry generator takes care of a carry across a 16-bit central processing array. Interrupt control units, bus drivers, and multimode latch buffers simplify the system design.

The material* in this chapter has been adapted in part from a publication of Intel Corporation. The material so published herein is the full responsibility of the author.

15.1. MICROCOMPUTER SET

General Features

The Intel bipolar microcomputer set is a family of Schottky bipolar LSI circuits which simplify the construction of microprogrammed central processors and device controllers. These processors and controllers are truly microprogrammed in the sense that their control logic is organized around a separate read only memory called the microprogram memory. Control signals for the various processing elements are generated by the microinstructions contained in the microprogram memory. In the implementation of a typical central processor, as shown in Fig. 15.1, the microprogram interprets a higher level of instructions, called macroinstructions, similar to those found in a small computer. For device controllers, the microprograms directly implement the required control functions (Fig. 15.1).

* Programs, figures, and tables are courtesy and copyright © 1975 by Intel Corporation. All rights reserved.

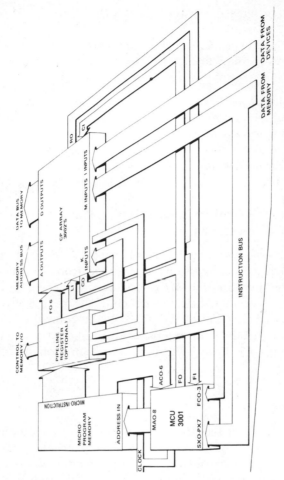

Figure 15.1. Block diagram of a typical system. (Courtesy of Intel Corporation).

563

15.2. MICROPROGRAM CONTROL UNIT (*MCU*) 3001

The INTEL 3001 microprogram control unit (*MCU*) controls the sequence in which microinstructions are fetched from the microprogram memory. Its functions include the following:

- Maintenance of the microprogram address register.
- Selection of the next microinstruction on the basis of the contents of the microprogram address register.
- Decoding and testing of data supplied via several input busses to determine the microinstruction execution sequence.
- Saving and testing of carry output data from the central processor (*CP*) array.
- Control of carry/shift input data to the *CP* array.
- Control of microprogram interrupts.

The *MCU* performs two major control functions. First, it controls the sequence in which microinstructions are fetched from the microprogram memory. For this purpose, the *MCU* contains a microprogram address register and the associated logic for selecting the next microinstruction address. The second function of the *MCU* is the control of the two flag flip-flops, which are included for interaction with the carry input and carry output logic of the *CP* array. The logical organization of the *MCU* is shown in Fig. 15.2.

Next Address Logic

The next address logic of the *MCU* provides a set of conditional and unconditional address control functions, used to implement a jump or jump/test operation as part of every microinstruction. In other words, each microinstruction typically contains a jump operation field that specifies the address control function and, hence, the next microprogram address.

To minimize the pin count of the *MCU* and to reduce the complexity of the next address logic, the microprogram address space is organized as a two-dimensional array or matrix. Each microprogram address corresponds to a unit of the matrix at a particular row and column location. Thus the 9-bit microprogram address is treated as specifying not one address, but two addresses—the row address in the upper 5 bits and the column address in the lower 4 bits. The address matrix can therefore contain, at most, 32 row addresses and 16 column addresses for a total of 512 microinstructions.

The next address logic of the *MCU* makes extensive use of this two-component addressing scheme. For example, from a particular row or column address, it is possible to jump unconditionally in one operation anywhere

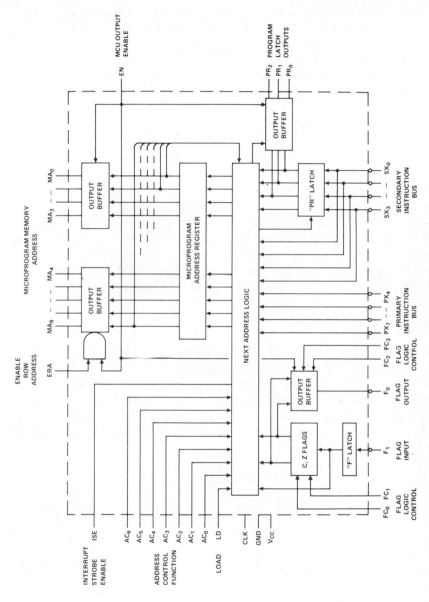

Figure 15.2. Block diagram of the microprogram control unit. (Courtesy of Intel Corporation).

565

in that row or column. It is not possible, however, to jump anywhere in the address matrix. In fact, for a given location in the matrix, there is a fixed subset of microprogram addresses that may be selected as the next address. These possible jump target addresses are referred to as a *jump set*. Each type of *MCU* address control (jump) function has a jump set associated with it.

Flag Logic

The flag logic of the *MCU* provides a set of functions for saving the current value of the carry output of the *CP* array and for controlling the value of the carry input to the *CP* array. These two distinct flag control functions are called flag input functions and flag output functions.

The flag logic is composed of two flip-flops, designated the C flag and the Z flag, along with a simple latch, called the F latch, which indicates the current state of the carry output line of the *CP* array. The flag logic is used in conjunction with the carry and shift logic of the *CP* array to implement a variety of shift/rotate and arithmetic functions.

Address Control Functions

The address control functions of the *MCU* are selected by the seven input lines, designated AC_0–AC_6. On the rising edge of the clock, the 9-bit microprogram address generated by the next address logic is loaded into the microprogram address register. The next microprogram address is delivered to the microprogram memory via the nine output lines, designated MA_0–MA_8. The microprogram address outputs are organized into row and column addresses as follows:

$$\underline{MA_8\ MA_7\ MA_6\ MA_5\ MA_4}$$
row address

$$\underline{MA_3\ MA_2\ MA_1\ MA_0}$$
column address

Each address control function is specified by a unique encoding of the data on the function input lines. From 3 to 5 bits of the data specify the particular function, while the remaining bits are used to select part of either the row or column address desired.

Figure 15.3 shows a typical application for the *MCU*: during the execution of a computer instruction, the instruction code is applied to the *MCU* over the memory data bus. The *MCU* generates the address MA_0–MA_8 and in this way selects in *PROM* the microprogram to implement the in-

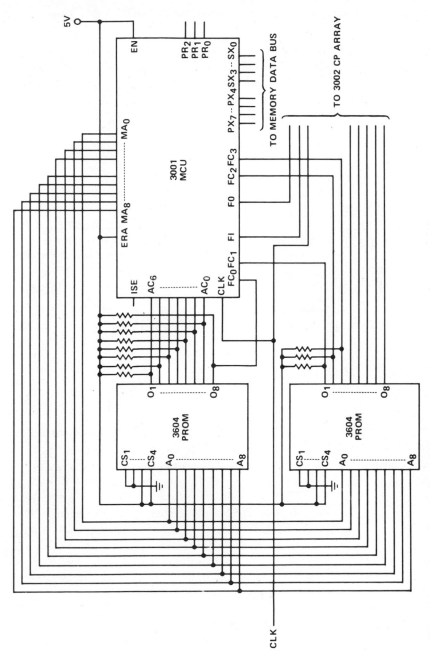

Figure 15.3. Configuration with microinstruction addressability. (Courtesy of Intel Corporation).

struction. Each step of the microprogram reads from *PROM*'s two pieces of information:

- The information needed to generate the address of the next microinstruction. The *MCU* receives this information over the AC_0–AC_6 bus.
- The information to control the central processor array, in order to execute the microinstruction.

15.3.   CENTRAL PROCESSING ELEMENT (*CPE*) 3002

General Features

The Intel 3002 central processing element (*CPE*) contains all the circuits that represent a 2-bit-wide slice through the data processing section of a digital computer. To construct a complete central processor for a given word width *N*, it is simply necessary to connect an array of $N/2$ *CPE*'s together. When wired together in such an array, a set of *CPE*'s provides the following capabilities:

- Two's complement arithmetic
- Logical AND, OR, NOT, and exclusive OR
- Incrementing and decrementing
- Shifting left or right
- Bit testing and zero detection
- Carry look-ahead generation
- Multiple data and address busses

The *CPE* provides the arithmetic, logic, and register functions of a 2-bit-wide slice through a microprogrammed central processor. Data from external sources such as main memory are brought into the *CPE* on one of the three separate input busses. Data being sent out of the *CPE* to external devices are carried on either of the two output busses. Within the *CPE*, data are stored in one of 11 scratch-pad registers or in the accumulator. Data from the input busses, the registers, or the accumulator are available to the arithmetic/logic section (*ALS*) under the control of two internal multiplexers. Additional inputs and outputs are included for carry propagation, shifting, and microfunction selection. The complete logical organization of the *CPE* is shown in Fig. 15.4.

F-, M-, and I-Bus Inputs

The seven microfunction bus input lines of the *CPE*, designated F_0–F_6, are decoded internally to select the *ALS* function, generate the scratch-pad address, and control the A- and B-multiplexers.

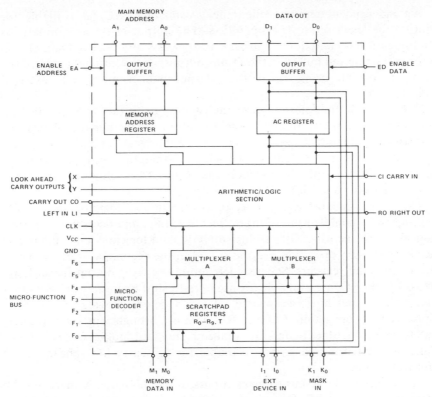

Figure 15.4. Central processing element. (Courtesy of Intel Corporation).

The M-bus inputs are arranged to bring data from an external main memory into the *CPE*. Data on the M-bus are multiplexed internally for input to the *ALS*.

The I-bus inputs are arranged to bring data from an external I/O system into the *CPE*. Data on the I-bus are also multiplexed internally, although independently of the M-bus, for input to the *ALS*. Separation of the two busses permits a relatively lightly loaded memory bus, even though a large number of I/O devices are connected to the I-bus. Alternatively, the I-bus may be wired to perform a multiple-bit shift (e.g., a byte exchange) by connecting it to one of the output busses. In this case, I/O device data are gated externally onto the M-bus.

Other Elements

The scratch pad contains 11 registers, designated R_0 through R_9 and T. The output of the scratch pad is multiplexed internally for input to the *ALS*. The *ALS* output is returned for input into the scratch pad.

An independent register called the *accumulator* (*AC*) is available for storing the result of an *ALS* operation. The output of the accumulator is multiplexed internally for input back to the *ALS* and is also available via a three-state output buffer on the D-bus outputs. Conventional usage of the D-bus is for data being sent to the external main memory or to external I/O devices.

The A and B multiplexers select the two inputs to the *ALS* specified on the microfunction bus. Inputs to the A-multiplexer include the M-bus, the scratch pad, and the accumulator. The B-multiplexer selects either the I-bus, the accumulator, or the K-bus. The selected B-multiplexer input is always logically ANDed with the data on the K-bus (see below) to provide a flexible masking and bit testing capability.

The *ALS* is capable of a variety of arithmetic and logic operations, including two's complement addition, incrementing, and decrementing, plus logical AND, inclusive OR, exclusive NOR, and logical complement. The result of an *ALS* operation may be stored in the accumulator or in one of the scratch pad registers. Separate left input and right output lines, designated LI and RO, are available for use in right shift operations. Carry input and carry output lines, designated CI and CO, are provided for normal ripple carry propagation. CO and RO data are brought out via two alternately enabled tristate buffers. In addition, standard look-ahead carry outputs, designated X and Y, are available for full carry look-ahead across any word length.

The ability of the K-bus to mask inputs to the *ALS* greatly increases the versatility of the *CPE*. During nonarithmetic operations in which carry propagation has no meaning, the carry circuits are used to perform a word-wise inclusive OR of the bits, masked by the K-bus, from the register or bus selected by the function decoder. Thus the *CPE* provides a flexible bit testing capability. The K-bus is also used during arithmetic operations to mask portions of the field being operated on. An additional function of the K-bus is to supply constants to the *CPE* from the microprogram.

Memory Address Register (*MAR*) and A-Bus

A separate *ALS* output is also available to the memory address register (*MAR*) and to the A-bus via a three-state output buffer. Conventional usage of the *MAR* and A-bus is for sending addresses to an external main memory. The *MAR* and A-bus may also be used, however, to select an external device when executing I/O operations.

During each microcycle, a microfunction is applied to F-bus inputs of the *CPE*. The microfunction is decoded, the operands are selected by the multiplexers, and the specified operation is performed by *ALS*. If a negative-going clock edge is applied, the result of the *ALS* operation is either deposited in the accumulator or written into the selected scratch-pad register. In addition: certain operations permit related address data to be deposited in the *MAR*. A new microfunction should only be applied following the rising edge of the clock.

By externally gating the clock input to the *CPE*, referred to as conditional clocking, the clock pulse may be selectively omitted during a microcycle. Since the carry, shift, and look-ahead circuits are not clocked, their outputs may be used to perform a variety of nondestructive tests on data in the accumulator or in the scratch pad. No register contents are modified by the operation because of the absence of the clock pulse.

The microfunction to be performed is determined by the function group (F group) or by register group (R group) selected by the data on the F-bus.

The typical configuration of *CPE*'s is shown in Fig. 15.5.

15.4. 3000 SYSTEM COMPONENTS

Look-Ahead Carry Generator (*LCG*)

The INTEL 3003 look-ahead carry generator (*LCG*) is a high-speed circuit capable of anticipating a carry across a full 16-bit 3002 central processing array. When used with a larger 3002 *CP* array, multiple 3003 carry generators provide high-speed carry look-ahead capability for any word length.

The *LCG* accepts eight pairs of active high-cascade inputs (*X, Y*) and an active low carry input and generates active low carries for up to eight groups of binary adders.

Multimode Latch Buffer

The INTEL 3212 multimode latch buffer is a versatile 8-bit latch with three-state output buffers and built-in device-select logic. It also contains an independent service request flip-flop for the generation of central processor interrupts. Because of its multimode capabilities, one or more 3212's can be used to implement many types of interface and support systems for series 3000 computing elements, including the interrupt control unit and the parallel bidirectional bus driver.

Interrupt Control Unit (*ICU*)

The Intel 3214 interrupt control unit (*ICU*) implements multilevel interrupt capability for systems designed with series 3000 computing elements.

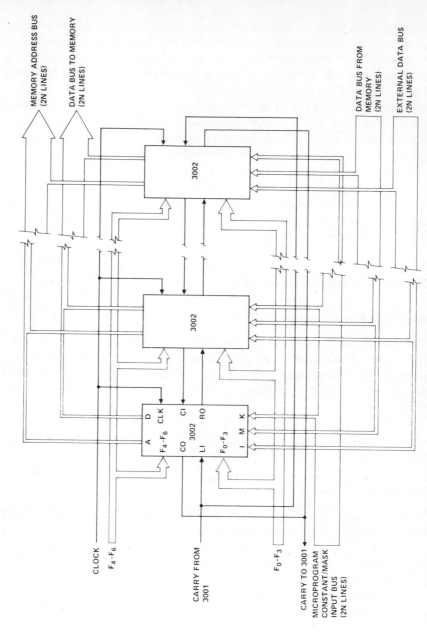

Figure 15.5. Ripple-carry Configuration composed of N 3002 *CPE*'s. (Courtesy of Intel Corporation).

MEMORY ADDRESS BUS (2N LINES)

DATA BUS TO MEMORY (2N LINES)

DATA BUS FROM MEMORY (2N LINES)

EXTERNAL DATA BUS (2N LINES)

CLOCK

F_4-F_6

CARRY FROM 3001

F_0-F_3

CARRY TO 3001

MICROPROGRAM CONSTANT/MASK INPUT BUS (2N LINES)

572

The *ICU* accepts an asynchronous interrupt strobe from the 3001 microprogram control unit or a bit in microprogram memory and generates a synchronous interrupt acknowledge and an interrupt vector, which may be directed to the *MCU* or *CP* array to uniquely identify the interrupt source.

The *ICU* is fully expandable in eight-level increments and provides the following system capabilities:

- Eight unique priority levels per *ICU*
- Automatic priority determination
- Programmable status
- *N*-level expansion capability
- Automatic interrupt vector generation

Parallel Bidirectional Bus Driver

The INTEL 3216 is a high-speed 4-bit parallel, bidirectional bus driver. Its three-state outputs enable it to isolate and drive external bus structures associated with series 3000 systems.

The 3216 driver and receiver gates have three-state outputs with *PNP* inputs. When the drivers or receivers are tristated, the inputs are disabled, presenting a low current load, typically less than 40 μA, to the system bus structure.

REFERENCE

1. Schottky Bipolar LSI Micro Computer Set, Data Sheets, Intel Corporation, Santa Clara, Ca., 1975.

16

IM6100 MICROPROCESSOR AND PDP-8 MINICOMPUTER

Chapter 16 presents Intersil IMP6100 microprocessor, which recognizes the instruction set of Digital Equipment Corporation's PDP8/E minicomputer. These are 12-bit machines. IMP6100 is designed in CMOS process. Low power and low voltage operations are important characteristics of CMOS. The instruction set is composed of memory reference, operate and input-output instructions. Four modes of addressing are available: direct, indirect current page, and zero page. Programmed and interrupt input-output transfers are described as well as the direct memory access.

The material* in this chapter has been adapted in part from a publication of Intersil Corporation. The material so published herein is the full responsibility of the author.

16.1. ARCHITECTURE

The IM6100 and IM6100A are single address, fixed word length, parallel transfer microprocessors using 12-bit, 2's complement arithmetic. The processors recognize the instruction set of Digital Equipment Corporation's PDP8/E minicomputer. The internal circuitry is completely static and is designed to operate at any speed between DC and the maximum operating frequency. Two pins are available to allow for an external crystal thereby eliminating the need for clock generators and level translators. The crystal can be removed and the processor clocked by an external clock generator. A 12-bit memory-accumulator ADD instruction is performed in 5 μsec by the IM6100 using a $+5$ volt supply and in 2.5 μsec by the IM6100A using a $+10$ volt supply. The device design is optimized to minimize the number of external components required for interfacing with standard memory and peripheral devices.

* Programs, figures, and tables are courtesy and copyright © 1975 by Intersil Corporation. All rights reserved.

574

PLA Output Latch

The PLA Output Latch latches the PLA output thereby permitting the PLA to be pipelined; it fetches the next control sequence while the CPU is executing the current sequence.

Memory and Device Control, ALU and REG Transfer Logic

The Memory and Device Control Unit provides external control signals to communicate with peripheral devices (DEVSEL), switch register (SWSEL), memory (MEMSEL) and/or control panel memory (CPSEL). During I/O instructions this unit also modifies the PLA outputs depending on the states of the four device control lines (SKP, C_0, C_1, C_2). The ALU and Register Transfer Logic provides the control signals for the internal register transfers and ALU operation.

Timing and State Control

The IM6100/A generates all the timing and state signals internally. A crystal is used to control the CPU operating frequency. The CPU divides the crystal frequency by two. With a 4MHz crystal, the internal states will be of 500ns duration. The major timing states are described in Fig. 16.2.

T_1 For memory reference instructions, a 12-bit address is sent on the DataX, DX, lines. The Load External Address Register, LXMAR, is used to clock an external register to store the

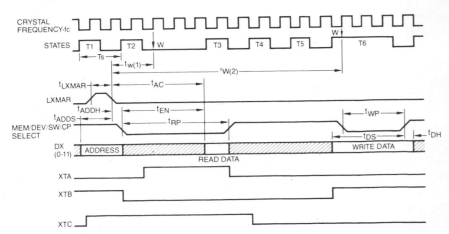

Figure 16.2 Basic timing (courtesy of Intersil Corporation).

The IM6100A has six 12-bit registers, a programmable logic array, an arithmetic and logic unit and associated gating and timing circuitry. A block diagram of the IM6100 is shown in Fig. 16.1.

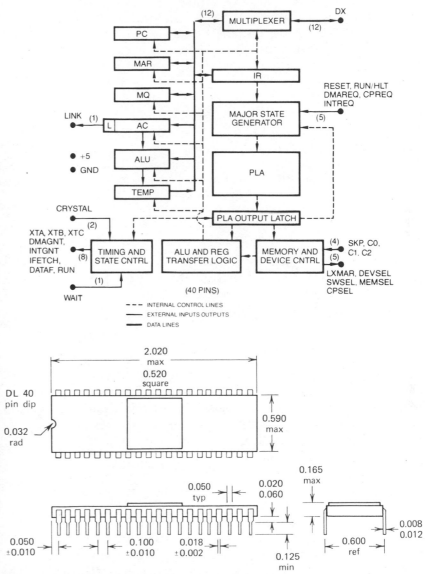

Figure 16.1 IMP 6100 block diagram and DIP (courtesy of Intersil Corporation).

Accumulator (*AC*)

The AC is a 12-bit register with which arithmetic and logical operations are performed. Data words may be fetched from memory to the AC or stored from the AC into memory. Arithmetic and logical operations involve two operands, one held in the AC and the other fetched from the memory. The result of the operation is left in the AC. The AC may be cleared, complemented, tested, incremented or rotated under program control. The AC also serves as an input-output register. All programmed data transfers pass through the AC.

Link (*L*)

The Link is a 1-bit flip-flop that serves as a high-order extension of the AC. It is used as a carry flip-flop for 2's complement arithmetic. A carry out of the ALU complements the Link. Link can be cleared, set, complemented and tested under program control and rotated as part of the AC.

MQ Register (*MQ*)

The MQ is a 12-bit temporary register which is program accessible. The contents of AC may be transferred to the MQ for temporary storage. MQ can be OR'ed with the AC and the result stored in the AC. The contents of the AC and the MQ may also be exchanged.

Memory Address Register (*MAR*)

While accessing memory, the 12-bit MAR register contains the address of the memory location that is currently selected for reading or writing. The MAR is also used as an internal register for microprogram control during data transfers to and from memory and peripherals.

Program Counter (*PC*)

The 12-bit PC contains the address of the memory location from which the next instruction is fetched. During an instruction fetch, the PC is transferred to MAR and the PC is then incremented by 1. When there is a branch to another address in memory, the branch address is set into the PC. Branching normally takes place under program control. However, during an input-output operation, a device may specify a branch address. A skip (SKP) instruction increments the PC by 1, thus causing the next instruction to be skipped. The SKP instruction may be unconditional or

conditional on the state of the AC and/or the Link. During an in operation, a device can also cause the next sequential instruc skipped.

Arithmetic and Logical Unit (*ALU*)

The ALU performs both arithmetic and logical operations—2's ment binary addition, AND, OR and complement. The ALU can a single position shift either to the left or to the right. A double implemented in two single bit shifts. The ALU can also shift by 3 to implement a byte swap in two steps. The AC is always one of th to the ALU. However, under internal microprogram control, AC gated off and all one's or all zero's gated in. The second input may one of the other registers under internal microprogram control.

Temporary Register (*TEMP*)

The 12-bit TEMP register latches the result of an ALU operation it is sent to the destination register to avoid race conditions. The is also used as an internal register for microprogram control.

Instruction Register (*IR*)

During an instruction fetch the 12-bit IR contains the instruction th to be executed by the CPU. The IR specifies the initial step of the m program sequence for each instruction and is also used as an inte register to store temporary data for microprogram control.

Multiplexer (*DX*)

The 12-bit Input/Output Multiplexer handles data, address and instructi transfers, into and out of, the CPU, from or into, the main memory an peripheral devices on a time-multiplexed basis.

Major State Generator and the Programmed Logic Array (*PLA*)

During an instruction fetch the instruction to be executed is loaded into the IR. The PLA is then used for the correct sequencing of the CPU for the appropriate instruction. After an instruction is completely sequenced, the major state generator scans the internal priority network. The state of the priority network decides whether the machine is going to fetch the next instruction in sequence or service one of the external request lines.

address information externally, if required. When executing an Input-Output I/O instruction, the instruction being executed is sent on the DX lines to be stored externally. The external address register then contains the device address and control information.

Various CPU request lines are priority sampled if the next cycle is an Instruction Fetch cycle. Current state of the CPU is available externally.

T_2

Memory/Peripheral data is read for an input transfer (READ). WAIT controls the transfer duration. If WAIT is active during input transfers, the CPU waits in the T_2 state. The wait duration is an integral multiple of the crystal frequency—250ns for 4MHz.

For memory reference instructions, the Memory Select, MEMSEL, line is active. For I/O instructions the Device Select, DEVSEL, line is active. Control lines, therefore, distinguish the contents of the external register as memory or device address.

External device sense lines, C_0, C_1, C_2, and SKP, are sampled if the instruction being executed is an I/O instruction.

Control Panel Memory Select, CPSEL, and Switch Register Select, SWSEL, become active low for data transfers between the IM6100 and Control Panel Memory and the Switch Register, respectively.

T_3, T_4, T_5 ALU operation and internal register transfers.
T_6 This state is entered for an output transfer (WRITE). The address is defined during T_1. WAIT controls the time for which the Write data must be maintained.

16.2. INSTRUCTION SET AND ADDRESSING

The IM6100 instructions are 12-bit words stored in memory. The IM6100 makes no distinction between instructions and data; it can manipulate instructions as stored variables or execute data as instructions when it is programmed to do so. There are three general classes of IM6100 instructions. They are referred to as Memory Reference Instruction (MRI), Operate Instruction (OPR) and Input/Output Transfer Instruction (IOT).

Before proceeding further, we will discuss the Specific Memory Organization with which the IM6100 interfaces.

Memory Organization

The IM6100 has a basic addressing capacity of 4096 12-Bit words. The addressing capacity may be extended by Extended Memory Control hardware. The memory system is organized in 4096 word blocks, called MEMORY FIELDS. The first 4096 words of memory are in Field 0. If a full 32K of memory is installed, the uppermost Memory Field will be numbered 7. In any given Memory Field every location has a unique 4 digit octal (12 bit binary) address, 0000_8 to 7777_8 (0000_{10} to 4095_{10}). Each Memory Field is subdivided into 32 PAGES of 128 words each. Memory Pages are numbered sequentially from Page 00_8, containing addresses 0000–0177_8, to Page 37_8, containing addresses 7600_8–7777_8. The first 5 bits of a 12-bit MEMORY ADDRESS denote the PAGE NUMBER and the low order 7 bits specify the PAGE ADDRESS of the memory location within the given Page.

During an instruction fetch cycle, the IM6100 fetches the instruction pointed to by the PC. The contents of the PC are transferred to the MAR. The PC is incremented by 1. The PC now contains the address of the 'next' sequential instruction. The MAR contains the address of the 'current' instruction which must be fetched from memory. Bits 0–4 of the MAR identify the CURRENT PAGE, that is, the Page from which instructions are currently being fetched and bits 5–11 of the MAR identify the location within the Current Page. (PAGE ZERO (0), by definition, denotes the first 128 words of memory, 0000_8–0177_8.)

Memory Reference Instructions (*MRI*)

The Memory Reference Instructions operate on the contents of a memory location or use the contents of a memory location to operate on the AC or the PC. The first 3 bits of a Memory Reference Instruction specify the operation code, or OPCODE, and the low order 9 bits, the OPERAND address, as shown in Fig. 16.3.

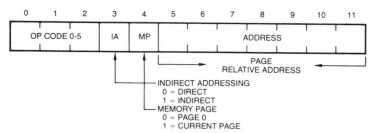

Figure 16.3 Memory reference instruction (courtesy of Intersil Corporation).

Bits 5 through 11, the PAGE ADDRESS, identify the location of the OPERAND on a given page, but they do not identify the page itself. The page is specified by bit 4, called the CURRENT PAGE OR PAGE 0 BIT. If bit 4 is a 0, the page address is interpreted as a location on Page 0. If bit 4 is a 1, the page address specified is interpreted to be on the Current Page.

For example, if bits 5 through 11 represent 123_8 and bit 4 is a 0, the location referenced is the absolute address 0123_8. However, if bit 4 is a 1 and the current instruction is in a memory location whose absolute address is 4610_8 the page address 123_8 designates the absolute address 4723_8, as shown below.

$$4610_8 \ = \ 100 \ 110 \ 001 \ 000 \ = \ PAGE \ 10 \ 011 \ = \ PAGE \ 23_8$$

Location 4610_8 is in PAGE 23_8. Location 123_8 in PAGE 23_8, CURRENT PAGE, will be:

$$10 \ 011 \ 1 \ 010 \ 011 \ = \ 100 \ 111 \ 010 \ 011 \ = \ 4723_8$$

PAGE	PAGE
NUMBER	ADDRESS
23_8	123_8

By this method, 256 locations may be directly addressed, 128 on PAGE 0 and 128 on the CURRENT PAGE. Other locations are addressed by utilizing bit 3. When bit 3 is a 0, the operand address is a DIRECT ADDRESS. An INDIRECT ADDRESS (pointer address) identifies the location that contains the desired address (effective address). To address a location that is not directly addressable, not in PAGE 0 or in the CURRENT PAGE, the absolute address of the desired location is stored in one of the 256 directly addressable locations (pointer address). Upon execution, the MRI will operate on the contents of the location identified by the address contained in the pointer location.

It should be noted that locations 0010_8–0017_8 in PAGE 0 are AUTO-INDEXED. If these locations are addressed indirectly, the contents are incremented by 1 and restored before they are used as the operand address. These locations may, therefore, be used for indexing applications.

Table 16.1 lists the mnemonics for the five memory reference instruction, their OPCODE, the operations they perform, the number of states and the execution time at $+5.0V$ and $+10.0V$, assuming a crystal frequency of 4MHz and 8MHz or a state time period of 500 ns and 250ns, respectively.

It should be noted that the data is represented in Two's Complement Integer notation. In this system, the negative of a number is formed by complementing each bit in the data word and adding "1" to the complemented number. The sign is indicated by the most significant bit. In the 12-bit word used by the IM6100, when bit 0 is a "0," it denotes a positive number and when bit 0 is a "1," it denotes a negative number. The maximum number ranges for this system are 3777_8 ($+2047$) and 4000_8 (-2048).

Notations applied in Table 16.1, are defined the same way as in the Section   3.2.

Operate Instructions

The Operate Instructions, which have an OPCODE of 7_8 (111), consists of 3 groups of microinstructions. Group 1 microinstructions, which are identified by the presence of a 0 in bit 3, are used to perform logical operations on the contents of the accumulator and link. Group 2 micro instructions, which are identified by the presence of a 1 in bit 3 and a 0 in bit 11, are used primarily to test the contents of the accumulator and then conditionally skip the next sequential instruction. Group 3 microinstructions have a 1 in bit 3 and a 1 in bit 11 and are used to perform logical operations on the contents of the AC and MQ.

Operate microinstructions from any group may be microprogrammed with other operate microinstructions of the same group. The actual code for a microprogrammed combination of two, or more, microinstructions is the bitwise logical OR of the octal codes for the individual microinstructions. When more than one operation is microprogrammed into a single instruction, the operations are performed in a prescribed sequence, with logical sequence number 1 microinstructions performed first, logical sequence number 2 microinstructions performed second, logical sequence number 3 microinstructions performed third and so on. Two operations with the same logical sequence number, within a given group of microinstructions, are performed simultaneously.

Three groups of operate instructions are listed in Tables 16.2, 16.3, and 16.4.

16.3.   INPUT/OUTPUT TRANSFER

The input/output transfer instructions, which have an OPCODE of 6_8, are used to initiate the operation of peripheral devices and to transfer data between peripherals and the IM6100. Three types of data transfer may be used to receive or transmit information between the IM6100 and one or more peripheral I/O devices. PROGRAMMED DATA TRANSFER provides a straightforward means of communicating with relatively slow I/O devices, such as Teletypes, cassettes, card readers and CRT displays. IN-

TERRUPT TRANSFERS use the interrupt system to service several peripheral devices simultaneously, on an intermittent basis, permitting computational operations to be performed concurrently with the data I/O operations. Both Programmed Data Transfers and Program Interrupt Transfers use the accumulator as a buffer, or storage area, for all data transfers. Since data may be transferred only between the accumulator and the peripheral, only one 12 bit word at a time may be transferred. DIRECT MEMORY ACCESS, DMA, transfers variable-size blocks of data between high-speed peripherals and the memory with a minimum of program control required by the IM6100.

IOT Instruction Format

The Input/Output Transfer Instruction format is represented in Fig. 16.4.

The first three bits, 0–2, are always set to 6_8 (110) to specify an IOT instruction. The next six bits, 3–8, contain the device selection code that determines the specific I/O device for which the IOT instruction is intended and, therefore, permit interface with up to 64 I/O devices. The last three bits, 9–11, contain the operation specification code that determines the specific operation to be performed. The nature of this operation for any given IOT instruction depends entirely upon the circuitry designed into the I/O device interface.

Programmed Data Transfer

Programmed Data Transfer is the easiest, simplest, most convenient and most common means of performing data I/O. For microprocessor applications, it may also be the most cost effective approach. The data transfer begins when the IM6100 fetches an instruction from the memory and recognizes that the current instruction is an IOT. This is referred to as IFETCH and consists of five (5) internal states. The IM6100 sequences the IOT instruction through a 2-cycle execute phase referred to as IOT_A and IOT_B. Bits 0–11 of the IOT instruction are available on DX 0–11 at $IOT_A \cdot$ LXMAR. These bits must be latched in an external address register. DEVSEL is active low to enable data transfers between the IM6100 and the peripheral device(s). The selected peripheral device communicates with the IM6100 through 4 control lines—C_0, C_1, C_2 and SKP. In the IM6100 the type of data transfer, during an IOT instruction, is specified by the peripheral device(s) by asserting the control lines, as shown in Table 16.5.

The control line SKP, when low during an IOT, causes the IM6100 to skip the next sequential instruction. This feature is used to sense the status of various signals in the device interface. The C_0, C_1, and C_2 lines are

MNE-MONIC	OP CODE	OPERATION	NUMBER OF STATES	EXECUTION TIME (μs)	
				IM6100 +5.0V	IM6100A +10.0V
AND	0_8	LOGICAL AND DIRECT (I = 0) Operation: (AC) <—(AC)$\land$(EA) Description: Contents of the EA are logically AND'ed with the contents of the AC and the result is stored in AC.	10	5.0	2.50
		INDIRECT (I = 1, PA ≠ $0010\text{-}0017_8$) Operation: (AC) <—(AC)$\land$(PA))	15	7.5	3.75
		AUTOINDEX (I = 1, PA = $0010\text{-}0017_8$) Operation: (PA) <—(PA) + 1; (AC) <—(AC)$\land$((PA))	16	8.0	4.00
TAD	1_8	BINARY ADD DIRECT (I = 0) Operation: (AC) <—(AC) + (EA) Description: Contents of the EA are ADD'ed with the contents of the AC and the result is stored in the AC; carry out complements the LINK. If AC is initially cleared, this instruction acts as LOAD from Memory	10	5.0	2.50
		INDIRECT (I = 1, PA ≠ $0010\text{-}0017_8$) Operation: (AC) <—(AC) + ((PA))	15	7.5	3.75
		AUTOINDEX (I = 1, PA = $0010\text{-}0017_8$) Operation: (PA) <—(PA) + 1; (AC) <—(AC) + ((PA))	16	8.0	4.00
ISZ	2_8	INCREMENT AND SKIP IF ZERO DIRECT (I = 0) Operation: (EA) <—(EA) + 1; if (EA) = 0000_8, PC <—PC + 1 Description: Contents of the EA are incremented by 1 and restored. If the result is zero, the next sequential instruction is skipped.	16	8.0	4.00
		INDIRECT (I = 1, PA ≠ $0010\text{-}0017_8$) Operation: ((PA)) <—((PA)) + 1; if ((PA)) = 0000_8, PC <—PC + 1	21	10.5	5.25
		AUTOINDEX (I = 1, PA = $0010\text{-}0017_8$) Operation: (PA) <—(PA) + 1; ((PA)) <—((PA)) + 1; if ((PA)) = 0000_8, PC <—PC + 1	22	11.0	5.50

584

Mnemonic	Opcode				
DCA	3_8	**DEPOSIT AND CLEAR THE ACCUMULATOR DIRECT (I = 0)** Operation: (EA) <—(AC); (AC) <—0000_8 Description: The contents of the AC are stored in EA and the AC is cleared.	11	5.5	2.75
		INDIRECT (I = 1, PA ≠ $0010\text{-}0017_8$) Operation: ((PA)) <—(AC); (AC) <—0000_8	16	8.0	4.00
		AUTOINDEX (I = 1, PA = $0010\text{-}0017_8$) Operation: (PA) <—(PA) + 1; ((PA)) <—(AC); (AC) <—0000_8	17	8.5	4.25
JMS	4_8	**JUMP TO SUBROUTINE DIRECT (I = 0)** Operation: (EA) <—(PC), (PC) <—EA + 1 Description: The contents of the PC are stored in the EA. The PC is incremented by 1 immediately after every instruction fetch. The contents of the EA now point to the next sequential instruction following the JMS (return address). The next instruction is taken from EA + 1.	11	5.5	2.75
		INDIRECT (I = 1, PA ≠ $0010\text{-}0017_8$) Operation: ((PA)) <—PC, (PC) <—(PA) + 1	16	8.0	4.00
		AUTOINDEX (I = 1, PA = $0010\text{-}0017_8$) Operation: (PA) <—(PA) + 1; ((PA)) <—PC, (PC) <—(PA) + 1	17	8.5	4.25
JMP	5_8	**JUMP DIRECT (I = 0)** Operation: (PC) <—EA Description: The next instruction is taken from the EA.	10	5.0	2.50
		INDIRECT (I = 1, PA ≠ $0010\text{-}0017_8$) Operation: (PC) <—(PA)	15	7.5	3.75
		AUTOINDEX (I = 1, PA = $0010\text{-}0017_8$) Operation: (PA) <—(PA) + 1; (PC) <—(PA)	16	8.0	4.00

MEMORY REFERENCE INSTRUCTIONS

MNEMONIC	OCTAL CODE	LOGICAL SEQUENCE	OPERATION	NUMBER OF STATES	EXECUTION TIME (μs) IM6100 +5.0V	EXECUTION TIME (μs) IM6100A +10.0V
NOP	7000	1	NO OPERATION—This instruction causes a 10 state delay in program execution, without affecting the state of the IM6100. It may be used for timing synchronization or as a convenient means of deleting an instruction from a program.	10	5.0	2.50
IAC	7001	3	INCREMENT ACCUMULATOR—The content of the AC is incremented by one (1) and carry out complements the Link (L).	10	5.0	2.50
RAL	7004	4	ROTATE ACCUMULATOR LEFT—The contents of the AC and L are rotated one binary position to the left. AC (1) is shifted to L and L is shifted to AC (11).	15	7.5	3.75
RTL	7006	4	ROTATE TWO LEFT—The contents of the AC and L are rotated two binary positions to the left. AC (1) is shifted to L and L is shifted to AC (10).	15	7.5	3.75
RAR	7010	4	ROTATE ACCUMULATOR RIGHT—The content of the AC and L are rotated one binary position to the right. AC (11) is shifted to L and L is shifted to AC (0).	15	7.5	3.75
RTR	7012	4	ROTATE TWO RIGHT—The contents of the AC and L are rotated two binary positions to the right. AC (10) is shifted to L and L is shifted to AC (1).	15	7.5	3.75
BSW	7002	4	BYTE SWAP—The right six (6) bits of the AC are exchanged or SWAPPED with the left six bits. AC (0) is swapped with AC (6), AC (1) with AC (7), etc. L is not affected.	15	7.5	3.75
CML	7020	2	COMPLEMENT LINK—The content of the link is complemented.	10	5.0	2.50

				10	5.0	2.50
CMA	7040	2	COMPLEMENT ACCUMULATOR—The content of each bit of the AC is complemented having the effect of replacing the content of the AC with its one's complement.	10	5.0	2.50
CIA	7041	2,3	COMPLEMENT AND INCREMENT ACCUMULATOR—The content of the AC is replaced with its two's complement. Carry out complements the LINK.	10	5.0	2.50
CLL	7100	1	CLEAR LINK—The link is loaded with a binary 0.	10	5.0	2.50
CLL RAL	7104	1,4	CLEAR LINK—ROTATE ACCUMULATOR LEFT.	15	7.5	3.75
CLL RTL	7106	1,4	CLEAR LINK—ROTATE TWO LEFT.	15	7.5	3.75
CLL RAR	7110	1,4	CLEAR LINK—ROTATE ACCUMULATOR RIGHT.	15	7.5	3.75
CLL RTR	7112	1,4	CLEAR LINK—ROTATE TWO RIGHT.	15	7.5	3.75
STL	7120	1,2	SET THE LINK—The LINK is loaded with a binary 1 corresponding with a microprogrammed combination of CLL and CML.	10	5.0	2.50
CLA	7200	1	CLEAR ACCUMULATOR—The accumulator is loaded with binary 0's.	10	5.0	2.50
CLA IAC	7201	1,3	CLEAR ACCUMULATOR—INCREMENT ACCUMULATOR.	10	5.0	2.50
GLT	7204	1,4	GET THE LINK—The AC is cleared; the content of L is shifted into AC (11), a 0 is shifted into L. This is a microprogrammed combination of CLA and RAL.	15	7.5	3.75
CLA CLL	7300	1	CLEAR ACCUMULATOR—CLEAR LINK.	10	5.0	2.50
STA	7240	1,2	SET THE ACCUMULATOR—Each bit of the AC is set to 1 corresponding to a micro-programmed combination of CLA and CMA.	10	5.0	2.50

GROUP 1 OPERATION MICROINSTRUCTIONS

MNEMONIC	OCTAL CODE	LOGICAL SEQUENCE	OPERATION	NUMBER OF STATES	EXECUTION TIME (μs)	
					IM6100 +5.0V	IM6100A +10.0V
NOP	7400	1	NO OPERATION—See GROUP 1 MICROINSTRUCTIONS	10	5.0	2.50
HLT	7402	3	HALT—Program stops at the conclusion of the current machine cycle. If HLT is combined with others in OPR 2, the other operations are completed before the end of the cycle.	10	5.0	2.50
OSR	7404	3	OR WITH SWITCH REGISTER—The content of the Switch Register if OR'ed with the content of the AC and the result is stored in the AC. The OSR INSTRUCTION TIMING is shown in Figure 7. The IM6100 sequences the OSR instruction through a 2-cycle execute phase referred to as OPR 2A and OPR 2B.	15	7.5	3.75
SKP	7410	1	SKIP—The content of the PC is incremented by 1, to skip the next sequential instruction.	10	5.0	2.50
SNL	7420	1	SKIP ON NON-ZERO LINK—The content of L is sampled, the next sequential instruction is skipped if L contains a 1. If L contains a 0, the next instruction is executed.	10	5.0	2.50
SZL	7430	1	SKIP ON ZERO LINK—The content of L is sampled, the next sequential instruction is skipped if L contains a 0. If the L contains a 1, the next instruction is executed.	10	5.0	2.50
SZA	7440	1	SKIP ON ZERO ACCUMULATOR—The content of the AC is sampled; the next sequential instruction is skipped if the AC has all bits which are 0. If any bit in the AC is a 1, the next instruction is executed.	10	5.0	2.50
SNA	7450	1	SKIP ON NON-ZERO ACCUMULATOR—The content of the AC is sampled; the next sequential instruction is skipped if the AC has any bits which are not 0. If every bit in the AC is 0, the next instruction is executed.	10	5.0	2.50
SZA SNL	7460	1	SKIP ON ZERO ACCUMULATOR, OR SKIP ON NON-ZERO LINK, OR BOTH	10	5.0	2.50

588

Mnemonic	Octal	Notes	Description	10	5.0	2.50
SNA SZL	7470	1	SKIP ON NON-ZERO ACCUMULATOR *AND* SKIP ON ZERO LINK	10	5.0	2.50
SMA	7500	1	SKIP ON MINUS ACCUMULATOR—If the content of AC (0) contains a 1, indicating that the AC contains a negative two's complement number, the next sequential instruction is skipped. If AC (0) contains a 0, the next instruction is executed.	10	5.0	2.50
SPA	7510	1	SKIP ON POSITIVE ACCUMULATOR—The contents of AC (0) are sampled. If AC (0) contains a 0, indicating that the AC contains a positive two's complement number, the next sequential instruction is skipped. If AC (0) contains a 1, the next instruction is executed.	10	5.0	2.50
SMA SNL	7520	1	SKIP ON MINUS ACCUMULATOR *OR* SKIP ON NON-ZERO LINK *OR* BOTH	10	5.0	2.50
SPA SZL	7530	1	SKIP ON POSITIVE ACCUMULATOR *AND* SKIP ON ZERO LINK	10	5.0	2.50
SMA SZA	7540	1	SKIP ON MINUS ACCUMULATOR *OR* SKIP ON ZERO ACCUMULATOR *OR* BOTH	10	5.0	2.50
SPA SNA	7550	1	SKIP ON POSITIVE ACCUMULATOR *AND* SKIP ON NON-ZERO ACCUMULATOR	10	5.0	2.50
SMA SZA SNL	7560	1	SKIP ON MINUS ACCUMULATOR *OR* SKIP ON ZERO ACCUMULATOR *OR* SKIP ON NON-ZERO LINK *OR* ALL	10	5.0	2.50
SPA SNA SZL	7570	1	SKIP ON POSITIVE ACCUMULATOR *AND* SKIP ON NON-ZERO ACCUMULATOR *AND* SKIP ON ZERO LINK	10	5.0	2.50
CLA	7600	2	CLEAR ACCUMULATOR—The AC is loaded with binary 0's.	10	5.0	2.50
LAS	7604	1,3	LOAD ACCUMULATOR WITH SWITCH REGISTER—The content of the AC is loaded with the content of the SR, bit for bit. This is equivalent to a microprogrammed combination of CLA and OSR.	15	7.5	3.75
SZA CLA	7640	1,2	SKIP ON ZERO ACCUMULATOR *THEN* CLEAR ACCUMULATOR	10	5.0	2.50
SNA CLA	7650	1,2	SKIP ON NON-ZERO ACCUMULATOR *THEN* CLEAR ACCUMULATOR	10	5.0	2.50
SMA CLA	7700	1,2	SKIP ON MINUS ACCUMULATOR *THEN* CLEAR ACCUMULATOR	10	5.0	2.50
SPA CLA	7710	1,2	SKIP ON POSITIVE ACCUMULATOR *THEN* CLEAR ACCUMULATOR	10	5.0	2.50

GROUP 2 OPERATE MICROINSTRUCTIONS

MNEMONIC	OCTAL CODE	LOGICAL SEQUENCE	OPERATION	NUMBER OF STATES	EXECUTION TIME (μs)	
					IM6100 +5.0V	IM6100A +10.0V
NOP	7401	3	NO OPERATION—See Group 1 Microinstructions	10	5.0	2.50
MQL	7421	2	MQ REGISTER LOAD—The content of the AC is loaded into the MQ, the AC is cleared and the original content of the MQ is lost.	10	5.0	2.50
MQA	7501	2	MQ REGISTER INTO ACCUMULATOR—The content of the MQ is OR'ed with the content of the AC and the result is loaded into the AC. The original content of the AC is lost but the original content of the MQ is retained. This instruction provides the programmer with an inclusive OR operation.	10	5.0	2.50
SWP	7521	3	SWAP ACCUMULATOR AND MQ REGISTER—The content of the AC and MQ are interchanged accomplishing a microprogrammed combination of MQA and MQL.	10	5.0	2.50
CLA	7601	1	CLEAR ACCUMULATOR	10	5.0	2.50
CAM	7621	3	CLEAR ACCUMULATOR AND MQ REGISTER—The content of the AC and MQ are loaded with binary 0's. This is equivalent to a microprogrammed combination of CLA and MQL.	10	5.0	2.50
ACL	7701	3	CLEAR ACCUMULATOR AND LOAD MQ REGISTER INTO ACCUMULATOR—This is equivalent to a microprogrammed combination of CLA and MQA.	10	5.0	2.50
CLA SWP	7721	3	CLEAR ACCUMULATOR AND SWAP ACCUMULATOR AND MQ REGISTER—The content of the AC is cleared. The content of the MQ is loaded into the AC and the MQ is cleared.	10	5.0	2.50

GROUP 3 OPERATE MICROINSTRUCTIONS

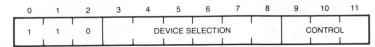

Figure 16.4 Input-output instruction format (courtesy of Intersil Corporation).

Table 16.5 Programmed I/O Control Lines

Control Lines				
C_0	C_1	C_2	Operation	Description
H	H	H	DEV $< -$AC	The contents of the AC is sent to the device.
L	H	H	DEV $< -$AC; CLA	The contents of the AC is sent to a device and then the AC is cleared.
H	L	H	AC $< -$AC V DEV	Data is received from a device, OR'ed with the data in the AC and the result is stored in the AC.
L	L	H	AC $< -$DEV	Data is received from a device and loaded into the AC.
*	H	L	PC $< -$PC $+$ DEV	Data from the device is added to the contents of the PC. This is referred to as a RELATIVE JUMP.
*	L	L	PC $< -$DEV	Data is received from a device and loaded into the PC. This is referred to as an ABSOLUTE JUMP.

*Don't Care

treated independently of the SKP line. In the case of a RELATIVE or ABSOLUTE JUMP, the skip operation is performed after the jump. The input signals to the IM6100, DX 0–11, C_0, C_1, C_2, and SKP, are sampled at IOT_A during $\overline{DEVSEL} \cdot XT_C$. The data from the IM6100 is available to the device(s) during $\overline{DEVSEL} \cdot \overline{XT}_C$. IOT_B cycle is internal to the IM6100 to perform the operations requested during IOT_A. Both IOT_A and IOT_B consist of six (6) internal states.

In summary, Programmed Data Transfer performs data I/O with a minimum of hardware support. The maximum rate at which programmed data transfers may take place is limited by the IM6100 instruction execution rate. However, the data rate of the most commonly used peripheral devices is much lower than the maximum rate at which programmed transfers can take place in the IM6100. The major drawback associated with Programmed Data Transfer is that the IM6100 must hang up in a waiting loop while the I/O device completes the last transfer and prepares for the next transfer. On the other hand, this technique permits easy hardware implementation and simple, economical interface design. For this reason, almost all devices except bulk storage units rely heavily on programmed data transfer for routine data I/O.

Program Interrupt Transfers

The program interrupt system may be used to initiate programmed data transfers in such a way that the time spent waiting for device status is greatly reduced or eliminated altogether. It also provides a means of performing concurrent programmed data transfers between the IM6100 and the peripheral devices. This is accomplished by isolating the I/O handling routines from the mainline program and using the interrupt system to ensure that these routines are entered only when an I/O device status is set, indicating that the device is actually ready to perform the next data transfer, or that it requires some sort of intervention from the running program.

The interrupt system allows certain external conditions to interrupt the computer program by driving the INTREQ input to the IM6100 Low. If no higher priority requests are outstanding and the interrupt system is enabled, the IM6100 grants the device interrupt at the end of the current instruction. After an interrupt has been granted, the Interrupt Enable Flip-Flop in the IM6100 is reset so that no more interrupts are acknowledged until the interrupt system is re-enabled under program control.

The current content of the Program Counter, PC, is deposited in location 0000_8 of the memory and the program fetches the instruction from location 0001_8. The return address is available in location 0000_8. This address must be saved in a software stack if nested interrupts are permitted.

Direct Memory Access (DMA)

Direct Memory Access, sometimes called data break, is the preferred form of data transfer for use with high-speed storage devices such as magnetic disk or tape units. The DMA mechanism transfers data directly between memory and peripheral devices. The IM6100 is involved only in setting up the transfer; the transfers take place with no processor intervention on a "cycle stealing" basis. The DMA transfer rate is limited only by the bandwidth of the memory and the data transfer characteristics of the device.

The device generates a DMA Request when it is ready to transfer data. The IM6100 grants the DMAREQ by activating the DMAGNT signal at the end of the current instruction. The IM6100 suspends any further instruction fetches until the DMAREQ line is released. The DX lines are tri-stated, all SEL lines are high, and the external timing signals XT_A,

XT_B, and XT_C are active. The device which generated the DMAREQ must provide the address and the necessary control signals to the memory for data transfers. The DMAREQ line can also be used as a level sensitive "pause" line.

Minicomputer PDP-8 and Its Software

In the last ten years tremendous software has been developed for the PDP-8. This software has been developed by both, Digital Equipment Corporation as well as thousands of users of the PDP-8. The PDP-8 also supports the high-level languages: FOCAL, FORTRAN and BASIC. Especially useful is the REAL-TIME BASIC. This language enables the user to program real-time operations using simple, high-level language statements. The statements exist for typical instrumentation and process control devices. It is interesting to notice that the PDP-8 is most probably the only computer entering into a second decade of successful applications. It has lived through many hardware versions, all of them software compatible. Today both, Digital Equipment Corporation and Intersil Corporation are delivering to the market place new machines from this interesting family.

REFERENCE

1. Intersil IM6100 CMOS 12 Bit Microprocessor, Intersil Corporation, Cupertino, Calif., 1975.
2. Small Computer Handbook, Digital Equipment Corporation, Maynard, Mass., 1974.

APPENDIX A

FLOWCHART SYMBOLS

Processing

Rectangular symbol represents the processing operation. The operation can be expressed with a number of instructions. Usually the process can be described in the rectangle, using algebraic or logical equation.

Decision

A comparison diamond is used at the point where program is split into few branches. Decision-making function usually compares the two quantities. This test is included within the diamond. The possible results of the test are used to label the branches going out of the diamond.

Predefined Process

This symbol is used to indicate a program segment which is discussed elsewhere, and is not detailed in the flowchart. The major subroutines and other routines discussed elsewhere are often represented in this way.

Connector

When the flowchart has to be broken in parts, the connector symbol can be used to show the flow of the program. Its sole purpose is to provide continuity. A number or a letter is enclosed to label the corresponding exits and entries. This symbol represents no processing or other program function.

Input-Output

This symbol is used to indicate the point in the program when the input or output of data is performed. This is a general symbol, which can be used for all kinds of input-output operation.

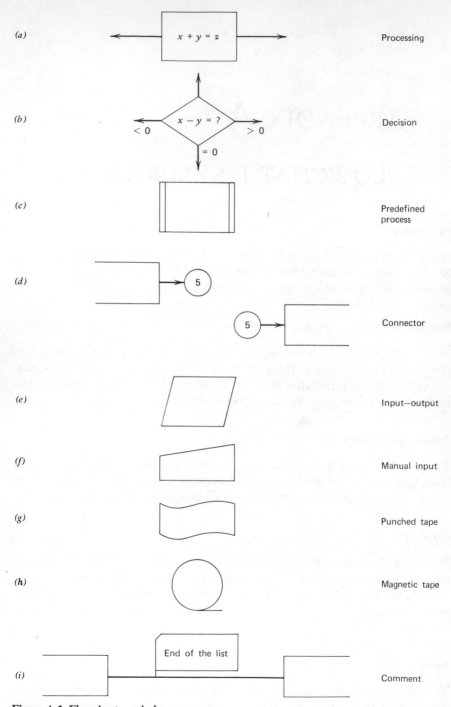

(a) $x + y = z$ Processing

(b) $x - y = ?$ < 0 > 0 $= 0$ Decision

(c)   Predefined process

(d)   5   5   Connector

(e)   Input–output

(f)   Manual input

(g)   Punched tape

(h)   Magnetic tape

(i)   End of the list   Comment

Figure A.1 Flowchart symbols.

596

Manual Input

This symbol is used to indicate the point in the program where the manual input of the information is performed. Manual input can be achieved by means of on-line keyboards, light pen, switch settings and so on

Punched Tape

The widely used medium for input-output, especially in connection with minicomputers, is the punched tape. As a result this special symbol is reserved for punched tape input-output.

Magnetic Tape

This symbol is used to indicate the reading or writing of information on magnetic tape.

Comment

Comment flag is used to keep the information pertinent to the processing, but which is not the part of the processing. Usually explanatory notes for clarification are included within this symbol.

APPENDIX **B**

SOFTWARE DEVELOPMENT MODULES FOR MICROPROCESSORS

Loaders

Loaders and bootstraps are short programs which, when in memory, enable the computer to accept and store other programs.

Editors

Editors are used to create and modify the source programs from the teletype keyboard. The editor provides easy manipulation of text by commands such as: create new text; delete old text; insert new text into old text; change section of the text; store text on the file.

Assemblers and Compilers

Assembler translates the source program written in symbolic language into an object binary program. Compiler translates the source program written in a high level language, such as PL/M, into an object binary program. For microcomputers, the transaction can be performed in the following way:

- Using the assembler loaded into Microcomputer Development System.
- Using the assembler available through the Time-Share terminals.
- Using the cross-assembler in a larger machine.

Cross-assemblers are available for 32-bit machines, and for 16-bit minicomputers, and they are usually written in FORTRAN. Cross-assembler reads the source program written in microcomputer's assembly language, and translates it into an object binary program. The object binary program is then loaded into the microcomputer for execution.

598

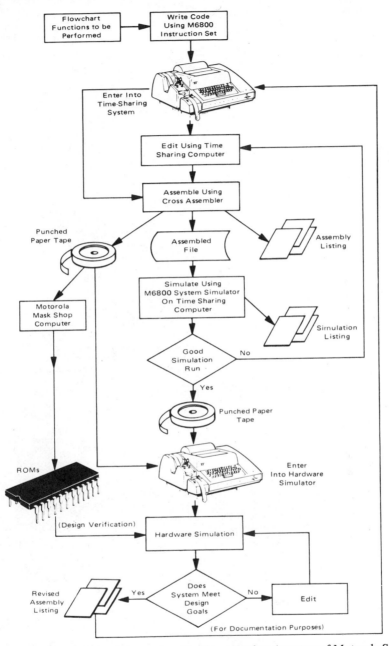

Figure B.1 System software design and verification procedure (courtesy of Motorola Semi-conductor Products, Inc.).

Simulators

Simulators are programs to simulate microprocessor operation. Input is object code from the assembler output. The operator can ask the simulator to start the program execution, to stop, to cycle, to interrupt, to display, or to punch the output results.

Figure B.1 shows typical software preparation cycle.

APPENDIX C

HARDWARE DEVELOPMENT MODULES AND TOOLS FOR MICROSYSTEMS

Logic Analyzers

Logic analyzers are specifically designed for analysis of digital logic circuits and signals. The analysis of a complex logic circuit by a designer is often a difficult task, particularly with asynchronous logic. The analyzer is usable for synchronous and asynchronous signals. It provides the ability to detect and store several digital signals. This information is then presented for display on an oscilloscope in a multitrace timing-diagram presentation.

Logic Clips and Probes

To simplify probing in compact digital circuits, small, dual purpose probes were developed for direct connection to dual in-line packages and various pins. Cabling problems are reduced by grouping the data probes. The probes are usually compatible with all familiar logic families (including TTL, DTL, ECL, HLL, and MOS). This will make analysis of mixed-logic systems possible.

Breadboard Systems

Removable breadboard presents the ideal tool for learning about digital circuits. Discrete components, actual IC's and standard hook-up wire interconnections simply plug into the breadboard thus eliminating the need for soldering, special modules and expensive cables.

Microcomputer Development Systems

Microcomputer modules are available as standard cards that may be purchased individually. Also self-contained systems, complete with Microprocessor, memory, I/O, crystal clock, power supplies, displays, control panel, and finished cabinet, are available. Many OEM systems could be designed in a short time, based on such modules.

The development systems come with a standard software package that includes a system monitor, editor and resident assembler. The programmer can prepare his program in mnemonic form, assemble it, and use the monitor to load the assembled program for execution.

PROM Programmers

PROM Programmers are small portable units designed for use in engineering laboratories or out in the field. Each Programmer can program, list, duplicate or verify data in PROM. Programming is done through the hexadecimal keyboard. Hexadecimal characters are used to define both, memory address and the data. Options include a teletype interface, a paper tape reader, and a built-in Ultraviolet light for erasing the PROMs.

Ultraviolet Light

An ultraviolet light is required to erase PROMs so they can be reused. Desirable features: built-in timer and enclosure to protect the eyes. Figure C.1 shows an example of hardware/software development tools.

1.   Minicomputer (Texas Instruments TI980B) with 48K of semiconductor memory and disk based operating system with following necessary software:
   a.   Source Editor
   b.   M6800 Crossassembler
   c.   Disc to PROM Transcription Program

2.   Disc Drive (Diablo)

3.   Cassette terminal (Texas Instruments Silent 700ASR) connected to TI980B minicomputer

4.   Ultraviolet light (Ultraviolet Products, Inc. S-52) for PROM erasure

5.   Universal PROM Programmer (Intel MDS-UPP-100) connected to TI980B minicomputer. Object output from Crossassembler that was stored on disk is transferred to the PROM using the program written in FORTRAN language with real-time extensions

6.   PROM (Intel 2708 Erasable Read Only Memory)

7.   Prototype microsystem built around Motorola's and Intel's chips

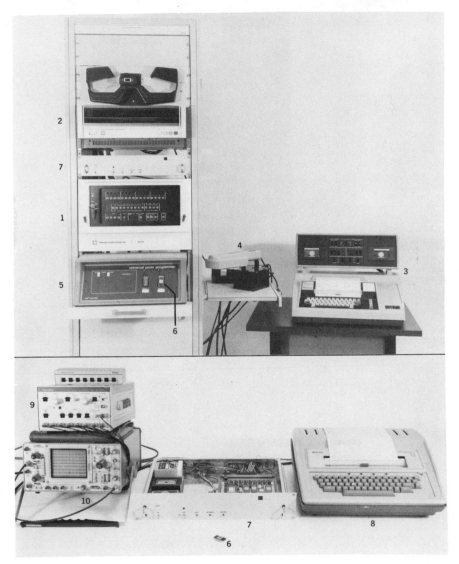

Figure C.1 Modern electronic laboratory equipped with well-balanced chain of tools for microprocessor system development (photograph by John C. Zeiss).

8.   Terminal (Texas Instruments Silent 700KSR) connected to proto-type microcomputer

9.   Logic Analyzer (Biomation 810-D Digital Logic Reader)

10.   Oscilloscope (Tektronix 465) displaying eight traces of data sampled and stored by the logic analyzer

INDEX

605